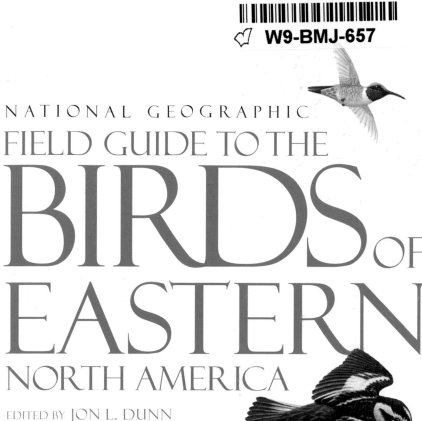

NATIONAL GEOGRAPHIC

FIELD GUIDE TO THE

BIRDS OF

EASTERN

NORTH AMERICA

EDITED BY JON L. DUNN
AND JONATHAN ALDERFER
WITH PAUL LEHMAN

NATIONAL GEOGRAPHIC

WASHINGTON, D.C.

Contents

Introduction

In this field guide, the division between East and West follows the general north-south line of the Rocky Mountains and incorporates state and provincial boundaries whenever possible.

Worm-eating Warbler: a species that breeds only in the eastern United States

adult ♂

♀

Yellow Warbler *aestiva*: a widespread North American breeder

In 2006, National Geographic released the fifth edition of *The Field Guide to the Birds of North America,* featuring 967 species, new artwork, and revised text reflecting the most current and accurate ornithological information. Building on that work, this volume, *The Field Guide to the Birds of Eastern North America,* provides annotated illustrations and detailed accounts specific to species found east of the Rocky Mountains.

We adhere to the Committee on Classification and Nomenclature of the American Ornithologists' Union (AOU) for issues of taxonomy and nomenclature—English and scientific names—as determined in the seventh edition of the AOU Check-list (1997) and its seven subsequent supplements, published annually in the July issue of the AOU journal, *The Auk.* We also follow either the American Birding Association Checklist Committee or the above-mentioned AOU committee in deciding which species to include. Apart from the list of exotics, the differences are few.

The area covered in this guide (see map at left and on back cover flap) follows important topographical features but uses state, provincial, and territorial lines when possible. Coverage extends 200 nautical miles offshore, which includes the French islands of St. Pierre and Miquelon. Although a companion volume, *The Field Guide to the Birds of Western North America,* covers birds from the Rocky Mountains and farther west, a number of western species are fully covered in this guide because they are of rare but regular occurrence as migrants on the western Great Plains.

If a species is regular, defined as very rare to abundant (see abundance terms, page 12), it receives full treatment in this guide. Many exotic species from other continents have been introduced into North America as game, park, or cage birds and are seen in the wild frequently. Those that have at least some degree of establishment (e.g., Purple Swamphen) are included here.

Found in the back of this book are two appendices. The first is an illustrated list of casual and accidental species that have occurred primarily in the East or are equally rare in the West. Most of these species originate from Mexico, the Caribbean, or Europe. The second is a brief list of western species that are casual or accidental in the East. These species receive full treatment in *The Field Guide to the Birds of Western North America.*

Museum specimens have been an essential resource in preparing detailed and accurate illustrations for both this guide and the *National Geographic Field Guide to the Birds of North America.* We are grateful to the many institutions that have loaned specimens to the artists (see Acknowledgments, page 417).

Families

Scientists organize animal species into family groups that share certain structural or molecular characteristics. Some bird families encompass more than a hundred members; others only one. Characteristics within a family are often helpful in identifying birds in the field. With their strong, sharp bills, strong claws, and short legs, members of the Picidae family, for example, are easily recognized as woodpeckers.

Brief family descriptions, with information applicable to all members of the family, can be found at the beginning of each group. Additionally, a description of a smaller group within a family is sometimes provided, such as that given for the *Empidonax* flycatchers, which share some distinguishing traits.

Scientific Names

Each species has a unique two-part scientific name, derived from Greek or Latin and written in italics. The first part, always capitalized, indicates the genus. For example, nine members of the family Picidae are placed in the genus *Picoides*. Together with the second part of the name (also referred to as the specific epithet), which is not capitalized, this identifies the species. *Picoides pubescens* is the name of one specific kind of woodpecker, commonly known as Downy Woodpecker.

Downy Woodpecker
Picoides pubescens

Subspecies

Since the latter half of the 19th century, species have been further divided into subspecies, or *races*, when populations from different geographical regions show recognizable differences. Each subspecies bears a third scientific name, or trinomial. Out of the three subspecies of American Three-toed Woodpecker, *Picoides dorsalis bacatus* (abbreviated as *P. d. bacatus*) identifies the dark-backed subspecies that inhabits the boreal forest of eastern North America. The paler-backed Rockies subspecies, *dorsalis,* has occurred as an accidental in southwest Kansas; a third and intermediate subspecies, *fasciatus,* is found east to Saskatchewan. Given the more uniform topography and climate of eastern North America, there is less geographical variation in the East than in the West, which has many mountain ranges, valleys, and deserts.

If the third part of a scientific name is the same as the second, the subspecies in question is known as the *nominate subspecies,* the type of the species originally described. The nominate subspecies of American Three-toed Woodpecker, *dorsalis,* was named and described in 1858, before *fasciatus* (1870) or *bacatus* (1900). For subspecies names, we have relied on the fifth edition of the AOU Check-list (1957), the last edition that treated subspecies.

This guide illustrates the extremes of variation within a species. For example, of the roughly seven subspecies of Horned Lark found in the East, we show the most typical or widespread—the nominate subspecies *alpestris,* also known as "Northern Horned Lark"—and also illustrate three other subspecies. For *polytypic species* (those having more than one subspecies) where the illustrations show mainly or entirely one subspecies, that subspecies' name appears italicized under the English name. If we include illustrations of other subspecies, those names appear next to the figures. Many species are *monotypic* (having no recognized subspecies), thus only the scientific binomial is used. For example, Cerulean Warbler is monotypic and is simply known by the scientific name *Dendroica caerulea.*

bacatus   dorsalis   fasciatus

Polytypic:
American Three-toed
Woodpecker

Monotypic:
Cerulean Warbler

How to Identify Birds

Field marks, a bird's physical features, are the clues by which birds are identified. They include plumage, or the bird's overall feathering; the shape of the body and its individual parts (see Parts of a Bird, page 10); and any actual markings such as bars, bands, spots, or rings. A field mark can be obvious, like a male Northern Cardinal's red plumage or a Killdeer's double breast bands. Other field marks are more subtle, such as the difference in head markings between a Clay-colored and a winter-plumaged Chipping Sparrow or the difference in head shapes of Greater and Lesser Scaup.

Lesser Scaup *(top)* and Greater Scaup *(bottom)* are best distinguished by head shape

Some plumage field marks are plainly visible only in good light, or from a certain angle, or when the bird is in flight. In this guide, the most distinctive features for each species in each plumage are usually listed first in the text account; boldface terms (e.g., ***adult female*** or ***first-winter male***) in the accounts correspond to the illustrated figures.

The most important thing when birding is to *look at the actual bird.* There will be plenty of time to consult the field guide later.

Behavior

juvenile

Both Short-billed *(above)* and Long-billed Dowitchers move their bills up and down like a sewing machine needle when feeding

Behavioral traits also provide many clues to species identity. Look, for example, at a bird's flight. Is it direct or undulating? Does the bird beat its wings rapidly or slowly? Observe feeding habits too. Does the bird forage on the ground or in the treetops? Does it peck at the water or drill the mud? Consider personality clues as well. Is the bird usually visible and approachable or shy and difficult to locate? Does it hop or walk? Does it flick its tail up or drop it down?

Voice

A bird's songs and calls reveal not only its presence, but also, in many cases, its identity. Some species—particularly nocturnal or secretive birds such as owls, nightjars, and rails—are more often heard than seen. A few species are most reliably identified by voice even when they are seen well.

When birds assemble or travel in flocks, they often keep in touch with a *contact* or *flight call* that may be markedly different from their other calls. Flight calls are especially important for identifying individuals (or flocks) overhead.

Molt and Plumage Sequence

The regular renewal of plumage, called *molt,* is essential to a bird's ability to fly and to its overall health. A molt produces a specific plumage, and not all birds go through the same sequence of plumages. Some species have a very simple sequence of plumages from juvenile to adult: for example, most raptors molt from juvenal plumage directly into adult plumage. Other species, such as many of the gulls, take more than three years to acquire

Alder Flycatcher *(top)* and Willow Flycatcher *(bottom)* are best separated by song

adult plumage and go through a complicated series of interim plumages. Shown in this guide are all of the most distinctive plumages likely to be encountered in the field.

The first coat of true feathers, acquired before a bird leaves the nest, is called the *juvenal plumage;* birds in this plumage are referred to as *juveniles.* True hawks and loons, as well as many other waterbirds, hold juvenal plumage well into winter. In many species, juvenal plumage is replaced in late summer or early fall by a *first-fall* or *first-winter* plumage that more closely resembles adult plumage. First-fall and any subsequent plumages that do not resemble the adult—known as *immature plumages*—may continue in a series that includes *first-spring* (when the bird is almost a year old), *first-summer,* and so on, until *adult plumage* is attained. When birds take several years to reach adult plumage, we label the interim plumages as *subadult* or note the specific year or season shown.

House Sparrows' appearance changes with wear

In adult birds, the same annual sequence of molt and plumages is repeated throughout the bird's life. Most adults undergo a complete molt, replacing all their feathers, in late summer or early fall, after breeding. For some species this is the only molt of the year, so adults of these species have the same plumage year-round. Other species undergo a partial molt—usually involving the head, body, and some wing coverts—in late winter or early spring, resulting in a more colorful *breeding plumage* that is seen in spring and summer. For species with two annual molts, the plumage attained after breeding is referred to as the *nonbreeding* or *winter plumage.* Some changes are evident only during the brief period of courtship. In herons, for example, the colors of bill, lores, legs, and feet may change. When these colors are at their height, the birds are said to be in *high breeding plumage.* After breeding, most ducks molt into a briefly held *eclipse plumage* in which males acquire a femalelike plumage and females show little change, although some become paler and duller.

Scarlet Tanagers undergo a complete molt from summer to fall

In addition, wear and fading of a bird's feathers can have a pronounced effect on its appearance. In species with a single annual molt in fall, the fresh colors exhibited right after molting are usually brighter than the faded colors seen at the end of the breeding season. For instance, adult Acadian Flycatchers are brightest from fall to spring; by late summer, their plumage becomes worn and faded. Plumage patterns can also be affected. In certain songbirds, such as Snow Bunting or House Sparrow, the more patterned spring plumage appears as the dull tips of the fresh fall plumage gradually wear away, with very little molt involved.

Often the fall molt occurs before migration, so we see these birds in fresh fall plumage even if they spend winter outside of North America. Certain species, including many shorebirds, suspend their molt during fall migration and complete it on arrival at the wintering grounds. Some species molt over a considerably longer period than others. Birds of prey, for instance, must rely on their wing feathers for successful hunting and thus molt very gradually so that only a few wing feathers are missing at any one time.

Acadian Flycatchers are in fresh plumage from fall to spring but appear worn by late summer

Parts of a Bird

Because the size, the shape, and the configuration of birds' various parts differ among families and species, birders should become familiar with their names and locations—bird topography. Nonpasserines are quite variable, and we give three examples: hummingbird, shorebird, and gull. Notice how the feathers overlap, and remember that a bird's posture and activity level can affect what feathers are visible.

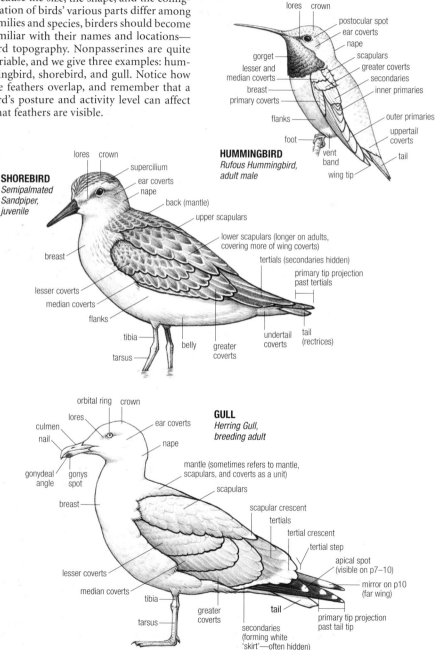

HUMMINGBIRD
*Rufous Hummingbird,
adult male*

lores   crown
postocular spot
ear coverts
nape
gorget
lesser and
median coverts
scapulars
greater coverts
secondaries
breast
inner primaries
primary coverts
flanks
outer primaries
foot
uppertail coverts
tail
vent band
wing tip

SHOREBIRD
*Semipalmated
Sandpiper,
juvenile*

lores   crown
supercilium
ear coverts
nape
back (mantle)
upper scapulars
lower scapulars (longer on adults, covering more of wing coverts)
breast
tertials (secondaries hidden)
primary tip projection past tertials
lesser coverts
median coverts
flanks
tibia
belly
greater coverts
undertail coverts
tail (rectrices)
tarsus

GULL
*Herring Gull,
breeding adult*

orbital ring   crown
lores
culmen
ear coverts
nail
nape
gonydeal angle
gonys spot
mantle (sometimes refers to mantle, scapulars, and coverts as a unit)
breast
scapulars
scapular crescent
tertials
tertial crescent
tertial step
apical spot (visible on p7–10)
mirror on p10 (far wing)
lesser coverts
median coverts
tibia
greater coverts
tail
primary tip projection past tail tip
tarsus
secondaries (forming white 'skirt'—often hidden)

Passerines show less variation in body shape and feather organization. The Lark Sparrow example illustrates all the features of the head and wings. Many species show wing bars, formed by the pale tips of the greater and/or median coverts when the wing is folded.

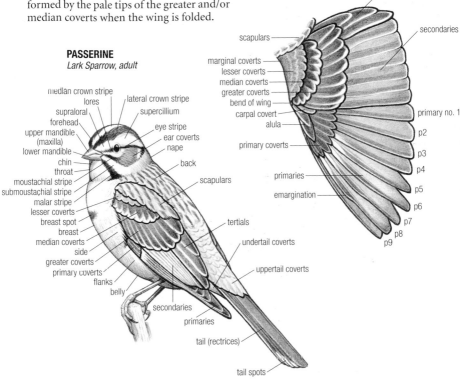

PASSERINE
Lark Sparrow, adult

median crown stripe
lores
supraloral
forehead
upper mandible (maxilla)
lower mandible
chin
throat
moustachial stripe
submoustachial stripe
malar stripe
lesser coverts
breast spot
breast
median coverts
side
greater coverts
primary coverts
flanks
belly

lateral crown stripe
supercillium
eye stripe
ear coverts
nape
back
scapulars
tertials
undertail coverts
uppertail coverts
secondaries
primaries
tail (rectrices)
tail spots

UPPER WING
Lark Sparrow, adult

tertials
secondaries
scapulars
marginal coverts
lesser coverts
median coverts
greater coverts
bend of wing
carpal covert
alula
primary coverts
primaries
emargination

primary no. 1
p2
p3
p4
p5
p6
p7
p8
p9

Some feather groups can be seen only when a bird is in flight. Other feather groups have special names when they are prominently marked, such as the carpal bar seen on a Common Tern (below). Most birds have twelve tail feathers. When you observe the folded tail from below, the two outermost tail feathers are visible.

wing lining
speculum
axillaries

American Black Duck

carpal bar

Common Tern, first summer

Myiarchus flycatcher
tails from below:
Great Crested, Ash-throated

12

Plumage Variation

Where adult males and females of a species are similar, we show only one. When male (♂) and female (♀) look different, we usually show both. If spring and fall, or *breeding* and *nonbreeding*, plumages differ only slightly, or if only one of these plumages is usually seen in North America, we tend to show only one figure. Juvenile and immature birds are illustrated when they hold a different-looking plumage after they are old enough to be seen away from their more easily recognizable parents.

A number of species have two or more *color morphs*—variations in plumage color occurring regionally or within the same population. For example, this guide shows three color morphs of Swainson's Hawk.

Some species (usually, but not always, of the same genus) occasionally breed with each other, producing *hybrid* offspring that may appear intermediate. Different subspecies also interbreed, resulting in *intergrade* individuals or populations.

Barrow's x Common Goldeneye hybrid

Measurements

Knowing the size of a bird is important. When identifying a kinglet, for example, it helps to know that the bird in question is tiny (only about four inches long). Relative size is also significant: In mixed flocks, Greater and Lesser Yellowlegs are easily distinguished from each other by size alone.

Body length and wingspread measurements are by their nature somewhat imprecise and may vary slightly from one source to another. However, we feel that these are the most useful measurements for birders in the field. Thus, average length (L) from tip of bill to tip of tail for each species is given. Where size varies greatly within a species, either because of sex or geographical variation among subspecies, a range of smallest to largest is provided. And for large birds often seen in flight, we give the wingspan (WS), measured from wing tip to wing tip.

Greater *(top)* and Lesser Yellowlegs *(bottom)* are distinguishable by size

Abundance and Habitat

Abundance must be considered in relation to habitat. Under the heading **Range**, the species accounts include supplemental information about habitat, abundance, and seasonal status that cannot be shown in a single map. Some species are highly local, found only in a very specialized habitat.

The following categories of abundance—given from most to least numerous—are used in this guide: *abundant, common, fairly common, uncommon, rare,* and *very rare.* Unlike rare species, *casual* species do not occur annually in North America, but a pattern of their occurrence is apparent over decades. *Accidental* species have been seen only once or a few times in an area that is far out of their normal range. In fact, it may be decades, or even centuries, before another one is seen there again.

Some other terms used herein include the following: *Vagrant* is a bird that is found well off its usual migration route. *Irruptive*

Casual: Redwing

Accidental: Red-footed Falcon

species are erratic in their movements over much of their range. One year they may be numerous in a given region and the next year, or even the next decade, they may be totally absent.

Range Maps

Maps are provided for all species with two general exceptions: (1) introduced species with very limited ranges that are described in the text and (2) species that do not breed in North America and are of rare, casual, or accidental occurrence here.

On each map, range boundaries are drawn where the species ceases to be regularly seen. Keep in mind that nearly every species will be rare at the edges of its range. The map key on the back cover flap explains the colors and symbols used. Many maps in this guide have been revised to reflect the most current information.

Birds are not, however, bound by maps. Their ranges continually expand and contract. Irruptive species move southward in some years in large or small numbers and for great or small distances. In some species, birds leave the nesting grounds in late summer and then move northward. These post-breeding wanderers, principally young birds, will subsequently migrate southward by winter. Range maps of pelagic species, which spend most of their time over the open sea, are somewhat conjectural.

Range information is based on actual sightings and therefore depends on the number of knowledgeable and active birders in each area. There is much to learn about bird distribution in every part of North America. Participation by birders is necessary to the monitoring of expanding and contracting ranges. Breeding-bird surveys and atlas projects make a vital contribution to the general fund of information about each species. The Cornell Laboratory of Ornithology has created eBird (www.ebird.org), a website where birders can post their observations of species and add to our understanding of status and distribution.

In the accounts of birds presently on the U.S. federal list of threatened or endangered species, we have placed the symbols **E** (endangered) or **T** (threatened). Canada also has its own list of threatened species, as do many states and provinces. Extinct species are indicated with the symbol **EX**.

How to Be a Better Birder

The time you spend studying your field guide at home will be repaid when you go out birding. In addition, a number of introductory books designed to help the beginning birder are available. One such book, *Birding Essentials,* published by National Geographic, covers all the basic skills and information.

Observing and studying birds can be an enriching, pleasurable experience with far-reaching rewards. With birding's increasing popularity, birders are becoming powerful advocates for the protection and stewardship of our natural resources. We urge you to get involved in conservation activities and to pass your knowledge and love of birds onto others.

THE EDITORS

Irruptive: Snowy Owl

Recent arrival:
Shiny Cowbird

Endangered species:
Red-cockaded
Woodpecker

Ducks, Geese, Swans (Family Anatidae)

Worldwide family. Web-footed, gregarious birds, ranging from small ducks to large swans. Largely aquatic, but geese, swans, and some "puddle ducks" also graze on land.

Greater White-fronted Goose *Anser albifrons*

L 28" (71 cm) Named for the distinctive white band at base of bill. Medium-size, grayish brown goose, with irregular black barring on underparts; orange feet and legs. Bill pink or orangish with whitish tip. In flight, note grayish blue wash on wing coverts and white, U-shaped rump band. Most *immatures* acquire white front above bill and white bill tip during first winter; acquire black belly markings by second fall; distinguished from similar vagrant Tundra and Taiga Bean-Geese by bill color and call; from Pink-footed Goose (a vagrant) by bill and leg color; compare also with immature blue-morph Snow Goose (next page). Color and size vary in *adults:* Pale, arctic tundra birds have heavy barring; Greenland's subspecies, *flavirostris,* rare in the Northeast, is darker, with heavier barring and a more orange bill.
Voice: Call is a high-pitched, laughing *kah-lah-aluck.*
Range: Large populations are found on Great Plains (fewer east to Mississippi Valley). Rare but regular migrant and winter visitor farther east.

Pink-footed Goose *Anser brachyrhynchus L 26" (66 cm)*

This East Coast vagrant from breeding grounds in eastern Greenland is distinguished from plain-bellied immature Greater White-fronted Goose by pink legs and variable dark base and tip to stubbier pinkish bill; neck shorter than Greater White-fronted. Juvenile is browner, looks more scaly than barred; legs duller. In flight, shows an extensive area of bluish gray on mantle and all wing coverts; darker head and neck contrast with grayish body; tail base is grayer and paler than Greater White-fronted Goose and Bean Goose.
Voice: High-pitched cackling calls given in flight.
Range: Primarily Old World species. A scattering of records between eastern Pennsylvania and Newfoundland; most sightings thought to involve wild birds.

IDENTIFYING: Subspecies of White-fronted Goose Greater White-fronted Geese of the tundra-breeding race *gambelli* are common in migration and winter on the Great Plains and western Gulf Coast southward well in to Mexico. They are uncommon east to the Mississippi River Valley and rare but regular at a few sites farther east still. A few spring migrants also wander east of their usual range. Scattered individuals are seen annually all the way to the East Coast, mostly in fall and winter. Another subspecies—*flavirostris*—known as the "Greenland White-fronted Goose" nests in western Greenland and winters primarily in Britain and Ireland. From the Appalachians and eastern Great Lakes eastward there is debate over what percentage of the White-fronteds seen are *gambelli* and how many are *flavirostris*. The latter clearly does occur very rarely south to the mid-Atlantic region, primarily in fall and winter. It differs from *gambelli* in being larger overall and in having a darker head and neck and a more orange (versus more pinkish) bill, which may become slightly pinker toward the tip. Problems arise when observers attempt to

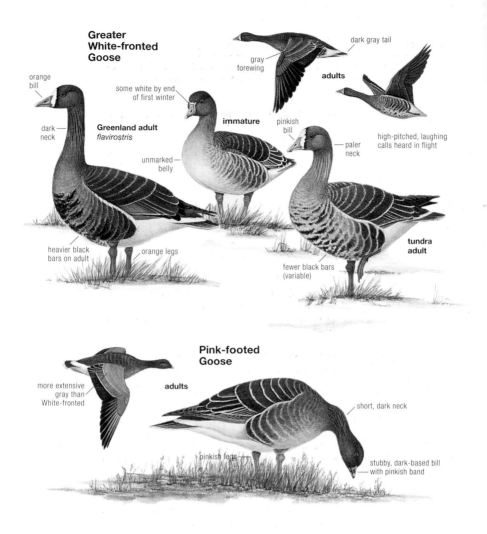

Greater White-fronted Goose

orange bill

dark neck

some white by end of first winter

Greenland adult *flavirostris*

unmarked belly

heavier black bars on adult

orange legs

gray forewing

immature

pinkish bill

adults

dark gray tail

adults

paler neck

high-pitched, laughing calls heard in flight

tundra adult

fewer black bars (variable)

Pink-footed Goose

more extensive gray than White-fronted

adults

short, dark neck

pinkish legs

stubby, dark-based bill with pinkish band

assign a subspecies name to some of these birds, however, because of color variation within both races and in differing perceptions of bill and neck colors by observers. Proper lighting is critical.

Other identification pitfalls involving gray geese at the *species* level involve vagrant Pink-footed Geese (see species account above) and domestic, barnyard-type Graylag Geese (page 44) seen in more natural habitats. These domestic geese are sometimes confused with immature Greater White-fronteds but tend to be larger overall, have a pot-bellied look, are larger billed, have

pinker legs, and give a lower, more nasal call.

The entire taxonomy and the ranges of some of the subspecies of Greater White-fronted are badly in need of revision. Earlier workers extended the range of slightly smaller *frontalis* over much of the breeding range of *gambelli*. Most now confine it to breeding in west and southwest Alaska and the Russian Far East. The Alaska breeders winter mainly in the Central Valley of California. Another Alaska breeding subspecies, *elegasi*, winters in the northern Central Valley of California and is the largest and darkest subspecies.

Snow Goose *Chen caerulescens* L 26-33" *(66-84 cm)*

Two color morphs; both are common in "Lesser Snow Goose" (*caerulescens*). Adults distinguished from smaller Ross's Goose by larger, pinkish bill with black "grinning patch." Flies with slower wingbeat than Ross's; rusty stains often visible on face in summer. **White-morph juvenile** is grayish above, with dark bill. **Blue-morph adult** has mostly white head and neck, brown back, variable amount of white on underparts. Juvenile has dark head and neck, overall slaty body coloring; distinguished from Greater White-fronted Goose (preceding page) by dark legs and bill and lack of white on face. Intermediates between white and blue morphs have mainly white underparts and whitish wing coverts.
Voice: Very vocal in flight, typically nasal cackling.
Range: Abundant. Occasionally hybridizes with Ross's Goose. A larger subspecies, *atlanticus,* "Greater Snow Goose" (not shown), breeds around Baffin Bay, winters only along mid-Atlantic coast; blue morph almost unknown. Smaller race, the "Lesser Snow Goose" (morphs shown here), is rare in winter throughout interior U.S. and in southern Canada outside mapped range. Blue morph is abundant in central North America; uncommon in East.

Ross's Goose *Chen rossii* L 23" *(58 cm)*

Stubby, triangular bill, mostly deep pinkish red with purplish blue-gray base (lacking in Snow Goose). More vertical demarcation between feathering and base of bill than in Snow. Neck shorter, head smaller and rounder than Snow; white head generally lacks rusty stains. Ross's has two color morphs. **White-morph juvenile** may have very pale gray wash on head, back, and flanks, but far less than juvenile white-morph Snow Goose. Extremely rare **blue morph** is darker than blue-morph Snow Goose; face and belly are white.
Voice: Like Snow Goose but higher pitched.
Range: Rare but regular east of Mississippi River Valley, east to Quebec and Vermont. Usually seen with Snow Geese.

Barnacle Goose *Branta leucopsis* L 27" *(69 cm)*

Vagrant from Greenland and Old World. Note distinctive head pattern and stubby bill. Bluish gray upperparts, barred with black, and white, U-shaped rump band. Silver-gray wing linings show in flight.
Voice: High-pitched cackling.
Range: Increasing Greenland population may be responsible for increase in reports from Maritimes to mid-Atlantic region. Also fairly common in captivity; thus most sightings from eastern North America are of uncertain origin, especially away from Atlantic seaboard. More of a land goose than the Brant, feeding in fields near the ocean.

Snow Goose
caerulescens

adults

black "grinning patch"

blue-morph adults

rusty stains

variably dark below

dark bill

darker than juvenile Ross's

white-morph juvenile

blue-morph juvenile

mostly dark brown

white-morph adult

rounder head than Snow

blue-morph adult

darker than blue-morph Snow

dark neck

adult

short neck

more rapid wingbeats than Snow

Ross's Goose

very similar to adult

white-morph juvenile

white-morph adult

stubby bill

Barnacle Goose

barred upperparts

white face

sharp contrast

bluish gray

usually seen with Canada Geese

Cackling Goose *Branta hutchinsii L 23-33" (58-84 cm)*

Formerly considered part of the Canada Goose complex, this species is smaller, with a rounder head and a stubbier bill. Its shorter neck is most obvious in flight. Four subspecies overall; the only one found regularly in eastern North America is *hutchinsii,* which typically shows a pale brown breast but only sometimes a partial white neck ring. Size of smallest Canada and largest Cackling overlap; identification criteria are still not adequately worked out. Records of uncertain origin of smallest and darkest Cackling Goose, *minima,* have occurred recently from the mid-Atlantic region.

Voice: Calls are higher pitched than Canada Goose.

Range: Rare but regular east to Atlantic seaboard. Exact status clouded by confusion with smallest, *parvipes* Canada.

Canada Goose *Branta canadensis L 30-43" (76-109 cm)*

Our most common and familiar goose. Black head and neck marked with distinctive white "chin strap," stretching from ear to ear. In flight, shows large dark wings; white undertail coverts; white, U-shaped rump band; and long neck. The approximately seven named subspecies in North America vary in overall color and size. Size decreases northward: The smallest subspecies, *parvipes* (**"Lesser Canada Goose"**), breeds from central Alaska to north-central Canada and winters mainly in central portions of U.S.

Voice: Call is a deep, musical *honk-a-lonk.*

Range: Flocks usually migrate in V-formations, stopping to feed in wetlands, grasslands, or agricultural areas. Breeding programs involving mixes of multiple subspecies have now produced expanding populations that are resident south of mapped range; explosive increase has prompted control measures in East.

Brant *Branta bernicla L 25" (64 cm)*

A small, dark, stocky sea goose. Note whitish patch on side of neck. White uppertail coverts almost conceal black tail. White undertail coverts conspicuous in flight. Wings comparatively long and pointed, wingbeat rather rapid. **Immature** birds show bold white edging to wing coverts and secondaries, and fainter neck patches than **adults.** Juveniles usually lack neck patches entirely. In eastern subspecies *hrota,* **"American Brant,"** pale belly contrasts with black chest, and neck patches do not meet in front. Western *nigricans,* **"Black Brant,"** a very rare East Coast visitor, has dark belly contrasting with whiter flanks, and neck patches meet in front.

Voice: Call is a low, rolling, slightly upslurred *raunk-raunk.*

Range: Primarily coastal goose; flocks fly low in ragged formation and feed on aquatic plants of shallow bays and estuaries. Locally common. Rare inland, but some are sighted during migrations through the Great Lakes and Appalachian regions, particularly in fall. Casual south of mapped range.

Cackling Goose
"Richardson's"
hutchinsii

rounded head

stubby bill

short neck

calls higher pitched than Canada

overall pale

flies with rapid, shallow wingbeats

short neck esp. noticeable in flight

flies with slower, deeper wingbeats than Cackling

Canada Goose

long, black neck

"Lesser"
parvipes

smallest Canada; compare carefully to Cackling

"Atlantic"
canadensis

honking calls lower pitched than Cackling

broken collar

adult

pale belly

flies with rapid, shallow wingbeats

adults

adult

complete white collar

Brant
"American Brant"
hrota

reduced collar

white fringes

dark belly

"Black Brant"
nigricans

immature

Mute Swan *Cygnus olor L 60" (152 cm)*

Prominent black knob at base of orange bill. *Juvenile* may be white or brownish; bill gray with black base. Darker juvenile begins to molt to white plumage by midwinter; bill becomes pinkish. Mute Swan often holds its long neck in an S-shaped curve, with bill pointed down. Often swims with wings arched over back.

Voice: Gives a variety of hisses and snorts, but generally silent. In flight, wingbeats make noticeable drone sound. (Other swans have silent wingbeats.)

Range: An Old World species, introduced in the U.S. Seen in parks. Most populations in the East are increasing, but Mute Swan is being systematically removed from the Great Lakes and other areas.

Trumpeter Swan *Cygnus buccinator L 60" (152 cm)*

Adult's black facial skin tapers to broad point at the eye, dips down in a V on forehead. Forehead slopes evenly to straight bill. *Juvenile* retains gray-brown plumage through first spring. Difficult to separate many Trumpeter and Tundra Swans; see box below.

Voice: Common call is a single or double *honk* that sounds like an old car horn.

Range: In Great Lakes and upper Midwest regions, reintroduced into perhaps part of former range and introduced elsewhere. A few of these individuals have wandered south in winter to the mid-South and mid-Atlantic regions, exceptionally even farther.

Tundra Swan *Cygnus columbianus L 52" (132 cm)*

In *adult,* black facial skin tapers to a point in front of eye and cuts straight across forehead; most birds have a yellow spot of variable size in front of eye. Head is rounded, bill slightly concave. *Juvenile* Tundras have variable black and pinkish coloring on the bill, becoming blacker over time; they molt earlier than immature Trumpeter Swans; appear much whiter by late winter. Difficult to separate many Trumpeter and Tundra Swans, especially lone individuals; see box below.

Voice: Call is a noisy, high-pitched whooping or yodeling.

Range: Nests on tundra or sheltered marshes; winters in flocks on shallow ponds, lakes, estuaries. Rare to uncommon in winter over parts of interior U.S.; casual south to the Gulf Coast and north to the Maritimes.

IDENTIFYING: Swans Distinguishing between Tundra and Trumpeter Swans in the field may be surprisingly difficult, particularly when dealing with a lone individual or small group, and size differences between the two species cannot be ascertained. Silent immatures are the most difficult to identify.

On adults, pay particular attention to the shape of the bill, the black facial skin in front of the eye, and the white forehead feathering. (And hope that the birds call!) Be aware that the yellow spot in front of the eye in some adult Tundras may be minimal or lacking and that this species may also show a suggestion of the fleshy line along the gape typical of Trumpeter. Trumpeter adults, however, never show the yellow spot. Juvenile

Mute Swan

sometimes arches wings

dark knob

adult

dark border

juvenile

darker than other juvenile swans

Trumpeter Swan

white forms V-shape on forehead

juvenile

adult

more concave shape than Trumpeter

juvenile

white feathering cuts straight across forehead; some lack yellow spot

eye stands out

adult

Tundra Swan
columbianus

Mute Swans—which lack the tell-tale bill-knob of the adult—may also be difficult to separate.

Through their first fall, young swans are typically accompanied by their parents; thus, the nearby adults make it easier to identify the juveniles. Although both species lighten as the winter progresses due to wear, Tundra juveniles average paler than Trumpeters. By late winter,

the former are largely whitish, whereas the latter are still largely grayish.

Bill patterns are helpful distinctions as well: Juvenile Tundra has a mostly pink bill base, darkening as it ages, although the exact amount of black and pink may vary from individual to individual; young Trumpeter and Mute Swans always show a noticeable dark base.

Whistling-Ducks

Named for their whistling calls, these gooselike ducks have long legs and long necks. Wingbeats are slower than ducks, faster than geese.

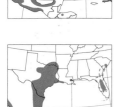

Fulvous Whistling-Duck *Dendrocygna bicolor*
L 20" (51 cm) Rich tawny color overall; back darker, edged with tawny. Bill and legs dark. Whitish rump band conspicuous in flight.
Voice: Call, a squealing *pe-chee.*
Range: Irregular summer wanderer north to dashed line on map; casual farther north. Declining overall. Forages in rice fields, marshes, shallow waters; often dives to feed. More active at night.

Black-bellied Whistling-Duck
Dendrocygna autumnalis L 21" (53 cm) Gray face with white eye ring, red bill. Legs red or pink; belly, rump, and tail black. White wing patch shows as broad white stripe in flight. *Juvenile* is paler, with gray bill.
Voice: Call is a high-pitched, four-note whistle.
Range: Increasing in southern Great Plains region, and introduced populations expanding in Florida, South Carolina. Casual north to Canada. Inhabits wetlands; nests in trees, nest boxes.

Perching Ducks

These surface-feeding, woodland ducks are equipped with sharp claws for perching in trees. They nest in tree cavities or nest boxes.

Wood Duck *Aix sponsa* L 18½" (47 cm)
Male's glossy, colorful plumage and sleek crest distinctive. Head pattern, bill colors retained in drab eclipse plumage. *Female* identified by short crest and large, white, teardrop-shaped eye patch; compare to female Mandarin (page 44). *Juvenile* resembles female but spotted below. In all plumages, flight profile distinctive: large head, bill angled downward; long, squared-off tail.
Voice: Male gives soft, upslurred whistle when swimming; female's squealing flight call is a rising *oo-eek.*
Range: Fairly common in open woodlands near water. Rare during winter throughout most of breeding range.

Muscovy Duck *Cairina moschata* L 26-33" (66-84 cm)
Large, blackish duck with green and purple gloss above with white patches on upper- and underwing. *Male* has blackish to dark reddish knob at base of bill, bare facial skin (usually brighter red in *domestic male,* whose color varies; can be all-white). Female is smaller, duller; lacks knob and bare facial skin. *Juvenile* even duller; slowly acquires wing patches in first winter. Wild Muscovies are shy, usually silent; seen mostly in flight at dawn and dusk.
Range: Tropical species; tame escaped birds found in parks continent-wide (established in Florida). A nest box program in Mexico helped wild Muscovies spread to lower Rio Grande area, Texas.

gooselike flight

adults

red bill

extensive white
on wing

**Fulvous
Whistling-
Duck**

blackish
rounded
wings

white
U-shaped
rump band

gray
bill

white lines
on sides
and flanks

**Black-bellied
Whistling-Duck**
autumnalis

juvenile

faint white
streaks on flanks

white around
and behind eye

♀

Wood Duck

♂

juvenile ♀

juvenile ♂

longish tail

♂

unique
pattern

gooselike
flight

female much
smaller than
male

juvenile ♀

knob

adult ♂

prominent
white

adult ♂

Muscovy Duck

highly
variable

**domestic
variety** ♂

Dabbling Ducks

Surface-feeding members of the genus *Anas:* the familiar "puddle ducks" of freshwater shallows and, chiefly in winter, salt marshes. Dabblers feed by tipping, tail up, to reach aquatic plants, seeds, and snails. They require no running start to take off but spring directly into flight. Most species show a distinguishing swatch of bright color, the speculum, on the secondaries. Many are known to hybridize.

American Wigeon *Anas americana L 19" (48 cm)*

Male's white forehead and cap are conspicuous in mixed flocks foraging in fields, marshes, and shallow waters; in flight, identified by mainly white wing linings and, in *adult male,* by large white patch on upperwing. Wing patches are grayish on *adult female* and immatures. Female lacks white on head, closely resembles gray-morph female Eurasian Wigeon; distinguishing field marks in flight are female American's white wing linings and contrast between gray throat and brown breast; Eurasian female's throat and breast are of uniform color.

Voice: Male gives piercing, three-note whistle; female call a much lower, single-syllable *quack.*

Range: A recently established local breeder on the East Coast. Rare in winter north to northern Great Lakes.

Eurasian Wigeon *Anas penelope L 20" (51 cm)*

Dark rufous head and gray back and sides make males conspicuous in flocks of American Wigeons; dusky wing linings are distinctive in all plumages. Hybridizes regularly with American Wigeon. *Adult male* has reddish brown head and neck with creamy crown; large white patches on upperwings. Many fall males retain some brown eclipse feathers but show distinctive reddish head. *Immature male* begins to acquire adult head and breast color but retains some brown juvenal plumage, particularly on forewing, similar to American Wigeon. *Gray-morph female* more closely resembles female American. *Rufous morph* has a more reddish head.

Voice: Male, like American Wigeon but even higher pitched.

Range: Eurasian Wigeon is a rare but regular migrant and winter visitor along the coast, rarer still in the interior.

Gadwall *Anas strepera L 20" (51 cm)*

Male is mostly gray, with white belly, black tail coverts, pale chestnut on wings. *Female*'s mottled brown plumage resembles female Mallard (page 28), but belly is white, forehead steeper, upper mandible gray with orange sides. Both sexes have white inner secondaries that may show as small patch on swimming bird and identify the species in flight.

Voice: Male's single-syllable call is loud and nasal; female's is a Mallard-like *quack.*

Range: Breeding sites very localized along Atlantic seaboard.

American Wigeon

adult ♂

white underwing coverts and axillaries

white or buffy white crown

adult ♂

♀

eclipse adult ♂

gray face contrasts with cinnamon-buff chest

bluish gray bill with dark tip

head and chest uniform in color

most with rusty cast

rufous-morph ♀

Eurasian Wigeon

dusky underwings and axillaries

adult ♂

gray-morph ♀

gray-morph ♀

cream

rufous

adult ♂

immature ♂

Gadwall

steep forehead

small white speculum patch

♂

even line of orange on sides of bill

♀

♂

black undertail coverts

white belly

American Black Duck   *Anas rubripes*   L 23" (58 cm)

Blackish brown, paler on face and foreneck. In flight, white wing linings contrast more sharply with otherwise dark plumage than in similar female Mallard. Violet speculum is bordered in black, may show a thin white trailing edge. *Male*'s bill is yellow; *female*'s dull green, may be flecked with black.

Voice: Similar to Mallard.

Range: Nesting pairs favor woodland lakes and streams, freshwater or tidal marshes. In many parts of range, especially deforested areas, Mallards are replacing American Black Ducks; the two species **hybridize** frequently.

Mottled Duck   *Anas fulvigula*   L 22" (56 cm)

Both sexes closely resemble American Black Duck but body is slightly paler, throat and face are buffy and unstreaked; speculum bluish. Note dark spot at gape. Differs from female Mallard by darker plumage and absence of white in tail or black on bill. Western Gulf Coast race, *maculosa*, is darker than nominate Florida race.

Voice: Similar to Mallard.

Range: Mottled Duck has been introduced to coastal South Carolina. Common year-round in coastal marshes. Very rare north to Kentucky and Kansas. Begins pairing in Jan. or Feb., earlier than the migratory American Black Ducks and Mallards. Some authorities consider the Mottled Duck to be a subspecies of the Mallard.

Northern Shoveler   *Anas clypeata*   L 19" (48 cm)

Large, spatulate bill, longer than head, identifies both sexes. Often seen feeding in groups, paddling in tight circles, straining food with bill. *Male* distinguished by green head, white breast, brown sides; in early *fall* has a white crescent on each side of face, like Blue-winged Teal. *Female*'s grayish bill is tinged with orange on cutting edges and lower mandible. In flight, both sexes show blue forewing patch.

Voice: Male gives a two-syllable nasal call; female gives a *quack*.

Range: Increasing in the East, where still only a very local breeder. Found in marshes, ponds, and bays.

IDENTIFYING: Female Mallard-Types
Female dabbling ducks that look a lot like a female Mallard—and that quack much like a female Mallard—include Gadwall, American Black Duck, and Mottled Duck. Although the presence of adult males alongside may help in the females' identification, mixed-species flocks are common and hybrid pairings occur (particularly between American Black Duck and Mallard). Be aware that juvenile males and adult males in eclipse plumage during the summer and early autumn may also add to the confusion. An eclipse male Mallard, for example, has a dull olive bill color close to that of a Mottled or an American Black Duck.

Females are best told apart by their wing and bill patterns. Note the exact color of the bill, the color contrast on the underwing, and both the exact color of the speculum and whether or not it is bordered fore and aft by white. The slightly smaller bill and steeper forehead are also important distinctions for the female Gadwall, as are its whiter belly and plainer face. A female Mallard typically has more distinct pale sides to the tail than found on Mottled and American Black Ducks.

American Black Duck x
Mallard hybrid ♂

underwings
contrast
strongly with
dark body

purplish
speculum not
bordered
by white in
front

American
Black Duck

♀

♂

streaked
face

greenish
yellow bill

unmarked
buffy face and
throat

black spot
at gape

♂

Mottled Duck
maculosa
western Gulf Coast

yellower
bill

mainly Florida
fulvigula

average paler overall
than *maculosa*

♂

blue
forewing

facial crescent,
compare to male
Blue-winged Teal

fall ♂

♂

Northern
Shoveler

♀

♀

orange
line

♂

large
spatulate bill

Mallard *Anas platyrhynchos* L 23" *(58 cm)*

Male readily identified by metallic green head and neck, yellow bill, narrow white collar, chestnut breast. Black central tail feathers curl up. Both sexes have white tail, white underwings, bright blue speculum with both sides bordered in white. *Female*'s mottled plumage resembles other *Anas* species; look for orange bill marked with black. *Juvenile* and *eclipse male* resemble female but bill is dull olive. Mallards in central Mexico north to Rio Grande region of south and western Texas, formerly considered a separate species, "Mexican Duck," are darker, lack distinctive male plumage; their bills are unmarked dull greenish to orange; *intergrades* occur in southwestern U.S. See also identification box on page 26.

Voice: Male gives a *quack* and a rasping *kreep*; female gives a series of *quack* notes.

Range: Frequents a wide variety of shallow-water environments. Abundant and widespread. Feral and domestic birds are permanent residents, often found on park ponds, including south of mapped range.

White-cheeked Pintail *Anas bahamensis* L 17" *(43 cm)*

A vagrant from the Caribbean region. White cheeks and throat contrast with dark forehead and cap; blue bill has a red spot near base. Long, pointed tail is buffy; tawny or reddish underparts are heavily spotted. Female is paler than *male*; tail slightly shorter. In flight, both sexes show green speculum broadly bordered on each side with buff.

Voice: Mostly silent.

Range: Casual vagrant from the West Indies to southern Florida. Sightings even from Florida are of uncertain origin; those away from Florida are most likely birds escaped from captivity.

Northern Pintail *Anas acuta* ♂L 26" *(66 cm)* ♀L 20" *(51 cm)*

Male's chocolate brown head tops long, slender white neck, the white extending in a thin line onto head. Black central tail feathers extend far beyond rest of long, wedge-shaped tail. *Female* is mottled brown, paler on head and neck; bill uniformly grayish. In both sexes, flight profile shows long neck; slender body; long, pointed wings; dark speculum bordered in white on trailing edge. In flight, female's mottled brown wing linings contrast with white belly; long, wedge-shaped tail lacks male's extended feathers.

Voice: Male gives a soft, whistled one- to three-syllable call; female gives one *quack* or a series of weak, hoarse *quack* notes.

Range: A common, widespread duck, found in marshes and open areas with ponds, lakes; in winter often feeds in grainfields. Much more common in West than in East. Rare in winter north to Great Lakes region.

Mallard

eclipse ♂

juvenile

speculum boldly bordered with white

underwings contrast less with body than Black Duck

♀

mostly white tail

dark saddle on orange bill

♀

yellow bill

♂

curled central tail feathers

male with yellow bill

♂

White-cheeked Pintail
bahamensis

sharply delineated white cheek and throat

♂

body darker than female Mallard

"Mexican Duck"- Mallard intergrade

grayish bill

♂

♀

Northern Pintail

white stripe

dark speculum with narrow white trailing edge

long pointed tail

♂

♀

Blue-winged Teal *Anas discors* L 15½" (39 cm)

Violet-gray head with white crescent on each side identifies *male*. *Female* distinguished from smaller female Green-winged Teal by larger bill, more heavily spotted undertail coverts, yellowish legs. Compare also with female Cinnamon Teal; note Blue-winged's grayer plumage, smaller bill, and bolder facial markings, including whiter lore and more prominent, broken eye ring. Male in eclipse plumage resembles female. In flight, wing patterns of both sexes match those of Cinnamon.
Voice: Male gives a high, whistled *peeu*; female gives a nasal *quack*.
Range: Fairly common in marshes and on ponds and lakes.

Cinnamon Teal *Anas cyanoptera* L 16" (41 cm)

Cinnamon head, neck, and underparts identify *male*. *Female* closely resembles female Blue-winged Teal but plumage is a richer brown; lore spot, eye line, and broken eye ring less distinct; bill longer and more spatulate. Compare also with Green-winged Teal. Young birds and males in eclipse plumage resemble female. Males more than a couple of months old have red-orange eyes; Blue-winged's eyes are dark. Wing pattern is almost identical to Blue-winged. Known to interbreed with Blue-winged Teal.
Voice: Male gives a chattering call; female gives a nasal *quack*.
Range: Common in marshes, ponds, and lakes. Regular from eastern Great Plains south to eastern Texas. Casual farther east. Some sightings may be escaped birds.

Green-winged Teal *Anas crecca* L 14½" (37 cm)

Our smallest dabbler. *Male*'s chestnut head has dark green ear patch outlined in white or buff. *Female* distinguished from other female teals by smaller bill and by largely white undertail coverts that contrast with mottled flanks. A fast-flying, agile duck. In flight, shows green speculum bordered in buff on leading edge, white on trailing edge. In the subspecies seen in most of North America, *carolinensis*, male has vertical white bar on side. Eurasian race, *crecca*, lacks the vertical bar, but has a white stripe on scapulars and slightly bolder buffy facial stripes.
Voice: Male gives liquid *preep* or *krick*; female gives a weak, high-pitched *quack*.
Range: Eurasian race rare to very rare in the East, mostly near the coast. Formerly considered a separate species, Common Teal.

IDENTIFYING: Female Teal Three species of teal are found regularly in eastern North America, though Cinnamon is casual east of the Great Plains. The smallest is Green-winged, which is readily identified by its whitish, not patterned, undertail coverts. The larger Blue-winged and Cinnamon are much more similar. The smaller-billed Blue-winged is overall paler and more mottled below with pale lores, a more prominent split eye ring, and a dark eye line. Cinnamon, which is a warmer brown color overall, is less patterned with a more blended face and a larger, more spatulate bill. Juvenile Cinnamon Teal, however, may appear more like Blue-winged. The iris of young male Cinnamon turns reddish during the fall; this is brown in Blue-winged.

The wing patterns of both are identical and very different from Green-winged; males of both have a prominent white bar separating the bluish forewing from the secondaries.

broken white
eye ring

eye
line

gray face

**Blue-winged
Teal**

♂

♀

smaller
bill than
Cinnamon

♀

white
crescent

♂

compare to immature
male Northern Shoveler

buffier face; less evident
eye line and eye ring than
female Blue-winged

♀

Cinnamon Teal

♂

larger spatulate bill
than Blue-winged

♂

white
horizontal bar

Green-winged Teal

♂ *crecca*

prominent
white facial
stripes

♂

♀

less white on
underwing than
Blue-winged
and Cinnamon

♂ *carolinensis*

♀ *carolinensis*

white
vertical bar

pale sides to
undertail coverts

Bay Ducks (Genus *Aythya*)

Diving ducks of the genus *Aythya* have legs set far back and far apart, which makes walking awkward. Heavy bodies require a running start on water for takeoff. Various species hybridize. Always carefully check potential vagrants to make sure they are not hybrids.

Canvasback   *Aythya valisineria* L 21" (53 cm)
Forehead slopes to long, black bill. *Male*'s head and neck are chestnut; back and sides are whitish. *Female* and eclipse male have pale brown head and neck, pale brownish gray back and sides. In flight, whitish belly contrasts with dark breast, dark undertail coverts. Wings lack contrasting pale stripe of smaller Redhead.
Voice: Mostly silent, except during display.
Range: Locally common in marshes, lakes, and bays; feeds in large flocks; has decreased substantially but decline has stabilized in most areas. Migrating flocks fly in irregular V-formations or in lines.

Redhead   *Aythya americana* L 19" (48 cm)
Rounded head and shorter, tricolored, mostly blue-gray bill separate this species from Canvasback. Bill is mostly pale blue (male) or slate (female), with narrow white ring bordering black tip. *Male*'s back and sides are smoky gray. Eye is paler (yellower) than in male Canvasback. *Female* and eclipse male are tawny brown, with slightly darker crown, pale patch bordering black bill tip, may show buffy eye ring; compare female scaup (next page) and female Ring-necked Duck (below). Redheads in flight show gray stripe on trailing edge of wings that contrasts with darker forewing.
Voice: Mostly silent, except during display.
Range: Locally common in marshes, ponds, and lakes; a substantial number winter on the Laguna Madre in coastal Texas; uncommon and local along Atlantic seaboard.

Ring-necked Duck   *Aythya collaris* L 17" (43 cm)
Peaked head; bold white ring near tip of bill. *Male* has second white ring at base of bill; white crescent separates black breast from gray sides. Narrow cinnamon collar is usually hard to see in the field. *Female* has dark crown, white eye ring; may have a pale line extending back from eye; face is mainly gray. In flight, all plumages show a gray stripe on secondaries.
Voice: Mostly silent, except during display.
Range: Fairly common in freshwater marshes and on woodland ponds; also on lakes; during winter, found also in southern coastal marshes. May breed south or winter north of mapped range.

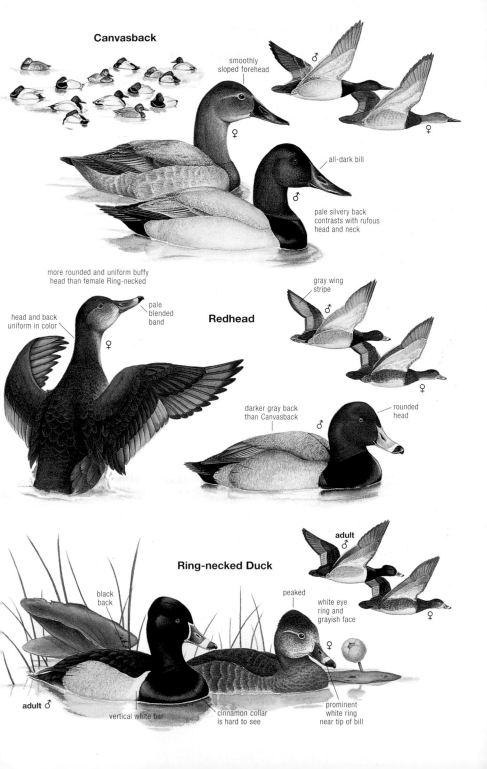

Canvasback

smoothly sloped forehead

♂

♀

all-dark bill

♀

pale silvery back contrasts with rufous head and neck

♂

more rounded and uniform buffy head than female Ring-necked

gray wing stripe

♂

pale blended band

Redhead

head and back uniform in color

♀

♀

darker gray back than Canvasback

♂

rounded head

Ring-necked Duck

adult

♂

black back

peaked

white eye ring and grayish face

♀

adult ♂

vertical white bar

cinnamon collar is hard to see

♀

prominent white ring near tip of bill

Greater Scaup *Aythya marila* L 18" *(46 cm)*

Larger size and smoothly rounded head help distinguish this species from Lesser Scaup. In close view, note Greater Scaup's slightly larger bill with wider black tip. *Male* averages paler on back and flanks; in good light, head may show a green gloss. In both species, *female* has bold white patch at base of bill, often slightly more extensive than in Lesser. Some female Greater Scaup, especially in spring and summer, have a paler head with a distinct whitish ear patch; some are also slightly paler brown overall than most Lessers. In flight, Greater Scaup typically shows a bold white stripe on secondaries and well out onto primaries, unlike Lesser Scaup.

Voice: Mostly silent, except during display.

Range: Locally common; found on large, open lakes and bays and inshore ocean waters. Migrates and winters in small or large flocks, often with Lesser Scaup. Rare to uncommon winter visitor along the Gulf Coast and on many larger island lakes and reservoirs.

Lesser Scaup *Aythya affinis* L 16½" *(42 cm)*

Smaller size and peaked crown help distinguish from Greater Scaup. In close view, note Lesser Scaup's slightly smaller bill with smaller black tip. In good light, *male*'s head may show a purple gloss, sometimes mixed with green. *Female* is brown overall, with bold white patch at base of bill. In some females, especially in spring and summer, head is paler, with whitish ear patch less distinct than in female Greater Scaup. In flight, Lesser Scaup shows bold white stripe on secondaries only.

Voice: Mostly silent, except during display.

Range: Common; breeds in marshes, small lakes, and ponds. In winter, found in large flocks on sheltered inshore ocean waters and bays, inlets, and lakes.

Tufted Duck *Aythya fuligula* L 17" *(43 cm)*

Old World species; very rare visitor. Head is rounded; crest distinct in *male,* smaller in *female* and immatures; may be absent in eclipse male. Gleaming white sides further distinguish male from male Ring-necked Duck. *First-winter male* has gray sides but lacks the white crescent conspicuous in male Ring-necked. Female is blackish brown above; lacks white eye ring and distinct white bill ring of female Ring-necked. Bills of both male and female Tufted have a wide black tip. Some females also have a small white area at base of bill. In flight, all plumages show a broad white stripe on secondaries and extending onto primaries. May hybridize with scaup.

Voice: Mostly silent, except during display.

Range: Regular visitor to Newfoundland and the Maritimes. Very rare in winter elsewhere along East Coast as far south as Maryland, casual in Great Lakes region. Found on ponds, rivers, bays, often with Ring-necked Ducks and especially scaup.

many females with prominent whitish auricular patches

♀

♀

larger, rounder head than Lesser

adult ♂

extensive white stripe

♀

Greater Scaup
nearctica

1st winter ♂

more black on bill tip than Lesser

adult ♂

Lesser Scaup

adult ♂

white restricted to secondaries

♀

smaller, peaked head than Greater

♀

less black on bill tip than Greater

adult ♂

Tufted Duck

♀

some females whitish here

crest

♀

broad black bill tip

extensive white like Greater Scaup

adult ♂

crest length variable on males and females

♀

dark brown back

1st winter ♂

black back

adult ♂

pure white sides

Common Eider *Somateria mollissima* L 24" *(61 cm)*
Female distinguished from female King Eider by larger size, sloping forehead, and evenly barred sides and scapulars. Feathering
extends along sides of bill to or beyond nostril, with minimal feathering on top of bill. Females range in overall color from rust to
gray. ***Male***'s head pattern is distinctive. A few eastern males show
a thin black V on throat; *v-nigrum* male has orange-yellow bill.
Eclipse and ***first-winter males*** are dark; first-winter has white on
breast; full adult plumage is attained by fourth winter. In flight,
adult male shows solid white back and wing coverts.
Voice: Mostly silent, except during display.
Range: Locally abundant on shallow bays, rocky shores. Rare in
winter to South Carolina; casual to Florida and on Great Lakes.

King Eider *Somateria spectabilis* L 22" *(56 cm)*
Female distinguished from female Common Eider by smaller size,
more rounded head, and crescent or V-shaped markings on sides
and scapulars. Feathering extends only slightly along sides of bill
but extensively down the top, making bill look stubby. ***Male***'s head
pattern is distinctive. In flight, shows partly black back, black wings
with white patches. ***First-winter male*** has brown head, pinkish or
buffy bill, buffy eye line; lacks white wing patches.
Voice: Mostly silent, except during display; croaking notes in flight.
Range: Common on tundra and coastal waters in northern part
of range; generally very rare on Great Lakes except on Lake Ontario,
where a few occur regularly. Rare on East Coast to Virginia; casual
to Florida, accidental on Gulf Coast.

Harlequin Duck *Histrionicus histrionicus* L 16½" *(42 cm)*
Small duck with rounded head, stubby bill. ***Male***'s colorful
plumage appears dark at a distance. ***Female*** has three white spots
on each side of head. Juvenile resembles adult female. Flight is
rapid, low. Compare female in flight with female Bufflehead.
Voice: Mostly silent, except during breeding season.
Range: Found along rocky coasts; inland along swift streams for
nesting. Rare south to Carolinas and on Great Lakes, casual elsewhere in interior.

IDENTIFYING: Common Eider Four subspecies of Common Eider can be found in eastern North America, although Pacific *v-nigrum*
is rare and confined to the far northern part of
the region. Atlantic *dresseri* and Hudson Bay
sedentaria are very similar, differing slightly in
the shape of the frontal lobes.

The more northerly Atlantic *borealis* winters
south regularly to Atlantic Canada and actually
is much more numerous at this season in Newfoundland than *dresseri*. This subspecies—
which is the smallest of the four—has a bright
orange-yellow bill and more narrow and
tapered frontal lobes.

"Atlantic Eider"   "Hudson Bay Eider"   "Northern Eider"   "Pacific Eider"
♂ *dresseri*   ♂ *sedentaria*   ♂ *borealis*   ♂ *v-nigrum*

eclipse adult ♂
v-nigrum

Common Eider
dresseri

adult ♂

♀

♀ *v-nigrum*

color variable

♀

white back

flat forehead

feathering extends to nostril

evenly barred

1st winter ♂

adult ♂

more rounded head than Common

buff-pink bill

1st winter ♂

King Eider

adult ♂

more restricted white on upperwing than Common

adult ♂

small points

feathering falls short of nostril

♀

crescent-shaped markings

round head with small bill

♀

Harlequin Duck

head spots develop over winter

adult ♂

1st winter ♂

white belly

♀

adult ♂

unique pattern

Sea Ducks

Stocky, short-necked diving ducks; most species breed in the far north and migrate in large, compact flocks to and from their coastal and Great Lakes wintering grounds.

Surf Scoter *Melanitta perspicillata* L 20" *(51 cm)*
Male's black plumage sets off colorful bill, white eye, white patch on forehead and nape; forehead is sloping, not rounded. *Female* is brown, with dark crown; usually has two white patches on each side of face, one primarily vertical and one more horizontal; feathering extends down top of bill only. Adult female and *first-winter male* may have whitish nape patch. All juveniles have whitish belly, usually white face patches. In flight, more uniform color of underwings helps distinguish Surf from Black Scoter; also orangish, not dark, legs and feet.
Voice: Mostly silent, except during display.
Range: Common; nests on tundra and in wooded areas near water. Rare inland migrant. Small groups winter on Great Lakes; most in coastal waters.

White-winged Scoter *Melanitta fusca* L 21" *(53 cm)*
White secondaries, conspicuous in flight, may show as a small white patch on swimming bird. Forehead slightly rounded. Feathering extends almost to nostrils on top and sides of bill. *Female* and juveniles lack contrasting dark crown and paler face of other scoters; white oval-shaped facial patches are distinct on juveniles, often indistinct on adult female. Juveniles and immatures are whitish below. *Adult male* has black knob at base of colorful bill; crescent-shaped white patch below white eye, brownish flanks.
Voice: Mostly silent, except during display.
Range: Fairly common on inland lakes in breeding season, coastal areas in winter. Uncommon inland migrant. Large numbers winter on Lake Ontario since introduction of zebra mussels. Rarest scoter in the South.

Black Scoter *Melanitta nigra* L 19" *(48 cm)*
Male is black, with orange-yellow knob at base of dark bill. *Female*'s dark crown and nape contrast with pale face and throat; feathering does not extend onto bill. In both, forehead is rounded. In flight, adult male's blackish wing linings contrast with paler flight feathers. Juveniles resemble females but are whitish on belly; *first-winter male* has some yellow at base of bill by winter.
Voice: Mostly silent, except during display.
Range: Nests on tundra. Small numbers seen in migration and winter on Great Lakes (most common on Lake Ontario, where some winter); rare elsewhere in eastern interior, mostly in fall.

Surf Scoter

feathering out culmen

white head patches

forward whitish patch vertically shaped

white nape on adult female

adult ♀

adult ♂

adult ♂

more uniformly dark wings than Black

immature ♀

white belly

1st winter ♂

1st winter ♀

bill shows color by December

White-winged Scoter
deglandi

1st winter ♀

juvenile of both sexes show whitish patches; forward patch horizontally shaped

adult ♂

only scoter with white in wings

white slash under eye

1st winter ♂

adult ♀

adult ♂

adult ♀

feathering extends out bill

white not always visible on folded wing

yellow-orange

round head

no feathering out on bill

pale face contrasts sharply with dark cap

adult ♂

secondaries and primaries paler than rest of wing

dull yellow

1st winter ♂

adult ♂

adult ♀

adult ♀

Black Scoter
americana

Long-tailed Duck *Clangula hyemalis*

♂L 22" *(56 cm)* ♀16" *(41 cm)* Formerly Oldsquaw. *Male*'s long tail is conspicuous in flight, may be submerged in swimming bird. Male in winter and spring largely white; breast, back dark brown; scapulars pearl gray; stubby bill shows pink band. By late spring, male mostly dark, with pale facial patch, bicolored scapulars. *Female* lacks long tail; bill is dark; plumage whiter in winter, darker in summer. *First-fall* birds are even darker. Long-taileds are identifiable at some distance by their swift, careening flight. Both sexes show uniformly dark underwings.
Voice: Loud, yodeling, three-part *calls,* heard all year.
Range: Away from Great Lakes rare in the interior, and south to Gulf Coast.

Bufflehead *Bucephala albeola* L 13½" *(34 cm)*
A small duck with a large, puffy head, steep forehead, short bill. *Male* is glossy black above, white below, with large white patch on head. *Female* is duller, with small, elongated white patch on each side of head. *First-winter male* and male in eclipse resemble female. In flight, males show white patch across entire wing; female has white patch only on inner secondaries.
Voice: Mostly silent, except during display.
Range: Generally common; nests on woodland lakes, ponds: winters on sheltered bays, rivers, lakes.

Common Goldeneye *Bucephala clangula* L 18½" *(47 cm)*
Male has round white spot on each side of face; scapulars are mostly white. *Female* and eclipse male closely resemble Barrow's Goldeneye. Head of Common is more triangular; forehead more sloped; bill longer. Female's head is slightly paler than female Barrow's; bill generally all-dark or with yellow near tip only; rarely completely dull yellow. In all plumages, subtle differences between the two species in white wing patches visible in flight.
Voice: Generally silent, except during display. Wings make whistling sound in flight.

Barrow's Goldeneye *Bucephala islandica* L 18" *(46 cm)*
Male has white crescent on each side of face; white patches on scapulars show on swimming bird as a row of spots; dark color of back extends in a bar partially separating white breast from white sides. *Female* and male in eclipse plumage closely resemble Common. Puffy, oval-shaped head, steep forehead, and stubby, triangular bill help identify Barrow's. Adult female's head slightly darker than female Common; bill mostly orangish yellow, except in young females, which may have only a yellow band near tip. In all plumages, white wing patches visible in flight differ subtly between the two species. *Hybrids* between the two species occur.
Voice: Generally silent, except during display. Male wings produce whistling sound in flight.
Range: Both goldeneye species summer on open lakes and small ponds; winter in sheltered coastal areas, inland lakes, and rivers. Overall, Barrow's is much less common; rare to casual outside mapped winter range.

1st winter ♂

males have pink band

small bill

early summer adult ♂

Long-tailed Duck

winter adult ♂

dark wings

long pointed tail

variably white on face

1st fall ♀

females have grayish bills

winter adult ♂

winter ♀

winter ♀

Bufflehead

extensive white head pattern

adult ♂

white cheek spot

small dark bill

1st winter ♂

adult ♂

♀

♀

Common Goldeneye
americana

mostly white scapulars

round white spot

adult
♂

adult ♂

1st winter ♂

pure white sides

♀

♀

Barrow's x Common hybrid

adult ♂

Barrow's Goldeneye

slightly less white on wing coverts than Common

many immature males have a shaded crescent by late December

adult
♂

1st winter ♂

steeper forehead and stubbier bill than Common

black scapulars with white spots

1st winter ♀

♀

white crescent

vertical black spur

adult ♂

adult ♀

Mergansers

Long, thin, serrated bills help these divers catch fish, crustaceans, and aquatic insects. Mergansers in flight show pointed wings.

Hooded Merganser Lophodytes cucullatus L 18" (46 cm)
Puffy, rounded crest; thin bill. **Male**'s bill is dark; white head patches are fan shaped and conspicuous when crest is raised. Compare with male Bufflehead (preceding page). **Female** brownish overall; upper mandible dark, lower yellowish. Rapid wingbeats in flight; both sexes show black-and-white inner secondaries. Crest is flattened in flight, male's head patch shows only as a white line.
Voice: Generally silent, except during display.
Range: Common over much of East. In breeding season, found on woodland ponds, rivers, and backwaters. Winters chiefly on fresh or brackish water.

Common Merganser Mergus merganser L 25" (64 cm)
Large duck with long, slim neck and thick-based, hooked, red bill. White breast and sides, often tinged with pink, and lack of crest distinguish **male** from Red-breasted Merganser. **Female**'s bright chestnut, crested head and neck contrast sharply with white chin, white breast. Adult male in flight shows white patch on upper surface of entire inner wing, partially crossed by a single black bar. Eclipse male resembles female but retains wing pattern. Female's white inner secondaries and greater coverts are partially crossed by a black bar. As in all species on this page, young male resembles adult female, but may show some darkening in face by spring.
Voice: Generally silent, except during display.
Range: Common Mergansers nest in woodlands near lakes and rivers; in winter, sometimes also found on brackish water, rarely salt. Casual to Gulf Coast.

Red-breasted Merganser Mergus serrator L 23" (58 cm)
Shaggy double crest, white collar, and streaked breast distinguish **male** from male Common Merganser. **Female**'s head and neck are duller than female Common; chin and foreneck whitish. Adult male in flight shows white patch on upper surface of inner wing, partly crossed by two black bars. Eclipse male resembles female but retains male wing pattern. Female's white inner secondaries and greater coverts are crossed by a single black bar. Smaller size and thinner bill help distinguish Red-breasted Merganser in mixed flocks.
Voice: Generally silent, except during display.
Range: Nests in woodlands near fresh water or in sheltered coastal areas; prefers brackish or salt water in winter. Abundant migrant on Great Lakes, where moderate numbers winter; elsewhere, fairly common to common migrant in interior.

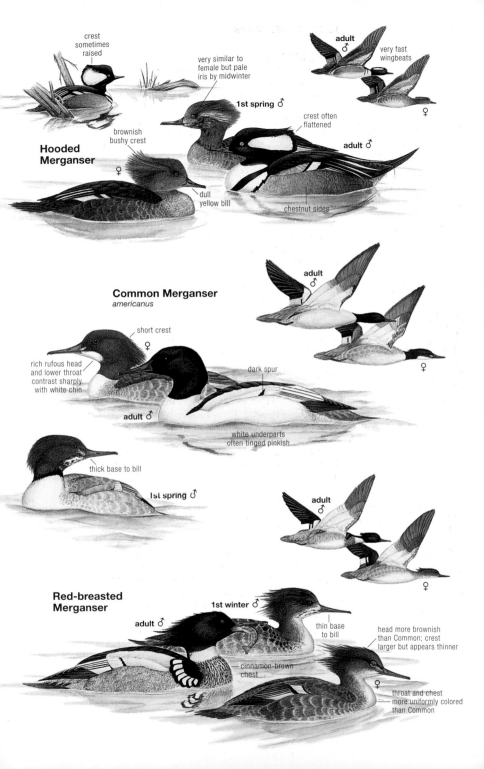

crest sometimes raised

very similar to female but pale iris by midwinter

adult ♂

very fast wingbeats

♀

1st spring ♂

crest often flattened

Hooded Merganser

brownish bushy crest

adult ♂

♀

dull yellow bill

chestnut sides

Common Merganser
americanus

adult ♂

short crest

♀

rich rufous head and lower throat contrast sharply with white chin

dark spur

♀

adult ♂

white underparts often tinged pinkish

thick base to bill

1st spring ♂

adult ♂

♀

Red-breasted Merganser

1st winter ♂

adult ♂

thin base to bill

head more brownish than Common; crest larger but appears thinner

cinnamon-brown chest

♀

throat and chest more uniformly colored than Common

Stiff-tailed Ducks

Long, stiff tail feathers serve as a rudder for these diving ducks. In both species, male's bill is blue in breeding season.

Ruddy Duck *Oxyura jamaicensis* L 15" (38 cm)
Small but chunky, with large head, broad bill, long tail, often cocked up. *Male*'s white cheeks are conspicuous both in *breeding* plumage and in dull *winter* plumage. In *female,* single dark line crosses cheek. Young resemble female through first winter.
Voice: Mostly silent. During display, male produces soft ticking and popping sounds.
Range: Common in much of range, though more local in Northeast; nests in dense vegetation of freshwater wetlands. During migration and winter, found on lakes and bays.

Masked Duck *Nomonyx dominicus* L 13½" (34 cm)
Tropical species. Shy; found on densely vegetated ponds. *Male*'s black face on reddish brown head is distinctive. In *female, winter male,* and *juvenile,* two dark stripes cross buffy face; barred back. Compare with Ruddy Duck (above).
Voice: Mostly silent.
Range: Rare and irregular visitor to southern and southeastern Texas; casual in Louisiana and Florida. Accidental in East, north to Wisconsin and New England.

Exotic Waterfowl

Many waterfowl species are brought into North America from other continents for zoos and private collections. Escapes are frequent. The species shown here are among those seen most frequently.

Ruddy Shelduck *Tadorna ferruginea* L 26" (66 cm)
Afro-Eurasian species often kept in captivity. A record of a flock of six on Southampton Island, Nunavut, Canada, may have been vagrants from Old World.

Common Shelduck *Tadorna tadorna* L 25" (64 cm)
Eurasian species. Female smaller, lacks knob on bill.

Egyptian Goose *Alopochen aegyptiacus* L 27" (68 cm)
African species. Widespread escape. Note white wing patches.

Mandarin Duck *Aix galericulata* L 16" (41 cm)
Asian species. Compare female to female Wood Duck (page 22).

Bar-headed Goose *Anser indicus* L 30" (76 cm)
Asian species. Fairly common in zoos and private collections.

Graylag Goose *Anser anser* L 34" (86 cm)
Eurasian species, progenitor of most domestic geese. A recent record of a wild bird off Newfoundland (page 398). Compare carefully to Greater White-fronted Goose (page 14).

Ruddy Duck

dark cap contrasts sharply with white face

winter ♂

long pointed tail often raised

winter ♀

breeding ♂

raised tail is spread in display

bright blue

breeding ♀

rufous body

single blurry line

breeding ♂

dark wings

flies low with rapid wing beats

♀

breeding ♂

white wing patches, but species seldom seen in flight

long pointed tail

♀

winter ♂

all plumages but breeding male have two dark bars

Masked Duck

smaller, stubbier bill than Ruddy

breeding ♀

juvenile

blackish head

winter ♀

body more richly colored than Ruddy

breeding ♂

Ruddy Shelduck

adult ♂

adult ♂

Common Shelduck

Egyptian Goose

adults

Mandarin Duck

♀

♂

compare to female Wood Duck

wild type

Graylag Goose

domestic type

Bar-headed Goose

adult

Ducks in Flight

Perching Ducks

Wood Duck

dark wings

long tail

♂

♀

Muscovy Duck

slow gooselike flight

juvenile ♀

large white wing patch

adult ♂

Dabbling Ducks

American Wigeon

white forewing

adult ♂

white underwing coverts and axillaries

♀

Eurasian Wigeon

white forewing

adult ♂

dusky underwing coverts and axillaries

gray-morph ♀

Mallard

♂

broad white borders to blue speculum

♀

Gadwall

white patch on inner secondaries

♂

white belly

♀

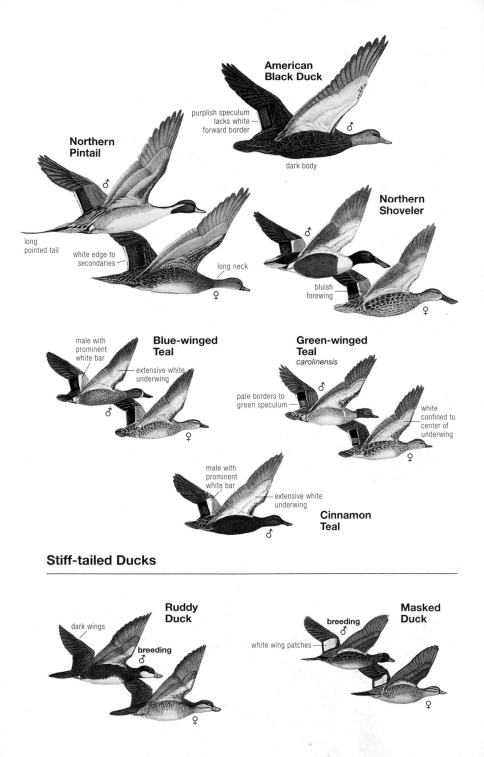

American Black Duck

purplish speculum lacks white forward border

dark body

♂

Northern Pintail

♂

long pointed tail

white edge to secondaries

long neck

♀

Northern Shoveler

♂

bluish forewing

♀

Blue-winged Teal

male with prominent white bar

extensive white underwing

♂

♀

Green-winged Teal
carolinensis

♂

pale borders to green speculum

white confined to center of underwing

♀

male with prominent white bar

extensive white underwing

Cinnamon Teal

♂

Stiff-tailed Ducks

Ruddy Duck

dark wings

breeding ♂

♀

Masked Duck

breeding ♂

white wing patches

♀

Ducks in Flight

Bay Ducks *(Aythya)*

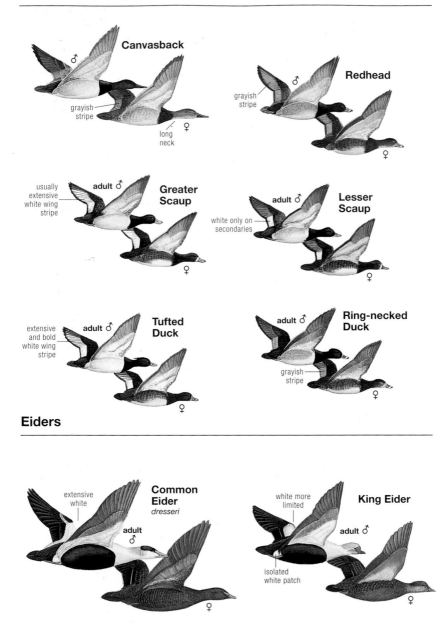

Canvasback

♂

grayish stripe

long neck ♀

Redhead

grayish stripe

♂

♀

usually extensive white wing stripe

adult ♂

Greater Scaup

♀

white only on secondaries

adult ♂

Lesser Scaup

♀

extensive and bold white wing stripe

adult ♂

Tufted Duck

♀

adult ♂

Ring-necked Duck

grayish stripe

♀

Eiders

extensive white

Common Eider
dresseri

adult ♂

♀

white more limited

King Eider

adult ♂

isolated white patch

♀

Sea Ducks

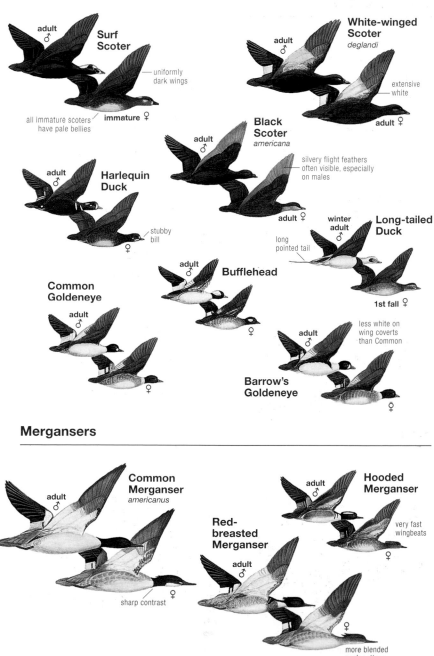

Surf Scoter
adult ♂
— uniformly dark wings
all immature scoters have pale bellies
immature ♀

White-winged Scoter
deglandi
adult ♂
extensive white
adult ♀

Harlequin Duck
adult ♂
stubby bill
♀

Black Scoter
americana
adult ♂
silvery flight feathers often visible, especially on males
adult ♀

Long-tailed Duck
winter adult ♂
long pointed tail
1st fall ♀

Common Goldeneye
adult ♂
♀

Bufflehead
adult ♂
♀

Barrow's Goldeneye
adult ♂
less white on wing coverts than Common
♀

Mergansers

Common Merganser
americanus
adult ♂
sharp contrast
♀

Red-breasted Merganser
adult ♂
♀
more blended neck pattern

Hooded Merganser
adult ♂
very fast wingbeats
♀

Curassows, Guans (Family Cracidae)

These tropical-forest birds have short, rounded wings and long tails. Generally secretive but highly vocal. One species of this family is found in the United States.

Plain Chachalaca *Ortalis vetula L 22" (56 cm)*

Gray to brownish olive above, buffier below, with small head, slight crest; long and rounded, lustrous, dark green tail tipped with white. Patch of bare skin on throat, usually grayish, is pinkish red in ***breeding male.*** Juvenile is duller. Chachalacas are found both foraging on the ground and hopping branch to branch up in trees. Almost always found in small flocks.
Voice: Male's call is a deep, ringing *cha-cha-lac*; female's voice is higher pitched; often given in a loud chorus—often synchronized—with other individuals. Also a low *krrr.*
Range: Inhabits subtropical woodlands, tall mesquite thickets, and even well-vegetated residential areas along the lower Rio Grande; feeds on the ground and in trees, chiefly on leaves and buds; often best seen at feeding stations, which many habituate. Introduced to Georgia's Sapelo Island.

Partridges, Grouse, Turkeys, Old World Quail
(Family Phasianidae)

Ground dwellers with feathered nostrils, short, strong bills, and short, rounded wings. Flight is brief but strong. Males perform elaborate courting displays. In some species, birds gather at the same strutting grounds, known as leks, every year.

Wild Turkey *Meleagris gallopavo*

♂*L 46" (117 cm)* ♀*L 37" (94 cm)* Largest game bird in North America; slightly smaller, more slender than the domesticated bird. Usually seen in flocks. ***Male*** has dark, iridescent body, flight feathers barred with white, red wattles, blackish breast tuft, spurred legs; bare-skinned head is blue and pink. Tail, uppertail coverts, and lower rump feathers are tipped with chestnut on eastern birds. ***Female*** and immature are smaller and duller than male, often lack breast tufts. Of the races seen in North America, *silvestris* predominates in the East. Birds from Kansas to Mexico (*intermedia*) are intermediate between *silvestris* and *merriami* of the Southwest; *intermedia* has buffy rather than whitish (*merriami*) tipping to the uppertail coverts and has a glossy black rump. Birds from Peninsular Florida (*osceola*) are like *silvestris,* but smaller.
Voice: In spring a male's gobbling call may be heard a mile away.
Range: Restocked in much of its former range and introduced in other areas. Birds of the open forest, forest openings, and field edges, Wild Turkeys forage mostly on the ground for seeds, nuts, acorns, and insects. Early and late in the day, groups may be seen foraging out into fields, pastures, and open agricultural land. At night they roost in trees.

breeding ♂

red
wattle

white tail tips

**Plain
Chachalaca**

long blackish tail

unfeathered
reddish head

displaying ♂

Wild Turkey
eastern *silvestris*

breast tuft —

♀
unfeathered
gray head

rufous
tipping

Ring-necked Pheasant *Phasianus colchicus*
♂ *L 33" (84 cm)* ♀ *L 21" (53 cm)* Introduced from Asia, this large, flashy bird has a long, pointed tail and short, rounded wings. *Male* is iridescent bronze overall, mottled with brown, black, and green; head varies from dark, glossy green to purplish, with fleshy red eye patches and iridescent ear tufts. Often shows a broad white neck ring. *Female* is buffy overall, much smaller and duller than male. Distinguished from female Sharp-tailed Grouse (page 56) by larger size, longer tail, lack of barring below, and lack of white in tail.

Voice: Male's territorial call is a loud, penetrating *kok-cack*. Both sexes give hoarse, croaking alarm notes. When flushed, rise almost vertically with a loud whirring of wings.

Range: Locally common; declining in parts of the East. Found in open country, farmlands, brushy areas, and woodland and marsh edges. Local hunting releases help maintain some populations and account for presence of some individuals outside normal range. The Japanese subspecies *"Green Pheasant,"* *versicolor,* introduced in tidewater Virginia and southern Delaware, is apparently gone.

Spruce Grouse *Falcipennis canadensis* L 16" (41 cm)
Male has dark throat and breast, edged with white; red eye combs. Over most of range, both sexes have black tail with chestnut tip. *Females* have two color *morphs,* red and *gray*; distinguished from Ruffed Grouse by lack of crest, different breast and tail pattern. Juveniles resemble red-morph female.

Voice: Both sexes give soft, low clucking notes. Female's high-pitched call is thought to be territorial. In courtship display, male spreads his tail, erects the red eye combs, and rapidly beats wings. In territorial flight display, male flutters upward on shallow wingstrokes.

Range: Widespread but tame and retiring, so easily overlooked. Spruce Grouse inhabit open coniferous and taiga forests with dense undergrowth. Frequents roadsides, especially in fall.

Ruffed Grouse *Bonasa umbellus* L 17" (43 cm)
Small crest; black ruff on sides of neck, usually inconspicuous; banded tail with wide, dark band near tip, incomplete in *female.* The two color *morphs, red* and *gray,* are most apparent by tail color. Red morphs predominate in the Appalachian region; gray morphs in the North. Ten subspecies recognized, five of which are found in the East.

Voice: In spring, the *male* displays by raising ruff and crest, fanning tail, and beating wings to make a hollow, accelerating, drumming noise. Both sexes give soft clucking notes. When flushed gives burst of wingbeats that may be startling.

Range: Uncommon to fairly common in deciduous and mixed woodlands. Numbers may fluctuate from year to year. Declining east of the Appalachians.

Ring-necked Pheasant

white neck ring

♀

♂

"Green Pheasant"
♂
♀

long tail—compare
carefully to female
Sharp-tailed Grouse

♀

Spruce Grouse

red comb

gray-morph ♀

displaying ♂

rufous
tail band

displaying
gray-morph ♂

crest

red-morph
♂

male with
solid band

Ruffed Grouse

red-morph ♀

female with
broken band

Gray Partridge *Perdix perdix L 12½" (32 cm)*
Grayish brown bird with rusty face and throat, paler in *female.*
Male has dark chestnut patch on belly; patch is smaller or absent in females. Flanks are barred with reddish brown; outer tail feathers rusty.
Voice: Includes a hoarse *kee-uck,* likened to a rusty gate.
Range: Widely introduced from Europe in early 1900s. Uncommon in most areas; has declined over parts of North American range. Inhabits open farmlands and grassy fields. In fall, forms coveys of 10 to 15 birds. Easiest to find when there is snow cover.

Willow Ptarmigan *Lagopus lagopus L 15" (38 cm)*
Largest ptarmigan. Mottled *summer* plumage of *male* is generally redder than in Rock Ptarmigan. White *winter* plumage lacks the black eye line of male Rock Ptarmigan; bill and overall size are slightly larger in Willow Ptarmigan. *Female* is otherwise difficult to distinguish from Rock Ptarmigan. Both species retain white wings and black tail year-round. Plumage is patchy white during *spring* and fall *molts.*
Voice: Includes low growls and croaks, noisy cackles. In courtship and territorial displays, male utters a raucous *go-back go-back go-backa go-backa go-backa.* Ptarmigans' red eye combs can be concealed or raised during courtship and aggression.
Range: Willow Ptarmigan is common on tundra, especially in thickets of willow and alder. In breeding season, generally prefers wetter, brushier habitat than Rock Ptarmigan. Irregular fall and winter movements slightly south of normal range. Casual in spring and winter to northern tier of U.S. states.

Rock Ptarmigan *Lagopus muta L 14" (36 cm)*
Mottled *summer* plumage is black, dark brown, or grayish brown; *male* generally lacks the reddish tones of male Willow Ptarmigan. There are many recognized subspecies, with color variations according to geography. In *winter* plumage, *male* has a black line from bill through eye, lacking in male Willow. Acquires breeding plumage later in spring than does Willow. In both sexes, bill and overall size are slightly smaller than in Willow. *Females* are otherwise difficult to distinguish from Willows. Plumage is patchy white during spring and fall molts. Both species retain white wings and black tail year-round.
Voice: Includes low growls and croaks and noisy cackles.
Range: The Rock Ptarmigan is common on high, rocky slopes and tundra. In breeding season, generally prefers higher and more barren habitat than does Willow Ptarmigan. May form flocks in winter. Irregular fall and winter movements slightly south of normal range. Accidental in northern Minnesota.

Gray Partridge

rufous face and throat

♀

rufous outer tail feathers

gray breast

dark belly

♂

summer ♂

dark rufous head and neck

thick bill

molting spring ♂

winter

Willow Ptarmigan

summer ♀

summer ♂

bold black eye line

winter ♂

winter ♀

slighter bill than Willow

summer ♀

Rock Ptarmigan

fall ♂

Greater Prairie-Chicken *Tympanuchus cupido*
L 17" (43 cm) Heavily barred with dark brown, cinnamon, and pale buff above and below. Short, rounded tail is all-dark in *male,* barred in *female.* Male has fleshy yellow-orange eye combs. Both sexes have elongated dark neck feathers, longer in males and erected during courtship to display inflated golden-orange neck sacs.
Voice: Courting males make a deep *oo-loo-woo* sound known as "booming," like blowing over top of an empty bottle.
Range: Uncommon, local, and declining. Found in areas of natural tallgrass prairie interspersed with cropland. A smaller, darker race, endangered "Attwater's Prairie-Chicken," *attwateri* (**E**) of southeastern Texas, is nearly extinct. The "Heath Hen" (nominate subspecies *cupido*), formerly resident along the Atlantic seaboard from Massachusetts to Virginia, is now extinct—last record on Martha's Vineyard in 1932.

Lesser Prairie-Chicken *Tympanuchus pallidicinctus*
L 16" (41 cm) Resembles Greater Prairie-Chicken, but slightly smaller, paler, less heavily barred below. Courting male displays orange-red neck sacs and erects dark neck tufts.
Voice: Male's "booming" sound slightly higher pitched than in Greater Prairie-Chicken.
Range: Uncommon, local, and declining in many parts of its range; found in sagebrush and shortgrass prairie country, especially where shinnery oak grows. Will forage in cropland.

Sharp-tailed Grouse *Tympanuchus phasianellus*
L 17" (43 cm) Similar to prairie-chickens, but underparts are scaled and spotted; tail is mostly white and pointed; yellowish eye combs are less prominent. Compare with female Ring-necked Pheasant (page 52). Birds are darkest in northern Canada (standing figure), palest in the Plains (flying figure). *Male*'s purplish neck sacs are inflated during courtship display.
Voice: Courting notes include cackling and a single, low *coo-oo* call accompanied by the rattling of wing quills.
Range: Inhabits grasslands, cropland, sagebrush, woodland edges, and clearcuts. Fairly common over much of range. Where ranges overlap, can hybridize with Greater Prairie-Chicken.

Greater Sage-Grouse *Centrocercus urophasianus*
♂L 28" (71 cm) ♀L 22" (56 cm) Blackish belly, long pointed tail feathers, and large size are distinctive. *Male* is larger than *female* and has yellow eye combs, black throat and bib, and large white ruff on breast. In flight, dark belly, absence of white outer tail feathers, and larger size distinguish it from Sharp-tailed Grouse; from female Ring-necked Pheasant by dark belly patch. *Displaying male* fans tail and rapidly inflates and deflates air sacs, emitting a loud, bubbling popping.
Voice: During display male gives gulping sounds.
Range: Uncommon and local in sagebrush areas of western Plains. Declining.

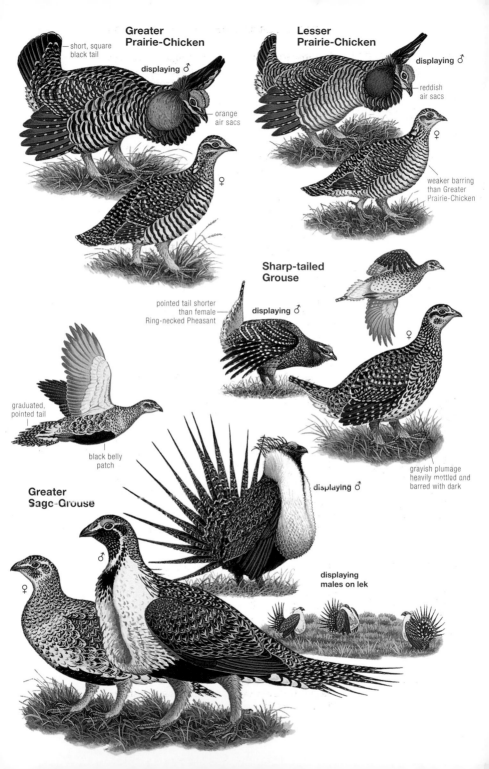

Greater Prairie-Chicken

short, square black tail

displaying ♂

orange air sacs

♀

Lesser Prairie-Chicken

displaying ♂

reddish air sacs

♀

weaker barring than Greater Prairie-Chicken

Sharp-tailed Grouse

pointed tail shorter than female Ring-necked Pheasant

displaying ♂

♀

grayish plumage heavily mottled and barred with dark

graduated, pointed tail

black belly patch

Greater Sage-Grouse

displaying ♂

displaying males on lek

♀

♂

58

New World Quail (Family Odontophoridae)

Scientific evidence has recently placed the New World Quail in their own family. All have chunky bodies and crests or head plumes. In North America, most live in the West.

Northern Bobwhite *Colinus virginianus L 9¾" (25 cm)*
Mottled, reddish brown quail with short gray tail. Flanks are striped with reddish brown. Throat and eye stripe are white in *male,* buffy in *female. Juvenile* is smaller and duller.
Voice: Male's call is a rising, whistled *bob-white,* heard chiefly in late spring and summer; whistled *hoy* call is heard year-round. Also soft clucking sounds.
Range: Uncommon to common in brushlands, open woodlands, agricultural land, and field edges, the bobwhite feeds and roosts in coveys except during nesting season. At northern edge of range, numbers have greatly declined over the last few decades. Recent hunting releases may be found in areas where the species is not truly established.

Montezuma Quail *Cyrtonyx montezumae L 8¾" (22 cm)*
Plump, short-tailed, round-winged quail. *Male* has distinctive facial pattern and rounded pale brown crest on back of head. Back and wings mottled black, brown, and tan; breast dark chestnut; sides and flanks dark gray with white spots. *Female* is mottled pinkish brown below with less distinct head markings. *Juvenile* is smaller, paler, with dark spotting on underparts.
Voice: Call given by male in breeding season is a loud, quavering, descending whistle.
Range: This secretive southwestern species barely enters the area covered by this guide along the western edge of the Edwards Plateau, in central Texas, where its small population inhabits grassy brushland. Uncommon, secretive, and local in grassy undergrowth of open juniper-oak savanna.

Scaled Quail *Callipepla squamata L 10" (25 cm)*
Grayish quail with conspicuous white-tipped crest. Bluish gray breast and mantle feathers have dark edges, creating a shingled or scaly effect. Female's crest is buffy and smaller. *Males* in southernmost Texas (*castanogastris*) tend to show a dark chestnut patch on belly, unlike the common subspecies, *pallida,* found over much of the U.S. range. *Juvenile* resembles adult but is more mottled above, with less conspicuous scaling.
Voice: During breeding season, both sexes give a location call when separated, a low, nasal *chip-churr,* accented on the second syllable.
Range: Uncommon; found in semidesert scrublands and grasslands with mixed scrub; often frequents roadsides. In fall, forms large coveys.

slight crest

white supercilium

white throat

buffy supercilium

buffy throat

♂

♀

juvenile

Northern Bobwhite

smaller and darker

Florida ♂ *floridanus*

dark buffy crest laid over nape

exotic head pattern

round white spots

solid blackish brown

♂

slightly crested look

Montezuma Quail

♀

juvenile

pale buffy top to crest

Scaled Quail

south Texas ♂ *castanogastris*

scaly breast

dark chestnut belly patch

juvenile

♂ *pallida*

60

Loons (Family Gaviidae)

In all species, juvenal-like plumage is held through the first summer.

Red-throated Loon *Gavia stellata* L 25" *(64 cm)*

Thin bill often appears slightly upturned; tends to hold head tilted up. ***Breeding adult*** has gray head with brick red throat patch that appears dark in flight; dark brown upperparts with no contrasting white patches on scapulars as in all other loons in breeding plumage. ***Winter adult*** has sharply defined white on face and extensive white spotting on back. ***Juvenile***'s head is grayish brown; throat may have dull red markings. In all plumages, white on flanks extends upward a bit on sides of rump, which may cause confusion with Arctic Loon, which is not yet recorded in East. In flight, shows smaller head and feet than Common and Yellow-billed Loon; wingbeat is quicker; often flies with drooping neck, unlike other loons.

Voice: Flight call, heard on breeding range, is a rapid, gooselike *kak-kak-kak*; otherwise, largely silent.

Range: Migrates coastally; also some overland where most numerous on northern and eastern Great Lakes. Casual in interior during winter.

Pacific Loon *Gavia pacifica* L 26" *(66 cm)*

In all plumages, has dark flanks, with no white extending upward on sides of rump. Bill is slim and straight; head smoothly rounded and held level. ***Breeding adult***'s head and nape are pale gray; white stripes on sides of neck show only moderate contrast; throat's iridescent purple patch, sometimes washed with green, usually appears black unless seen clearly on swimming bird. ***Juvenile***'s crown and nape are slightly paler than back, unlike Common Loon; in juvenile and ***winter adult***, dark cap extends to eye. Winter adults and most juveniles have a thin, brown "chin strap," though it may be faint in juveniles. Compare to juvenile Red-throated Loon, with which this species is sometimes confused. In flight, resembles Common, but head and feet are smaller.

Voice: Largely silent.

Range: Very rare on Great Plains, in Midwest, and along western Gulf Coast; casual on East Coast.

IDENTIFYING: Winter Loons Observing winter loons can be tricky, especially when birds are distant or it is hard to establish size. Characteristics to look for include posture, bill shape, and the degree of contrast in the head and neck. The widespread Common Loon is large and blocky, with a big bill and a dark patch on the sides of the neck. The smaller Red-throated Loon has a paler face than Common; the adult Red-throated is strikingly white, and the juvenile is marked with brownish. Red-throated often holds its head up a bit, like Yellow-billed (casual in the East), but unlike Common or Pacific, the latter of which is rare in the East. Pacific, which is similar in size to Red-throated, is colored more like Common. It shows a clean and even line of separation of dark and white on the neck; the leading edge of the dark color is the darkest, often appearing as a subtle, broad, dark vertical line. Many Pacifics show a chin strap, which should not be confused with the dusky wash across the upper neck shown by many juvenile Red-throated Loons.

winter adult

in flight, neck often droops

1st spring

Red-throated Loon

bill slightly upturned and often holds head up

breeding adult

reddish throat often looks dark

face and neck washed with dusky

extensive pure white face

white speckling on back

juvenile

winter adult

swimming juveniles for comparison

Common   **Yellow-billed**   **Pacific**   **Red-throated**

winter adult

some young birds lack chin straps

juveniles

Pacific Loon

white scaling

winter adult

dark chin strap

sharp and even division between front and rear of neck

dark upperparts

winter adult

faint white vertical streaks

pale gray nape

breeding adult

Common Loon   *Gavia immer*   L 32" *(81 cm)*

Large, thick-billed loon with slightly curved culmen. Bill is black in **breeding** plumage, blue-gray in **winter adult** and **juvenile,** but the culmen remains dark. In winter plumage, crown and nape are darker than back; dark on nape extends around sides of neck, but note the white indentation above this. In winter adult the white extends up and around the eye; the face pattern is more blended in juveniles. Forehead is steep, crown is peaked at front. Holds head level. Juvenile Common and Yellow-billed Loons have whitish scalloping on their scapulars, distinguishing them from the plainer-backed winter adults. Full juvenal plumage is kept through most of the winter, with a partial molt in spring. Most winter adults retain at least a few spotted coverts, often visible on swimming birds. Under most conditions, Common and Yellow-billed fly quite high above the water when migrating, while the other loon species fly lower. Note their slower wingbeats and the paddle-shaped feet that are usually visible beyond the tail. Winters mainly in coastal waters or on large, ice-free inland bodies of water. In flight, large head and feet help distinguish Common from Pacific and Red-throated Loons.

Voice: Loud yodeling calls delivered on water and in flight are heard all year, but most often on breeding grounds.

Range: Fairly common; nests on large lakes. Migrates overland as well as coastally.

Yellow-billed Loon   *Gavia adamsii*   L 34" *(86 cm)*

Breeding adult has straw-yellow bill, usually longer than in Common Loon; culmen is straight, giving bill a slightly uptilted look; head often tilted back, which enhances this effect. Crown is peaked at front and rear, giving a subtle double-bump effect. Bill is duskier at the base in **winter adult** and **juvenile,** but always shows strong yellow cast toward the tip, including the culmen (dark in Common). Note also pale face and distinct, variably shaped dark mark behind eye; eye is smaller, back and crown are paler and browner than in Common.

Voice: Calls are similar to Common.

Range: Yellow-billed Loon breeds on tundra lakes and rivers. Migrates coastally; casual east to Great Lakes region and Pennsylvania, and south to Texas and Georgia.

IDENTIFYING: Loons in Flight Loons are periodically seen in flight, routinely so during migration, especially from coastal headlands. Common is most likely to fly high, and its large feet are usually prominent. Red-throated Loon often flies lower and often drops its neck below the horizontal line of the body.

Pacific Loon is quite gregarious in the West, often migrating in flocks, but in the East it is strictly a rarity. In breeding plumage, all species except Red-throated show striking white markings on the scapulars; Red-throated is uniformly brownish above. Common and Yellow-billed (casual in the East) show a distinct white collar. Pacific shows a pale gray nape, which contrasts with the blackish throat area; it also shows a thick black line down the sides and flanks that separates the white underwings from the white under body. Size can be helpful, particularly if more than one species is present.

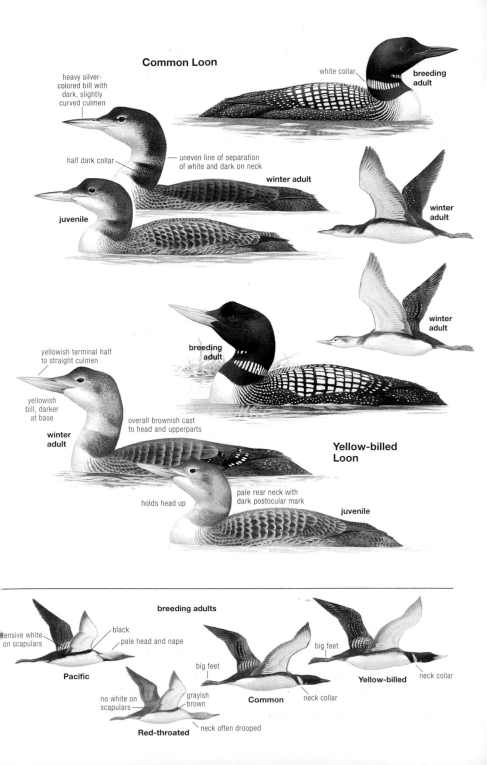

Common Loon

heavy silver-colored bill with dark, slightly curved culmen

white collar

breeding adult

half dark collar

uneven line of separation of white and dark on neck

winter adult

juvenile

winter adult

winter adult

yellowish terminal half to straight culmen

breeding adult

yellowish bill, darker at base

overall brownish cast to head and upperparts

winter adult

Yellow-billed Loon

holds head up

pale rear neck with dark postocular mark

juvenile

breeding adults

tensive white on scapulars

black

pale head and nape

big feet

big feet

Pacific

no white on scapulars

grayish brown

neck collar

neck collar

Yellow-billed

Red-throated

neck often drooped

Common

neck collar

Grebes (Family Podicipedidae)

A worldwide family of aquatic diving birds. Lobed toes make them strong swimmers. Grebes are infrequently seen on land or in flight.

Least Grebe *Tachybaptus dominicus* L 9¾" (25 cm)

A small, short-necked grebe with golden yellow eyes, a slim, dark bill, and purplish gray face and foreneck. ***Breeding adult*** has blackish crown, hindneck, throat, and back. ***Winter*** birds have white throat, paler bill, less black on crown. In flight, shows large white wing patch. Compare with nonbreeding Pied-billed Grebe.
Voice: Usually silent; sometimes utters nasal notes.
Range: Rather uncommon and local; may hide in vegetation near shores of ponds, sloughs, ditches. May nest at any season.

Pied-billed Grebe *Podilymbus podiceps* L 13½" (34 cm)

A short-necked, big-headed grebe. ***Breeding adult*** is brown overall, with black ring around stout, whitish bill; black chin and throat; pale belly. ***Winter*** birds lose bill ring; chin is white, throat tinged with pale rufous. ***Juvenile*** resembles winter adult but throat is much redder, head and neck streaked. In flight, shows almost no white on wing.
Voice: On breeding grounds gives distinctive loud series of gulping notes.
Range: Nests around marshy ponds and sloughs; sometimes hides from intruders by sinking until only its head shows. Winters on fresh or salt water.

Horned Grebe *Podiceps auritus* L 13½" (34 cm)

Breeding adult has chestnut foreneck, golden "horns." In ***winter*** plumage, white cheeks and throat contrast with dark crown and nape; some are dusky on lower foreneck. Black on nape narrows to a thin stripe. All birds show a pale spot in front of eye. In flight, white secondaries show as patch on trailing edge of wing. Bill is short and straight, thicker than Eared Grebe's, and often shows pale tip; neck is thicker too, crown flatter. Most often confused when in transitional plumage in early spring. Smaller size and shorter, dark bill separate winter Horned from Red-necked.
Voice: Mostly silent away from breeding grounds.
Range: Breeds on lakes and ponds. Winters mostly on salt water but also on ice-free lakes.

Eared Grebe *Podiceps nigricollis* L 12½" (32 cm)

Breeding adult has blackish neck, golden "ears" fanning out behind eye. In ***winter*** plumage, throat variably dusky; cheek dark; whitish on chin extends up as a crescent behind eye; compare with Horned Grebe. Note Eared's thinner bill; thinner neck; more peaked crown. Lacks pale spot in front of eye. Generally rides higher in the water than Horned, exposing fluffy white undertail coverts. In flight, shows white patch on trailing edge of wing.
Voice: Mostly silent away from breeding grounds.
Range: Nests on marshy lakes. Rare in most of East.

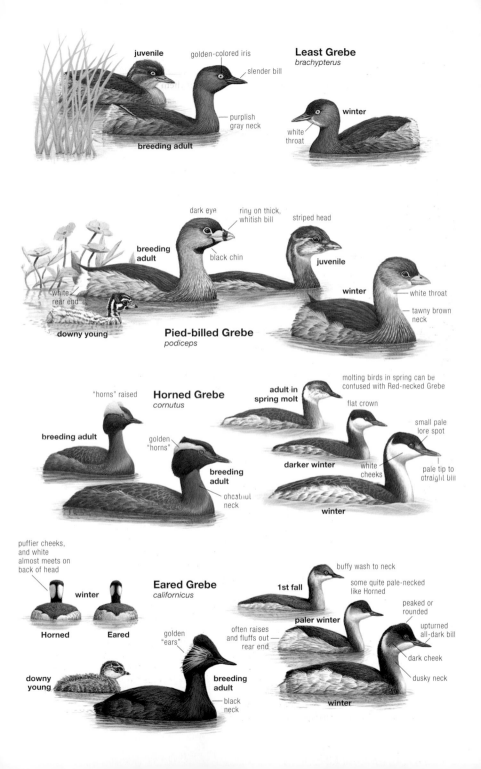

Least Grebe
brachypterus

juvenile
golden-colored iris
slender bill
purplish gray neck
breeding adult

winter
white throat

Pied-billed Grebe
podiceps

dark eye
ring on thick, whitish bill
breeding adult
black chin
striped head
juvenile
winter
white throat
tawny brown neck
white rear end
downy young

Horned Grebe
cornutus

"horns" raised
breeding adult
golden "horns"
breeding adult
chestnut neck

molting birds in spring can be confused with Red-necked Grebe
adult in spring molt
flat crown
darker winter
white cheeks
small pale lore spot
pale tip to straight bill
winter

Eared Grebe
californicus

puffier cheeks, and white almost meets on back of head
winter
Horned   Eared

golden "ears"
often raises and fluffs out rear end
breeding adult
black neck
downy young

buffy wash to neck
1st fall
some quite pale-necked like Horned
paler winter
peaked or rounded
upturned all-dark bill
dark cheek
dusky neck
winter

Red-necked Grebe *Podiceps grisegena* L 20" (51 cm)

Large grebe with heavy, tapered, mostly yellowish bill almost as long as the head. ***Breeding adult****'s* whitish throat and cheeks contrast with reddish foreneck. In **winter** plumage, throat is dusky, white of chin extends onto rear of face in a crescent. ***First-winter*** bird has rounder head, paler eye; lacks strong facial crescent. ***Juvenile*** has striped head, darker bill. In flight, Red-necked Grebe shows a white leading and trailing edge on inner wing; thick neck is often held slouched down. Generally solitary.

Voice: Calls, usually heard only on breeding grounds, include a *crick-crick* note and drawn out braying calls.

Range: Breeds on shallow lakes; winters mostly along coasts. Rare in interior south of northern tier of states; occasionally, moderate numbers winter in mid-Atlantic region, especially in years when Great Lakes freeze. Casual south to Southwest and Gulf Coast states.

Clark's Grebe *Aechmophorus clarkii* L 25" (64 cm)

Resembles Western Grebe but bill is yellow-orange; back and flanks are paler; black cap does not extend to eye in ***breeding*** plumage; ***downy young*** are paler. In **winter adult,** lore region acquires more dark color, pattern looks more like Western; best distinction then is bill color. In flight, Clark Grebe's white wing stripe is more extensive than on Western.

Voice: Call is a single, two-syllabled, upslurred *kree-eek* note.

Range: Limits of range in both species are not well known; Clark's occupies same general area and habitat as Western but is much less common in northern and eastern part of range. Accidental to eastern North America. Formerly considered one species with Western; hybrids are sometimes noted.

Western Grebe *Aechmophorus occidentalis* L 25" (64 cm)

Large grebe, strikingly black and white, with a long, thin neck and long bill. Resembles Clark's Grebe but bill is yellow-green; black cap extends to include eyes; back and flanks are darker; ***downy young*** are darker. In **winter adult,** lore region acquires more whitish color, and pattern can closely resemble winter Clark's. In flight, Western Grebe's white wing stripe is less extensive than Clark's.

Voice: Call is a loud, two-note *crick-kreek.*

Range: Gregarious; nests in reeds along broad, freshwater lakes. Winters on seacoasts and sheltered bays and large inland bodies of water. Occupies same general range and habitat as Clark's but greatly predominates in northern and eastern part of range. Casual during migration and winter to eastern North America. Formerly considered one species with Clark's; hybrids are regularly noted.

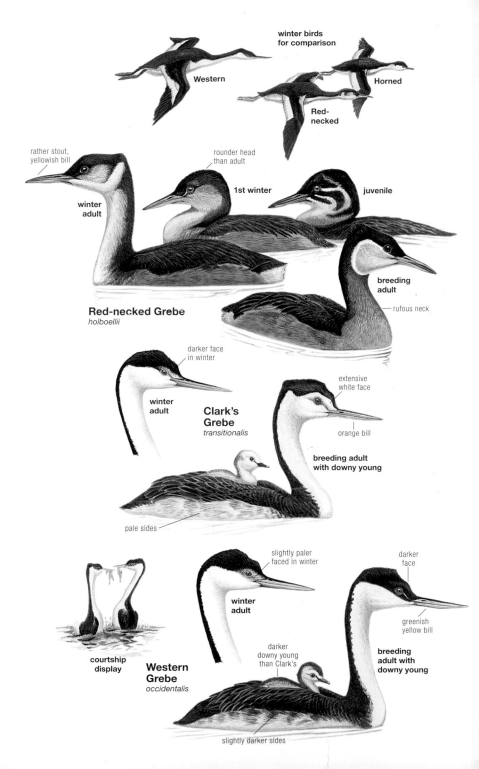

winter birds
for comparison

Western

Horned

Red-
necked

rather stout,
yellowish bill

rounder head
than adult

1st winter

juvenile

winter
adult

Red-necked Grebe
holboellii

breeding
adult

rufous neck

darker face
in winter

winter
adult

**Clark's
Grebe**
transitionalis

extensive
white face

orange bill

**breeding adult
with downy young**

pale sides

slightly paler
faced in winter

darker
face

winter
adult

greenish
yellow bill

courtship
display

**Western
Grebe**
occidentalis

darker
downy young
than Clark's

**breeding
adult with
downy young**

slightly darker sides

Shearwaters, Petrels (Family Procellariidae)

These pelagic seabirds are rarely seen from shore. They fly with rapid wingbeats, stiff-winged glides. Some may arc up and down well off the surface of the water in a roller-coaster fashion. Flight style may vary depending on wind conditions and whether the individual is in search of food or in direct flight. Most species are generally silent at sea. Their bills have nostril tubes.

Northern Fulmar *Fulmarus glacialis*
L 19" (48 cm) WS 42" (107 cm) Atlantic birds (*glacialis*) are thicker billed than Pacific birds (*rogersii*) and show a uniformly colored tail and rump; also the color morphs are not as dark (illustrated *dark morphs* are more typical of Pacific birds) or as pale as the various Pacific morphs. *Intermediate* morphs of all shades also occur. Unlike the Pacific populations, dark and intermediate morphs predominate at high latitudes in the North Atlantic, while more southerly breeders are all **light morphs**. Many authorities only recognize one subspecies in the North Atlantic. All birds show pale inner primaries. Distinguished from gulls by short, thick bill with nostril tubes, and shearwater-like flight; from shearwaters by thick, yellow bill, stockier shape, thicker neck, and rounder wings.
Voice: Although mostly silent when at sea, fulmars will give harsh grunting sounds when squabbling over food.
Range: Nests on sea cliffs. Prefers cold waters. Uncommon south of Newfoundland. Within winter range, numbers fluctuate annually; some nonbreeders summer south to Gulf of Maine. Casual on Hudson Bay.

IDENTIFYING: Pelagic Birds Pelagic birds constitute the order Procellariiformes, which in the Northern Hemisphere is divided into the albatrosses, petrels and shearwaters, and storm-petrels. As a group, they are popularly known as the "tubenoses" for their unique tubed nostrils. Other characteristics of the order include hooked bills made up of separate bill plates, webbed feet, large olfactory glands, the ability to excrete excess salt (typically through the nostril tubes), and highly developed powers of flight. Their diet includes fish, squid, and zooplankton; many tubenoses are attracted to fishing boats and chum. All are essentially oceanic in lifestyle, coming onshore only to breed. Most species are rarely if ever seen from shore during the nonbreeding season, although some are visible from land, occasionally in large numbers. Only six species of tubenoses breed in North America, and only three of these do so in the northwest Atlantic. Most of the others are visitors to our waters from nesting grounds on distant, often remote islands, many in the Southern Hemisphere. Despite the huge distances they travel, several of these species—such as Greater and Sooty Shearwaters and Wilson's Storm-Petrel—can be surprisingly numerous in our waters during *their* nonbreeding season, which is *our* late spring, summer, and early autumn.

The identification of pelagic birds is challenging. Most North American observations are made at sea, where rocking boats, great distances, and generally drab plumage can exasperate even experienced seabirders. Observers should focus on the light-dark patterns, overall size and shape, wing proportions, and the flight style. Such identification skills are gained only through field experience. Flight style in the albatrosses, petrels, and shearwaters is usually a series of wingbeats interspersed with stiff-winged glides. The speed, duration, and depth of the wingbeats and the frequency and duration of the glides define a species' flight style, as does the amount of arcing up and down.

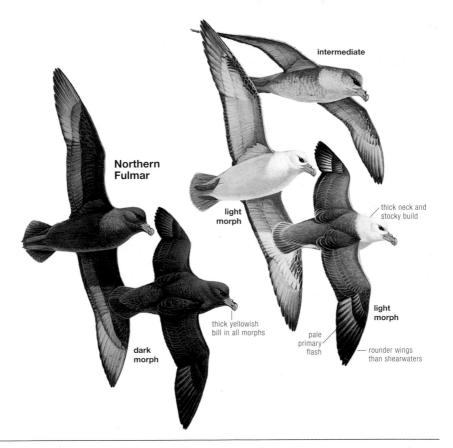

Northern Fulmar

intermediate

light
morph

thick neck and
stocky build

light
morph

thick yellowish
bill in all morphs

dark
morph

pale
primary
flash

rounder wings
than shearwaters

Storm-Petrels stay closer to the surface, and
their flight is typically more swallowlike, though
this is variable among the species. In all
tubenoses, wind speed and a bird's activity will
alter its flight style. Whether the winds are strong
or light, whether the bird is flying into or with the
wind, and whether it is feeding or carrying out
direct traveling flight are all factors that con-
tribute to the variability seen.

Black-browed
Albatross

Band-rumped
Storm-Petrel

Black-capped
Petrel

Cory's
Shearwater

Gadfly Petrels

Fast-flying petrels with arcing, acrobatic flight in high winds. Unlike shearwaters, they typically hold their wings slightly forward from the shoulder and bent sharply back at the "wrist." The four species found off our Atlantic and Gulf coasts are largely tied to Gulf Stream waters, with the majority of records from off North Carolina.

Black-capped Petrel *Pterodroma hasitata*
L 16" (41 cm) WS 37" (94 cm) Distinct dark cap; white collar; broad white band on uppertail coverts and base of tail. White wing lining, with variable dark diagonal bar on leading edge. Wing and bill shape, white forehead, broader band on tail, and languid, arching flight distinguish this species from Greater Shearwater (page 72). Some birds have less white at base of tail and duskier collar. Black-capped usually seen singly and typically does not approach boats closely.
Range: Breeds on Hispaniola and Cuba. Common in Gulf Stream off North Carolina from late May to mid-Oct.; uncommon in winter; casual north to Nova Scotia and in Gulf of Mexico. Recorded from shore and inland after hurricanes.

Fea's Petrel *Pterodroma feae* *L 14" (36 cm) WS 37" (94 cm)*
Fea's is brownish gray above with dark M pattern, pale uppertail coverts and tail. White below; partial breast band; mostly dark underwings.
Range: Breeds in the Madeira and Cape Verde Islands off West Africa. Rare but annual visitor off North Carolina in late May and early June, casual into the fall; accidental to Nova Scotia. Sightings (supported by excellent photos but no specimens) in this case believed to be Fea's, not Zino's Petrel (*P. madeira*, a highly endangered species breeding only on Madeira), based on larger bill size and likelihood.

Bermuda Petrel *Pterodroma cahow* **E**
L 15" (38 cm) WS 35" (89 cm) Species believed extinct, but rediscovered in 1951; population increasing, now estimated at about 200. Note that larger Black-capped Petrel has heavier bill and disproportionately shorter wings. Bermuda Petrel's whitish rump, sometimes lacking, is restricted to base of uppertail coverts. It is slightly smaller and its body and wings are slightly slimmer than Black-capped. Without Black-capped's white collar, dark on head is more like cowl than cap; Bermuda more buoyant in flight, with darker underwings than Black-capped.
Range: Nests only on islets off Bermuda; since mid-1990s, about 20 well-documented records in late spring (mostly) and summer off Outer Banks, North Carolina.

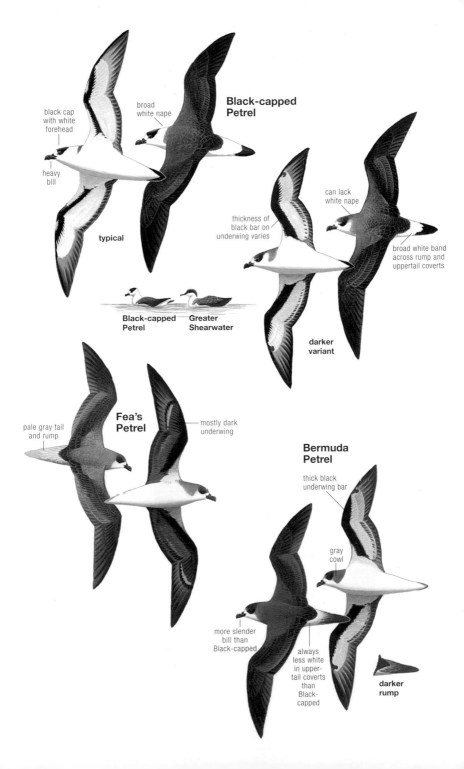

black cap with white forehead

broad white nape

Black-capped Petrel

heavy bill

typical

can lack white nape

thickness of black bar on underwing varies

broad white band across rump and uppertail coverts

darker variant

Black-capped Petrel Greater Shearwater

pale gray tail and rump

Fea's Petrel

mostly dark underwing

Bermuda Petrel

thick black underwing bar

gray cowl

more slender bill than Black-capped

always less white in uppertail coverts than Black-capped

darker rump

Herald Petrel *Pterodroma arminjoniana*
L 15½" (39 cm) WS 37½" (95 cm) Long-winged, slender-bodied species with languid wingbeats. Occurs in three morphs; ***dark morph,*** predominant in U.S., has pale-based flight feathers and greater primary coverts on underwing. Compare to chunkier Sooty Shearwater with its shorter tail, thinner bill, paler underwings, and faster wingbeats. ***Light morph*** has brownish gray head and chest, variably whitish throat, white belly, pale underwings. ***Intermediate morphs*** are variably mottled below.
Range: Tropical Southern Hemisphere species. South Atlantic birds of the nominate race nest on islands off Brazil; mid-Atlantic region sightings likely from these populations. Rare but annual visitor late May to late Sept. in Gulf Stream off North Carolina. Accidental inland after hurricanes.

Shearwaters

Most shearwaters nest on isolated offshore islands far from our shores. Their diet is predominantly fish and squid.

Cory's Shearwater *Calonectris diomedea*
L 18" (46 cm) WS 46" (117 cm) Grayish brown upperparts merge into white underparts without sharp contrast; bill is yellowish. Flight is more languid than most other shearwaters, wings are slightly more crooked.
Range: Prefers warmer waters. Nominate *diomedea* breeds in the Mediterranean; slightly larger *borealis* breeds on the Azores, Canary, and Salvage Islands. Underside of primaries darker in *borealis*. Both occur (*borealis* much more common) off East Coast, mainly late spring through fall; they are sometimes seen from shore. Uncommon in Gulf of Mexico. Rare well off coast of Atlantic provinces.

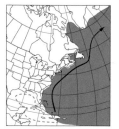

Greater Shearwater *Puffinus gravis*
L 18" (46 cm) WS 44" (112 cm) Dark brown cap contrasts with grayish brown upperparts and white cheeks. Rump usually shows a narrow, white, U-shaped band. Bill is dark; underparts white with indistinct dusky patch on belly. Many Greater Shearwaters have a white nape. Slightly smaller than Cory's Shearwater. Similar to Black-capped Petrel (page 70), but lacks white forehead and wide black bar on underwing; also has shorter, less wedge-shaped tail with less extensive white at base.
Range: Breeds in South Atlantic. Fairly common off the East Coast during migration, chiefly in spring. Summers in large numbers from the Gulf of Maine north. Sometimes seen from shore. Casual in Gulf of Mexico.

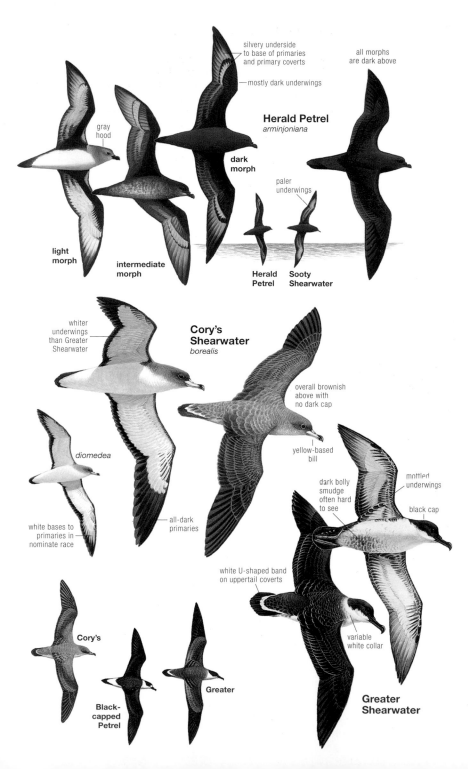

silvery underside
to base of primaries
and primary coverts

mostly dark underwings

all morphs
are dark above

gray
hood

Herald Petrel
arminjoniana

dark
morph

paler
underwings

**light
morph**

**intermediate
morph**

**Herald
Petrel**

**Sooty
Shearwater**

whiter
underwings
than Greater
Shearwater

**Cory's
Shearwater**
borealis

overall brownish
above with
no dark cap

diomedea

yellow-based
bill

mottled
underwings

dark bolly
smudge
often hard
to see

black cap

white bases to
primaries in
nominate race

all-dark
primaries

white U-shaped band
on uppertail coverts

variable
white collar

Cory's

**Black-
capped
Petrel**

Greater

**Greater
Shearwater**

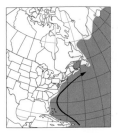

Sooty Shearwater *Puffinus griseus*
L 18" (46 cm) WS 40" (101 cm) Whitish underwing coverts contrast with Sooty Shearwater's overall dark plumage. White on underwings is usually most prominent on primary coverts. Flies with fast wingbeats and, except in windy weather, with short glides.
Range: Prefers colder waters. Breeds in Southern Hemisphere. Fairly common off East Coast in spring; fairly common in summer off New England and Atlantic Provinces. Casual in Gulf of Mexico. Sometimes seen from shore.

Manx Shearwater *Puffinus puffinus*
L 13½" (34 cm) WS 33" (84 cm) Blackish above, white below with white wing linings. Pure white undertail coverts extend to end of short tail. White wraps around dark ear coverts.
Range: Most breed on islands around the United Kingdom; one small colony in Newfoundland. Nesting also strongly suggested but not proven elsewhere in Atlantic Canada and New England. Winters mostly off eastern South America. Fairly common off the northern Atlantic coast in summer. Rare in winter from Maryland south. Sometimes seen from shore.

Audubon's Shearwater *Puffinus lherminieri*
L 12" (31 cm) WS 27" (69 cm) Dark brown above, white below, with long tail, dark undertail coverts (a few with pale ones). Small white area in front of eye. Flight fairly rapid and usually close to water; rarely arcs high off surface.
Range: Prefers warmer waters. Breeds on Caribbean islands. Common off the southern Atlantic coast, uncommon to fairly common in Gulf of Mexico, chiefly from late April through Oct. Rare in winter. Small numbers found most years in late summer north to waters off southern New England. Rarely seen from shore.

IDENTIFYING: Small Shearwaters The larger shearwaters and petrels use a flight style in moderate to strong winds known as dynamic soaring, a roller-coaster, arcing path also discussed on pages 68-69. The two smaller shearwaters—Manx and Audubon's—only rarely use this flight style. Manx will do so under stronger winds, but both species—particularly Audubon's—are known for their rapid wingflaps and short glides; they typically remain close to the surface, only rarely arcing high.

These two species are difficult to separate in the field. Manx Shearwater, which prefers cool water, is slightly blacker above than Audubon's Shearwater; it also has white undertail coverts and is proportioned more like a small Greater Shearwater. Audubon's, partial to warm water, is often associated with the so-called pelagic drift community, feeding on items that live and move with floating mats of *sargassum* algae. It is slightly shorter winged but longer tailed than Manx. When close-up views can be attained, note the distribution of light feathering on the head: Manx shows a pale crescent curling up behind the cheek; Audubon's often shows white in front of the eye.

Small numbers of Manx Shearwaters may be seen off the Southeast coast, where Audubon's is fairly common; the two species have sometimes been seen together in mixed-species shearwater flocks. Conversely, a few Audubon's Shearwaters wander north most years in late summer, when ocean temperatures are at their warmest, as far as the waters off New York or southern New England, where Manx is regular.

worn birds
appear browner

**Sooty
Shearwater**

whitish wing
linings and
primary coverts

**Manx
Shearwater**

white
underwings

white wraps
around
ear coverts

white
undertail
coverts

**Audubon's
Shearwater**
lherminieri

short
wings

dark
undertail
coverts

longer tail
than Manx

Storm-Petrels (Family Hydrobatidae)

These small seabirds hover close to the water, pattering or hopping across the waves to feed. Some species follow ships. Identification, which is often difficult, can be made by size when multiple species present and by flight behavior, depending on weather and activity. Mostly silent at sea.

White-faced Storm-Petrel *Pelagodroma marina*
L 7½" (19 cm) WS 17" (43 cm) Flies with stiff, shallow wingbeats and short glides. Habitually angles to water at 45 degrees, then bounces off the surface with long legs in a pogo-stick or kangaroo fashion. Distinctive white underparts, wing linings, and face. Dark eye stripe, crown, and upperparts; paler rump.
Range: Rare off the Atlantic coast in Aug. and Sept.

European Storm-Petrel *Hydrobates pelagicus*
L 5½-6½" (14-17 cm) WS 15" (38 cm) Small, compact, dark storm-petrel with white underwing bar; upperwing entirely dark; feet do not project beyond tail.
Range: Nests in eastern Atlantic and Mediterranean. Specimen record from Nova Scotia, and recent records in late spring off North Carolina.

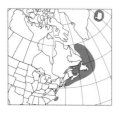

Leach's Storm-Petrel *Oceanodroma leucorhoa*
L 8" (20 cm) WS 18" (46 cm) Distinctive erratic flight, with deep strokes of long, pointed wings. In strong winds may fly more like a shearwater. In close view, note dusky line dividing white rump band on most birds.
Range: Fairly common from Maine northward; also off North Carolina; rare and remains well offshore elsewhere. Casual onshore and inland following hurricanes and nor'easters.

Wilson's Storm-Petrel *Oceanites oceanicus*
L 7¼" (18 cm) WS 16" (41 cm) Flies with shallow, fluttery wingbeats. Wings short and rounded; long legs; in flight, feet trail behind tip of squarish or rounded tail. Often hovers to feed, pattering its yellow-webbed feet on the water. Bold white, U-shaped rump band extends onto undertail coverts; visible even on sitting bird.
Range: Common off Atlantic coast from May to Sept.; regularly seen from shore from mid-Atlantic northward; very rare in Gulf of Mexico. Breeds Antarctic waters.

Band-rumped Storm-Petrel *Oceanodroma castro*
L 9" (23 cm) WS 17" (43 cm) Rather shallow wingstrokes followed by stiff-winged glides, like the flight of a shearwater but unlike the typical erratic flight of Leach's Storm-Petrel or the fluttery flight of Wilson's. White rump patch narrower than on Wilson's. Tail squarish or very slightly notched. Larger, longer winged than Wilson's; fainter carpal bar and thicker bill than Leach's.
Range: Breeds in eastern Atlantic. Fairly common from late May to late Aug. in Gulf Stream off North Carolina; uncommon in Gulf to Mexico; rare or casual elsewhere. Accidental onshore and inland following hurricanes.

White-faced Storm-Petrel

pale gray rump

yellow webs

habitually bounces off water like a kangaroo

long legs

bold white supercilium

white underparts and underwings

European Storm-Petrel

most lack carpal bar

small size and short wings

white bar on underwing

short wings

long legs; feet project beyond tail

rounded tail

Wilson's Storm-Petrel

prominent carpel bar

forked tail

Leach's Storm-Petrel
leucorhoa

little or no white below level of tail

often patters ("dances") with long legs

white wrap around

yellow foot webbing hard to see

Wilson's

Band-rumped

Leach's

usually dusky center to rump

dark tips to uppertail coverts

deeply notched tail

Band-rumped Storm-Petrel

muted carpal bar

heavy bill

slightly forked tail

white band usually with no dusky center

78

Frigatebirds (Family Fregatidae)

These large, dark seabirds have the longest wingspan, in proportion to weight, of all birds.

Magnificent Frigatebird *Fregata magnificens*
L 40" (102 cm) WS 90" (229 cm) Long, forked tail; long, narrow wings. **Male** is glossy black; orange-red throat pouch becomes bright red when inflated in courtship display. **Female** is blackish brown, with white at center of underparts. **Juvenile** shows varying amount of white on head and underparts; require four to six years to reach adult plumage. Frigatebirds skim the sea, snatching up food from surface; also harass other birds in flight, forcing them to disgorge food.
Voice: Silent except at breeding colonies.
Range: Generally seen along coast, but also casual inland, especially after storms. Breeds on Dry Tortugas off Florida. Rare on East Coast north to North Carolina, casual farther north.

Tropicbirds (Family Phaethontidae)

Long central tail feathers identify adults. These birds are usually seen far out at sea, where they plunge dive for fish.

White-tailed Tropicbird *Phaethon lepturus*
L 30" (76 cm) WS 37" (94 cm) Smaller than Red-billed Tropicbird; distinctive black stripe on upperwing coverts; primary coverts mostly white; primaries show less black than in Red-billed; long tail streamers often have a yellowish cast. Bill orange in Atlantic subspecies (*catesbyi*) **adult. Juvenile** lacks tail streamers; upperparts are boldly barred; bill more yellowish.
Voice: Mostly silent at sea.
Range: Tropical species, rare but regular in Gulf Stream off North Carolina in summer; casual near Dry Tortugas, Florida, and elsewhere off East Coast.

Red-billed Tropicbird *Phaethon aethereus*
L 40" (102 cm) WS 44" (112 cm) Flies with rapid, stiff, shallow wingbeats, unlike other tropicbirds, whose flight is more ternlike. **Adult** has red bill, black primaries and primary coverts, barring on back and wings, white tail streamers. **Juvenile** has black collar; lacks streamers; tail is tipped with black; barring on upperparts is finer than in other young tropicbirds. Also bill is yellowish, but soon becomes orange-red.
Voice: Mostly silent at sea.
Range: Tropical species; very rare in Gulf of Mexico and off Atlantic coast to North Carolina; casual to Maine.

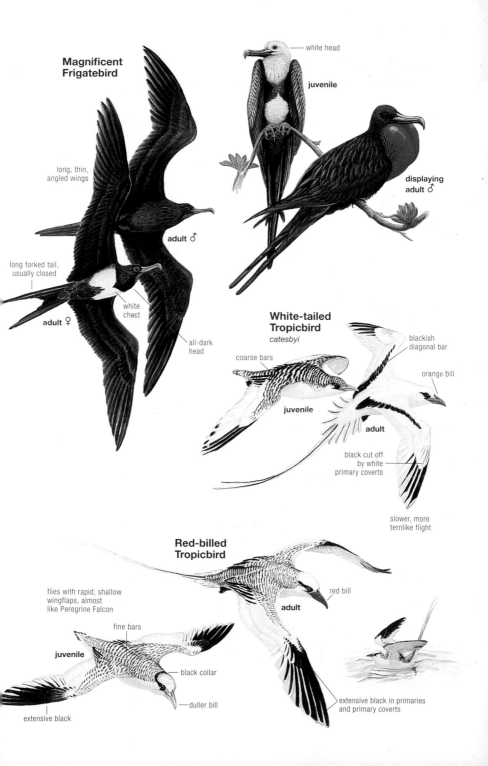

Magnificent Frigatebird

white head

juvenile

long, thin, angled wings

adult ♂

displaying adult ♂

long forked tail, usually closed

adult ♀

white chest

all-dark head

White-tailed Tropicbird
catesbyi

blackish diagonal bar

orange bill

coarse bars

juvenile

adult

black cut off by white primary coverts

slower, more ternlike flight

Red-billed Tropicbird

flies with rapid, shallow wingflaps, almost like Peregrine Falcon

fine bars

red bill

adult

juvenile

black collar

duller bill

extensive black

extensive black in primaries and primary coverts

Boobies, Gannets (Family Sulidae)

High-diving seabirds that plunge into water. Gregarious, nesting in colonies on small islands. The rest of the year, gannets roost at sea, boobies primarily on land.

Red-footed Booby Sula sula
L 28" (71 cm) WS 60" (152 cm) Smallest booby, with rounded head. All *adults* show bright coral red feet, and blue and pink at base of bill. Four principal morphs occur: **brown morph, white-tailed brown morph, white morph,** and **black-tailed white morph;** note that white morphs have black primaries, secondaries, and underwing median primary coverts. All *juveniles* and *subadults* are brownish overall with darker chest band, with darker trailing edge to upperwing, mainly dark underwings and flesh pink or pale orangey legs and feet.
Voice: Mostly silent at sea.
Range: Tropical species; very rare visitor to Florida's Dry Tortugas, casual elsewhere in state.

Brown Booby Sula leucogaster
L 30" (76 cm) WS 57" (145 cm) **Adults** of nominate race have dark brown heads and necks with sharply contrasting white bellies and underwing coverts. Adult female's bill, facial skin, legs, and feet are bright yellow; male's soft parts washed with grayish green, throat bluish. *Juveniles* are dark brown, with little or no contrast between breast and belly; underwing muted. *Subadults* show white on belly and sharp line of contrast with darker neck.
Voice: Mostly silent at sea.
Range: A few found regularly on Dry Tortugas and nearby navigation towers; rare north off both Florida coasts. Very rare through Gulf of Mexico and off North Carolina; casual north to Nova Scotia. Breeds in Caribbean.

Masked Booby Sula dactylatra
L 32" (81 cm) WS 62" (158 cm) Proportionately, the shortest tailed booby. *Adult* distinguished from Northern Gannet by yellowish bill and extensive black facial skin; black tail; and solid black trailing edge to wing. On *juvenile,* note more white on underwing, with contrasting dark median primary coverts and pale collar. *Subadult* has paler head and broader collar; note yellow on bill.
Voice: Mostly silent at sea.
Range: Breeds on Dry Tortugas, Florida, and in Caribbean. Rare to uncommon in Gulf of Mexico mostly in summer; rare in summer in Gulf Stream north to North Carolina. Casual farther north.

Red-footed Booby

some bluish in lores

juvenile

some pink in bill

gentle, round head

dull pinkish feet

black-tailed white-morph adult

red feet

black underwing median primary coverts

white-morph adults

brown-morph adult

white-tailed brown-morph adult

brown-morph subadult

dark underwing coverts

juvenile

Brown Booby
leucogaster

flatter head shape

yellow facial skin

adult ♀

underwing pattern muted

juvenile

contrast can be difficult to see

subadult ♀

sharply contrasting white belly and underwing

adult ♂

blue facial skin

yellow legs and feet

Masked Booby
dactylatra

dark extends to body

adult

mostly dark underwing

Northern Gannet immature

mostly white underwing

dark bill

adult

all-white wing linings

black mask

adult

juvenile

juvenile

dull yellow-green bill

white collar on most young birds

subadult

subadult

82   PELICANS

Northern Gannet *Morus bassanus*
L 37" *(94 cm)* WS 72" *(183 cm)* Large, white seabird with long, black-tipped wings, pointed white tail. *Juvenile* is dark gray above, with pale speckling; grayish below. *First-year* birds are whiter below; distinguished from juvenile and immature Masked Booby by more uniformly dark underwings and, at close range, by different feathering pattern around the bill. Full *adult* plumage is acquired in three to four years.
Voice: Mostly silent at sea except when excited at feeding frenzy.
Range: Common; breeds in large colonies on rocky cliffs; winters at sea. Often seen from shore. Casual in Great Lakes region in late fall.

Pelicans (Family Pelecanidae)

These large, heavy waterbirds have massive bills and huge throat pouches used as dip nets to catch fish. In flight, pelicans hold their heads drawn back.

American White Pelican *Pelecanus erythrorhynchos*
L 62" *(158 cm)* WS 108" *(274 cm)* White, with black primaries and outer secondaries. *Breeding adult* has pale yellow crest; bill is bright orange, usually with a fibrous plate on upper mandible. Plate is shed after eggs are laid; crown and nape become grayish. Juvenile is white with brownish wash on head, neck, and lesser coverts; soft parts more dully colored. White Pelicans do not dive for food but dip their bills into the water while swimming. Usually found in flocks.
Voice: Mostly silent away from breeding colonies.
Range: *Nonbreeding* birds are seen in summer throughout area enclosed by dashed line on map. Vagrants may appear almost anywhere, increasingly in Northeast.

Brown Pelican *Pelecanus occidentalis*
L 48" *(122 cm)* WS 84" *(213 cm)* **Nonbreeding adult** has white head and neck, often washed with yellow; grayish brown body; blackish belly. In *breeding* bird, hindneck is dark chestnut; yellow patch appears at base of foreneck. On eastern race, *carolinensis* (shown here), gular pouch is usually grayish. Molt during incubation and *chick feeding* produces speckled head and foreneck. Adult eye color is light except during chick feeding, when it darkens. Juvenile is grayish brown above, tipped with pale buff; underparts whitish. *Immatures* are browner; acquire adult plumage by third year. Dives from the air after prey, capturing fish in its pouch.
Voice: Mostly silent.
Range: Very rare to casual, but widely recorded from interior U.S. and southern Canada. Wanderers are seen regularly, mainly in spring and summer, to limit of dashed line on map, casually to Nova Scotia.

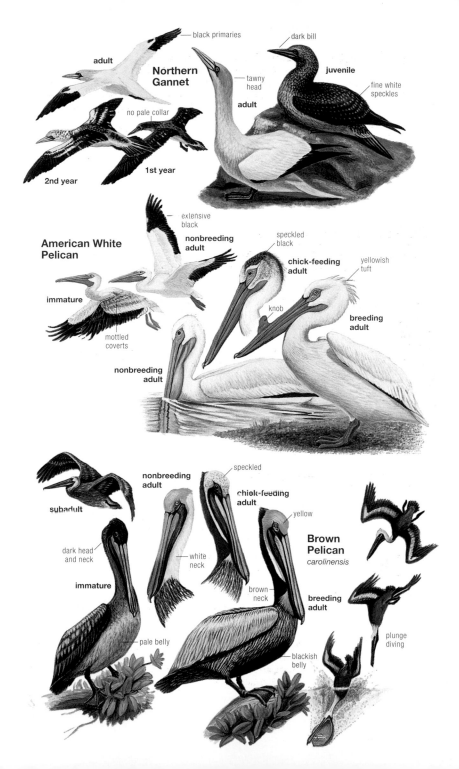

Northern Gannet

black primaries

adult

dark bill

tawny head

adult

juvenile

fine white speckles

no pale collar

2nd year

1st year

American White Pelican

extensive black

nonbreeding adult

speckled black

chick-feeding adult

yellowish tuft

immature

knob

breeding adult

mottled coverts

nonbreeding adult

subadult

nonbreeding adult

speckled

chick-feeding adult

yellow

Brown Pelican
carolinensis

dark head and neck

white neck

immature

brown neck

breeding adult

plunge diving

pale belly

blackish belly

Cormorants (Family Phalacrocoracidae)

Dark birds with set-back legs; long, hooked bill; and colorful bare facial skin and throat pouch. Dive from the surface for fish. May briefly soar; may swim partially submerged.

Great Cormorant *Phalacrocorax carbo*
L 36" (91 cm) WS 63" (160 cm) Large, short-tailed cormorant with small, lemon yellow throat pouch broadly bordered with white feathering. **Breeding adult** shows white flank patches and wispy white plumes on head. Smaller Double-crested Cormorant has orange throat pouch; lacks flank patches; note also Great Cormorant's larger, blockier head and heavier bill. **Juvenile** birds are brown above; white belly contrasts with streaked brown neck, breast, and flanks. Second-year immatures resemble nonbreeding adults more closely but have a brown tinge above; compare with young Double-crested, which has a slimmer bill, deeper orange facial skin, and, often, a darker belly.
Voice: Mostly silent away from breeding colonies.
Range: Winters in small numbers regularly south to North Carolina, very rarely as far south as Florida. Casual on Lake Ontario.

Neotropic Cormorant *Phalacrocorax brasilianus*
L 26" (66 cm) WS 40" (102 cm) Small, long-tailed cormorant with white-bordered, yellow-brown or dull yellow throat pouch that tapers to a sharp point behind bill. In **breeding** plumage, **adult** acquires short white plumes on sides of neck. Distinguished from Double-crested Cormorant by smaller size, longer tail, and smaller, angled throat pouch that usually does not extend around eye. Neotropic **juvenile** is overall browner than adult, particularly on underparts.
Voice: Mostly silent away from breeding colonies.
Range: Fairly common; found at marshy ponds or shallow saltwater bays and inlets often near perching pilings, stumps, and snags. Casual to western Midwest; accidental in mid-Atlantic region. Formerly called Olivaceous Cormorant.

Double-crested Cormorant *Phalacrocorax auritus*
L 32" (81 cm) WS 52" (132 cm) Large, rounded throat pouch is yellow-orange year-round. **Breeding adult** has a tuft curving back on either side of its head from behind eyes. Tufts are largely black and inconspicuous in eastern birds. **Juvenile** is brown above, variably pale below, but usually palest on upper breast and neck. Compare with immature Great Cormorant. Immature Double-cresteds sometimes have pouch edged with white, which can cause confusion with Neotropic Cormorant.
Voice: Mostly silent away from breeding colonies.
Range: Common and widespread; found along coasts, inland lakes, and rivers. Breeding populations in the interior have greatly increased in the last three decades.

Great Cormorant
carbo

dark

white feathers soon lost

breeding

large blocky head

yellowish

white

long, heavy bill

white more diffuse

dark neck

olive-bronze sheen

white belly

juvenile

nonbreeding adult

white flank patch

breeding adult Great

short tail

adult Double-crested

white

long tail

adult Neotropic

breeding adult

smaller bill

dark orange gular with white border

yellowish

juvenile

slender build

feathers more pointed

juvenile Neotropic

yellow-orange above dark lores

more acute angle

juvenile Double-crested

yellow-orange stripe above dark loral stripe

Neotropic Cormorant
mexicanus

long tail

nonbreeding adult

Double-crested Cormorant
auritus

juvenile

winter adult

pale breast

dark belly

wispy black crest

orangish

breeding adult

mostly dark

2nd year

1st year

some 1st years have white bordering gular pouch

1st year

some 1st years have paler bellies

Darters (Family Anhingidae)

Long, slim neck helps to distinguish anhingas from cormorants. Anhingas often swim submerged to the neck. Sharply pointed bill is used to spear fish.

Anhinga *Anhinga anhinga L 35" (89 cm) WS 45" (114 cm)*
Black above, with green gloss; silvery white spots and streaks on wings and upper back. During breeding season, *male* acquires pale, wispy plumes on upper neck; bill and bare facial skin become brightly colored. *Female* has buffy neck and breast. Immatures resemble adult female but are browner overall. Anhingas prefer freshwater habitats; often seen perched on branches or stumps with wings spread. In flight, profile looks headless. Flies with slow, regular wingbeats and circles like raptor on thermals. Sometimes soaring Double-crested Cormorants with slightly splayed tails are mistaken for Anhingas.
Voice: Mostly silent; may give occasional croaks and rattles.
Range: Casual wanderer north of breeding range.

Herons, Bitterns, Allies (Family Ardeidae)

Wading birds; most have long legs, neck, and bill for stalking food in shallow water. Graceful crests and plumes adorn some species in breeding season.

American Bittern *Botaurus lentiginosus*
L 28" (71 cm) WS 42" (107 cm) Mottled brown upperparts and brownish neck streaks. Contrasting dark flight feathers are conspicuous in flight; note also that wings are longer, narrower, and more pointed, not rounded as in night-herons. *Juvenile* lacks neck patches. When alarmed, freezes with bill pointing up, or flushes with rapid wingbeats.
Voice: Distinctive spring and early summer song, *oonk-a-lunk,* is most often heard at dusk in dense marsh reeds. Also a nasal *arrk* call in flight.
Range: Uncommon and declining; casual breeder south of range.

Least Bittern *Ixobrychus exilis L 13" (33 cm) WS 17" (43 cm)*
Buffy inner wing patches identify this small, rather secretive heron as it flushes briefly from dense marsh cover. When alarmed, it may freeze with bill pointing up. In *male* back and crown are black; in *female* they are browner. *Juvenile* resembles female but has more prominent streaking on back and breast. Rare dark morph, *"Cory's Least Bittern"* not documented since mid-20th century, is chestnut where typical plumage is pale. Uncommon.
Voice: Least Bittern's calls include a series of (usually three) harsh *kek* notes, which might be confused with call of Virginia or larger Clapper and King Rails; song, a softer series of soft *ku* notes, is heard only on the breeding ground.
Range: Uncommon in freshwater marshes and ponds with stands of reeds.

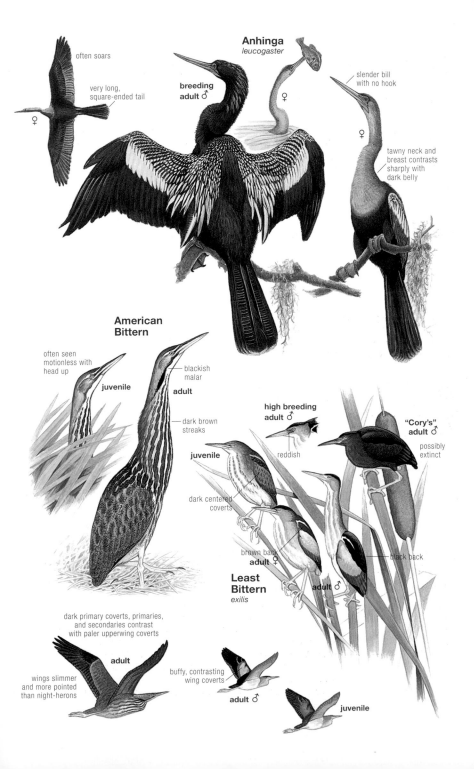

Anhinga
leucogaster

often soars

very long,
square-ended tail

♀

breeding
adult ♂

♀

slender bill
with no hook

♀

tawny neck and
breast contrasts
sharply with
dark belly

American Bittern

often seen
motionless with
head up

juvenile

blackish
malar

adult

dark brown
streaks

high breeding
adult ♂

reddish

"Cory's"
adult ♂

possibly
extinct

juvenile

dark centered
coverts

brown back
adult ♀

black back

Least Bittern
exilis

adult ♂

dark primary coverts, primaries,
and secondaries contrast
with paler upperwing coverts

adult

wings slimmer
and more pointed
than night-herons

buffy, contrasting
wing coverts

adult ♂

juvenile

Green Heron *Butorides virescens*

L 18" (46 cm) WS 26" (66 cm) Small, chunky heron with short legs. Back and sides of *adult*'s neck are deep chestnut; green on upperparts is mixed with blue-gray; center of throat and neck white. Greenish black crown feathers, sometimes raised to form shaggy crest. Legs are usually dull yellow but in male turn bright orange in high breeding plumage. *Juvenile* is browner above; white throat and underparts heavily streaked with brown. When alarmed, raises crest and flicks tail. Compare with Least Bittern (preceding page).

Voice: Common call is a loud, sharp *kyowk*.

Range: Usually solitary; found in a variety of habitats, but prefers streams, ponds, and marshes with woodland or bushy cover; often perches in trees. Generally common; a few winter north of resident limit. Very rare visitor north to much of southern Canada.

Great Egret *Ardea alba* *L 39" (99 cm) WS 51" (130 cm)*

Large white heron with heavy yellow bill, blackish legs and feet. In *breeding* plumage, long plumes trail from back, extending beyond tail. In immature and *nonbreeding adult,* bill and leg colors are duller, plumes absent. Distinguished from most other white herons by large size; from white morph of the larger Great Blue Heron by black legs and feet.

Voice: Occasional deep croaks.

Range: Common in wetlands, occasionally in moist fields. Partial to open habitats for feeding; stalks prey slowly, methodically. Occasionally breeds far north of usual range. Spring overshoots and post-breeding wanderers reach far north of mapped breeding range.

Great Blue Heron *Ardea herodias*

L 46" (117 cm) WS 72" (183 cm) Large, gray-blue heron; black stripe extends above eye; white foreneck is streaked with black. *Breeding adult* has yellowish bill and ornate plumes on head, neck, and back. Nonbreeding adult lacks plumes; bill is yellower. *Juvenile* has black crown, no plumes. All-white morph found in southern Florida formerly considered a separate species, *"Great White Heron."* Note the pale legs and heavy bill, which help differentiate it from Great Egret (above). *"Wurdemann's Heron"* morph, which is found chiefly in Florida Keys, has all-white head.

Voice: Occasional deep croaks.

Range: Common. A few winter far north into breeding range; also may wander at other seasons north of mapped breeding range. "Great White Heron" has occurred casually north of Florida and west, mostly in summer and early fall.

adult

Green Heron
virescens

short
yellowish
legs

juvenile

brown

streaked
neck

dark cap

adult

lime green facial skin

very long
neck

**high breeding
adult**

yellow facial
skin

long
yellow bill

nonbreeding

Great Egret
egretta

dark legs and feet

black
remiges

adult

long and heavy
yellowish bill

**Great Blue
Heron**
herodias

**"Great White
Heron"**

white crown
with black lateral
crown stripe

**breeding
adult**

dark cap

white head

pale legs

**"Wurdemann's Heron"
breeding adult**

rufous
thighs

juvenile

Snowy Egret *Egretta thula L 24" (61 cm) WS 41" (104 cm)*
White heron with slender black bill, yellow eyes, black legs, bright golden yellow feet. Graceful plumes on head, neck, and back (where they curve upward) are striking in ***breeding adult***. In ***high breeding*** plumage, lores turn red, feet orange. Nonbreeding plumage is similar but plumes are shorter; also note yellow on backs of legs. Compare to Little Egret. ***Juvenile*** resembles nonbreeding adult, but lacks plumes and shows some bluish gray at base of lower mandible. Can be confused with immature Little Blue Heron (next page); note young Snowy's slimmer, mostly black bill; yellow lores; predominantly dark legs; white wing tips. Active feeders.
Voice: Low, raspy note, mostly at nest site.
Range: Common in various wetland habitats. A few found north of mapped range in spring and after breeding season.

Little Egret *Egretta garzetta L 24" (60 cm) WS 36" (91 cm)*
Old World species. Closely resembles Snowy Egret, but often appears larger, with longer neck; longer, thicker bill and legs, the latter always entirely black; mostly grayish lores; and more extensive throat feathering out on lower mandible. Little Egret's crown is flatter; feet are yellow, like Snowy, but average slightly duller. In ***breeding*** plumage, lore color is variable, but can be yellow. Note the two or three long, tapering plumes, rather than Snowy's many curved plumes. Often feeds less frenetically than Snowy.
Voice: Similar to Snowy Egret.
Range: Casual spring and summer visitor to East Coast, from Newfoundland to mid-Atlantic states.

Cattle Egret *Bubulcus ibis L 20" (51 cm) WS 36" (91 cm)*
Small, stocky white heron with large, rounded head; note throat feathering extends far out on bill. ***Breeding adult*** is orange-buff on crown, back, and foreneck. At height of breeding season, bill is red-orange, legs dusky red. ***Nonbreeding adult*** (opposite) has short yellow bill, yellowish legs. Juvenile's bill is black. In flight, resembles Snowy but is smaller; bill, legs shorter; wingbeats faster.
Voice: Mostly silent.
Range: Often seen among livestock in fields, feeding on insects. An Old World species, Cattle Egret came to South America from Africa, spread to Florida in the early 1950s. In spring, summer, and especially fall, may wander well north of breeding range.

IDENTIFYING: White Egrets Separating various white egret species is fairly straightforward as long as a few features are kept in mind. Great Egret is the largest species; Cattle, the smallest, has disproportionately short legs. Young juvenile Cattle Egrets can be tricky to identify when their bills are dark. With their sharply separated pink-based bill and shaggy head plumes during the breeding season, White-morph Reddish Egrets are easily identified. In contrast, immatures and winter adults have entirely dark bills. The "dancing" feeding behavior is an excellent differentiating characteristic for this species. Immature Little Blue Herons during their first fall and winter closely resemble Snowy Egrets, but they have duller lores and a somewhat thicker and more obviously bicolored bill. Most, but not all, have some dusky in the wing tips, often only visible in flight. They also have more uniformly greenish yellow legs and feed more deliberately than Snowy Egrets.

Little Blue Heron juvenile

dusky in wing tips of many birds

Snowy Egret

short legs

Cattle Egret nonbreeding

Snowy Egret
thula

black bill

juvenile

shaggy crest

high breeding adult

breeding adult

yellow feet

legs of immatures and nonbreeding adults have greenish up back of leg

sometimes yellowish lores

grayish lores

longer bill than Snowy

breeding adult

two long plumes

nonbreeding adult

buffy on head, back, and breast in breeding plumage

bill red and yellow in high breeding

yellow bill

Little Egret
garzetta

immature

dark legs turn yellow by fall

entirely black legs

high breeding adult

Cattle Egret
ibis

pinkish legs, otherwise yellow rest of the year

sharply contrasting yellow feet

Tricolored Heron *Egretta tricolor*
L 26" (66 cm) WS 36" (91 cm) White belly and foreneck contrast with mainly dark blue upperparts; bill long and slender. During breeding season, lores and base of bill turn cobalt blue. *Juvenile* has chestnut hindneck and wing coverts.
Voice: Mostly silent; some low croaking at nest site.
Range: Fairly common inhabitant of salt marshes and mangrove swamps of the East and Gulf Coasts. Rare inland, but has bred from Dakotas to Oklahoma. Very rare visitor north to southern Canada.

Little Blue Heron *Egretta caerulea*
L 24" (61 cm) WS 40" (102 cm) Slate blue overall. During most of the year, plumage, head, and neck are dark purple; legs and feet dull green. In high **breeding** plumage, head and neck become reddish purple, legs and feet black. *Juvenile* is easily confused with immature Snowy Egret (preceding page); note Little Blue Heron's dull greenish yellow legs and feet; two-toned bill with thicker, gray base and dark tip; mostly grayish lores; and, often, narrow, dusky primary tips. During first spring, juvenile's white plumage begins gradual *molt* to adult plumage, during which time the mottled birds are said to be in their "calico phase." Little Blue Herons are slow, methodical feeders. They are often seen motionless with neck bent at a 45-degree angle, awaiting prey.
Voice: Mostly silent; some low croaking and squawking, mostly at nest site.
Range: Fairly common at freshwater ponds, lakes, and marshes and coastal saltwater wetlands. Some birds are found north of mapped range in spring and during post-breeding dispersal, very rarely to southern Canada.

Reddish Egret *Egretta rufescens*
L 30" (76 cm) WS 46" (117 cm) While feeding, this heron often lurches, dashing about with wings spread in a canopy. **Dark-morph breeding adult** has shaggy plumes on rufous head, neck. Bill is pink with black tip; legs cobalt blue. Nonbreeding plumage varies, but in general duller, with shorter plumes, darker bill. **Dark-morph juvenile** is gray; some pale cinnamon on head, neck, inner wing; bill is dark. **White-morph adult** resembles immature Little Blue Heron or Snowy Egret (preceding page); note larger size, longer bill, dark legs and feet. A few dark-morph birds have much white on wings and resemble molting immature Little Blue Heron.
Voice: Mostly silent; some low grunts at nest site.
Range: Uncommon. Inhabits shallow, open salt pans; occasionally salt marshes. Wanders along Gulf Coast in post-breeding dispersal; casual inland to Midwest and up the Atlantic coast to New England, mostly in late summer.

Tricolored Heron
ruficollis

juvenile

rufous on neck and wing coverts

breeding adult

long bill

long, slim neck

white belly

mottled plumage seen on one-year-old birds in spring and summer

bicolored bill with grayish lores

molting immature

Little Blue Heron

maroon

breeding adult

juvenile

blue base to bill

greenish yellow legs

nonbreeding adult

very deliberate feeding behavior

thick-based, slightly downcurved bill

some juveniles show dusky wing tips; best viewed in flight

only birds in breeding plumage have pink-based bills

white-morph breeding adult

when feeding, rushes about with wings open

canopy feeding

overall buffy-gray

dark-morph juvenile

Reddish Egret
rufescens

dark-morph breeding adult

distinctly larger than Little Blue Heron

dark gray legs

Black-crowned Night-Heron *Nycticorax nycticorax*

L 25" (64 cm) WS 44" (112 cm) Stocky heron with short neck and legs. ***Adult*** has black crown and back; white hindneck plumes are longest in breeding season. In high breeding plumage, legs turn bright pink. ***Juvenile*** distinguished from young Yellow-crowned Night-Heron by browner upperparts with bolder white spotting; thicker neck and stockier overall body shape; paler, less contrasting face with smaller eyes; and longer, thinner bill with mostly pale lower mandible. In flight, legs barely extend beyond tail. Full adult plumage is not acquired until third year. Compare immature in flight also to American Bittern (page 86).
Voice: Calls include a low, harsh *woc,* more guttural than in Yellow-crowned.
Range: Mainly nocturnal feeder, hunts quietly in a variety of wetlands and in harbors. Typically roosts in trees, often in groups. Very local in much of northern part of range. Declining in some regions. Occurs very rarely north of mapped range.

Yellow-crowned Night-Heron *Nyctanassa violacea*

L 24" (61 cm) WS 42" (107 cm) ***Adult*** has buffy white crown, black face with white cheeks; acquires head plumes in breeding season. ***Juvenile*** distinguished from young Black-crowned Night-Heron by grayer upperparts with less conspicuous white spotting; longer neck; stouter, mostly dark bill, although recently fledged juveniles have some yellow at bill base; and larger eyes. In flight, its legs extend well beyond its tail and it shows darker flight feathers and trailing edge on wings. Overall less stocky than Black-crowned, with thinner, more pointed wings. Full adult plumage is acquired in third year.
Voice: Calls include a short *woc,* higher and less harsh than in Black-crowned.
Range: Uncommon to fairly common; roosts in trees in wet woods and swamps. Single pairs may be found nesting well away from heron colonies. Casual north to dashed line on map, mostly as a spring overshoot and during post-breeding dispersal.

IDENTIFYING: Immature Night-Herons
Separating Black-crowned and Yellow-crowned Night-Herons in adult plumage is fairly straightforward. Full adult plumage in night-herons is not acquired until the bird's third calendar year. During the second year, however, it attains some telltale signs of an adult. It is the juvenile—seen between summer fledging and the following late winter—that causes the most identification difficulties. Young Yellow-crowned Night-Herons are slimmer and lankier than Black-crowneds, appearing in shape like most other herons. They have longer legs, with the entire foot and some of the lower leg projecting beyond the tail in flight; in Black-crowned, only most of the foot projects. Yellow-crowned

also has a thicker bill that is almost entirely dark gray, with only minimal greenish or other paling at the very base of the lower mandible; Black-crowned has extensive greenish yellow on the lower mandible. Other differences include Yellow-crowned's slightly grayer plumage, smaller white spotting on the wing, and narrower streaking on the breast.

A species that may be confused with young night-herons is American Bittern (page 86), which lacks the pale spotting on the wing coverts shown by juvenile night-herons. In flight, note the bittern's upperwing pattern (more similar to young Yellow-crowned than to Black-crowned), its pointier wing tip, and its slightly shallower and more rapid wingbeat.

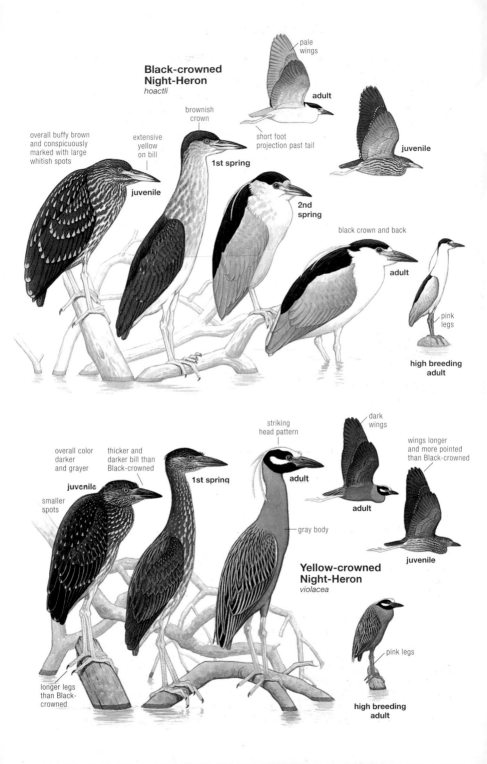

Black-crowned Night-Heron
hoactli

pale wings

adult

short foot projection past tail

juvenile

brownish crown

1st spring

extensive yellow on bill

overall buffy brown and conspicuously marked with large whitish spots

juvenile

2nd spring

black crown and back

adult

high breeding adult

pink legs

overall color darker and grayer

juvenile

smaller spots

thicker and darker bill than Black-crowned

1st spring

striking head pattern

adult

dark wings

wings longer and more pointed than Black-crowned

adult

juvenile

gray body

Yellow-crowned Night-Heron
violacea

longer legs than Black-crowned

high breeding adult

pink legs

Ibises, Spoonbills (Family Threskiornithidae)

Gregarious, heronlike birds, these long-legged waders feed with long, specialized bills: slender and curved downward in ibises, wide and spatulate in spoonbills.

Glossy Ibis Plegadis falcinellus

L 23" (58 cm) WS 36" (91 cm) **Breeding adult**'s chestnut plumage is glossed with green or purple; looks all-dark at a distance. Distinguished from White-faced Ibis by brown eye, gray-green legs with red joints, and lack of distinct white border to bare facial skin. Blue edge to gray facial skin does not extend behind eye or under chin. **Winter adult** closely resembles winter White-faced; look for gray facial skin partially bordered by blue line. **Juvenile** closely resembles juvenile White-faced Ibis, but note gray facial skin and at least trace of blue line on most birds. Adult breeding plumage is acquired in second spring.
Voice: Occasional low grunts.
Range: Glossy Ibises inhabit freshwater and saltwater marshes. Fairly common but local. Recent substantial increase in records west to Texas and Great Plains, chiefly in spring.

White-faced Ibis Plegadis chihi

L 23" (58 cm) WS 36" (91 cm) **Breeding adult** distinguished from Glossy Ibis, with which it sometimes hybridizes, by bronzer tones in chestnut plumage, reddish bill, red eye, mostly red legs, and white feathered border around pinkish red facial skin; border extends behind eye and under chin. **Winter adult** plumage is like Glossy, but lacks pale blue line from eye to bill; facial skin is pale pink. **Juvenile** closely resembles juvenile Glossy until winter, when facial skin turns pinkish; look for lack of blue line (or a hint of white border) and reddish tinge to eye.
Voice: Occasional low grunts.
Range: Breeds in freshwater marshes. Very rare in Midwest and East Coast north to New England in spring and summer.

White Ibis Eudocimus albus L 25" (64 cm) WS 38" (97 cm)

Adult's white plumage and pink facial skin are distinctive. In **breeding adult,** facial skin, bill, and legs turn scarlet. Dark tips of primaries most easily seen in flight. Immatures have white underparts and wing linings, pinkish bill; gradually molt into adult plumage by second fall. Closely related **Scarlet Ibis** (E. ruber), a South American species introduced or escaped in Florida, hybridizes with White Ibis; offspring are various shades of pink or scarlet.
Voice: Occasional low grunts.
Range: Locally common in coastal salt marshes, swamps, mangroves. Expanding north, now breeds to Virginia. Casual north to New Jersey, Midwest; accidental to southern Canada.

Glossy Ibis

juvenile

juvenile

all ages have dark eyes

winter adult

most juveniles show bluish lines that are similar to those on adults

powder blue lines don't extend around eye

reddish joints

breeding adult

breeding adult

red iris

pinkish skin on lores

winter adult

often with faint whitish supraloral line; iris red by late winter

facial skin grayish, sometimes with some pinkish by fall

juvenile

White-faced Ibis

breeding adult

red facial skin bordered by white feathered margin

extensively reddish legs

Scarlet Ibis adult

Juvenile

breeding adult

black wing tips

red face and white eye

White Ibis

dark eye

pinkish red bill

white belly

juvenile

breeding adult

red legs

1st spring

Roseate Spoonbill *Platalea ajaja*

L 32" (81 cm) WS 50" (127 cm) ***Adult*** has pink body with red highlights; long, spatulate bill; unfeathered greenish head. The head may become buffy during courtship. ***Juvenile*** has white feathering on head; body is mostly pale pink. Spoonbills feed in shallow waters, swinging their bills from side to side.

Voice: Mostly silent; occasional low grunts.

Range: Locally fairly common in swamps and marshes along the Gulf Coast; a few wander north in summer to Oklahoma; casual north to mid-Atlantic and Midwest regions.

Storks (Family Ciconiidae)

Large, long-legged birds that fly with slow beats of their long, broad wings, soaring and circling like hawks.

Wood Stork *Mycteria americana* **E**

L 40" (102 cm) WS 61" (155 cm) Black flight feathers and tail contrast with white body. ***Adult*** has bald, blackish gray head; thick, dusky, downcurved bill. ***Juvenile***'s head is feathered largely with grayish brown; bill is yellow.

Voice: Mostly silent. Some bill clacking at nest site.

Range: Uncommon. Wood Storks inhabit wet meadows, swamps, ponds, and coastal shallows. A few wander north in summer and fall, including flocks from Mexican breeding grounds to Texas and lower Mississippi Valley; casual north to Dakotas and Maine.

Flamingos (Family Phoenicopteridae)

Large waders with big, bent bills, which are used to strain food from the waters of shallow lakes and lagoons.

Greater Flamingo *Phoenicopterus ruber*

L 46" (117 cm) WS 60" (152 cm) Note pink legs, black flight feathers, tricolored bill. ***Immature*** is grayer, with pink wash below; paler bill.

Voice: Mostly silent; occasional honking notes.

Range: Birds seen in New World are of the nominate race, treated by some as separate species, which breeds as close to Florida as southern Bahamas, Cuba, and the Yucatan Peninsula. A few seen most years in fall and winter in Florida Bay; casual on Texas coast; others, especially away from these regions, more likely escapes. In addition, escapes include a widespread Old World subspecies (*roseus*), with pink-and-white plumage; the Chilean Flamingo (*P. chilensis*), with grayish legs with pink joints; and the Lesser Flamingo (*Phoeniconaias minor*), with dark red bill and blotchy red wing coverts and axillaries.

Roseate Spoonbill

crimson marginal coverts

juvenile

breeding adult

breeding adult

pale pink wings

juvenile

spoon-shaped bill

Wood Stork

extensive black

juvenile

tawny feathers

yellowish bill

adult

adult

unfeathered head and neck

long, heavy downcurved bill

yellow feet

largely pinkish, strongly downcurved bill is whitish at base, blackish at tip

adult

black remiges

immature

fast, ducklike wingbeats

Greater Flamingo
ruber

very long, pink legs

New World Vultures (Family Cathartidae)

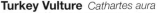

Small, unfeathered head and hooked bill aid in consuming carrion.

Turkey Vulture *Cathartes aura*
L 27" (69 cm) WS 69" (175 cm) In flight, rocks side to side with minimal flapping (flaps are rather deep and slow) and wings held upward in a shallow V; dark wing linings contrast with silvery flight feathers. Rather long tailed. *Adult* has red head, white bill, brown legs; *juvenile*'s head and bill are dark, legs are paler. Feeds chiefly on carrion and refuse.
Voice: Silent except at nest site, where kissing sounds made.
Range: Common in mapped range. Has expanded both summer and winter ranges northward.

Black Vulture *Coragyps atratus*
L 25" (64 cm) WS 57" (145 cm) In flight, shows large white patches at base of primaries. Tail is shorter than Turkey Vulture; wings shorter and broader; legs white; feet usually extend to edge of tail or beyond. Flight includes rapid flapping and short glides, usually with wings flat. Gregarious and aggressive, but less efficient at spotting carrion than Turkey Vulture.
Voice: Silent except at nest site, where kissing and groaning sounds made.
Range: Common in open country and near human settlements, often scavenges in garbage dumps. Range expanding in the Northeast; casual north to Ontario and Maritimes.

Hawks, Kites, Eagles, Allies (Family Accipitridae)

Worldwide family of diurnal birds of prey, with hooked bills and strong talons.

Osprey *Pandion haliaetus*
L 22-25" (56-64 cm) WS 58-72" (147-183 cm) Dark brown above, white below, with white head, prominent dark eye stripe. Females average darker streaking on neck; *juvenile* plumage is fringed with pale buff above. In flight, long, narrow wings are bent back at "wrist," dark carpal patches conspicuous; wings slightly arched in soaring.
Voice: Call is a series of loud, whistled *kyew* notes.
Range: Nests near fresh or salt water; eats mostly fish. Hovering over water, dives down, then plunges feetfirst to snatch prey. Bulky nests are built in trees, on sheds, poles, docks, and special platforms. Conservation programs successful, and the species is now fairly common.

Turkey Vulture

reddish head

adult

grayish

juvenile

adults

soars on slight dihedral, wingflaps are slow and deep

long tail

two-toned underwings

soars on flat wings, wingflaps are rapid and shallow

adult

extensive white base to outer primaries

gull-like flight

long angled wings

dark wrist

barred flight feathers

pale wing linings

adult

pale grayish legs

short tail

Black Vulture

bold dark eye stripe

uniformly dark above

Osprey
carolinensis

prominent pale tips

juvenile

adult

Mississippi Kite *Ictinia mississippiensis*

L 14½" (37 cm) WS 35" (89 cm) Long, pointed wings with first primary distinctly shorter; long, flared tail. Dark gray above, paler below, with pale gray head, averaging paler on *male. Female* with white shaft on outer tail feather and often whitish in vent region. White secondaries show in flight as white wing patch. Black tail readily distinguishes Mississippi from White-tailed Kite. Compare also with male Northern Harrier (next page); note Mississippi never hovers. *Juvenile* is heavily streaked and spotted, with pale bands on tail, but pattern and overall darkness highly variable on underparts, underwings, and tail. *First-summer* bird (page 124) more like adult but retains juvenal flight feathers. At all ages, may be confused with Peregrine Falcon ; compare wing and tail shapes. Mississippi Kites capture and eat their prey, mainly insects, on the wing. Gregarious; often hunt in groups, nest in loose colonies.

Voice: Downslurred whistle, given mainly on breeding grounds.

Range: Found in woodlands, swamps, rangelands, some residential areas. Regular straggler (chiefly immatures in spring and early summer) to mid-Atlantic states. Casual north to Great Lakes region and New England. Winters in South America.

White-tailed Kite *Elanus leucurus*

L 16" (41 cm) WS 42" (107 cm) Long, pointed wings; long tail. White underparts and mostly white tail distinguish *adults* from similar Mississippi Kite. Compare also with male Northern Harrier (next page). *Juvenile*'s underparts and head are lightly streaked with rufous, which rapidly fades. In all ages, black shoulders show in flight as black leading edge of inner wings from above, small black patches from below. Hovers while hunting, unlike any other North American kite. Eats mainly rodents, insects.

Voice: Regularly gives whistled call; also grating notes.

Range: Populations fluctuate. Fairly common in grasslands, farmlands, even highway median strips. Casual north of mapped range to northern Great Plains, Midwest, and Northeast, and New York. Often forms winter roosts of more than a hundred birds.

Swallow-tailed Kite *Elanoides forficatus*

L 23" (58 cm) WS 48" (122 cm) Seen in flight, deeply forked tail and sharply defined pattern of black and white are like no other large bird except the young Magnificent Frigatebird (page 78). Perched, Swallow-tailed Kite's coloring more closely resembles White-tailed and Mississippi Kites; again, note long, forked tail. Juvenile is similar to *adult,* but tail is shorter, flight feathers and tail narrowly tipped with white. Agile and graceful, Swallow-tailed snatches flying insects; also drops down upon snakes, lizards, young birds; does not hover. Often eats prey in flight; also drinks in flight, skimming the water like a swallow. Found in open woods, bottomlands, and wetlands. Nests near the tops of tall trees. Somewhat social; several may hunt in the same territory.

Voice: Mostly silent.

Range: Casual in spring and summer as far north as Ontario and Nova Scotia. Most winter in South America.

Mississippi Kite

never hovers

adult ♂

whitish secondary patch

dark wings

adult ♀

black tail

pale gray head

juvenile

adult ♂

usually seen in flight; white body and wing linings contrast with black flight feathers

adult

long forked black tail

Swallow-tailed Kite

habitually hovers when foraging

dark spot

adults

long whitish tail

juvenile

buffy on chest

adult

black shoulders

adult

White-tailed Kite
majusculus

Snail Kite *Rostrhamus sociabilis* **E**

L 17" (43 cm) WS 46" (117 cm) This kite's wings are paddle shaped, bill thin and deeply hooked. *Male* is gray-black above and below, with white uppertail and undertail coverts; square, white tail with broad, dark band and paler terminal band; legs orange-red; eyes and facial skin reddish. *Female* is dark brown, with distinctive head pattern. *Juvenile* has dark brown eyes, duller facial skin and legs, streaked crown and underparts. Hunting flight is slow, with considerable flapping of wings, and head held down as the kite searches for apple snails, its chief and perhaps only food.
Voice: Mostly silent; occasionally a nasal grating sound.
Range: A tropical species. Endangered; uncommon and local resident in southern Florida; accidental in Texas, South Carolina.

Hook-billed Kite *Chondrohierax uncinatus*

L 18" (46 cm) WS 36" (91 cm) Plumage varies considerably, but look for large, heavy bill with long hook, white eyes, banded tail, and heavily barred underparts, including underwings. *Male* is generally gray overall. *Female* is brown, with a rufous collar and rufous, barred underparts and wing linings. *Juvenile* has brown eyes, white collar, and whitish underparts with variable dark brown barring. In the *black morph,* rarely seen in the U.S., *adult* is all-black except for a single white or grayish tail band and whitish tail tip; *black-morph juvenile* is mostly brownish black, with two or more grayish tail bands. Hook-billed Kite flies with deep, languid wingbeats, its "wrists" slightly cocked upward and "hands" angled down. Wings are paddle shaped, slightly tapered in at the base. It eats insects and small amphibians, but prefers snails of various kinds. A pile of broken snail shells beneath a tree may indicate a favorite perch or a nest site above.
Voice: Mostly silent.
Range: Tropical species. Rare resident in lower Rio Grande Valley from Santa Ana to Falcon Dam. Found in dense woodlands, from which it thermals upward in midmorning.

Northern Harrier *Circus cyaneus*

L 16-20" (41-51 cm) WS 38-48" (97-122 cm) White uppertail coverts and owl-like facial disk distinctive in all ages and both sexes. Body slim; wings long and narrow with somewhat rounded tips; tail long. *Adult male* is grayish above; mostly white below with variable chestnut spotting; has black wing tips and black tips to secondaries. *Female* is brown above, whitish below with heavy brown streaking on breast and flanks, lighter streaking and spotting on belly. *Juvenile* resembles adult female but is cinnamon below, fading to creamy buff by spring; streaked only on the breast; wing linings are cinnamon; inner secondaries are darker. Harriers generally perch low and fly close to the ground, wings upraised, as they search for birds, mice, frogs, and other prey. Seldom soar high except during migration and in acrobatic courtship display.
Voice: Occasionally gives a high, downslurred call; also a series of *keee* notes when agitated.
Range: Uncommon to fairly common in wetlands and open fields.

adult ♂

whitish superculium and chin

long, thin curved bill

strong eye line

adult ♂

white

adult ♀

heavy streaks

white tail base

gray tip

Snail Kite
plumbeus

juvenile

adult ♂

hooked bill

black-morph adult

black-morph juvenile

rufous wing linings

adult ♀

juvenile

adult ♂

barred grayish underparts

white

variable dark barring

adult ♀

rufous collar

barred rufous underparts

Hook-billed Kite
uncinatus

white

juvenile

gray above

roundish owl-like head

white underwing with dark wing tip and trailing edge

juvenile

darker secondaries

adult ♂

adult ♂

unstreaked belly

barred remiges

adult ♀

juveniles

streaked belly

long tail

adult ♂

whitish rump

Northern Harrier
hudsonicus

long, thin wings with rounded tips

Eagles

These two species, our largest diurnal birds of prey, share a soaring behavior—on the lookout for prey—although their preferred food differs. The subject of human persecution for well over a century, their numbers are now steady or increasing.

Golden Eagle *Aquila chrysaetos*
L 30-40" (76-102 cm) WS 80-88" (203-224 cm) Brown, with variable yellow to tawny brown wash over back of head and neck; bill is mostly horn colored; tail is faintly banded. Tawny greater upperwing coverts form a bar. *Juveniles,* seen in flight from below, show well-defined white patches at base of primaries, white tail with distinct dark terminal band. Compare with juvenile Bald Eagle, which has a larger head and bill, a shorter tail, and a blotchier tail and underwing pattern. *Adult* plumage is acquired in four years. Golden Eagle often soars with wings slightly uplifted.
Voice: Mostly silent away from nest.
Range: Found singly or in pairs. Inhabits mountainous or hilly terrain, hunting over open country for small mammals, snakes, birds, and carrion. Also found in valleys, on western plains, and at wetlands, especially in migration and winter. Nests on cliffs or in trees. Uncommon to rare in the East.

Bald Eagle *Haliaeetus leucocephalus* **T**
L 31-37" (79-94 cm) WS 70-90" (178-229 cm) *Adults* readily identified by white head and tail, large yellow bill. *Juveniles* are mostly dark, may be confused with juvenile Golden Eagle; compare blotchy white on underwing coverts, axillaries, and tail with Golden Eagle's more sharply defined pattern; note also Bald Eagle's disproportionately larger head and bill, shorter tail. Flat-winged soar distinguishes young Bald Eagle from Turkey Vulture (page 100). Bald Eagles require four or five years to reach full adult plumage. The various interim "subadult" plumages may be highly variable; some *second-* and *third-year* birds show an Osprey-like dark patch through the eye.
Voice: A variety of call including a series of high-pitched twitterings or whistles.
Range: Seen most often on seacoasts or near rivers and lakes. Feed mainly on fish in breeding season, regularly on carrion, injured waterfowl, and on roadkill in winter. Nest in tall trees or on cliffs. Most numerous in winter along Mississippi and Missouri Rivers and at large reservoirs. Florida-raised birds may wander north as far as southern Canada. Banning of pesticide use and intense recovery programs have increased populations of Bald Eagles that had been seriously diminished in the East.

Golden Eagle
canadensis

golden nape

juvenile

whitish wing patch

short head projection

adult

whitish tail base

adult

dark or faintly barred tail

adult

juvenile

2nd year

whitish underwing coverts and axillaries

longer head projection than Golden

Bald Eagle

3rd year

larger bill than Golden

white head

juvenile

white tail

adults

tail shorter than Golden

Accipiters

Comparatively long tails and short, rounded wings give these three woodland hawks great agility. Flight is several quick wingbeats and a glide. The three species in North America are confusingly similar. Generally silent, except at nest site.

Sharp-shinned Hawk *Accipiter striatus*
L 10-14" (25-36 cm) WS 20-28" (51-71 cm) Distinguished from Cooper's Hawk by shorter, squared tail, often appearing notched when folded, thinner legs, and by smaller head and neck. **Adult** lacks Cooper's strong contrast between crown and back. **Juveniles** are whitish below, some streaked with brown (like Cooper's), others spotted with reddish brown. Note also the pale eyebrows, narrow white tip on tail, entirely white undertail coverts, less tawny head than other accipiters. In flight (page 125), again compare smaller head and proportionately shorter tail than Cooper's; wingbeats quick and choppy, slower on Cooper's.
Range: Sharp-shinned Hawk is fairly common over much of its range; found in mixed woodlands. Preys chiefly on small birds, often at feeders. Migrates singly or in loose groups.

Cooper's Hawk *Accipiter cooperii*
L 14-20" (36-51 cm) WS 29-37" (74-94 cm) Distinguished from Sharp-shinned Hawk by longer, rounded tail, larger head, and, in **adult,** stronger contrast between back and crown. **Juvenile** has whitish or buffy underparts with fine streaks on breast, streaking reduced or absent on belly; tawny rufous color on head is much richer and white tip on tail is broader than in Sharp-shinned; undertail coverts entirely white. Note that some juveniles may have a pale eyebrow like Sharp-shinned. In flight (page 125), again compare larger head and longer tail.
Range: Inhabits broken woodlands or streamside groves, especially deciduous. Preys largely on songbirds, often at feeders, also some small mammals. Often perches on telephone poles, unlike Sharp-shinned. Usually migrates singly. Rare, mainly in fall, in Maritimes.

Northern Goshawk *Accipiter gentilis*
L 21-26" (53-66 cm) WS 40-46" (102-117 cm) Conspicuous eyebrow, flaring behind eye, separates **adult**'s dark crown from blue-gray back. Underparts are white with dense gray barring; appear gray at a distance; has wedge-shaped tail with fluffy undertail coverts. Note disproportionately shorter tail, longer wings, than Cooper's Hawk. **Juvenile** is brown above, buffy below, with thick, blackish brown streaks, heaviest on flanks; tail has wavy dark bands bordered with white and a thin white tip; undertail coverts usually have dark streaks. In flight (page 125), note tawny bar on upperwing coverts. Juvenile also can be confused with Gyrfalcon (page 122) and Red-shouldered Hawk (page 114).
Range: Inhabits deep, conifer-dominated, mixed woodlands; preys on birds and mammals as large as hares. Uncommon; winters irregularly south of mapped range when southward irruptions occur in some years.

Sharp-shinned Hawk
velox

small head

juvenile ♀

adult ♂

thin legs

Cooper's Hawk

larger head, longer neck, and tawny nape

juvenile ♀

adult ♂

curved leading edge

head projects

long rounded tail

straight leading edge

juvenile

long wings for an accipiter

juvenile

juvenile

shorter square tail

prominent pale supercilium

juvenile ♀

juvenile

streaked undertail coverts

long, pale gray supercilium contrasts sharply with dark auriculars

adult ♂

Northern Goshawk
atricapillus

dark barred underparts

thin, pale, wavy bands border dark bands

Common Black-Hawk *Buteogallus anthracinus*

L 21" (53 cm) WS 50" (127 cm) Wings broad and rounded; tail short, broad. **Adult** blackish overall; tail has broad white band. Legs and cere orange-yellow. Distinguished from Zone-tailed Hawk by broader wings; broader, less banded tail; larger bill; more orange-yellow in lore region. **Juvenile** has strong face pattern; heavily streaked underparts; many-banded tail; buffy wing panel visible from above and below.

Voice: Call is a series of loud whistles.

Range: Found along waterways. Very rare visitor to southern and central Texas.

Harris's Hawk *Parabuteo unicinctus*

L 21" (53 cm) WS 46" (117 cm) Chocolate brown overall, with chestnut shoulder patches, leggings, and wing linings; has white at base and tip of long tail; also has rounded wing tips. **Juvenile** is heavily streaked below; chestnut shoulder patches are less distinct.

Voice: Call is a harsh, grating *eeaarrr*.

Range: May straggle north of mapped range to central Great Plains, but many other individuals far outside the normal range may be escapes. Inhabits semiarid woodland and brushland. Gregarious; sometimes hunts in small, cooperative groups.

Buteos

These high-soaring hawks use rising thermals for energy-efficient flight; they are among the easiest of our birds of prey to spot. All have broad wings and relatively short tails. Most species also hunt from perches. Many species were persecuted by humans until the mid-1900s.

Zone-tailed Hawk *Buteo albonotatus*

L 20" (51 cm) WS 51" (130 cm) Grayish black overall, with barred flight feathers. Legs and cere are yellow. Slimmer winged than Common Black-Hawk; also has longer tail, which is variably banded according to sex and age. Flies like Turkey Vulture, which it resembles; this similarity may keep prey from recognizing it. But compare Zone-tailed's banded tail, smaller bill, yellow cere, and larger, feathered head. **Juvenile** has grayish tail and some white flecking on breast.

Voice: Call is a squealing whistle.

Range: Uncommon; found in mesa and mountain country, often near watercourses; drops from low glide on small birds, rodents, lizards, and fish. Uncommon breeder on the Edwards Plateau in central Texas. Rare in southern Texas, mostly in winter. Accidental to Nova Scotia, Louisiana, and Florida.

Common Black-Hawk
anthracinus

finely banded remiges

juvenile

banded tail

whitish patch

adult

stocky body shape with short tail

longer tail than adult

juvenile

short tail with single, broad, white band

adult

broad short wings

short rounded wings

juvenile

adult

streaked below

Turkey Vulture for comparison

long, narrow wings

flies with dihedral very similar to Turkey Vulture

Harris's Hawk
harrisi

white tail base and tip

chestnut wing linings

juvenile

finely banded

barred remiges differ from Turkey Vulture

adult ♂

adult

chestnut wing coverts

smaller bill than Common Black-Hawk

long tail with heavy black band

ng tail ith hite tip

chestnut thighs

white undertail coverts

Zone-tailed Hawk

adult

Roadside Hawk *Buteo magnirostris*

L 14" (36 cm) WS 30" (75 cm) A small, slim, long-legged raptor with banded tail. *Adult* with brown bib, barred belly. *Juvenile* with some streaking on chest. Flies with stiff, rapid wingbeats; wing tips rounded with rufous patch on inner primaries. Compare with Gray Hawk and with Broad-winged and Red-shouldered Hawks. **Voice:** Mostly silent in U.S.
Range: Tropical species, casual in winter in lower Rio Grande Valley, Texas.

Gray Hawk *Buteo nitidus*

L 17" (43 cm) WS 35" (89 cm) Gray upperparts, gray-barred underparts and wing linings, and rounded wing tips distinguish Gray from Broad-winged (next page). Accipiter-like flight: several rapid, shallow wingbeats and a glide. *Juvenile* resembles juvenile Broad-winged, but has longer tail projection, stronger face pattern with outlined white cheek, and white, U-shaped rump band; dark trailing edge on wings is smaller or absent.
Voice: Calls include a loud, descending whistle.
Range: Tropical species. Resident in woodlands with nearby open land in lower Rio Grande Valley, Texas. Rare in summer upriver to Big Bend.

Short-tailed Hawk *Buteo brachyurus*

L 15½" (39 cm) WS 35" (89 cm) Small hawk with two color morphs. Secondaries seen from below are darker than primaries. *Light morph* has dark helmet and underwing resembling Swainson's Hawk (page 116), wings and tail are shorter, broader; lacks chest band. *Adults* have wide, dark subterminal tail band; of equal width on juveniles. Faint streaks on sides of light morph; spotted with white on wing linings and underparts on dark-morph juveniles. Exclusively an aerial hunter, it is most often seen in flight.
Voice: Mostly silent away from nest site.
Range: Found in woodland, savanna, and swamps; in winter even some suburbs. Casual to south Texas in spring and summer; accidental Michigan.

IDENTIFYING: Buteos in Flight The genus *Buteo* comprises large, wide-winged, short-tailed, soaring hawks, often seen circling on thermals or riding mountain updrafts. Some are forest dwellers and others are found in open country. Sexes are similar in appearance, although females are slightly larger than males, and juveniles have different plumage than adults.

Plumage variation *within* many species of buteos is substantial, a result of differing subspecies, color morphs, and age. (This variation is greatest from the Great Plains westward.) Thus, it is very important to learn the basic shapes of the species, including shape in flight,

particularly the relatively widespread Red-tailed, Red-shouldered, and Broad-winged Hawks, as well as some of the more uniquely shaped buteos such as the long- and pointy-winged Swainson's. Also note underwing and tail patterns. Raptors molt their plumage once per year, usually in spring. The timing of this molt can be delayed or protracted. Buteos and other birds of prey molt their flight feathers sequentially — the same primary on each wing, for example — so they remain "balanced" and fully flightworthy at all times. Be aware that some species when worn or in active wing molt may give the impression of having unusual pale plumage.

short rounded wings

Roadside Hawk

pale eye

adult

adult

short, pale supercilium

brown bib

barred rufous patch on inner primaries

juvenile

streaked breast

long legs

long banded tail

distinct head pattern with dark eye line, dark malar, and pale cheeks

juvenile

longer tail than Broad-winged

juveniles

whitish uppertail coverts

Gray Hawk
plagiata

fine gray bars

banded black-and-white tail

juvenile

adult

adult

dark helmet

rarely seen perched

white wing linings

Short-tailed Hawk
fuliginosus

light-morph adult

uniform white underparts

dark-morph adult

Broad-winged Hawk *Buteo platypterus*

L 16" (41 cm) WS 34" (86 cm) Pointed wing tips; white under-wings have dark borders; tail has broad black and white bands, with last white band broader than the others. Wings broad but more pointed than in Red-shouldered Hawk; wing linings buffy or white; tail shorter, broader. *Juvenile* Broad-winged typically has black moustachial streak; dark-bordered underwings, indistinct bands on tail; very similar to juvenile eastern Red-shouldered but paler below; may have a pale area at base of primaries, especially when in worn condition, but lack the distinct pale crescent. Rare *dark morph* breeds in western and central Canada. Identify by same overall size and shape and tail pattern as light morph. Flies with relatively slow wingflaps, unlike the Gray Hawk, which has an accipiter-like flight with quick flaps and glides.

Voice: Call, heard on breeding and winter grounds, is a thin, shrill, slightly descending whistle: *pee-teee.*

Range: Broad-winged is a woodland species; may be seen perched on poles and power lines near forest edges. Preys primarily on small mammals, amphibians, reptiles, birds, and large insects. Often migrates in very large flocks. Most winter in South America; a few winter in southern Florida and south Texas. Dark-morph Broad-wingeds are seen only casually east of the Great Plains.

Red-shouldered Hawk *Buteo lineatus*

L 15-19" (38-48 cm) WS 37-42" (94-107 cm) Relatively long tailed and long legged. In flight, shows pale crescent at base of primaries. *Adult* has reddish shoulders and wing linings and extensive pale spotting above. Widespread eastern nominate race *lineatus* shows dark streaks on reddish chest. Southeastern *alleni* (not shown) is smaller, with grayish cast to head and back; usually lacks breast streaking. South Florida *extimus* is the smallest and palest race. Central Texas *texanus* (not shown) is decidedly more rufous below. *Juveniles* show extensive variations; *lineatus* shows more finely streaked breast and more closely resembles juvenile Broad-winged Hawk; other eastern races show more coarsely marked underparts. Flight of *lineatus,* with slow wingbeats, like Broad-winged.

Voice: Call is an evenly spaced series of clear, high *kee-ah* or *kah* notes.

Range: Found in moist, mixed woodlands, including woodlots bordering residential areas; often seen near water. Preys primarily on small mammals, amphibians, reptiles, and crawfish. Florida birds more apt to be seen perched in the open. Migratory *lineatus* is an early spring and late fall migrant. Very rare in Maritime Provinces.

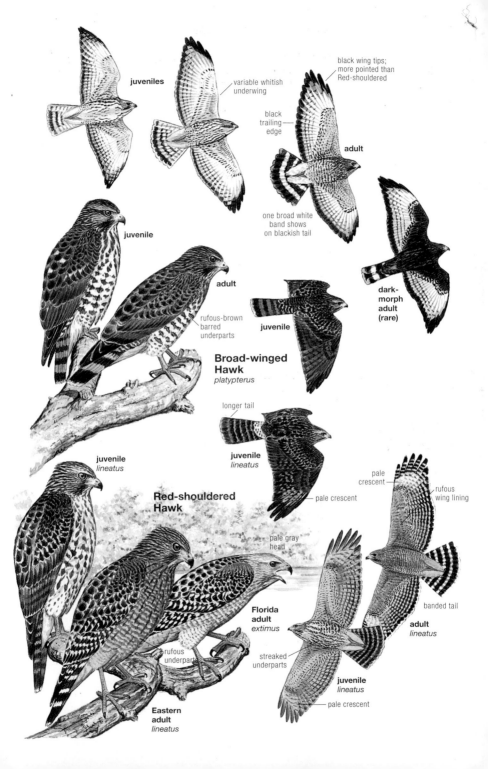

juveniles

variable whitish underwing

black wing tips; more pointed than Red-shouldered

black trailing edge

adult

one broad white band shows on blackish tail

juvenile

adult

rufous-brown barred underparts

juvenile

dark-morph adult (rare)

Broad-winged Hawk
platypterus

longer tail

juvenile
lineatus

Red-shouldered Hawk

juvenile
lineatus

pale crescent

pale gray head

pale crescent

rufous wing lining

juvenile
lineatus

Florida adult
extimus

rufous underparts

banded tail

adult
lineatus

streaked underparts

juvenile
lineatus

pale crescent

Eastern adult
lineatus

Red-tailed Hawk *Buteo jamaicensis*

L 22" (56 cm) WS 50" (127 cm) Our most common buteo; wings broad and fairly rounded; plumage extremely variable. Looks heavy billed, unlike Rough-legged (next page) and Swainson's. Variable pale mottling on scapulars contrasts with dark mantle, often forming a broad-sided V on perched birds. Most **adults** in the East show a belly band of dark streaks on whitish underparts; dark bar on leading edge of underwing, contrasting with paler wing linings (page 126). Note reddish upper tail; paler red under tail. Great Plains race *krideri,* **"Krider's Red-tailed,"** has paler upperparts and whitish tail with pale reddish wash; in flight, shows pale rectangular patches at base of primaries on upperwing. Dark and rufous morphs of western race, *calurus* (not shown), may be found in winter east to Mississippi River Valley, very rarely farther east; they have dark wing linings and underparts, obscuring the bar on leading edge and belly band; tail is dark reddish above. In *harlani,* **"Harlan's Hawk,"** formerly considered a separate species, dark morph has dusky white tail, diffuse blackish terminal band; shows some white streaking on its dark breast; may lack scapular mottling; rare *harlani* light morph has typical tail pattern, but plumage resembles *krideri.* "Harlan's Hawk" breeds in Alaska and east to northwestern Canada; winters primarily in central U.S. **Juveniles** of all morphs except *harlani* have gray-brown tails with many blackish bands; otherwise heavily streaked and spotted with brown below.
Voice: Distinctive call, a harsh, descending *keeeeer.*
Range: Habitat variable: woods with nearby open land, plains, agricultural areas. Preys primarily on rodents, also on reptiles, amphibians, and birds.

Swainson's Hawk *Buteo swainsoni*

L 21" (53 cm) WS 52" (132 cm) Distinguished from most other buteos by long, narrow, pointed wings; plumage extremely variable. Lacks Red-tailed's pale mottling on scapulars; bill smaller. All but darkest birds show contrast between paler wing linings and dark flight feathers; most show pale uppertail coverts. In *light morph,* whitish or buffy white wing linings contrast with darkly barred brown flight feathers; dark bib; underparts otherwise whitish to pale buff. *Dark-morph adult* dark brown with white undertail coverts; shows less sharp contrast between wing linings and flight feathers; darkest birds show none. Compare with dark juvenile White-tailed (next page). *Intermediate* colorations between light and dark morphs include a rufous morph. Intermediate and *light-morph juveniles* have dark moustachial stripe and conspicuous whitish eyebrows that meet on the forehead; variable streaking below, very heavy on dark morphs. Show less contrast between wing linings and flight feathers than adults (page 126). Soars with uptilted wings in teetering, vulturelike flight.
Voice: Mostly silent, except near nest site.
Range: Nests on plains and prairie. Very rare spring and, primarily, fall migrant in eastern North America. Gregarious; usually migrates in large flocks, often with Broad-winged Hawks (preceding page). Winters chiefly in South America; rarely in southern Florida and south Texas.

Red-tailed Hawk

eastern adult *borealis*

whitish on scapulars

eastern juvenile *borealis*

rufous tail

"Harlan's Hawk" adult *harlani*

whitish spots on breast

whitish base to tail

pale head

"Krider's Red-tailed" adult *krideri*

paler rufous tail

rufous tail

rather rounded wing tip

dark patagial bar

wings more slender than adult's

juvenile *borealis*

streaked belly

adult *borealis*

long, narrow pointed wings

smaller bill than Red-tailed

light-morph juvenile

often with darker lateral breast patches

Swainson's Hawk

dark-morph adult

whitish underwing coverts contrast with dark flight feathers

light-morph adult

brown breast band

light-morph adult

broad dark subterminal band

intermediate-morph adult

Rough-legged Hawk *Buteo lagopus*

L 21" (53 cm) WS 53" (135 cm) White tail with dark band or bands helps to identify this hawk in all plumages; bill small. Thin legs are feathered to the toes, the feathering barred in adults, unbarred in juveniles. **Adult male** has multibanded tail with a broad blackish subterminal band. **Adult female**'s tail is brown toward tip with a thin, black subterminal band. **Juvenile** has a single broad, brown tail band. Wings are long, fairly narrow. Seen in flight from above, white at base of tail is conspicuous; note also the small white patches at base of primaries on upperwings. In the common light morph, pale head contrasts with darker back and dark belly band, especially in females and immatures. Adult male has darker breast markings that may create a bib effect; belly is paler. Observe the square, black carpal patches at the "wrists" of the wings. **Dark morph** is less common. Often hovers while hunting.
Voice: During breeding season gives a soft, plaintive whistle. Alarm call is a loud screech or squeal.
Range: Inhabits open country, also marshes in winter. Numbers, southern limit of winter range vary from year to year.

Ferruginous Hawk *Buteo regalis*

L 23" (58 cm) WS 56" (142 cm) Pale headed; extended "gape line" goes back under eye; tail is a mixture of pale rust, white, and gray. Long, broad, pointed wings; note large, white, crescent-shaped patches on upperwing surface. Seen from below, flight feathers lack barring. **Adults** show rusty color on back, shoulders; rusty leggings form a conspicuous V against whitish underparts spotted with rufous. Rare **dark morph** varies from dark rufous to dark brown, with dark undertail coverts. Absence of dark tail bands separates it from dark-morph Rough-legged. **Juvenile** almost or entirely lacks rusty leggings and is less rufous above; resembles "Krider's Red-tailed" (preceding page), but wings longer, more pointed. Often hovers when hunting or soars in a dihedral. Often sits on ground.
Voice: Harsh alarm calls, *kree-a* or *kaah,* given chiefly in breeding season.
Range: Inhabits dry, open country. Casual east to western Great Lakes, Mississippi River; accidental to Virginia, Florida.

White-tailed Hawk *Buteo albicaudatus*

L 20" (51 cm) WS 51" (130 cm) Wings fairly long and pointed; at rest, appears long legged and **adult**'s wing tips project well beyond end of short tail; tail is white with single black band and other finer bands. Rusty shoulders contrast with dark gray upperparts. Underparts and wing linings vary from white on most to lightly barred. Females darker above, more barred below. **Juveniles** brown above, variable below from mostly blackish to paler; most show a white breast patch; tail pale gray; undertail and uppertail coverts whitish, the latter forming a pale U at tail base. Compare with dark-morph Swainson's (preceding page) and Ferruginous Hawks.
Voice: Mostly silent, except near nest site.
Range: Resident in open coastal grasslands and semiarid brush country. Casual to southwest Louisiana and west Texas.

Rough-legged Hawk
sanctijohannis

small bill

squarish
carpal
patch

adult ♀

dark-morph
adult ♂

adult ♂

feathered
tarsus

juvenile with pale head
and blackish belly

white tail base with broad,
black subterminal band

adult males with
multiple blackish
bands at tail base

juvenile

juveniles
whiter below
than adults

**Ferruginous
Hawk**

pale head

juvenile

variable rufous
feathering in
underwing coverts

extended
gape

dark
morph adult

adults

rufous
underparts

whitish
tail lacks
bands

all show broad
whitish crescents

adult

rufous leggings

White-tailed Hawk
hypospodius

grayish head
and back

juvenile

long pointed
wings

rufous
scapulars and
marginal
coverts

adult

white
below

short white
tail with
black
subterminal
tail band

dark
juvenile

adult

juvenile

some juveniles
all-dark below
except for
undertail coverts

whitish
tail base

pale tail

Caracaras, Falcons (Family Falconidae)

Falcons are distinguished from hawks by their long wings, which are bent back at the "wrist" and, except in the Crested Caracara, narrow and pointed. Females are larger than the males.

Crested Caracara *Caracara cheriway* **T**
L 23" (58 cm) WS 50" (127 cm) Large head, long legs. Blackish brown overall; white throat and neck; red-orange to yellow bare facial skin; underparts barred with black. *Juvenile* browner; upperparts edged and spotted with buff; underparts streaked with buff, unlike *adult* barring. In flight, shows whitish patches near ends of rounded wings. Flapping, ravenlike flight; soars with flat wings.
Voice: Calls include a low rattle and a single *wuck* note.
Range: Inhabits open brushlands. Feeds on carrion; also hunts insects, small animals. Fairly common in Texas; rare in Louisiana. Records from well outside known range are of debatable origin.

Aplomado Falcon *Falco femoralis* **E**
L 15-16½" (38-42 cm) WS 40-48" (102-122 cm) In flight, often hovers; long, pointed wings and long, banded tail; underwings are dark, with pale trailing edge. Note slate gray crown, boldly marked head. Dark patches on sides sometimes extend across breast. *Juvenile* is cinnamon below with a streaked breast, and browner above.
Voice: Call a series of *kek* notes.
Range: Once found in open grasslands in southern Texas. Disappeared by the early 20th century. Reintroduction project under way in south coastal Texas.

American Kestrel *Falco sparverius*
L 10½" (27 cm) WS 23" (58 cm) Smallest, most common of our falcons. Russet back and tail, double black stripes on white face. In flight, *males* show a row of white, circular spots on trailing edge of wings. Male has blue-gray wing coverts; compare with Merlin and much larger Peregrine Falcon. Hovers over prey before plunging. Often perches on telephone wires; frequently bobs its tail.
Voice: Call is a shrill *killy killy killy.*
Range: Found in open country; feeds on insects, reptiles, small mammals, and birds.

Merlin *Falco columbarius* *L 12" (31 cm) WS 25" (64 cm)*
Adult male gray-blue above; *female* and juveniles usually dark brown. Lacks the strong facial markings and russet upperparts of kestrels; has broader wings. Plumage varies geographically. Widespread nominate breeds in the taiga region. Pale *richardsonii* breeds on northern Great Plains. Shows strongly barred tail in flight, unlike the much larger Peregrine and Prairie Falcons. Underparts, underwings darker than in kestrels, particularly in *columbarius;* head larger. All *richardsonii* have pale cheeks; male paler blue-gray above; female and juvenile pale brown, the latter with wide, pale tail bands. Powerful flyer; does not hover. Catches birds in flight.
Voice: Mostly silent, except at from nest site.
Range: Generally uncommon.

blackish cap

pink facial skin

slight crest

adult

barred white chest

conspicuous white patches

long white-based tail

adult ♀

dark belly band and underwing coverts

long tail

juvenile

Crested Caracara

black belly

bold white supercilium and breast

adult ♂

blackish side patches

long lowish legs

juvenile

juvenile ♀

Aplomado Falcon
septentrionalis

adult ♂   frequently hovers

all with two dark facial stripes

uniformly rufous-brown

American Kestrel

adult ♂

adult ♀

♀

adult ♂   rapid, powerful flight with no hovering

rufous tail

juvenile ♂

faint moustache

♀

Merlin
columbarius

dark bluish

dark brown

male has bluish gray wings

adult ♂

♀ *richardsonii*

pale brown upperparts

adult ♂
richardsonii

pale bluish gray

Prairie Falcon *Falco mexicanus*

L 15½-19½" (39-50 cm) WS 35-43" (89-109 cm) Pale brown above; creamy white and heavily spotted below. Brown crown, dark moustachial, and broad pale area below and behind eye; facial markings narrower and plumage paler overall than Peregrine Falcon. Compare also with female and juvenile male Merlin (preceding page), especially subspecies *richardsonii*. In flight, all ages show distinctive dark axillaries and dark bar on wing lining, broader on females. Juvenile streaked below (not spotted), darker above; bluish cere. Preys chiefly on birds, small mammals.

Voice: Mostly silent away from nest site.

Range: Uncommon. Inhabits dry, open country, prairies. Rare migrant and winter visitor to western Midwest. Casual elsewhere in Midwest and Southeast.

Peregrine Falcon *Falco peregrinus*

L 16-20" (41-51 cm) WS 36-44" (91-112 cm) Crown and nape black; black wedge extends below eye, forming a distinctive helmet, absent in Prairie Falcon and smaller Merlin (preceding page). Tail is shorter than in Prairie; wing tips almost reach the end; also lacks dark bar and axillaries on underwings. Plumage pale in migratory subspecies *tundrius* breeding in the North. More sedentary *anatum* race has thicker moustachial stripe; **adult** shows rufous wash below; **juvenile** is dark brownish above, and underparts are heavily streaked. Juvenile *tundrius* has a pale eyebrow and larger pale area on side of face; underparts more finely streaked.

Voice: Gives harsh *cack* notes when agitated at nest site.

Range: Peregrines inhabit open wetlands near cliffs; prey chiefly on birds. Use of pesticides helped eliminate eastern *anatum* breeding populations; now reintroduced in parts of former range. Now established also in cities, where seen year-round; nest on bridges, tall buildings. Most East Coast sightings in the fall are of *tundrius*.

Gyrfalcon *Falco rusticolus*

L 20-25" (51-64 cm) WS 42-52" (107-132 cm) Heavily built; wings broader based than in other falcons. **Adult** has yellow-orange eye ring, cere, and legs (bluish gray in juveniles). Tail broad and tapered; may be barred or unbarred; in perched bird, tail extends far beyond wing tips, unlike other falcons. Compare also with Northern Goshawk (page 108). Plumages vary from **white morph** to **gray morph,** to very **dark morph,** with paler gray morphs intermediate between typical gray and white. Facial markings range from none on white morph to all-dark cheeks on dark morph. Juveniles of white and gray morphs are much browner above; **juveniles** of gray and dark morphs show darker wing linings and paler flight feathers. Flies with slow, powerful wingbeats. Preys chiefly on birds.

Voice: Mostly silent during nonbreeding season; gives harsh *cack* notes when agitated at nest site.

Range: Gyrfalcon inhabits open tundra near rocky outcrops and cliffs. Scarce; winters irregularly south to dashed line on map. Casual to southern Great Plains, southern Great Lakes, and mid-Atlantic regions.

Prairie Falcon

head pattern differs from Peregrine Falcon

adults

pale brown

blackish axillaries and underwing coverts

adult *anatum*

uniform underwing

Peregrine Falcon

broad, dark moustachial stripe

juvenile *anatum*

thinner dark moustache than *anatum*

juvenile *tundrius*

dark brown

long wing tips extend nearly to tail tip

adult *anatum*

adult *tundrius*

faint moustache

gray-morph adult

dark-morph juvenile

very dark brown

Gyrfalcon

darker wing coverts contrast with slightly paler remiges

gray-morph juvenile

long tail extends well beyond wing tips

white-morph adult

Female Hawks in Flight

Kites

White-tailed Kite
dark patch
adult
long white tail

mostly dark gray body
falconlike wing shape
Mississippi Kite
1st summer
long tail

Hook-billed Kite
unique wing shape
adult
rufous underparts and wing linings
long banded tail

rounded wing tips
Snail Kite
adult
long, slightly forked tail with extensive white base

Falcons

long, pale rufous tail
American Kestrel

Merlin
shorter and darker banded tail
columbarius

dark helmet
uniform underwing
Peregrine Falcon
adult

dark underwing coverts
Gyrfalcon
gray-morph juvenile
long tail

blackish axillaries and wing coverts
Prairie Falcon
adult

Accipiters, Harrier, Smaller Buteos

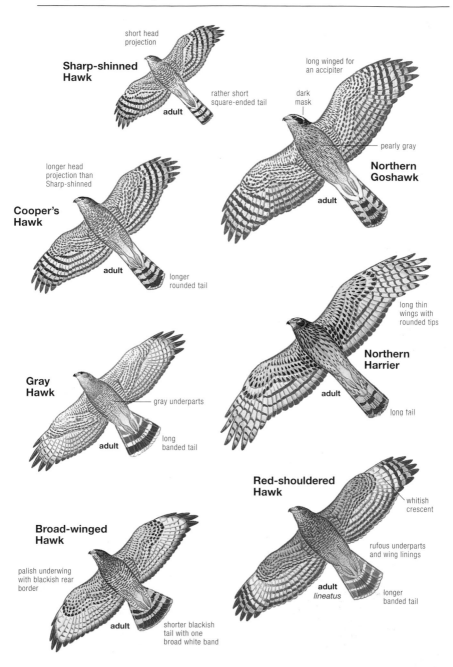

Sharp-shinned Hawk
short head projection
rather short square-ended tail
adult

Northern Goshawk
long winged for an accipiter
dark mask
pearly gray
adult

Cooper's Hawk
longer head projection than Sharp-shinned
longer rounded tail
adult

Gray Hawk
gray underparts
long banded tail
adult

Northern Harrier
long thin wings with rounded tips
long tail
adult

Broad-winged Hawk
palish underwing with blackish rear border
shorter blackish tail with one broad white band
adult

Red-shouldered Hawk
whitish crescent
rufous underparts and wing linings
longer banded tail
adult
lineatus

Female Hawks in Flight

Larger Buteos, Black-Hawk

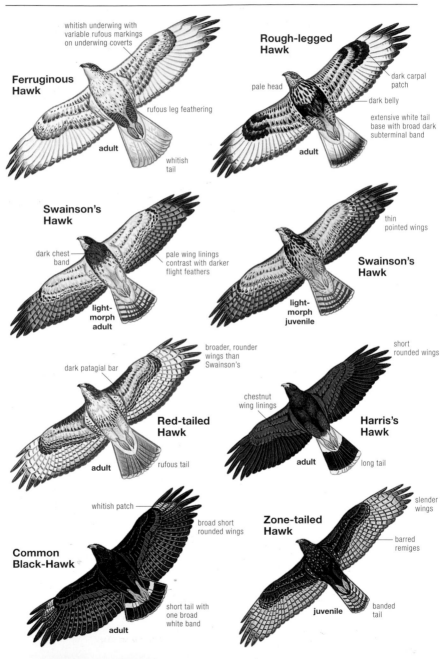

Ferruginous Hawk
whitish underwing with variable rufous markings on underwing coverts
rufous leg feathering
adult
whitish tail

Rough-legged Hawk
pale head
dark carpal patch
dark belly
extensive white tail base with broad dark subterminal band
adult

Swainson's Hawk
dark chest band
pale wing linings contrast with darker flight feathers
light-morph adult

thin pointed wings
Swainson's Hawk
light-morph juvenile

Red-tailed Hawk
dark patagial bar
broader, rounder wings than Swainson's
rufous tail
adult

short rounded wings
chestnut wing linings
Harris's Hawk
long tail
adult

Common Black-Hawk
whitish patch
broad short rounded wings
short tail with one broad white band
adult

Zone-tailed Hawk
slender wings
barred remiges
banded tail
juvenile

Osprey, Eagles, Caracara

Osprey

long angled wings

adult

Bald Eagle

long head projection

whitish in underwing coverts and on belly

shorter tail projection

2nd year

Crested Caracara

white wing patch

white throat and breast

extensive whitish tail base

adult

Golden Eagle

adults rather uniformly dark on body and on underwing

longer tail projection

adult

New World Vultures

Turkey Vulture

long narrow wings

small reddish head

two-toned underwings

unmarked remiges

adult

Black Vulture

large whitish primary patch with dusky tips

short tail

shorter, broad wings

adult

Limpkins (Family Aramidae)

Large, long-necked wading bird, named for its unusual limping gait.

Limpkin *Aramus guarauna* L 26" (66 cm)
Chocolate brown overall, densely streaked with white above. Long bill, slightly downcurved. Long legs and large, webless feet are dull grayish green. Juvenile is paler than *adult.*
Voice: Call, heard chiefly at night, is a wailing *krr-oww.*
Range: Uncommon in swamps and wetlands, where it wades or swims in search of snails, frogs, and insects. Casual in southern Georgia; accidental north to Maryland and Nova Scotia.

Rails, Gallinules, Coots (Family Rallidae)

These marsh birds have short tails and short, rounded wings. Most species are local and secretive. Some, especially the rails, are identified chiefly by call and habitat.

Yellow Rail *Coturnicops noveboracensis* L 7¼" (18 cm)
A small, very secretive, dark rail, deep tawny yellow above with wide dark stripes crossed by white bars. In flight, shows a large white patch on trailing edges of wings. Compare to juvenile Sora (below), which is not as black above; its upperparts are streaked, not barred, with white. *Juvenile* is darker than adult.
Voice: Distinctive call, heard chiefly in breeding season, a four- or five-note *tick-tick, tick-tick-tick* in alternate twos or twos and threes, sounds like tapping two pebbles together.
Range: Uncommon and local; secretive. Breeds in grassy marshes, damp fields; not found in deep-water marshes or swamps. Winters in fresh, brackish, or salt marshes, rice fields, dry fields.

Sora *Porzana carolina* L 8¾" (22 cm)
Short, thick bill, yellow or greenish yellow. *Breeding adult* coarsely streaked above. Face and center of throat and breast are black. In *winter* plumage, black throat is somewhat obscured by gray edgings. *Juvenile* lacks black on face and throat; underparts are paler.
Voice: Calls, heard year-round, a descending whinny and a sharp, high-pitched *keek;* a whistled *ker-wheer* heard on breeding grounds.
Range: Common in freshwater and brackish marshes, rice fields, grainfields; found in saltwater marshes during migration, winter.

Black Rail *Laterallus jamaicensis* L 6" (15 cm)
Very small, extremely secretive. Blackish above, with white speckling; chestnut nape. Bill short and black. Underparts grayish black, with narrow white barring on flanks. Newly hatched juveniles of other rails resemble Black Rail.
Voice: Most vocal in the middle of the night. Distinctive call, heard chiefly in breeding season, is a repeated *kik-kee-do* or *kik-kee-derr;* sometimes four notes: *kik-kik-kee-do.*
Range: Uncommon and local; inhabits marshes, swamps, wet meadows. Very irregular inland; range speculative.

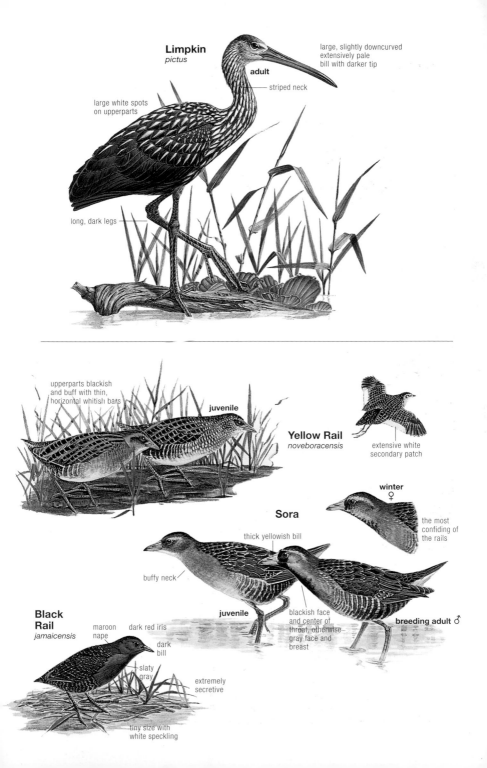

Limpkin
pictus

adult

large, slightly downcurved
extensively pale
bill with darker tip

striped neck

large white spots
on upperparts

long, dark legs

upperparts blackish
and buff with thin,
horizontal whitish bars

juvenile

Yellow Rail
noveboracensis

extensive white
secondary patch

winter
♀

Sora

the most
confiding of
the rails

thick yellowish bill

buffy neck

**Black
Rail**
jamaicensis

maroon
nape

dark red iris

dark
bill

slaty
gray

juvenile

extremely
secretive

blackish face
and center of
throat, otherwise
gray face and
breast

breeding adult ♂

tiny size with
white speckling

Clapper Rail *Rallus longirostris* L 14½" (37 cm)

Much larger than Virginia Rail (below). Plumage variable but always has grayish edges on brown-centered back feathers, olive wing coverts. East Coast subspecies such as *crepitans* are much duller than King Rail: buffy below; cheeks gray; flanks less strongly barred than in King. Gulf Coast races such as *scottii* are brighter cinnamon below and thus much more likely to be confused with King.

Voice: Clapper's call is a series of ten or more dry *kek kek kek* notes, like King but accelerating and then slowing, and a dry *kit kit krrr*. Also a series of grunting notes.

Range: Common in coastal salt marshes. Casual north to Maritimes. Accidental inland.

King Rail *Rallus elegans* L 15" (38 cm)

Large freshwater rail with long and slightly downcurved bill. Much larger than similar Virginia Rail (below). Adult is distinguished from Clapper Rail by tawny edges on black-centered back feathers and tawny wing coverts. Head slate, with buffy cheeks, buffy eyebrow; underparts cinnamon; flanks strongly barred black-and-white. Clapper Rails have more blended flanks. *Juvenile* is darker above, paler below. King Rail favors wet ditches and freshwater and brackish swamps and marshes, but is hard to see.

Voice: As with Clapper Rail, most often heard at dusk and dawn. Usually distinctive call is a series of fewer than ten *kek kek kek* notes, fairly evenly spaced. Also a series of grunting notes. Some calls of the two are identical.

Range: Uncommon in freshwater habitat near Gulf Coast; generally rather rare and very local well inland north to the Canadian border region. Has disappeared from some regions. Some birds winter in coastal marshes with Clapper Rails. Hybridizes with Clapper Rail in narrow zone of overlap and identification of at least some birds from areas where the two species meet is problematical.

Virginia Rail *Rallus limicola* L 9½" (24 cm)

Similar to King Rail (above) but much smaller; cheeks grayer; wings richer chestnut; legs and bill often redder. *Juvenile* is blackish brown above, mottled black or gray below.

Voice: Song is a series of *kid kid kidick kidick* phrases, heard chiefly in breeding season. Also a *tic tic tic turrr*. Common call, heard year-round, is a descending, accelerating series of raspy *oink* notes.

Range: Fairly common but a bit secretive; found in freshwater and brackish marshes and in wetlands; also found in coastal salt marshes.

grayish face

all races have brown-
centered upperpart feathers
with grayish edges

crepitans

**Clapper
Rail**

scottii

feathers on
upperparts with
buffy edges and
black centers

buffy
face

adult

juvenile

rich tawny
breast

King Rail
elegans

gray
cheek

long, thin
reddish bill

juvenile

Virginia Rail
limicola

Purple Gallinule *Porphyrio martinica L 13" (33 cm)*

Bright purplish blue head, neck, underparts; pale blue forehead shield; red-and-yellow bill. Legs, feet bright yellow. *Juvenile* buffy brown overall, with brownish olive back, greenish wings; bill mostly dark olive, legs and feet dull olive. Molts into winter plumage after fall migration but may retain traces of juvenal plumage into first spring. In all ages, all-white undertail coverts are conspicuous.
Voice: Call is a sharp *keek*; also a series of grunting notes.
Range: Fairly common in overgrown swamps, lagoons, marshes. Regularly perches in bushes, trees. Highly migratory; winters from southern Florida to Argentina. Wanderers are seen in all seasons far north of mapped range; sometimes breeds north of area shown.

Purple Swamphen *Porphyrio porphyrio*

L 18-20" (45-50 cm) Old World species. Resembles a huge Purple Gallinule with reddish bill and frontal shield, iris, legs. Various subspecies groups recognized, some may deserve treatment as separate species. Florida birds appear to belong to the *poliocephalus* group (three races) from southern Asia with grayish blue neck, or possibly closely allied *viridis* (mainland southeast Asia), but some swamphens with bluer heads likely represent other subspecies.
Voice: Calls similar to moorhen's but much lower pitched.
Range: Found from southern Europe to island groups in tropical South Pacific. Introduced into south Florida in 1996 and has spread, but eradication under way in some areas.

Common Moorhen *Gallinula chloropus L 14" (36 cm)*

Black head and neck, with red forehead shield, red bill with yellow tip. Back brownish olive; underparts slate; white along flanks is diagnostic. Outer undertail coverts white, inner ones black. Legs and feet yellow. *Juvenile* is paler, browner; throat whitish; bill and legs dusky. *Winter adult* has brownish facial shield and usually a brownish bill with dusky yellow tip.
Voice: A high *keek*; also a series of nasal clucking notes.
Range: Common in freshwater marshes, ponds, placid rivers; now uncommon to rare and declining from much of interior range.

American Coot *Fulica americana L 15½" (39 cm)*

Overall blackish, darker on head and neck; outer undertail coverts white. Whitish bill has dark subterminal band; note reddish brown forehead shield. Leg color ranges from greenish gray in *juvenile* birds to yellow or orangish in adults. Toes are lobed, unlike gallinules. Juvenile is quite pale; by first winter more like adult, but still paler, with whitish feather tips, especially below. In flight, white trailing edge on most of wing is distinctive. A few *variant* American Coots have extensively white facial shields like Caribbean Coot, *F. caribaea*, of the West Indies. Regarded by some as a subspecies of American, Caribbean has not yet been verified in Florida.
Voice: Variety of grunting and clucking calls; also a sharp *krrp*, slightly lower pitched than Moorhen call.
Range: Nests in freshwater marshes, wetlands, or near lakes and ponds; winters in both fresh and salt water; also grazes on golf courses and park lawns, often in large flocks. Often dives to feed.

light violet shield

green above, bright
purplish blue
on head and below

juvenile

**Purple
Gallinule**

overall buffy
color

long yellow
legs and toes

darker
bill

winter

light violet-gray neck

thick
red bill

red bill with
yellow tip

breeding

bronze-
brown back

juvenile

**Purple
Swamphen**
poliocephalus

large size

**Common
Moorhen**
cachinnans

thin
whitish
stripe

whitish
bill

juvenile

some lack
dark top
to shield

variant

**American
Coot**
americana

lobed feet

swims like
a duck most
of the time

Cranes (Family Gruidae)

Tall birds with long necks and legs. Tertials droop over the rump in a "bustle" that distinguishes cranes from herons. Cranes fly with their necks fully extended and circle in thermals like raptors. Courtship includes a frenzied, leaping dance.

Sandhill Crane Grus canadensis

L 34-48" (86-122 cm) WS 73-90" (185-229 cm) Races vary in size: northern nominate race smallest; more southerly *tabida* largest. Resident Florida race, *pratensis,* and Gulf Coast race, *pulla* (**E**), are intermediate. *Adult* is gray, with dull red skin on crown and lores; whitish chin, cheek, and upper throat; and slaty primaries. *Juvenile* lacks red patch; head and neck vary from pale to tawny; gray body irregularly mottled with brownish red; full adult plumage reached after two and a half years. Sometimes confused with Great Blue Heron (page 88), which lacks bustle. Preening with muddy bills, cranes may stain feathers of upper back, lower neck, and breast with ferrous solution in mud.

Voice: Common call is a trumpeting, rattling *gar-oo-oo,* audible for more than a mile. Young birds give a wholly different, cricket-like call.

Range: Locally common; breeds on tundra and in marshes and grasslands. In winter, regularly feeds in dry fields, returning to water at night. Rare on East Coast. Migrating flocks fly at great heights.

Common Crane Grus grus

L 44-51" (112-130 cm) WS 79-91" (202-231 cm) Eurasian species, casual vagrant on the Great Plains, accidental farther east; almost always with migrating flocks of Sandhill Cranes. Some records involve a mixed Common-Sandhill pair with accompanying hybrid young. *Adult* distinguished from Sandhill Crane by blackish head and neck marked by broad white stripe. *Juvenile* like juvenile Sandhill; may show trace of white head stripe by spring. In flight, in all ages, black primaries and secondaries show as a broad black trailing edge on gray wings.

Voice: Gives a far-carrying trumpeting call.

Whooping Crane Grus americana E

L 52" (132 cm) WS 87" (221 cm) *Adult* is white overall, with red facial skin; black primaries show in flight. *Juvenile* bird is whitish, with pale reddish brown head and neck, scattered reddish brown feathers over the rest of its body; begins to acquire adult plumage after first summer. A few abnormally colored Sandhill Cranes have been taken for Whooping Cranes; check wing-tip pattern.

Voice: Call is a shrill, trumpeting *ker-loo ker-lee-loo.*

Range: Sparse population breeds in marshes of Wood Buffalo National Park, Canada; winters in Aransas National Wildlife Refuge on Gulf Coast. Wild population is now about 200, including introductions. Intensive management and protection seem to be slowly succeeding. Small populations of both migratory and nonmigratory birds have been introduced in Florida, some migrate to Wisconsin.

all cranes have tertial "bustles"

juvenile

red crown

adult

Sandhill Crane
rowani

stained adult

adult

dark dusky remiges

juvenile

white stripe

yellowish bill

adult

black neck

adult

blackish remiges

Common Crane
lilfordi

red crown

adult

black wing tips

adult

juvenile

Whooping Crane

Lapwings, Plovers (Family Charadriidae)

These compact birds run and stop abruptly when foraging. Shape and behavior identify plovers in general.

Black-bellied Plover *Pluvialis squatarola* L 11½" (29 cm)
Black-and-white **breeding male** has frosty crown and nape, white belly region; *female* averages less black. *Winter* and *juvenile* birds distinguished from American Golden-Plover by larger size, larger bill, and grayer plumage (including crown); underparts streaked rather than softly barred, but note that juvenile can be speckled with gold above. In flight, shows black axillaries and white uppertail coverts, barred white tail, and bold white wing stripe.
Voice: Call is a drawn-out, three-note whistle, the second note lower pitched.
Range: Nests on Arctic tundra. Common migrant in Great Lakes region; uncommon to rare elsewhere in interior.

American Golden-Plover *Pluvialis dominica*
L 10¼" (26 cm) Smaller and slimmer, with a smaller bill than Black-bellied Plover; darker crown; wing stripe is indistinct, and underwings are smoky gray with no black in axillaries; no contrasting white rump. Note the approximately four evenly spaced primary tips. **Breeding male** shows broad white patches on sides of neck; underparts otherwise black. *Female* has less black. Mar. arrivals are in winter plumage; breeding plumage acquired on migration north.
Voice: Flight call is a shrill *ku-wheep.*
Range: Nests on tundra; migrants found on short-grass, plowed fields, mudflats, and, rarely, beaches. Fairly common migrant through Great Plains east to Mississippi River Valley. Very rare along East Coast in spring; more numerous in fall. Winters in South America.

European Golden-Plover *Pluvialis apricaria*
L 11" (28 cm) Spring vagrant to Atlantic Canada. Similar to American Golden-Plover; note larger size, plumper body shape, white underwings; also bolder wing bar. Small bill. On **breeding males,** white nearly meets on front of breast; sides, flanks, and undertail coverts are white; note dense pattern of smaller gold spots on upperparts, unlike coarser pattern of larger spots on American Golden-Plover.
Voice: Call is a mournful, drawn-out whistle.
Range: Breeds from Greenland and Iceland to northwestern Russia. Winters from Europe to North Africa. Irregular spring migrant to Newfoundland and Labrador; casually to eastern Quebec and Nova Scotia.

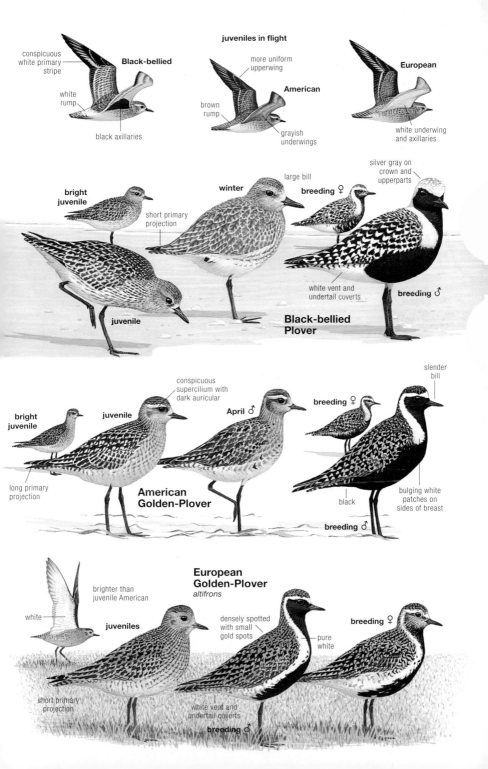

juveniles in flight

Black-bellied
- conspicuous white primary stripe
- white rump
- black axillaries

American
- more uniform upperwing
- brown rump
- grayish underwings

European
- white underwing and axillaries

Black-bellied Plover

bright juvenile
- short primary projection

winter
- large bill

breeding ♀
- silver gray on crown and upperparts

juvenile
- white vent and undertail coverts

breeding ♂

American Golden-Plover

bright juvenile
- long primary projection

juvenile
- conspicuous supercilium with dark auricular

April ♂

breeding ♀
- slender bill

breeding ♂
- black
- bulging white patches on sides of breast

European Golden-Plover
altifrons

- brighter than juvenile American
- white

juveniles
- short primary projection

- densely spotted with small gold spots
- pure white

breeding ♂
- white vent and undertail coverts

breeding ♀

Killdeer *Charadrius vociferus L 10½" (27 cm)*
Double breast bands are distinctive. Bright reddish orange rump is visible in flight. Downy young Killdeer have only one breast band.
Voice: Loud, piercing call, *kill-dee* or *dee-dee-dee.*
Range: Common in grassy fields and on shores. Nests on open ground, usually on gravel, even on rooftops. May form loose flocks and linger into early winter in summer range. Vagrant north of breeding range.

Wilson's Plover *Charadrius wilsonia L 7¾" (20 cm)*
Long, heavy, black bill; broad neck band is black in **breeding male,** brown in **female** and winter male; legs grayish pink. **Juvenile** resembles adult female but note scaly-looking upperparts. Breeding male may have cinnamon-buff ear patch. Compare with very young Killdeer.
Voice: Call is a sharp, whistled *whit.*
Range: Uncommon and declining on barrier islands, sandy beaches, and mud flats. Recorded casually north to the Maritime Provinces and accidental far inland to Great Lakes and Great Plains regions.

Semipalmated Plover *Charadrius semipalmatus*
L 7¼" (18 cm) Dark back distinguishes this species from Piping and Snowy Plovers; bill much smaller than in Wilson's Plover. At very close range, Semipalmated shows partial webbing between toes. **Breeding male** often lacks white above eye; also shows orangish eye ring. **Juvenile** has darker legs than adults do.
Voice: Distinctive call is a whistled, upslurred *chu-weet;* song a series of same.
Range: Common on beaches, lakeshores, and tidal flats; seen throughout the continent in migration.

Common Ringed Plover *Charadrius hiaticula*
L 7½" (19 cm) Almost identical to Semipalmated Plover and best distinguished by voice. Breast band averages slightly broader in center than in Semipalmated. White eyebrow is more distinct, particularly in male; orbital ring is partial or lacking altogether; webbing between toes less extensive. Bill is slightly longer, of more even thickness, and shows more orange at base; black on face meets bill where mandibles join.
Voice: Call is a soft, fluted *pooee;* song, delivered in display flight, is a series of these notes.
Range: Nests on Baffin Island, Greenland; migrates to and from Old World. Casual in Newfoundland, accidental on East Coast south to Virginia.

long tail and reddish orange rump

Killdeer

two breast bands

Wilson's Plover
wilsonia

juvenile

thick breast band

breeding ♂

long thick bill

♀

juvenile

dull fleshy legs

winter

complete orangish orbital ring

dark brown upperparts

Semipalmated Plover

always with complete band

breeding ♀

breeding ♂

juvenile

juvenile

bold white supercilium

orbital ring absent or incomplete

Common Ringed Plover

bill slightly longer than Semipalmated with more extensive orange base

breeding ♂

breeding ♀

Snowy Plover *Charadrius alexandrinus* L 6¼" (16 cm)
Pale above, very pale in eastern Gulf Coast birds; thin dark bill; dark or grayish legs; partial breast band; dark ear patch. **Females** and **juveniles** resemble Piping Plover; note Snowy Plover's thinner bill, darker legs.
Voice: Calls include a low *krut* and a soft, whistled *ku-wheet.*
Range: Inhabits barren sandy beaches and flats. Uncommon and declining on Gulf Coast. Western *nivosus,* breeding east to Great Plains and Texas, is threatened (**T**).

Piping Plover *Charadrius melodus* **E** L 7¼" (18 cm)
Very pale above; orange legs; white rump conspicuous in flight. In **breeding** plumage, shows dark narrow breast band usually complete in *circumcinctus,* sometimes incomplete, especially in **females** and paler-faced East Coast birds, *melodus.* In **winter,** bill is all-dark. Distinguished from Snowy Plover by thicker bill, paler back; legs are brighter than in both Snowy and Semipalmated Plovers.
Voice: Distinctive call, a clear *peep-lo.*
Range: Found on sandy beaches, lakeshores, and dunes. Endangered: generally uncommon; local and declining breeder and rare migrant in interior. In winter, *melodus* winters mainly on south Atlantic coast and northern Bahamas; *circumcinctus* on Gulf Coast.

Northern Lapwing *Vanellus vanellus* L 12½" (32 cm)
Eurasian vagrant. Most sightings of birds in **winter** plumage: dark, iridescent above, white below, with black breast; wispy but prominent crest. Wings broad and rounded, with white tips, white wing linings.
Voice: Flight call is a whistled *pee-wit.*
Range: Casual primarily in late fall and early winter in northeast states and provinces; accidental elsewhere in East; recorded south to Florida.

Mountain Plover *Charadrius montanus* L 9" (23 cm)
In **breeding** plumage, unbanded white underparts separate this plover from all other brown-backed plovers. Buffy tinge on breast is more extensive in **winter** plumage; compare with winter American Golden-Plover (page 136). In flight, Mountain Plover shows white underwings; American Golden-Plover's are grayish.
Voice: Calls heard on breeding grounds include low, drawn-out whistles and harsh notes. In migration and winter, gives a harsh *krrr* note.
Range: Inhabits plains; local and declining in many areas. Rarely seen during migration. Gregarious in winter; usually found on grassy or bare dirt fields.

Snowy Plover

upperparts darker
than Piping, paler than
Semipalmated

slender
bill

juvenile

♀

western
nivosus

♂

very pale
upperparts,
like Piping

dark lateral
patch

dark legs

Gulf Coast ♂
tenuirostris

**Piping
Plover**
melodus

gray breast band
incomplete

thicker bill

very pale gray
upperparts

winter

breeding ♂

long rounded wings
with white tips

orange legs

**interior
breeding ♂**
circumcinctus

breeding ♀

winter

white wing linings
and tail base

long wispy
crest

black lores and
black forecrown bar
with white forehead

winter

flashy white
underwing

uniform tan
upperparts

broad black
breast band

lateral
brown patch

**Mountain
Plover**

rich buff
undertail
coverts

winter

breeding

**Northern
Lapwing**

winter

juvenile

Oystercatchers (Family Haematopodidae)

These chunky shorebirds have laterally flattened, heavy bills that can reach into mollusks and pry the shells open; they also probe mud and sand for worms and crabs.

American Oystercatcher *Haematopus palliatus*
L 18½" (47 cm) Large red-orange bill. Black head and dark brown back; white wing and tail patches, white underparts. *Juvenile* appears scaly above; dark tip on bill is kept through first year.
Voice: Call a loud, whistled *queep*, given singly or in a series.
Range: Birds feed in pairs and flocks on coastal beaches and mudflats. Expanding northward in the East; recently established as a breeder in Maine and southern Nova Scotia. Accidental inland.

Stilts, Avocets (Family Recurvirostridae)

Sleek and graceful waders with long, slender bills and spindly legs. Two species inhabit North America.

American Avocet *Recurvirostra americana L 18" (46 cm)*
Black-and-white above, white below; head and neck rusty in breeding plumage, gray in winter. *Juvenile* has cinnamon wash on head and neck. Avocets feed by sweeping their bills from side to side through the water. *Male*'s bill is longer, straighter than *female*'s.
Voice: Common call is a loud *wheet*.
Range: Fairly common on shallow ponds, marshes, and lakeshores. A few migrants are regular north to Long Island and Great Lakes; very rare farther north, mostly in fall.

Black-necked Stilt *Himantopus mexicanus L 14" (36 cm)*
Male's glossy black back and bill contrast sharply with white underparts, long red or pink legs. Female is browner on back. *Juvenile* is brown above, with buffy edgings.
Voice: Common call is a loud *kek kek kek*.
Range: Breeds and winters in a wide variety of wet habitats; breeding range is spreading north. Casual north to Great Lakes and southern New England.

Jacanas (Family Jacanidae)

Extremely long toes and claws allow these tropical birds to walk on lily pads and other floating plants.

Northern Jacana *Jacana spinosa L 9½" (24 cm)*
Mexican and Central American species. *Adult* has chestnut and black body and wings; yellow frontal shield. Often raises its wings, revealing yellow flight feathers.
Voice: Call is a series of harsh staccato notes, usually given in flight.
Range: Casual visitor to ponds and marshes in southern Texas, where it has probably bred.

gold eye

long red bill

black neck contrasts
sharply with white belly

brown back

bold white
wing stripe

adults

darker
bill

juvenile

**American
Oystercatcher**
palliatus

breeding ♀

cinnamon head
and neck

male has
longer and
straighter bill

upturned bill

breeding ♀

white
scapular
patch

juvenile ♂

winter ♂

buffy neck

**American
Avocet**

long grayish
legs

juvenile

**Northern
Jacana**
gymnostoma

yellow flight
feathers

yellow
forehead shield
and long bill

**Black-necked
Stilt**

blackish
neck

♂

long,
thin
bill

adult

immature

very long,
pinkish red legs

long toes

white
supercilium
and
underparts

Sandpipers, Phalaropes, Allies (Family Scolopacidae)

The majority of these shorebirds have three distinct plumages. Most begin molting to winter plumage as they near or reach their winter grounds.

Spotted Sandpiper *Actitis macularius* L 7½" (19 cm)
Striking in **breeding** plumage, with barred upperparts, spotted underparts. **Juvenile** and **winter** birds lack spotting below. In juvenile and first-winter birds, barred wing coverts contrast with back. Flies with stiff, rapid, fluttering wingbeats. On the ground, nods and teeters constantly.
Voice: Calls include a shrill *peet-weet* and, in flight, a series of *weet* notes, lower pitched than the calls of Solitary Sandpiper.
Range: Spotted is common and widespread, found at sheltered streams, ponds, lakes, or marshes. Generally seen singly; may form small flocks in migration. Most winter in Central and South America. Rare in winter to southern edge of breeding range.

Solitary Sandpiper *Tringa solitaria* L 8½" (22 cm)
Dark brown above, heavily spotted with buffy white. White below; lower throat, breast, and sides streaked with blackish brown. Bolder white eye ring and shorter, olive legs distinguish Solitary Sandpiper from Lesser Yellowlegs (next page). In flight, shows dark central tail feathers, white outer feathers barred with black. Underwing is dark. Often keeps wings raised briefly after alighting; on the ground, often bobs its tail. Two subspecies: nominate *solitaria* (illustrated) from East is spotted with white in breeding plumage; spots more cinnamon-buff in more western *cinnamomea*.
Voice: Calls include a shrill *peet-weet*, higher pitched than calls of Spotted Sandpiper.
Range: Generally seen singly or in small flocks. Fairly common at shallow backwaters, pools, small estuaries, even rain puddles.

Willet *Tringa semipalmata* L 15" (38 cm)
Large, plump, and grayish overall with grayish legs. In flight, note black-and-white wing pattern. Two subspecies: eastern *semipalmata* is smaller, darker, browner, and thicker billed than western *inornata* in all plumages. **Breeding** *semipalmata* is more heavily barred below with more pinkish-based bill than *inornata*. **Juvenile** *semipalmata* has more contrasting scapulars than *inornata*. Separating winter birds to subspecies best done by structural features and range. Winter-plumaged *semipalmata* typically not seen in North America, except for early Mar. arrivals on Gulf Coast.
Voice: Territorial call is *pill-will-willet*, distinctly faster and higher pitched in nominate race. Other raucous calls are given year-round, all averaging higher pitched in the nominate race.
Range: Nominate *semipalmata* nests in coastal Atlantic and Gulf salt marshes; *inornata* in interior marshes. In fall *semipalmata* is an early migrant, most departing by late Aug., and winters entirely outside North America (mainly South America).

dark lateral
breast patches

**1st
winter**

**Spotted
Sandpiper**

juvenile

flies with
rapid, shallow,
stiff wingbeats

pink bill
with dark tip

barred wing coverts

juvenile

heavily spotted
underparts

breeding

white eye ring

breeding

juvenile

dark center
to rump
and tail

**Solitary
Sandpiper**
solitaria

dark
grayish
brown
breast

juvenile

short greenish legs

short pinkish-based bill

brownish cast
to upperparts

Willet

contrasting
scapulars

**early March
in molt**

eastern
semipalmata

western

eastern

heavily
barred

breeding

juvenile

striking wing pattern
in flight

winter

western Willets
are larger and
have a longer,
darker bill

**worn
breeding**

western
inornata

paler above

less heavily
marked
below

plainer and paler
upperparts

juvenile

breeding

winter

Lesser Yellowlegs *Tringa flavipes* L 10½" *(27 cm)*

Legs yellow to rarely orange. Smaller than Greater Yellowlegs; all-dark bill is shorter, thinner, straighter. In *breeding* plumage, not nearly as heavily as marked as Greater, especially on sides and flanks. *Juvenile* and *winter* birds are overall darker than Greater; juvenile Lessers are washed with grayish brown across the neck and lack the streaks that are present in Greater. A more sedate feeder than Greater, leisurely picks at prey from a more vertical position.

Voice: Call is one to three *tew* notes, a little higher than Greater Yellowlegs, the individual notes more clipped and all on one pitch.

Range: Common. Nests on tundra or in woodland. On nesting grounds, like Greater, often perches in trees and yelps at intruders. Most winter in South America, a few in U.S.

Greater Yellowlegs *Tringa melanoleuca* L 14" *(36 cm)*

Legs yellow to orange. Larger than Lesser Yellowlegs; bill longer, stouter, often slightly upturned; in all plumages except breeding, bill two-toned. In *breeding* plumage, throat and breast are heavily streaked; sides and belly are spotted and barred with black; bill is all black. In *juvenile* birds the neck is distinctly streaked. Behavior is more active than Lesser Yellowlegs, often racing about with extended neck while pursuing prey (often very small fish).

Voice: Call is a loud, slightly descending series of three or more *tew* notes.

Range: Fairly common; nests on muskeg, winters in wetland habitats. Compared to Lesser Yellowlegs, Greater is overall a later fall migrant and much more capable of wintering at interior locations.

Upland Sandpiper *Bartramia longicauda* L 12" *(31 cm)*

Small head, with large, dark, prominent eyes; long, thin neck, long tail, long wings. Legs yellow. Prefers fields, where often only its head and neck are visible above the grass. Also perches on posts on breeding grounds. In flight, blackish primaries contrast with mottled brown upperparts.

Voice: Calls, a rolling *pulip pulip,* and a call like a wolf whistle, heard in flight on breeding grounds.

Range: Nests in prairies, fallow fields, airports; migrants also found in farm fields, at sod farms. Fairly common except in easternmost range, where very local and declining.

IDENTIFYING: Yellowlegs When the two yellowlegs species are together, identification by size alone is easy, but identifying single birds can pose problems, even for experienced birders. Greater has a longer, slightly upturned bill that—except in breeding plumage—is grayer at the base than at the tip. Greaters are often quite active and chase prey (such as small fish) about, whereas Lessers feed sedately, picking at the water surface. In breeding plumage Greaters are much more strongly and extensively marked below. Lesser is paler below, with streaks only on the neck and inner sides. In juvenal plumage Greaters have streaks on the neck, while Lessers are washed with grayish across the neck and breast and any streaking is very blurry. The standard call notes are completely diagnostic, a *tew* or *tew-tew* in Lesser, whereas Greater gives a ringing and descending three-note call. Both species can occasionally have reddish orange legs and have been confused with redshanks.

both Lesser and Greater
Yellowlegs have whitish
rumps and barred tails

always with slim,
short, dark bill

breeding

**Lesser
Yellowlegs**

winter

winter

juvenile

faintly
marked
sides and
flanks

grayish wash
across chest

yellow legs

winter

bill all-dark in
breeding plumage

breeding

winter

long, slightly
upturned bill,
grayish at base

heavily
barred
flanks

**Greater
Yellowlegs**

juvenile

yellow legs

distinctly
streaked
breast

dark eye
stands out in
plain face

**Upland
Sandpiper**

long
neck

adult

juvenile

short,
straight,
mostly
yellowish
bill

dark outer
half of wing

long tail

juvenile

Eskimo Curlew *Numenius borealis* **E** *L 14" (36 cm)*

Formerly common, now probably extinct. Resembles a small Whimbrel, but upperparts darker, bill less curved; wing linings pale cinnamon. Closer in size to Upland Sandpiper.

Voice: Calls are poorly known; one call reportedly a rippling *tr-tr-tr* and a soft whistle.

Range: Formerly bred on Arctic tundra. Only known nesting area was Anderson River region, Northwest Territories (nests found 1862-1866), but breeding range may have extended west to Alaska and perhaps Russian Far East. Wintered mainly on the Pampas of Argentina. Migrated up through Great Plains in spring; to northeast Arctic Canada and then over the Atlantic to South America in fall. The last certain record was of an adult female shot by a "sportsman" on Barbados on 4 Sept. 1963 (specimen eventually secured). Other more recent sightings not adequately documented. Main cause of likely extinction was unregulated market hunting, especially prevalent on central Great Plains in the two decades following the Civil War. Rare by 1900, thought possibly extinct by 1940; but a few persisted, as up to two were well photographed in Mar. and Apr. from 1959 to 1962 at Galveston Island, Texas, the last verified North American records.

Whimbrel *Numenius phaeopus* *L 17½" (45 cm)*

Bold, dark-striped crown; dark eye line extending through lores; long downcurved bill. In flight, North American *hudsonicus* shows dark rump and underwings; European *phaeopus,* casual vagrant to East (mainly Atlantic coast), white rump and underwings. Some argue that based on distinct plumage and genetic differences, the Palearctic subspecies should be split from North American Whimbrels; however, all subspecies give similar vocalizations.

Voice: Call is a series of hollow whistles on one pitch.

Range: Fairly common; nests on open tundra; winters on coasts; most winter south of U.S. Generally rare in interior, except Great Lakes.

Long-billed Curlew *Numenius americanus* *L 23" (58 cm)*

Cinnamon-brown above, buff below, with very long, strongly downcurved bill. Lacks dark head stripes of Whimbrel. Males and juveniles have shorter bills. Cinnamon-buff wing linings and flight feathers, visible in flight, distinctive in all plumages. At rest closely resembles the smaller Marbled Godwit, if bill is hidden; note paler legs. Bill length extremes are substantial and shorter-billed juveniles look much more Whimbrel-like in structure.

Voice: Call is loud musical, ascending *cur-lee.*

Range: Nests in dry grasslands; winters in agricultural fields and on mudflats and sandy beaches. Rare east of Great Plains, Texas coast; casual north to Midwest and New England.

smaller size and
shorter billed
than Whimbrel

**Eskimo
Curlew**

adult

adult

buffy underwing
coverts

strong dark lateral
crown and eye stripes

decurved bill

Whimbrel
hudsonicus

hudsonicus

fairly uniform
brown above

dark
underwings

phaeopus

whitish
rump

whitish underwing
coverts

faint head
pattern

juvenile ♂

bill length
varies greatly

adult

barred
remiges

cinnamon
underwing
coverts
and flight
feathers

**Long-billed
Curlew**

adult ♀

Godwits

These large shorebirds have slightly or noticeably upcurved bills.

Black-tailed Godwit Limosa limosa L 16½" (42 cm)

Eurasian species. Long, bicolored bill is straight or only slightly upcurved. Tail is mostly black, uppertail coverts white. In *breeding* plumage, shows chestnut head and neck and heavily barred sides and flanks. East Coast records are of *islandica*, which in the breeding male is a deep and extensive reddish color below. *Winter* birds are gray above, whitish below. In all plumages, white wing linings and broad wing stripe are conspicuous in flight.
Voice: Flight call a two- or three-note *vi-vi-vi*.
Range: Casual along Atlantic coast; accidental Ontario, Louisiana.

Hudsonian Godwit Limosa haemastica L 15½" (39 cm)

Long, bicolored bill, slightly upcurved. Tail is black, uppertail coverts white. *Breeding male* is dark chestnut below, finely barred. *Female* is larger and duller. *Juvenile*'s buff feather edges give upperparts a scaly look. Winter adult resembles Black-tailed Godwit; dark wing linings and narrower white wing stripe are distinctive in flight.
Voice: Mostly silent away from breeding grounds.
Range: Breeding range not fully known. Migrates through central and eastern Great Plains in spring, much farther east in fall.

Bar-tailed Godwit Limosa lapponica L 16" (41 cm)

Eurasian species. Long, bicolored bill, slightly upcurved. *Breeding male* is reddish brown below; lacks heavy barring of Black-tailed Godwit. *Female* larger, much paler than male. In *winter* plumage, Bar-tailed resembles Marbled Godwit but lacks cinnamon tones. Note also shorter bill and shorter legs. Black-and-white barred tail distinctive but hard to see at rest. *Juvenile* resembles winter adult but is buffier overall. Two subspecies occur in North America. European *lapponica*, very rare migrant along Atlantic coast, has a whitish rump, white wing linings, and brown-barred axillaries. Alaska-breeding *baueri* recorded from Massachusetts; rump is heavily mottled, wing linings brown with white barring.
Voice: Mostly silent away from breeding grounds.

Marbled Godwit Limosa fedoa L 18" (46 cm)

Long, bicolored bill, slightly upcurved. Tawny brown; mottled with black above, barred below. Barring is much less extensive on *winter* birds and juveniles. Wing coverts also less patterned on juveniles. Legs are longer than in Bar-tailed Godwit. In flight, cinnamon wing linings and cinnamon on primaries and secondaries are distinctive. Legs black (gray in Long-billed Curlew).
Voice: Flight call a slightly nasal *kah-wek*. Also a repeated *ga-wi-da, ga-wi-da*.
Range: Nests in grassy meadows, near lakes and ponds. Fairly common on Texas coast and in Florida, locally elsewhere on Gulf and southern Atlantic coasts; rare but regular farther north.

Black-tailed Godwit

bold white stripe

juvenile

white wing linings

black-and-white tail

juvenile

winter

nearly straight bill

extensive deep chestnut

black bars

breeding ♂
islandica

long, slender, pointed wings

moderate wing stripe

juvenile

black-and-white tail

black wing linings

Hudsonian Godwit

juvenile

upturned bill

molting fall adult ♂

breeding ♀

breeding ♂

female larger and grayer than male

dark chestnut breast and belly

grayish brown remiges

mottled gray rump and underwing

winter
baueri

whitish underwing

whitish rump

winter
lapponica

streaked upperparts

juvenile

winter

upturned bill

breeding ♀

Bar-tailed Godwit
baueri

short legs

breeding ♂
rufous underparts

female larger and duller than male

rufous wing linings and remiges

long upturned bill

Marbled Godwit
fedoa

winter

breeding ♂

winter ♀

rich buffy coloration

dark legs separate Marbled Godwit from similarly plumaged Long-billed Curlew

Ruddy Turnstone *Arenaria interpres* L 9½" (24 cm)

Striking black-and-white head and bib, black-and-chestnut back, and orange legs mark this stout bird in *breeding* plumage. Female is duller than *male.* Bib pattern and orange leg color are retained in *winter* plumage. *Juvenile* resembles winter adult but back has a scaly appearance. Turnstones use their bills to flip aside shells and pebbles in search of food. In flight, complex pattern on back and wings identifies Ruddy Turnstones.
Voice: Distinctive call is a low-pitched, guttural rattle.
Range: Nests on coastal tundra. Winters on mudflats, sandy beaches, rocky shores. Rare inland migrant except in Great Lakes region, where much more numerous.

Red Knot *Calidris canutus* L 10½" (27 cm)

Chunky and short legged. *Breeding adult* is dappled brown, black, and chestnut above, with buffy chestnut face and breast. In *winter,* back is pale gray; underparts white. Distinguished from dowitchers (page 162) by shorter bill, paler crown, and, in flight, by whitish rump finely barred with gray. *Juveniles* similar to winter adults but have scaly-looking upperparts and, when fresh, a light buff wash on breast.
Voice: Mostly silent; sometimes gives a soft *ka-whit* in flight.
Range: Nests on tundra. Feeds along sandy beaches and mudflats. Eastern populations (subspecies *rufa*) depend on very few staging areas during migration for refueling. In spring this is mainly from the mid-Atlantic coast, such as along shores of Delaware Bay, where they are dependent on horseshoe crab eggs. Unregulated overharvesting of these eggs for commercial fertilizer caused a severe and rapid population crash. Very rare migrant in the interior, though slightly more regular from the Great Lakes. Winters locally south to South America.

Sanderling *Calidris alba* L 8" (20 cm)

Palest sandpiper of *winter;* pale gray above, white below. Bill, legs black. Bold white wing stripe shows in flight. In *breeding* plumage (acquired late Apr. to late May), head, mantle, and breast are rusty. *Juveniles* are blackish above, with pale edges near tips of feathers, resulting in checkered pattern. In both juveniles and winter birds, note the dark leading edge to the wing (shoulder).
Voice: Call is a *kip,* often in a series.
Range: Nests on tundra; feeds on sandy beaches, running to snatch mollusks and crustaceans exposed by retreating waves, usually in flocks; sometimes found roosting on jetties with other shorebirds; more rarely found feeding on mudflats and rocks. Inland a regular migrant in Great Lakes and northern Great Plains regions, scarce elsewhere.

Ruddy Turnstone

juvenile

striking wing pattern

harlequin head and breast pattern

breeding ♂

extensive rufous; female duller

winter

breeding ♂

orange-red legs

whitish rump barred with gray

Red Knot

whitish supercilium and dark eye line

plain gray

winter

spotted chest

winter

pale vent and undertail coverts

chunky body with short, straight bill

subterminal dark edges with pale fringes

rufous

breeding

juvenile

winter

dark marginal coverts

bold white wing stripe

strongly patterned with black-and-white above

Sanderling

very pale above

short, straight bill

juvenile

winter

rufous upperparts, head, and breast

breeding

no hind toe

runs on sand

Peeps

These are seven species of small *Calidris* sandpipers that are difficult to identify. Collectively known as stints by Old World English speakers, they can be roughly divided into four Old World and three New World species. Sometimes the larger Baird's and White-rumped Sandpipers are also included. Keys to identification include learning overall structure and feather topography, behavior, and the distribution patterns of each. It is essential to thoroughly learn our three common species before attempting to identify one of the Eurasian ones.

Semipalmated Sandpiper   *Calidris pusilla* L 6¼" *(16 cm)*

Black legs; tubular-looking, straight bill, of variable length. Easily confused with Western Sandpiper. In *breeding* birds, note Semipalmated usually lacks spotting on flanks, shows only a tinge of rust on crown, ear patch, scapulars. *Juveniles* distinguished by stronger supercilium contrasting with darker crown and ear coverts and by more uniform upperparts. Some brighter above than illustrated. *Winter* plumage (in North America seen most often on Gulf Coast in late Mar.) of these two species is very similar, but rounder-headed Semipalmated is plumper; note bill shape; face shows slightly more contrast; center of breast never shows the faint streaks visible on some winter Westerns.
Voice: Call is a short *churk*.
Range: A common migrant in eastern half of continent; very rare in winter in south Florida; no valid winter records elsewhere.

Western Sandpiper   *Calidris mauri* L 6½" *(17 cm)*

Black legs; tapered bill, of variable length (longer in females); distal portion usually slightly drooped. Easily confused with Semipalmated Sandpiper, but blockier-headed Western has more attenuated body. In *breeding* plumage, Western has arrow-shaped spots along sides, rufous at base of scapulars, and a bright rufous wash on crown and ear patch. *Juvenile* is distinguished from juvenile Semipalmated by less prominent supercilium, paler crown and face, and brighter rufous edges on back and inner scapulars. *Winter* plumage is very similar. Note structure (especially bill shape). In North America, especially away from south Florida, any winter-plumaged individual in fall or winter is likely to be this species.
Voice: Call is a raspy *jeet*.
Range: Scarce fall-only migrant in eastern Canada and New England. Surprisingly rare in upper Midwest, northern Great Plains.

Least Sandpiper   *Calidris minutilla* L 6" *(15 cm)*

Note small size and short, thin bill, slightly downcurved. Always darker above than Western and Semipalmated Sandpipers. Legs are yellowish, but can appear dark in poor light or when smeared with mud. In *winter* plumage, has prominent brown breast band. *Juvenile* has strong buffy wash across breast. Feeds in a variety of wet habitats, but forages less in the water, often preferring to feed back from the shore's edge.
Voice: Call is a high plaintive *kreee*.
Range: Breeds in tundra and taiga. Common migrant.

Semipalmated Sandpiper

breeding

birds breeding in eastern Canada have largest bills

breeding ♀

short, straight, tubular bill

more uniform upperparts than juvenile Western

dark ear coverts

pale supercilium

round head

partially webbed toes

juvenile

winter

thicker neck and flatter crown than Semipalmated

winter

rufous-edged inner scapulars contrast with duller coverts

juvenile

Western Sandpiper

partially webbed toes

rufous crown and ear coverts

slender, slightly downcurved bill

breeding

arrow-shaped spots extend to flanks

brownish breast band

winter

Least Sandpiper

breeding

thin, slightly decurved bill

juvenile

yellowish legs

distinct streaks

White-rumped Sandpiper *Calidris fuscicollis*

L 7½" (19 cm) Long primary tip projection beyond tertials and tail on standing bird. Similar to Baird's Sandpiper structurally, but grayer overall and usually has an entirely white rump. In **breeding** plumage, streaking extends to flanks. *Juvenile* shows rusty edges on crown and back.
Voice: Call note, a very high-pitched insectlike *jeet.*
Range: Feeds on mudflats. Common spring and rare fall migrant through Great Plains; uncommon along East Coast, more numerous in fall in Northeast. Spring migration late, extends to late June; juveniles don't migrate south until the end of Sept. Winters in southern South America; no valid midwinter records for North America.

Baird's Sandpiper *Calidris bairdii L 7½" (19 cm)*

Long primary tip projection beyond tertials and tail on standing bird gives the bird a horizontal profile. Buff-brown above and across breast. Pale fringing on *juvenile*'s back gives a scaly appearance. Distinguished from White-rumped Sandpiper by more buffy brown color and uniform plumage; in flight by dark rump. Distinguished from Least Sandpiper by much larger size, longer and straighter bill, and primary projection.
Voice: Call, a low raspy *kreep,* similar to Pectoral's, but less rich.
Range: Fairly common to common; found on upper beaches, lakeshores, wet fields, sod. Migration is through Great Plains. Uncommon (usually juveniles) to East Coast in fall. Winters in South America; accidental in North America in midwinter.

Dunlin *Calidris alpina L 8½" (22 cm)*

Medium size; long bill, curved at tip; in flight shows dark center to rump. **Breeding** plumage with reddish upperparts, black belly. Subspecies differ in size, structure, breeding plumage: more ventrally streaked in *hudsonia,* found in eastern North America. Three races from Greenland and western Palearctic (*arctica, schinzii, alpina*) are smaller, shorter billed, and darker above in breeding plumage; *arctica* and *alpina* accidental on East Coast. In **winter** plumage, upperparts and chest brownish gray. *Juveniles* rusty above, spotted below. In North America, adults and juveniles stay north and molt into winter plumage, then migrate south.
Voice: Call is a harsh, reedy *kree.*
Range: Feeds on mudflats. Rare on Great Plains.

Curlew Sandpiper *Calidris ferruginea L 8½" (22 cm)*

Eurasian species. Long, downcurved bill has whitish area at base. In **breeding** plumage, rich chestnut underparts, mottled chestnut back distinctive. Female slightly paler than male, may appear slightly barred. Many sightings are of birds in patchy spring plumage or molting to winter plumage, showing grayer upperparts and partly white underparts. *Juvenile* appears scaly above; shows rich buff wash across breast; compare with winter Dunlins. White rump is conspicuous in flight.
Voice: Call is a soft, rippling *chirrup.*
Range: Rare migrant on East Coast, casual elsewhere.

White-rumped Sandpiper

juvenile

dull rufous edges

breeding

white rump normally only visible in flight

juvenile

fall-molting adult

long wings and primary projection

streaking extends to flanks

shape like White-rumped, but browner

breeding

whitish fringe on upperparts

juvenile

juvenile

like White-rumped, long wings extend beyond tail

Baird's Sandpiper

dark rump

winter

breeding *schinzii*

rufous upperparts

Dunlin *hudsonia*

long, downcurved bill

juvenile

black belly

breeding

gray wash across breast, faint streaks on flanks

winter

Curlew Sandpiper

long, downcurved bill

juvenile

pale fringes on upperparts

buffy wash

overall chestnut coloration

white rump with dark gray tail

juvenile

breeding ♂

winter

longer legs than Dunlin

Pectoral Sandpiper *Calidris melanotos* *L 8¾" (22 cm)*
Prominent streaking on breast, darker in **male,** contrasts
sharply with clear white belly. Male is slightly larger than *female.*
Juvenile has buffy wash on streaked breast, brighter rusty
crown. Compare with Baird's Sandpiper (preceding page) and
Least Sandpiper (page 154).
Voice: Call is a rich, low *churk.*
Range: Often feeds in wet meadows, marshes, pond edges,
moist turf. Common in Midwest; uncommon to fairly common
on East Coast, where most numerous in fall; scarcer on western Great Plains. Breeds on Arctic tundra from central Canada
west thousands of miles to the Taymyr Peninsula of central
Arctic Russia. These westerly breeders, which also migrate
through the Midwest, probably migrate farther than any other
species. Winters in South America.

Buff-breasted Sandpiper *Tryngites subruficollis*
L 8¼" (21 cm) Dark eye stands out prominently on buffy face;
underparts paler buff with dark spotting on the sides of the
breast; feathering extends out lower mandible; legs orange-
yellow. In flight, shows flashy white wing linings. These wing
linings are also exhibited in breeding displays where the wings
are raised. They are also flashed in migration, especially when
interacting with other Buff-breasteds. *Juveniles* are paler below,
with scaly white fringing to feathers above.
Voice: Mostly silent away from breeding grounds.
Range: Prefers plowed fields, turf farms, and wet rice fields.
Migrates through the interior of the continent. In fall, rare to
uncommon in the East; most sightings west or east of eastern
Great Plains are of juveniles. Winters in South America.

Ruff *Philomachus pugnax* ♂*L 12" (31 cm)* ♀*L 10" (25 cm)*
Old World species. Males substantially larger than females.
Breeding males acquire dramatic ruffs in colors that range from
black to rufous to white. **Female** lacks ruff, is smaller, and has
a variable amount of black below. Both sexes have a plump body,
small head, and white underwings. Leg color may be yellow,
greenish, orange, or red. *Juvenile* is buffy below, has prominently fringed feathers above. In flight, the U-shaped white
band on rump is distinctive in all plumages.
Voice: Mostly silent away from breeding grounds.
Range: Frequents marshes and grassy edges to lakes and ponds.
Rare migrant along East Coast, very rare in Great Lakes region.
Casual elsewhere. Most birds seen along the Atlantic Coast are
adults, and most are seen from Apr. to May and from July to
Aug. In contrast, the few juveniles are found later in fall, pri-
marily in Sept.

breeding ♂

breeding ♀

darker breast

long wings and primary projection

Pectoral Sandpiper

pectoral band of streaks

yellowish legs

juveniles

displaying adult

dark crescent

scaly upperparts

juvenile

dark eye stands out in blank face

whitish underwing

spots on sides of breast

juvenile

white U-shaped band

juvenile ♀

Buff-breasted Sandpiper

breeding adult

yellow legs

buffy underparts

feathering extends out lower mandible

displaying breeding males

♀

scaly upperparts

buffy neck and breast

summer molting ♂

back feathers often raised

Ruff

juvenile ♀

small head and plump body

whitish lores and forehead

summer molting ♀

leg color variable: greenish to bright orange

winter ♂

often with colored bill base

Purple Sandpiper *Calidris maritima L 9" (23 cm)*
Breeding adult has tawny buff crown, streaked with black; back is edged with white and tawny buff; breast and flanks spotted with blackish brown. Long, slender bill is slightly downcurved, base orange-yellow. Legs orange-yellow. In flight and in ***winter,*** adult resembles Rock Sandpiper.
Voice: Call a scratchy *keesh;* also a chatter.
Range: Migrates late in fall. Rare fall migrant on Great Lakes. Casual elsewhere inland and in winter on the Gulf Coast. Winters on rocky shores and jetties, often with Ruddy Turnstones and Sanderlings.

Stilt Sandpiper *Calidris himantopus L 8½" (22 cm)*
Breeding adult has pale eyebrow, chestnut on head, slender, slightly downcurved bill, and heavily barred underparts. In ***winter,*** adult is grayer above, whiter below; ***juvenile*** has more sharply patterned upperparts; the two resemble Curlew Sandpiper (page 156), but note straighter bill, yellow-green legs, and, in flight, lack of prominent wing stripe, paler tail; early juvenile has a buffy wash on breast. Feeds like dowitchers, with which it often associates, but note smaller size and disproportionately longer legs.
Voice: Call is a low, hoarse *querp.*
Range: Common migrant through Great Plains and Mississippi River Valley; fairly common to East in fall, rare in spring.

American Woodcock *Scolopax minor L 11" (28 cm)*
Chunky, with long bill, barred crown, large eyes set high in head. Rounded wings. Nocturnal, secretive. Flies up abruptly; wings make a twittering sound. Males give an elaborate flight display; visible at dusk and dawn.
Voice: Call is heard mainly in spring, a nasal *peent.* During display also gives chirping sounds.
Range: Common; nests in moist woodlands and bogs. In migration and winter often seen at dawn and dusk near woodland edges and field edges. In mild winters, a few are found farther north than mapped.

Wilson's Snipe *Gallinago delicata L 10¼" (26 cm)*
Stocky, with very long bill; boldly striped head; barred flanks.
Voice: Usually seen when flushed, as it gives a harsh two-syllable *ski-ape* call in rapid, twisting flight. Where breeding, males deliver loud *wheet* notes from perches. In swooping display flight, vibrating outer tail feathers make quavering hoots, like song of Boreal Owl.
Range: Nests in swamps, bogs, and wet grassy fields. In migration and winter also feeds at marshes, lakeshores, muddy fields, and ditches.

Purple Sandpiper

juvenile

bright orange base to bill

winter

overall dark slate gray

streaked sides and flanks

heavily and extensively spotted below

breeding

orange legs

winter

whitish rump and grayish tail

feet project well beyond tail

juvenile

winter

chestnut cheek and crown

Stilt Sandpiper

distinct pale supercilium

juvenile

long, slightly downcurved bill

barred underparts

breeding

molting juvenile

paler, smaller and slimmer than dowitchers; faintly streaked below

long, greenish legs

Wilson's Snipe

dark underwing

chunky, with short, rounded wings

American Woodcock

dark bands

large eyes

displaying

underwing

strongly striped head

bold pale stripes on upperparts

rich buffy underparts

heavily barred sides and flanks

Dowitchers

Medium-size, chunky, dark shorebirds, dowitchers have long, straight bills and distinct pale eyebrows. Feeding in mud or shallow water, they probe with a rapid jabbing motion. Dowitchers in flight show a white wedge from barred tail to middle of back. Separating the two species is easiest with juveniles, more difficult with breeding adults, and very difficult in winter except by distinctive calls. Both species give the same song, a rapid *di di da doo,* year-round.

Short-billed Dowitcher Limnodromus griseus
L 11" (28 cm) In flight, tail usually looks paler than in Long-billed. **Breeding** plumage varies among the three subspecies, two of which occur east of the Rockies: *griseus* (which breeds in northeast Canada) and *hendersoni* (central and western Canada). Unlike Long-billed, most Short-billed show some white on the belly, especially *griseus,* which also has a heavily spotted breast and may have densely barred flanks. In *hendersoni,* which may be mostly reddish below, foreneck much less heavily spotted than in Long-billed; sides have less or no barring; upperparts brighter. In all subspecies, *juvenile* brighter above, buffier and more spotted below than juvenile Long-billed; tertials, visible greater wing coverts have broad reddish-buff edges and internal bars, loops, or stripes. **Winter** birds brownish gray above, white below, with gray breast; at close range note fine dark speckling on, below the breast on many birds. **Voice:** Call is a mellow *tu tu tu,* repeated in a rapid series as an alarm call.
Range: Common in migration along the Atlantic coast (*griseus*); from the eastern plains to Atlantic coast from New Jersey south (*hendersoni*); a few *griseus* are seen on eastern Great Lakes and eastern Gulf Coast, a few *hendersoni* north to New England (fall only). Fall migration begins earlier than Long-billed, usually in late June or early July for adults; early Aug. for juveniles. Migrant juveniles are seen through early Oct.

Long-billed Dowitcher Limnodromus scolopaceus
L 11½" (29 cm) **Male**'s bill is no longer than on Short-billed, **female**'s is. In flight, tail usually looks darker than in Short-billed. **Breeding** plumage is entirely reddish below; foreneck heavily spotted; sides usually barred. Bold white scapular tips in spring help separate from Short-billed. **Juvenile** darker above, grayer below than Short-billed; tertials, greater wing coverts are plain, with thin gray edges and rufous tips; some birds show two pale spots near the tips. In **winter** birds, breast unspotted, more extensively dark than on most Short-billeds. Adult Long-billeds go to favored locations in late summer to molt; Short-billeds molt at winter grounds.
Voice: Call a sharp, high-pitched *keek,* singly or in a rapid series.
Range: Common in migration in western half of continent; less common in the East in fall, rare in spring. Fall migration begins later than Short-billed, in late July. Juveniles migrate later than adults; rare before Sept. Dowitchers seen inland after mid-Oct. are almost certainly Long-billed.

juvenile tertials

internal bars and stripes

Short-billed Dowitcher

worn breeding *griseus*

spots on sides of breast

white belly

extensive buffy markings above

breeding *griseus*

breeding *hendersoni*

molting juvenile

bold internal marks on tertials and greater coverts

juvenile

faint spots

winter

both dowitcher species have white stripe up back

griseus

winter *hendersoni*

Long-billed Dowitcher

molting juvenile

winter

tail averages darker, especially than Short-billed *hendersoni*

very faint, if any, internal markings on tertials and greater coverts

juvenile

winter

winter

overall very similar to winter Short-billed, but is slightly darker and has plainer breast

juvenile tertials

white scapular fringes when fresh

worn breeding ♀

fresh breeding ♂

bars on sides of breast

males have shorter bills

Phalaropes

These elegant shorebirds have partially lobed feet and dense, soft plumage. Feeding on the water, phalaropes often spin like tops, stirring up larvae, crustaceans, and insects. Females, larger and more brightly colored than the males, do the courting; males incubate the eggs and care for the chicks. In fall, adults and juveniles (particularly Wilson's and Red Phalaropes) rapidly molt to winter plumage; many are seen in transitional plumage farther south.

Wilson's Phalarope *Phalaropus tricolor* L 9¼" (24 cm)

Long, thin bill; bold blackish stripe on face and neck. In *winter* plumage, upperparts are gray, underparts white; note also lack of distinct dark ear patch; legs yellowish. Briefly held *juvenal* plumage resembles winter adult but back is browner with buffy edge to feathers, breast buffy. In flight, white uppertail coverts, whitish tail, and absence of white wing stripe distinguish juvenile and winter birds from other phalaropes.
Voice: Calls include a hoarse *wurk* and other low, croaking notes.
Range: Wilson's is chiefly an inland phalarope, nesting on grassy borders of shallow lakes and marshes. Feeds as often on land as on water. Uncommon to rare east of Great Plains.

Red-necked Phalarope *Phalaropus lobatus*

L 7¾" (20 cm) Chestnut on front and sides of neck distinctive in *breeding female,* less prominent in *male.* Both have dark back with bright buff stripes along sides; bill shorter than in Wilson's Phalarope, thinner than in Red Phalarope. *Winter* birds are bluegray above with whitish stripes; underparts and front of crown white; dark patch extends back from eye. In flight, show white wing stripe, whitish stripes on back, dark central tail coverts. Fresh *juvenile* resembles winter adult but is blacker above, with bright buff stripes.
Voice: Call is a high, sharp *kit,* often given in a series.
Range: Breeds on Arctic and subarctic tundra; winters chiefly at sea in Southern Hemisphere. Rare inland in Midwest, East; uncommon off East Coast; more numerous off Maine and Maritimes.

Red Phalarope *Phalaropus fulicarius* L 8½" (22 cm)

Bill shorter and thicker than in other phalaropes; yellow with black tip in breeding adult, usually all-dark in juvenile and winter adult. *Female* in breeding plumage has black crown, white face, chestnut red underparts. *Male* is duller. *Juvenile* resembles male but is much paler below; juveniles seen in southern Canada and the U.S. are *molting* to winter plumage; more closely resemble Red-necked Phalaropes. *Winter* bird is pale gray above. In flight, shows a bolder white wing stripe than Red-necked's.
Voice: Call is a sharp *keip,* is higher pitched than Red-necked's.
Range: Breeds on Arctic shores; winters at sea. Very rare inland, chiefly seen in fall. Very uncommon off much of East Coast, more numerous off Maine and Maritimes.

Wilson's Phalarope

juvenile

short, yellowish legs

molting juvenile

pale gray **winter**

whitish rump and pale gray tail

winter

dark maroon neck

long, thin needlelike bill

breeding ♀

breeding ♂

buffy streaks above

breeding adults with juvenile

Red-necked Phalarope

white wing stripe **winter**

juvenile

faint pale streaks on back

molting juvenile

dark eye patch

needlelike bill

winter

reddish neck

breeding ♀

breeding ♂

molting fall adults

bolder wing stripe than Red-necked **winter**

juvenile

Red Phalarope

white cheek

breeding ♀

red underparts

molting juvenile

plain gray upperparts

dark eye patch

thicker bill than Red-necked

winter

breeding ♂

Shorebirds in Flight

Plovers

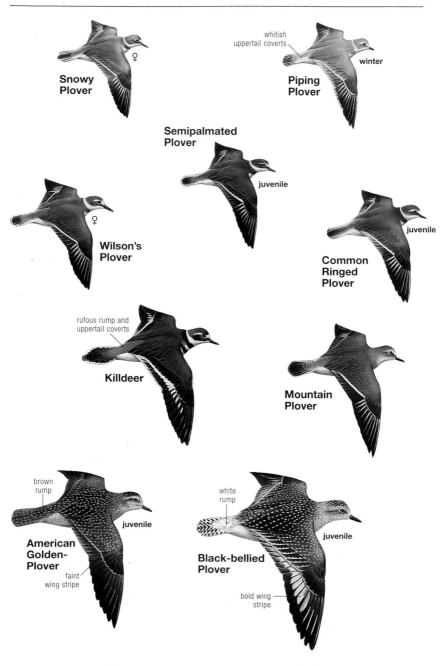

Snowy Plover ♀

whitish uppertail coverts

Piping Plover winter

Semipalmated Plover juvenile

Wilson's Plover ♀

Common Ringed Plover juvenile

rufous rump and uppertail coverts

Killdeer

Mountain Plover

brown rump

American Golden-Plover juvenile

faint wing stripe

white rump

Black-bellied Plover juvenile

bold wing stripe

Godwits and Curlews

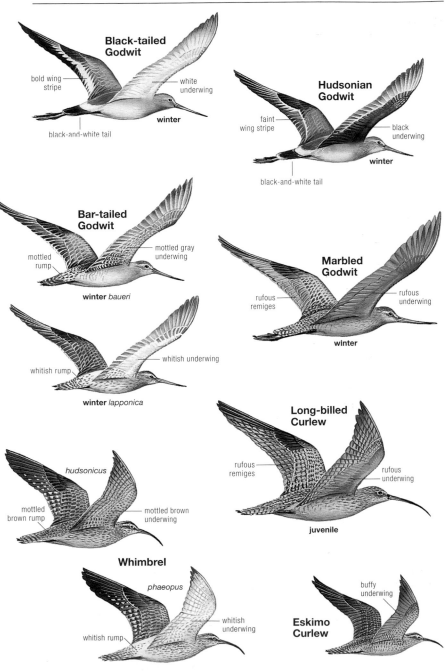

Black-tailed Godwit
bold wing stripe
white underwing
winter
black-and-white tail

Hudsonian Godwit
faint wing stripe
black underwing
winter
black-and-white tail

Bar-tailed Godwit
mottled rump
mottled gray underwing
winter *baueri*
whitish rump
whitish underwing
winter *lapponica*

Marbled Godwit
rufous remiges
rufous underwing
winter

Long-billed Curlew
rufous remiges
rufous underwing
juvenile

hudsonicus
mottled brown rump
mottled brown underwing

Whimbrel
phaeopus
whitish rump
whitish underwing

Eskimo Curlew
buffy underwing

Shorebirds in Flight

Tringa and Other Sandpipers

Lesser Yellowlegs
whitish rump
winter

bold wing pattern
winter
Willet
inornata

whitish rump
winter
Greater Yellowlegs

dark center to rump with barred outer tail feathers
juvenile
Solitary Sandpiper

long tail
juvenile
Upland Sandpiper

white U-shaped band
juvenile ♀
Ruff

white stripe up back
winter
Short-billed Dowitcher

juvenile
Buff-breasted Sandpiper

Phalaropes

white wing stripe and dark center to rump
winter
Red Phalarope

thinner white wing stripe and dark center to rump
winter
Red-necked Phalarope

whitish rump, pale gray tail
winter
plain wings
Wilson's Phalarope

Calidris Sandpipers

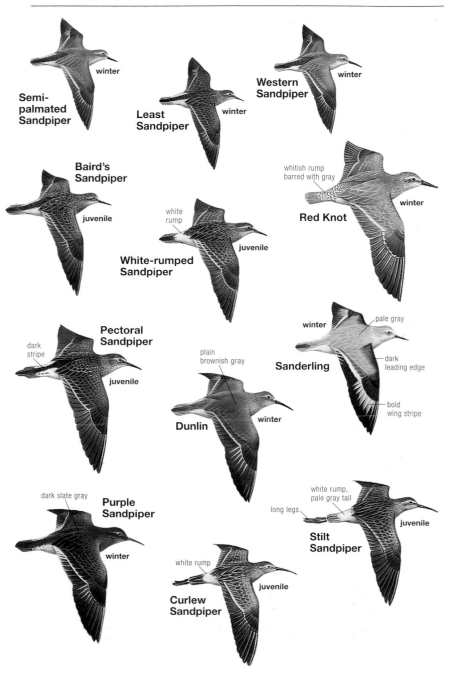

Semi-palmated Sandpiper — winter

Least Sandpiper — winter

Western Sandpiper — winter

Baird's Sandpiper — juvenile

White-rumped Sandpiper — white rump — juvenile

Red Knot — whitish rump barred with gray — winter

Pectoral Sandpiper — dark stripe — juvenile

Dunlin — plain brownish gray — winter

Sanderling — winter — pale gray — dark leading edge — bold wing stripe

Purple Sandpiper — dark slate gray — winter

Curlew Sandpiper — white rump — juvenile

Stilt Sandpiper — white rump, pale gray tail — long legs — juvenile

Gulls, Terns, Skimmers (Family Laridae)

A large, diverse family with strong wings and powerful flight. Some species are largely pelagic; others frequent coastal waters or inland lakes and wetlands. Gulls take from about two to four years to reach adult plumage; immatures are often variable and hard to identify. In general, male gulls are larger than females.

Laughing Gull *Larus atricilla*

L 16½" (42 cm) WS 40" (102 cm) Three-year gull. **Breeding adult** has black hood, white underparts, slate gray wings with black outer primaries. In *winter*, shows gray wash on nape; compare with the half-hood of Franklin's Gull. Second-summer bird has partial hood, some spotting on tip of tail. *Second-winter* bird is similar to second-summer but has gray wash on sides of breast, lacks hood. *First-winter* bird has extensively gray sides, complete tail band, gray wash on nape, slate gray back, dark brown wings; compare with first-winter Franklin's Gull. *Juvenile* is like first-winter bird but brown on head and body.
Voice: Calls include a crowing series of *hah* notes; also a single nasal *kow* or *ka-ha*.
Range: Common along Gulf and Atlantic coasts; rare well inland and in Atlantic Provinces.

Franklin's Gull *Larus pipixcan*

L 14½" (37 cm) WS 36" (91 cm) Three-year gull. **Breeding adult** has black hood, white underparts variably tinged with pink, slate gray wings with white bar and black-and-white tips on primaries. Distinguished from Laughing Gull by white bar and large white tips on primaries, pale gray central tail feathers, and broader white eye crescents. All *winter* birds have a dark half-hood, more extensive than in any winter Laughing Gull. Second-summer Franklin's has partial or no bar on primaries, thus is particularly apt to be confused with adult or near-adult Laughing. *First-summer* bird is like winter adult but lacks white primary bar; bill and legs black. *First-winter* bird resembles first-winter Laughing; note white outer tail feathers, half-hood, broader eye crescents, white underparts, and, in flight, pale inner primaries. Juvenile is like first-winter bird but back is brown. At all ages, distinguished from Laughing Gull by smaller size, smaller bill with less prominent hook, rounder forehead, less extensive dark on underside of primaries; shorter legs and wings give a stocky look when standing.
Voice: Call like Laughing Gull's but slightly higher and softer.
Range: Rare to very rare east of Mississippi River, mostly in fall. Winters primarily off South America; very rare in winter along Gulf Coast.

dark underside to primaries

breeding adult

has dark "ear muffs," but no half-hood like Franklin's

winter adult

2nd winter

long bill with slightly thicker tip

breeding adult

2nd winter

long wings

1st winter

dark "ear muffs," but no hood

gray across breast and down sides and flanks

overall brownish color

juvenile

Laughing Gull

1st winter

broad, complete tail band

Gulls

distinctive black-and-white wing tip pattern

thick white eye crescents in all plumages

bill shorter than Laughing

paler underwing than Laughing

breeding adult

no white band as in adult

breeding adult

winter adult

white hind-neck

bold, dark half-hood

1st summer

bold, white apical spots

often with pink tint to underparts

1st winter

Franklin's Gull

shorter winged than Laughing

1st winter

narrow dark tail band with white outer tail feathers

Little Gull *Larus minutus* *L 11" (28 cm) WS 24" (61 cm)*

Two- to three-year gull. **Breeding adult** has black hood, black bill, pale gray mantle, white wing tips, white underparts, red legs. **Winter adult** has dusky cap, dark spot behind eye. Short, rounded wings uniformly pale gray above, dark gray to black below, with white trailing edge. Some **second-winter** birds are like adult but underwing pattern is incomplete; show some dusky slate in primaries. **First-winter** is like Bonaparte's but primaries blackish above, lack white wedge; wings show strong blackish W; crown shows more black.

Voice: Occasional nasal and ternlike calls.

Range: Western Palearctic species, has bred irregularly from Great Lakes to Hudson Bay. Generally rare but regular on Great Lakes in migration and in winter on East Coast; very rare to casual elsewhere in North America.

Bonaparte's Gull *Larus philadelphia*

L 13½" (34 cm) WS 33" (84 cm) Two-year gull. **Breeding adult** has slate black hood, black bill, gray mantle with black wing tips that are pale on underside; white underparts, orange-red legs. In flight, shows white wedge on wing. **Winter** bird lacks hood. **First-winter** bird has a dark brown carpal bar on leading edge of wing, dark band on secondaries, black tail band; compare with juvenile Black-legged Kittiwake (page 186). First-summer bird may show partial hood; wings and tail are like first-winter. Flight is buoyant, wingbeats rapid.

Voice: Call a nasal or raspy ternlike *kerrr* or *gerrr*.

Range: Breeds at taiga ponds and marshes; winters on inshore ocean waters, estuaries, large lakes, rivers, sewage ponds. Winters north to Great Lakes during mild years.

Black-headed Gull *Larus ridibundus*

L 16" (41 cm) WS 40" (102 cm) Two-year gull. **Breeding adult** has dark brown hood; maroon-red bill and legs; mantle slightly paler gray than Bonaparte's Gull; black wing tips; white underparts. **Winter adult** lacks hood; bill brighter red. **First-winter** birds have orange-red or pinkish red bill, pale legs, dark tail band, dark brown carpal bar. Distinguished from Bonaparte's by larger size and bill color. **First-summer** bird's hood varies from minimal, like first-winter's, to nearly complete; wings and tail like first-winter. In all plumages, shows dark underside of primaries in flight, darker on adults; compare with Bonaparte's.

Voice: Calls ternlike; a grating or screechy *ree-ah*.

Range: Colonizer from Europe. Fairly common in winter in Newfoundland, where a few breed; small numbers are regular in Maritimes and coastal New England, rare south to North Carolina; casual elsewhere in North America.

head pattern like
Bonaparte's but
with slight capped
appearance

Little Gull

winter
adult

breeding
adult

full solid
black
hood

pale
wing tips

breeding
adult

uniformly pale
gray primaries
with white tips;
dark underwing

2nd winter

bold black
carpal bar

1st winter

1st winter

extensive
blackish
coverts

blackish
hood with
gray cast

breeding
adult

postocular
spot

**Bonaparte's
Gull**

winter
adult

winter
adult

white primaries
above and
below with thin
black tips

1st winter

dark
carpal bar

1st winter

dark
brown
hood

breeding
adult

**Black-headed
Gull**

winter
adult

long
reddish bill

1st
winter

dark slate
underside to
primaries, paler
in immature

winter
adult

pinkish
base with
dark tip

dark inner
primaries

1st summer

slightly paler
above than
Bonaparte's

1st winter

Black-tailed Gull *Larus crassirostris*
L 18½" (47 cm) WS 47¼" (120 cm) Vagrant from East Asia. Three-year or four-year gull, about size of Ring-billed Gull (page 176); bill and wings long; legs short. Distinctive white eye crescents except on **breeding adult** and third-winter bird. Adult has black ring near red tip of bill; yellow iris, red orbital ring. Mantle dark slate gray; tail has broad black subterminal band. Head of **winter adult** heavily streaked. Compare also with larger Lesser Black-backed Gull (page 180). **First-winter** bird has white on face, otherwise heavily washed with brown.
Voice: North American birds have been largely silent.
Range: Casual along East Coast from Newfoundland to Virginia; accidental on Texas Gulf coast and in the interior.

Mew Gull *Larus canus* *L 16" (41 cm) WS 43" (109 cm)*
Three-year gull. North American race *brachyrhynchus* is the smallest of three subspecies found here; has least black on wing tips; in flight, shows much more white on primaries than Ring-billed Gull (next page). European nominate race, *canus* ("Common Gull") has more extensive black on wing tips, especially on p8. All **adults** have white head, washed with brown in **winter;** dark gray mantle; thin yellow bill may have dusky subterminal smudge in winter; most have large, dark eyes. **Second-winter** bird is like adult but has two-toned bill; has less white on primaries; variably spotted tail band. **First-winter** *brachyrhynchus* is heavily washed with brown below, almost solid brown on belly; spotted with white on breast. The head and nape are washed with soft brown; mantle dark gray; primaries light brown with pale edges. Tail is almost entirely brown, with heavily barred tail coverts; wing linings evenly pale brown (page 188). Compare to young Ring-billed with retained juvenal plumage. **Juvenile** is like first-winter, but brown on the back and head, darker below. European *canus* resembles Ring-billed Gull in first winter; but note *canus*'s mostly white tail with dark subterminal band, unbarred white tail coverts, darker gray back, white wing linings mottled with brown. Mew Gulls average smaller than Ring-billed Gulls, especially *brachyrhynchus,* with rounder heads, larger eyes, thinner bills.
Voice: Calls include a wheezy *kyap* and shrill *sur;* also a mewing *kii-uu.*
Range: North American race very rare east to Great Lakes and casual to Atlantic coast regions. European race found on East Coast mostly in winter, rare but annual in Newfoundland and almost annual in Maritimes; casual south to coastal New York; accidental south to coastal North Carolina. European *canus,* along with a closely related larger race *heinei,* from farther east, may represent a distinct species from North American *brachyrhynchus.* The situation is complicated by yet another subspecies, *kamtschatschensis* of east Asia, the largest race, which shows somewhat intermediate plumage characteristics between *canus* and *brachyrhynchus.*

Black-tailed Gull

pale eye

long bill with
black subterminal
band and red tip

breeding
adult

broad,
bold black
tail band

overall smooth
brown color
with whitish
in face

breeding
adult

winter
adult

pink-based bill
with dark tip

long
wings

rather dark slaty
gray upperparts

1st
winter

2nd
winter

yellowish
legs

Mew Gull
brachyrhynchus

2nd winter

1st winter

breeding
adult

brownish
underwing

overall brownish
compared to
juvenile Ring-billed

brownish
wash

winter
adult

most with dark eye

2nd
winter

short,
slender,
yellow bill

brown coverts
with pale fringes

juvenile

darker above
than Ring-billed

often with
darker ring
on bill

long
wings

more
spotted
neck

breeding
adult

winter adult
canus

more extensive
black in primaries,
especially p8, than
brachyrhynchus

1st winter

1st winter

black tail band
contrasts
sharply with
white tail base

tail nearly
entirely dark

adult
canus

Ring-billed Gull *Larus delawarensis*

L 17½" (45 cm) WS 48" (122 cm) Three-year gull. **Adult** has pale gray mantle; yellow bill with black subterminal ring; pale eyes; yellowish legs; head streaked and spotted with brown in **winter**. **Second-winter** birds are like winter adult but bill has broader band, black on primaries is more extensive, tail usually has some blackish terminal spots. **First-winter** bird has gray back, brown wings with dark blackish-brown primaries, brown-streaked head and nape; underparts white with brown spots and scalloping on breast and throat; tail has medium-wide but variable brown band and extensive mottling above band; uppertail and undertail coverts are lightly barred; secondary coverts medium gray; wing linings mostly white, with some barring. Distinguished from first-winter Mew Gull (*brachyrhynchus*) by white underparts spotted on breast and throat, tail pattern, darker primaries, heavier bill, and paler back. **Juvenal** plumage may be largely kept into early winter; resembles first-winter but back is brown, spotting below more extensive, bill has more black.
Voice: Calls include a mewing *kee-ew,* sharper *kyow,* and whining *sseeaa.* Also an extended "long call."
Range: Abundant and widespread; winters uncommonly outside mapped range.

California Gull *Larus californicus*

L 21" (53 cm) WS 54" (137 cm) Four-year gull. **Adult** has darker gray mantle than Herring Gull (next page), paler than Lesser Black-backed Gull (page 180); white head, heavily streaked with brown in winter; dark eyes; yellow bill with black and red spots; black spot often smaller in breeding season; gray-green or greenish-yellow legs, brighter yellow in breeding season. In flight, shows dusky trailing edge on underwing. Third-winter plumage is like adult but bill is more extensively smudged with black; wings show some brown; tail has some brown spotting. **Second-winter** has gray back, brown wings, grayish to blue-green legs, two-toned bill; compare to first-winter Ring-billed Gull (above). **First-winter** is brown overall with veiled gray on scapulars; usually palest on throat, breast, and upper belly; legs pinkish; two-toned bill, the colors sharply defined. In flight, first-winter birds show double dark bar on inner half of wing, caused by darker secondaries and greater secondary covert bases. Compare first-winter birds to first- and second-winter Herring and Lesser Black-backed. **Juveniles** are variably pale below, lack pale bill base.
Voice: Calls include a *kyow* and higher *kii-ow;* also a long, slightly nasal, trumpeting "long call." All lower pitched than Ring-billed.
Range: Casual visitor east of Dakotas as far as East and Gulf coasts.

spots on head

winter adult

paler underwing than Mew

1st winter

2nd winter

black subterminal band

pale eye

breeding adult

2nd winter

Ring-billed Gull

breeding adult

pale gray

pale underside to secondaries

outer wing pattern differs from Mew

small mirror

yellow legs

may have tail markings

dark eye

1st winter

1st winter tail

juvenile

small dark centers to coverts

pinkish legs

tail pattern variable

1st winter tail

black and red spots on bill

dark-based greater coverts

1st winter

breeding adult

rather slender wings

dark secondaries

no obvious pale window

extensive black in primaries

darker gray than Ring-billed or Herring

California Gull

dark eye

heavy brown wash

2nd winter

breeding adult

slender pinkish bill with blackish tips

winter adult

yellowish green legs

juvenile has blackish bill until September

gray secondaries compare to Herring and Ring-billed

1st winter

pale juvenile

dark juvenile

Herring Gull *Larus argentatus*

L 25" (64 cm) WS 58" (147 cm)   Highly variable four-year gull. Widespread North American race is *smithsonianus*. *Adult* has pale gray mantle; white head streaked with brown in winter; legs and feet pink; bill yellow with red spot. *Third-winter* plumage is like winter adult but with black smudge on bill, some brown on body and wing coverts. *Second-winter* bird has pale gray back; brown wings; pale eyes; two-toned bill. *First-winter* birds are brown over-all, with dark brownish black primaries and tail band, dark eyes, dark bill, with variable pink at base; some may have bill like first-winter California Gull (preceding page); but usually distinguished by darker bill, paler face and throat, and, in flight, by pale panel at base of primaries and single dark bar on secondaries. Distinguished from first-winter Lesser Black-backed Gull (next page) by browner, less-contrasting body plumage, usually darker belly, and, in flight, by pale primary and outer secondary coverts and less-contrasting rump pattern. European race, *argenteus*, from western Europe and slightly darker mantled *argentatus* from farther east are most distinct from *smithsonianus* in first-winter plumage. European birds are paler and more checkered above and are whiter on the rump region and tail base. They are casual to Newfoundland, and there is a specimen record from Ontario.

Voice: Series of bugling calls makes up "long call." Also a full *kyow*.

Range: Frequents a wide variety of habitats, from offshore waters to coasts, farm fields, parking lots, and dumps. Common in much of eastern North America.

Yellow-legged Gull *Larus michahellis*

L 24" (61 cm) WS 57" (144 cm)   Palearctic species. Size similar to Herring Gull, but Yellow-legged has squarer head, peaked at rear of crown; bill stouter and shorter. Adult mantle darker gray than *smithsonianus* Herring. From above, wing tip darker than Herring; from below more gray, less black, on outermost primaries. Red gonys spot often extends onto upper mandible; orbital ring is redder than on Herring. Yellow legs distinctive, but some *smithsonianus* Herrings may show some yellow during winter and early spring. In Yellow-legged, fainter winter head streaking is restricted to nape and crown, making white head stand out; by midwinter most *adults* are white headed. *First-winter* birds are much paler on head and underparts than first-winter Herring; blocky head and extensive white on uppertail coverts and base of tail suggests same-age Great Black-backed Gull (next page). Compare also to first-winter Lesser Black-backed. Molt to first-winter occurs earlier than in Herring; by fall, young Yellow-legged often appear worn. Eastern Atlantic islands subspecies, *atlantis*, is smaller and darker than *michahellis* of western Europe and the Mediterranean. North American sightings have not been assigned to subspecies with certainty, but a specimen from Quebec has been referred to as *atlantis*.

Voice: Similar to Herring Gull but slightly deeper.

Range: Casual winter visitor to northeastern coast from New-foundland to mid-Atlantic, possibly south Texas.

white tail base

paler than *smithsonianus*

1st winter *argenteus*

obvious pale window

1st winter *smithsonianus*

Herring Gull *smithsonianus*

breeding adult

pale underside to secondaries

striking pale eye

extensive streaking

pale gray upperparts

juvenile

winter adult

pink legs

often pale headed

1st winter

2nd winter

3rd winter

often more adultlike

apical spots small or absent

some dark in tail

1st winter

pale eye by late 2nd winter

Yellow-legged Gull *michahellis*

no pale window

1st winter

white tail base

1st winter

stouter bill than Herring

winter adult

breeding adult

darker gray than Herring

yellow legs

Lesser Black-backed Gull *Larus fuscus*

L 21" (53 cm) WS 54" (137 cm) A four-year gull. ***Adult*** has white head, heavily streaked with brown in winter; white underparts; yellow legs. Third-winter bird has dark smudge on bill; some brown in wings. ***Second-winter*** bird resembles second-winter Herring Gull (preceding page) but note dark gray back, much darker underwings. ***First-winter*** bird similar to first-winter Herring Gull but head and belly are paler, upperparts more contrastingly dark and light; bill is always entirely black. Identified in flight by darker primary and secondary coverts, more extensively dark primaries and white outer tail feathers; paler rump contrasts with back. Much smaller than Great Black-backed Gull. Smaller and slimmer on average than Herring Gull, with smaller bill, but there is substantial range of overlap; also note longer wings. Most birds seen here are of northern European race *graellsii*. A few darker mantled adults in eastern North America likely of Baltic race *intermedius*.
Voice: Like Herring Gull but slightly deeper.
Range: Western Palearctic species; generally rare to locally uncommon, with the largest numbers in mid-Atlantic and Florida regions.

Great Black-backed Gull *Larus marinus*

L 30" (76 cm) WS 65" (165 cm) Four-year gull. Large overall size, bill distinctive. ***Adult***'s white head virtually unstreaked in winter; black upperparts; white underparts; variably pale eyes; pink legs. In flight, note extensive white on outer primary that merges with white spot on second primary to form solid white area. ***Third-winter*** bird like adult but shows some dark on bill, some brown in wings, sometimes dark in tail. ***Second-summer*** bird has pale eye, black back; wings and tail are like first-winter. Second-winter is like first-winter, but base of bill is paler, secondary coverts more evenly brown. ***First-winter*** bird resembles Herring Gull (preceding page) but head and body are much paler, back and wings have a checkered look; shows almost white rump, checkered tail band.
Voice: Calls, such as *kyow*, are deep and hoarse. "Long call" lower pitched and slower than Herring's.
Range: Breeding range expanding southward on Atlantic coast. Fairly common on eastern Great Lakes, rare elsewhere well inland and on Gulf Coast; casual west to Great Plains.

IDENTIFYING: Parts of a Gull

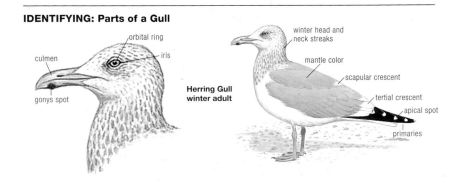

orbital ring
culmen
iris
gonys spot

Herring Gull winter adult

winter head and neck streaks
mantle color
scapular crescent
tertial crescent
apical spot
primaries

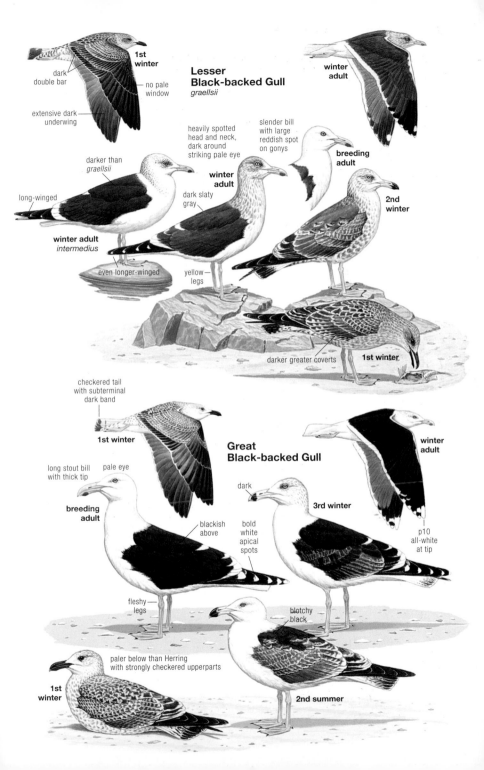

1st winter

dark double bar

no pale window

extensive dark underwing

Lesser Black-backed Gull
graellsii

winter adult

heavily spotted head and neck, dark around striking pale eye

slender bill with large reddish spot on gonys

breeding adult

darker than *graellsii*

winter adult

dark slaty gray

2nd winter

long-winged

winter adult
intermedius

even longer-winged

yellow legs

darker greater coverts   **1st winter**

checkered tail with subterminal dark band

1st winter

Great Black-backed Gull

winter adult

long stout bill with thick tip

pale eye

breeding adult

dark

3rd winter

blackish above

bold white apical spots

p10 all-white at tip

fleshy legs

blotchy black

paler below than Herring with strongly checkered upperparts

1st winter

2nd summer

Iceland Gull *Larus glaucoides*

L 22" (56 cm) WS 54" (137 cm) Highly variable four-year gull. *Adults* have white heads, suffused with brown in winter; most have yellow eyes, a few brown. Late *second-winter* birds have pale eyes, gray back, two-toned bill. *First-winter* birds are buffy to mostly white; chiefly dark bill is short; eyes dark; wing tips white or irregularly washed with brown. Canadian-breeding adult *kumlieni* have wing tips variably marked with gray; a few are pure white. Greenland breeding *glaucoides* is slightly smaller and paler overall in all plumages; adults are slightly paler mantled and have pure white wing tips; most migrate southeast to Iceland, a few to Europe; rare or casual to northeast North America. First-winter birds distinguished from Thayer's by paler primaries, checkered tertials, usually paler body plumage and on some by checkered tail; from Glaucous by usually darker bill and structural features (smaller size, rounder head, and longer wings that extend beyond tail at rest).
Voice: Mostly silent in nonbreeding season; otherwise calls close to Herring's.
Range: Uncommon to rare on Great Lakes; casual to Gulf Coast and Great Plains.

Glaucous Gull *Larus hyperboreus*

L 27" (69 cm) WS 60" (152 cm) Heavy-bodied, four-year gull. All have translucent tips to white primaries. *Adult* has very pale gray mantle, yellow eye. Head is streaked with brown in winter. Late *second-winter* bird has pale gray back and pale eye. *First-winter* birds may be buffy or almost all-white; bill is bicolored. Distinguished from Iceland Gull by size; heavier, longer bill; flatter crown; slightly paler mantle of adults; disproportionately shorter wings, barely extending beyond tail.
Voice: Similar to Herring Gull; some calls actually higher pitched.
Range: Very rare in winter south to Gulf states. Occasionally hybridizes with Herring Gull.

IDENTIFYING: Gull Age Classes When identifying many species of gulls, one must *first* properly *age* the bird. It is important to understand the fundamental changes in plumage and bare-part color and pattern that take place in two-year, three-year, and four-year gulls, as well as the effects that abrasion, wear, and bleaching have on a bird's feathers. It is also crucial to understand the overall timing of molts in gulls, which is complicated by the variation between individuals of the same species that results in varying plumage patterns and bare-part colors among birds of similar age. Some of the larger species may be in almost continuous molt before they reach adulthood.

In this guide, gull ages are linked to a bird's physical age: For instance, a first-winter bird is in its late first and early second calendar year, and a second-winter individual is in its late second and early third calendar year. Some other books use the terms "first cycle," "second cycle," and so on, terms based on molts.

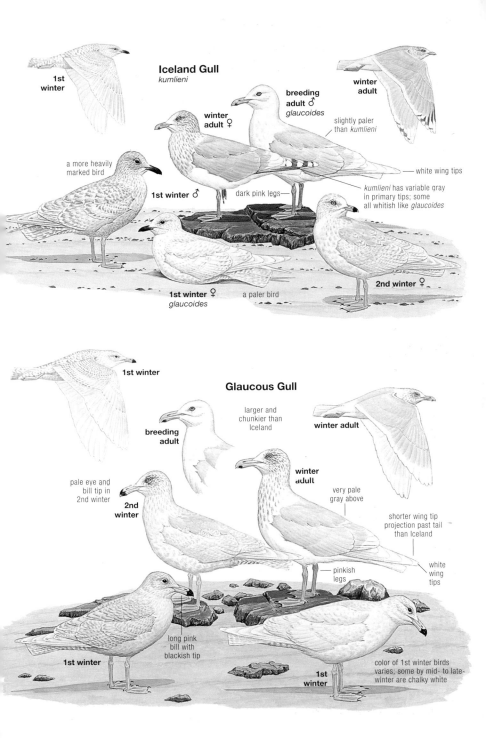

Iceland Gull
kumlieni

1st winter

winter adult

breeding adult ♂
glaucoides

winter adult

slightly paler than *kumlieni*

white wing tips

kumlieni has variable gray in primary tips; some all whitish like *glaucoides*

a more heavily marked bird

1st winter ♂

dark pink legs

1st winter ♀
glaucoides

a paler bird

2nd winter ♀

Glaucous Gull

1st winter

breeding adult

larger and chunkier than Iceland

winter adult

pale eye and bill tip in 2nd winter

2nd winter

winter adult

very pale gray above

shorter wing tip projection past tail than Iceland

white wing tips

pinkish legs

1st winter

long pink bill with blackish tip

1st winter

color of 1st winter birds varies; some by mid- to late-winter are chalky white

Thayer's Gull *Larus thayeri*
L 23" (58 cm) WS 55" (140 cm) Variable four-year gull. In most **adults,** eye is dark brown, mantle is slightly darker than Herring Gull or Iceland Gull (preceding page); bill is yellow with dark red spot; legs are darker pink than Herring. Primaries are pale gray below, with thin, dark trailing edge; show some black or slaty gray from above. Many have paler eyes. ***Second-winter*** has gray mantle, contrasting gray-brown tail band, dark eye. ***First-winter*** is variable but primaries always entirely pale below, darker than mantle above. Distinguished from Herring Gull by smaller size, paler checkered markings in plumage, and paler primaries with whitish edges; distinguished from Iceland Gull by generally darker plumage; primaries, which are darker than mantle; mostly solid brown tertials; more distinct dark secondary bar; and usually unspeckled tail.
Voice: Calls similar to those of Herring and Iceland Gulls.
Range: Rare but regular winter visitor to Great Plains and Great Lakes regions, very rare farther east and south through the interior to Gulf Coast. Casual on East Coast. Considered by some a race of Iceland Gull.

Kelp Gull *Larus dominicanus*
L 23" (58 cm) WS 53" (135 cm) Widespread Southern Hemisphere species; casual to Gulf Coast, accidental farther north. A few Kelps nested on Chandeleur Islands off southeast Louisiana for about a decade starting in early 1990s. This resulted in pure Kelp pairings, and mixed pairings with Herring Gull that produced **hybrids.** Accidental elsewhere. Three-year gull. **Adult** Kelp has black back and dull greenish legs; head streaking in winter indistinct. Eye color variable. Note restricted white in outer primaries, unlike Great Black-backed (page 180). Compare also with Lesser Black-backed Gull (page 180). Change to adult plumage rapid; mantle blackish by ***second summer.***

Ivory Gull *Pagophila eburnea* *L 17" (43 cm) WS 37" (94 cm)*
Two-year Arctic gull, ghostly pale. **Adults** in all plumages are strikingly white with a yellow-tipped greenish bill, black eyes, black legs. ***First-winter*** birds show a variable amount of speckling on the body, heaviest and often patchy on the face, forming a smudge; have tail band, and spots on tips of primaries. A short-necked, stocky gull with long wings.
Voice: Rarely heard away from breeding grounds. Gives a high, mewing *kew.*
Range: Closely associated with pack ice. Winters primarily in Arctic seas. Casual along the Atlantic coast to New York, and inland to the northern tier of states. Accidental south to Tennessee. Global warming imperils species.

Thayer's Gull

1st winter

dark secondary bar

pale underwing

brownish on outer webs from above

2nd winter

eye color variable

winter adult

winter adult

head and neck washed with brownish

narrow dark line

large white mirrors with little blackish

dark pink legs

breeding adult

some are quite dark and very similar to 1st winter Herrings

1st winter

short bill

1st winter

mostly brownish tertials

brownish primaries with pale fringes

Kelp Gull

plumage suggests Lesser Black-backed but chunkier with bigger bill

heavy bill

Kelp x Herring hybrid winter adult

slaty gray

one white mirror

winter adult

molting juvenile

2nd summer

greenish legs

blackish upperparts as dark or darker than Great Black-backed

breeding adult

Ivory Gull

dark eye

greenish bill with yellow-orange tip

long, narrow, rather pointed wings

adult

pure white

1st winter

dusky face

short black legs

black markings on primary tips and near tail tip

adult

Black-legged Kittiwake *Rissa tridactyla*

L 17" (43 cm) WS 36" (91 cm) Pelagic three-year gull. *Adult* has white head, nape smudged with gray in *winter;* dark eye; yellow bill; white body with gray mantle. Inner primaries are pale, wing tips inky black; legs black. Second-year bird is like adult but with more black on outermost primary. *Juvenile* has dark half collar, retained into early winter; black bill; black spot behind eye; dark tail band; and, in flight, dark M across the wings. Distinguished from young Sabine's Gull by half collar, dark carpal bar. A very few young birds have pinkish legs.

Voice: Call is a series of *kittiwake*'s, given mostly on nesting grounds. Also a nasal *awk.*

Range: Nests in large cliff colonies; winters at sea. Seen rarely from shore south of breeding range. Rare in late fall on Great Lakes, otherwise casual inland south to Gulf Coast. A few non-breeders seen in summer south to Gulf of Mexico.

Sabine's Gull *Xema sabini* *L 13½" (34 cm) WS 33" (84 cm)*

Two-year gull with striking black-gray-and-white wing pattern in all ages. *Breeding adult* has dark gray hood with thin black ring at bottom; black bill with yellow tip; forked tail. First-summer bird is like adult but hood not complete; faint dusky nape. In *juvenal* plumage, wing pattern is like adult; crown and nape are soft gray-brown; bill black; tail has dark band. Most adults migrate out of North America before acquiring white head and dark nape of winter plumage. Juveniles depart before acquiring more adultlike plumage.

Voice: Call a ternlike *kiew,* only occasionally heard away from nesting areas.

Range: Sabine's Gull winters at sea mainly in the Southern Hemisphere. Very rare in fall east to Great Lakes region and southern Quebec. Casual on and off East Coast and in the South.

Ross's Gull *Rhodostethia rosea*

L 13½" (34 cm) WS 33" (84 cm) Two-year gull. Variably pink below; upperwing pale gray; underwing pale to dark gray. *Breeding adult* has black collar, partial or absent in winter. *Winter adult* has partial gray collar that contrasts with white head. *First-winter* bird has black at tip of tail, dark spot behind eye; acquires black collar by first summer; in flight, shows M pattern like Little Gull. In all plumages, note long, pointed wings; long, wedge-shaped tail; and broad, white trailing edge to wings.

Voice: Mostly silent away from Arctic, where it gives ternlike chitters and a mellow yapping.

Range: Arctic species of the Russian Far East, has bred in northern Canada and Greenland in last three decades. Presumably winters at sea. Casual south to northern U.S., with records south to Nebraska, Indiana, Maryland, and Delaware.

Black-legged Kittiwake

black wing tips

breeding adult

dusky postocular bar and wash on nape

unmarked yellow bill

winter adult

juvenile

blackish bill

black collar

blackish M-pattern across wings

juvenile

short blackish legs

tail band

dark bill with yellow tip

gray hood with black border

molting adult

breeding adult

adults and juveniles have distinctive upperwing pattern

large white apical spots

forked tail

breeding adult

Sabine's Gull

dark bill

juvenile

brownish or grayish on crown, nape, and upperparts; scaly above

juvenile

1st winter

compare to Little Gull

Ross's Gull

black collar

breeding adult

1st winter

wedge-shaped tail

winter adult

in all birds, underparts variably washed with pink

dark gray underwing with bulging white trailing edge

Immature Gulls in Flight

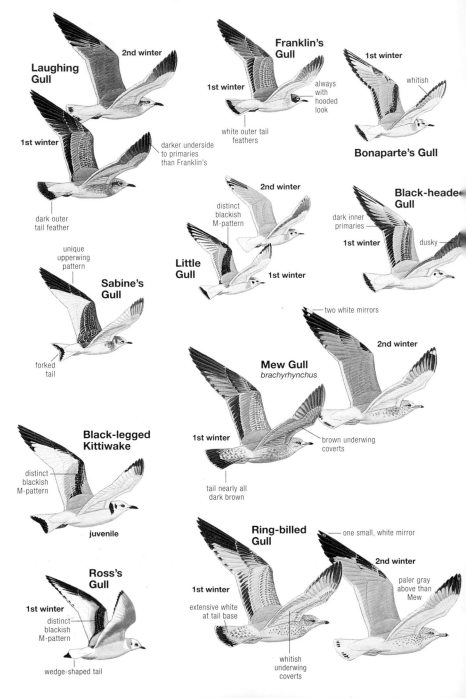

Laughing Gull
2nd winter
1st winter
dark outer tail feather
darker underside to primaries than Franklin's

Franklin's Gull
1st winter
always with hooded look
white outer tail feathers

1st winter
whitish
Bonaparte's Gull

Black-headed Gull
dark inner primaries
1st winter
dusky

Sabine's Gull
unique upperwing pattern
forked tail

Little Gull
2nd winter
distinct blackish M-pattern
1st winter

two white mirrors
2nd winter

Mew Gull
brachyrhynchus
1st winter
brown underwing coverts
tail nearly all dark brown

Black-legged Kittiwake
distinct blackish M-pattern
juvenile

Ross's Gull
1st winter
distinct blackish M-pattern
wedge-shaped tail

Ring-billed Gull
one small, white mirror
2nd winter
paler gray above than Mew
1st winter
extensive white at tail base
whitish underwing coverts

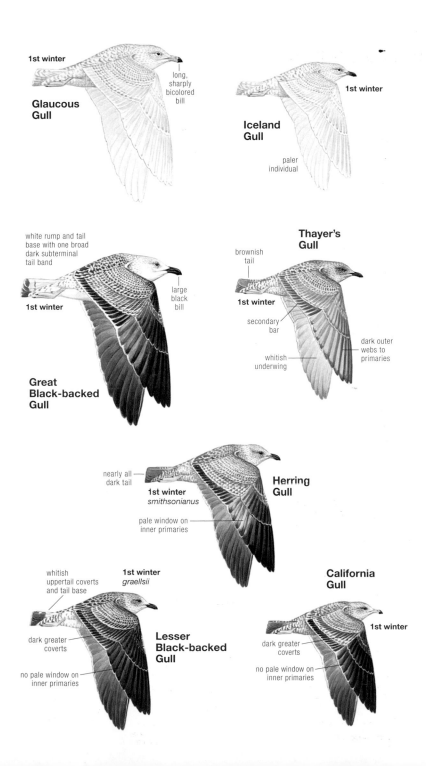

1st winter

Glaucous Gull

long, sharply bicolored bill

1st winter

Iceland Gull

paler individual

white rump and tail base with one broad dark subterminal tail band

1st winter

large black bill

Great Black-backed Gull

Thayer's Gull

brownish tail

1st winter

secondary bar

whitish underwing

dark outer webs to primaries

nearly all dark tail

1st winter
smithsonianus

pale window on inner primaries

Herring Gull

whitish uppertail coverts and tail base

1st winter
graellsii

dark greater coverts

no pale window on inner primaries

Lesser Black-backed Gull

California Gull

dark greater coverts

no pale window on inner primaries

1st winter

Terns

Distinguished from gulls by long, pointed wings and bill and by feeding technique. Most terns plunge-dive into the water after prey, primarily small fish. Most species have a forked tail.

Brown Noddy   *Anous stolidus*
L 15½" (39 cm) WS 32" (81 cm)   Overall dark gray-brown with whitish gray cap, blending at back; *immature* shows only a whitish line on forehead. Unlike other terns, noddies have long, wedge-shaped tail with only a small notch at tip.
Voice: Usually silent; a crowlike *karrk* call is heard mostly around the breeding colonies.
Range: Nests in a colony on Dry Tortugas, Florida. Casual to Gulf Coast and off Outer Banks, North Carolina. Accidental elsewhere following hurricanes.

Black Noddy   *Anous minutus*   L 13½" (34 cm) WS 30" (76 cm)
Black Noddy is smaller than Brown Noddy, with shorter legs; bill is thinner and disproportionately longer; overall color is slightly blacker. In *immatures,* white area on head is very sharply defined, wing coverts worn and brownish.
Voice: Birds found in U.S. are mostly silent.
Range: Tropical species, rare and irregular visitor among Brown Noddies on Dry Tortugas (mostly immatures). Casual on Texas Gulf Coast.

Bridled Tern   *Onychoprion anaethetus*
L 15" (38 cm) WS 30" (76 cm)   Note white collar between brownish gray upperparts and black cap on *breeding adult.* Similar to Sooty Tern, but slimmer; wings more pointed; underwings and tail edges more extensively white; tail grayer. Bridled's white forehead patch extends behind the eye, while Sooty's stops at the eye. *Juvenile* has pale mottling above.
Voice: Typical call a soft, nasal *weeep.*
Range: Nests in the West Indies and locally irregularly off Florida Keys. Regular in summer well offshore in the Gulf of Mexico, and in the Gulf Stream to North Carolina; rarely to off New Jersey; after tropical storms, casual to New England, accidental inland. Many reports pertain to Sooty Terns.

Sooty Tern   *Onychoprion fuscatus*
L 16" (41 cm) WS 32" (81 cm)   Blackish above, white below; white forehead. Lacks white collar of Bridled Tern. Tail is deeply forked, edged with white. *Juvenile* is sooty brown overall, with whitish stippling on back; pale lower belly and undertail coverts; pale wing linings.
Voice: Typical call is a high, nasal *wacky-wack.* Also nasal *ipp.*
Range: Large breeding colony on Dry Tortugas, Florida; also a few may nest on islands off Texas and Louisiana. Regular in summer well offshore in the Gulf of Mexico and to North Carolina. Tropical storms can carry birds inland to Great Lakes and north to Maritime Provinces.

Brown Noddy
stolidus

long, pointed tail

overall chocolate brown color

blended white crown

adult

adult

very limited white

immature

adult

smaller and blacker than Brown Noddy

bill more slender than Brown Noddy

white crown sharply delineated at rear

Black Noddy
americanus

immature

extensive whitish underside to primaries

grayish brown cast above

Bridled Tern
melanoptera

breeding adult

head pattern diluted

juvenile

white extends behind eye

pale collar

extensive white in outer tail when spread

Sooty Tern
fuscatus

black above

pale underwing unlike noddy terns

juvenile

dark underparts

whitish undertail coverts

white does not extend behind eye

breeding adult

restricted white in outer tail

Common Tern *Sterna hirundo*
L 14½" (37 cm) WS 30" (76 cm) Medium gray above, with black cap and nape; paler below (though grayish in breeding plumage). Bill red, usually tipped with black. Slightly stockier than the Arctic Tern, with flatter crown, longer neck and bill. In flight, usually displays a dark wedge, variably shaped, near tip of upperwing; in late summer all outer primaries can appear dark. Note also that head projects farther than in Arctic. Common Tern's shorter tail gives it a chunkier look. Also compare with Forster's Tern. Early *juvenile* shows some brown above, white below; mostly dark bill. Juvenile's forehead is white, crown and nape blackish, secondaries dark gray; compare with juvenile Forster's Tern (next page). All immature and winter plumages have a dark shoulder bar. Full *adult breeding* plumage is acquired by third spring.
Voice: Calls are a sharp *kip* and a distinctive low, piercing, drawn-out *kee-ar-r-r-r.*
Range: Common Terns nest in large colonies. Declining in some areas due to nest disturbance. Uncommon migrant over much of interior.

Arctic Tern *Sterna paradisaea*
L 15½" (39 cm) WS 31" (79 cm) In *breeding adult,* medium gray above, with black cap and nape; gray below. Bill deep red. Slightly slimmer than Common Tern, with rounder head, shorter neck and bill. In flight, upperwing appears uniformly gray, lacking dark wedge of Common; underwing shows very narrow black line on trailing edge of primaries; all flight feathers appear translucent. Note also that tail is longer and head does not project as far as in Common. *Juvenile* largely lacks brownish wash of early juvenile Common; shoulder bar less distinct; secondaries whitish and a portion of coverts whitish too, creating an effect like Sabine's Gull (page 186). Forehead is white, crown and nape blackish; compare juvenile Forster's Tern (next page). Full adult breeding plumage is acquired by third spring.
Voice: Calls include a raspy *tr-tee-ar,* higher than Common Tern's call. Also a sharp *keet.*
Range: Arctic Terns migrate well offshore; casual inland during migration, especially in late spring.

IDENTIFYING: *Sterna* Terns The four species of eastern *Sterna* terns—Common, Arctic, Roseate, and Forster's—present identification challenges. Not only do all four of these species look alike, but within each species there is substantial change in appearance from season to season and between different age categories. Useful field marks for one plumage (such as grayness versus whiteness of the breast, exact color of the primaries) may be of little or no use in another. Therefore, it is important to learn the features that do not vary with age or season: size

and structure (including bill size and leg length) and vocalizations. Differences in size and structure are somewhat subtle, however, so they are best appreciated when multiple tern species are found together, which is often the case.

As in the study of gulls, being able to properly age an individual *Sterna* tern and to understand both the basics of tern molt and how wear may affect appearance are important first steps in properly identifying these birds. Fresh juveniles in late summer show variable brownish backs in which the intensity of color (e.g., little brown

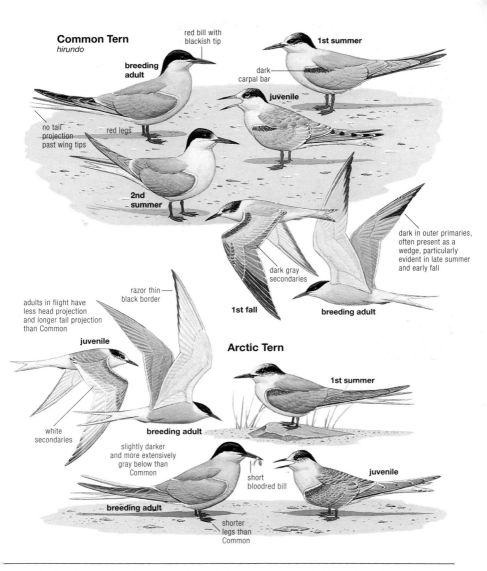

Common Tern
hirundo

red bill with blackish tip

breeding adult

1st summer

dark carpal bar

juvenile

no tail projection past wing tips

red legs

2nd summer

dark in outer primaries, often present as a wedge, particularly evident in late summer and early fall

razor thin black border

dark gray secondaries

adults in flight have less head projection and longer tail projection than Common

juvenile

1st fall

breeding adult

white secondaries

breeding adult

Arctic Tern

1st summer

slightly darker and more extensively gray below than Common

short bloodred bill

juvenile

breeding adult

shorter legs than Common

in juvenile Arctic) and patterning (e.g., distinct scallops in Roseate) are useful characteristics. This color and patterning largely wear away to gray by autumn.

The presence or absence of a dark carpal (shoulder) bar is another important marker to use in all birds, except breeding adults. First-summer individuals—those that are approximately one year of age—do not breed, so many remain on or close to the wintering grounds, though a few return north to breeding areas. These first-summer terns resemble winter adults but have

more worn-looking wings. Second-summer birds (which are in their third calendar year) more closely resemble full adults, although they retain some white flecking on the forehead as well as possibly a trace of the dark carpal bar. Birds of this age may breed.

Other characteristics to emphasize when identifying *Sterna* terns include primary color and pattern of molt, tail length and color, bill and leg color, breast color, and cap pattern. Vocalizations, once learned, can be very useful, too. All give species-specific calls.

Roseate Tern *Sterna dougallii* **E**

L 15½" (39 cm) WS 29" (74 cm) **Breeding adult** is white below with slight, variable pinkish cast visible in good light; pale gray above with black cap and nape. Much paler overall than Common and Arctic Terns (preceding page). Lacks dark trailing edge on underside of outer wing. Bill mostly black; during summer more red appears at base. Wings shorter than in Common and Arctic; flies with rapid wingbeats suggestive of Least Tern (next page). Deeply forked all-white tail extends well beyond wings in standing bird. Legs and feet bright red-orange. **Juvenile**'s brownish cap extends over forehead; mantle looks coarsely scaled, lower back barred with black; bill and legs black. **First-summer** bird has white forehead; lacks dark secondaries of immature Common. Full adult plumage is attained by second spring.

Voice: Call is an abrupt *chi-weep* or *ki-vit;* alarm signal a drawn-out *zra-ap,* like ripping cloth.

Range: Uncommon, local, and highly maritime, Roseate Terns usually come ashore only to nest. Rare on mid-Atlantic coast in late spring and summer.

Forster's Tern *Sterna forsteri*

L 14½" (37 cm) WS 31" (79 cm) **Breeding adult** is snow white below, pale gray above, with black cap and nape; mostly orange bill, orange legs and feet. Wingbeat much slower than in Roseate Tern. Legs and bill longer than in Common and Arctic Terns (preceding page). Long, deeply forked gray tail has white outer edges. In flight, shows pale upperwing area formed by silvery primaries; white rump contrasts with gray back, gray tail. **Winter** plumage resembles Common and Arctic but is acquired by mid- to late Aug., much earlier than those species, which molt chiefly after migration out of U.S. Note also lack of dark shoulder bars; most have dark eye patches not joined at nape as in Common, but many have dark streaks on nape. **Juvenile** and **first-winter** bird have shorter tails than adults and more dark color in wings. Juvenile has ginger brown cap and dark eye patch; shoulder bar is faint or absent.

Voice: Calls include a hoarse *kyarr,* lower and shorter than in Common. Also a higher *ket.*

Range: Forster's Terns nest in widely scattered colonies in marshes. Rare but regular late-summer and fall visitor to New England and Atlantic Canada.

Gull-billed Tern *Gelochelidon nilotica*

L 14" (36 cm) WS 34" (86 cm) **Breeding adult** is white below, pale gray above, with black crown and nape, stout black bill, black legs and feet. Stockier and paler than Common Tern (preceding page); wings broader; tail shorter and only moderately forked. **Juveniles** and **winter** birds appear largely white headed apart from some fine streaking. Juvenile has pale edgings on upperparts, bill brownish.

Voice: Adult call is a raspy, sharp *kay-wack;* call of juvenile is a faint, high-pitched *peep peep.*

Range: Nests in salt marshes and on beaches; often seen hunting for insects over fields and marshes. Does not hover or dive in water. Casual in interior, New England, and Atlantic Canada.

Roseate Tern
dougallii

darkish crown

strongly marked with blackish above

juvenile

breeding adult

dark in outer primaries

shallow, rapid wingbeats

slight pinkish tint to white underparts

juvenile

long tail projection past wing tips

bill mostly black

breeding adult

1st summer

Forster's Tern

long, orange-based bill with dark tip

breeding adult

white below

long orange legs

juvenile

1st winter

winter adult

dark mask; does not extend around nape as in Common

thick black bill

breeding adult

juvenile

Gull-billed Tern

stocky body with "heavy flight"

very whitish overall, including head

rather long black legs

winter adult

short tail

Least Tern *Sterna antillarum* **E**
L 9" (23 cm) WS 20" (51 cm) Smallest North American tern. **Breeding adult** is gray above, with black cap and nape, white forehead, yellow bill with dark tip; underparts are white; legs orange-yellow. By late summer, bill base is more greenish. In flight, black wedge on outer primaries is conspicuous; note also short, deeply forked tail. *Juvenile* shows brownish, U-shaped markings; crown dusky; wings show dark shoulder bar. By first fall, upperparts gray, crown whiter, but dark shoulder bar retained. *First-summer* birds are more like adults but have dark bill and legs, shoulder bar, black line through eye, dusky primaries. Flight is rapid and buoyant.
Voice: Calls include high-pitched *kip* notes, a shrill *chir-ee-eep.*
Range: Nests in colonies on beaches and sandbars; also on rooftops. Fairly common but local on East and Gulf Coasts; declining inland. Winters from Central America south.

Black Tern *Chlidonias niger* *L 9¾" (25 cm) WS 24" (61 cm)*
Breeding adult is mostly black, with dark gray back, wings, and tail; white undertail coverts. In flight, shows uniformly pale gray underwing and fairly short tail, slightly forked. Bill is black in all plumages. *Juvenile* and winter birds are white below, with dark gray mantle and tail; dark ear patch extends from dark crown; flying birds show dark bar on side of breast. Some juveniles show a contrastingly paler rump. Shoulder bar on upperwing is much darker than in juvenile White-winged Tern. First-summer birds can be like winter adults or may have some dark feathers on head and underparts; second-summer birds are like breeding adults, but show some whitish on head; full breeding plumage is acquired by third spring. *Molting fall adult* appears patchy black-and-white as it acquires winter plumage in late summer; easily confused with the White-winged Tern.
Voice: Calls include a metallic *kik* and a slurred *k-seek.*
Range: Black Terns nest on lakeshores and in marshes; declining over part of range. Migrants may be seen well offshore. Winters mostly in South America.

White-winged Tern *Chlidonias leucopterus*
L 9½" (24 cm) WS 23" (58 cm) Casual visitor from Eurasia. Bill and tail shorter than in Black Tern; tail less deeply notched. In *breeding* plumage, bill usually black, but sometimes red; white tail, whitish upperwing coverts, and black wing linings are distinctive; upperwing shows black outer primaries. *Molting* birds are patchy black-and-white, but whitish tail and rump are distinctive; black wing linings often last until late summer. *Winter adult* has white wing linings; lacks dark breast bar of Black Tern; crown, speckled rather than solid black, not usually connected to dark ear patch. First-summer bird resembles winter adult; second-summer usually like breeding adult; adult plumage reached by third spring. *Juvenile*'s head pattern resembles Black's, but browner back shows greater contrast with grayish wing coverts and whitish rump.
Voice: Mostly silent away from breeding grounds.
Range: Casual to East Coast; accidental to Great Lakes region.

Least Tern *antillarum*

wingbeats very shallow and rapid

breeding adult

breeding adult

white forehead

yellow bill with black tip

juvenile

dark carpal bar

1st summer

dark gray above

dark ear patch extends from crown

pale underwings

molting fall adult

juvenile

dark bar on sides

gray flanks

breeding adult

Black Tern *surinamensis*

black body

breeding adult

juvenile

white vent and undertail coverts

breeding adult

paler upperwing than Black Tern

White-winged Tern

juvenile

brownish back contrasts with white rump

black wing linings with white remiges

bill color variable, sometimes dark red

red legs

molting adult

winter adult

blackish postocular spot; head paler than Black Tern

pale rump

tail shorter and squarer than Black Tern

pure white below

Caspian Tern *Hydroprogne caspia*

L 21" (53 cm) WS 50" (127 cm) Large, stocky; bill orange to coral red with dark near tip, much thicker than in Royal Tern. In flight, shows dark underside of primaries; tail less deeply forked than Royal. *Adult* acquires black cap in *breeding* season; in *winter adult* and *juvenile,* crown streaked; never shows fully white forehead of Royal.
Voice: Adult's calls include a harsh, raspy *kowk* and *ca-arr;* immature's a distinctive, whistled *whee-you.*
Range: Small colonies nest on coasts, in wetlands.

Royal Tern *Thalasseus maximus*

L 20" (51 cm) WS 41" (104 cm) Orange-red bill, thinner than Caspian. In flight, shows mostly pale underside of primaries; tail more deeply forked than Caspian. *Adult* shows white crown most of year; black cap acquired briefly early in *breeding* season. In *winter adult* and *juvenile,* black on nape does not usually extend to encompass eye.
Voice: Calls include a bleating *kee-rer* and a ploverlike whistled *tourreee.*
Range: Nests in dense colonies. Uncommon to rare north of breeding range along Atlantic coast in late summer; casual in North American interior.

Sandwich Tern *Thalasseus sandvicensis*

L 15" (38 cm) WS 34" (86 cm) Slender, black bill, tipped with yellow. *Breeding adult* is pale gray above with black crown, short black crest. In flight, shows some dark in outer primaries. White tail is deeply forked, comparatively short. Adult in *winter* plumage, seen as early as July, has a white forehead, streaked crown, grayer tail. *Juvenile*'s tail less deeply forked; bill often lacks yellow tip, in a few it is entirely yellow. By late summer, juvenile loses dark V-shaped markings and spots on back and scapulars.
Voice: Calls include abrupt, grating *gwit gwit* and *skee-rick* notes.
Range: Nests on coastal beaches and islands. Regular visitor north to New Jersey. Casual farther north, accidental inland, particularly following tropical storms.

Black Skimmer *Rynchops niger*

L 18" (46 cm) WS 44" (112 cm) No other bird has a lower mandible longer than the upper. A long-winged coastal bird, it furrows the shallows with its red, black-tipped bill. Black above and white below; red legs and bill shape are distinctive. Female is smaller than the male. *Juvenile* is mottled dingy brown above. *Winter adults* show a white collar.
Voice: Typical call is a nasal *ip* or *yep.*
Range: Nests on sandy beaches and islands. Casual north to Atlantic Canada and inland.

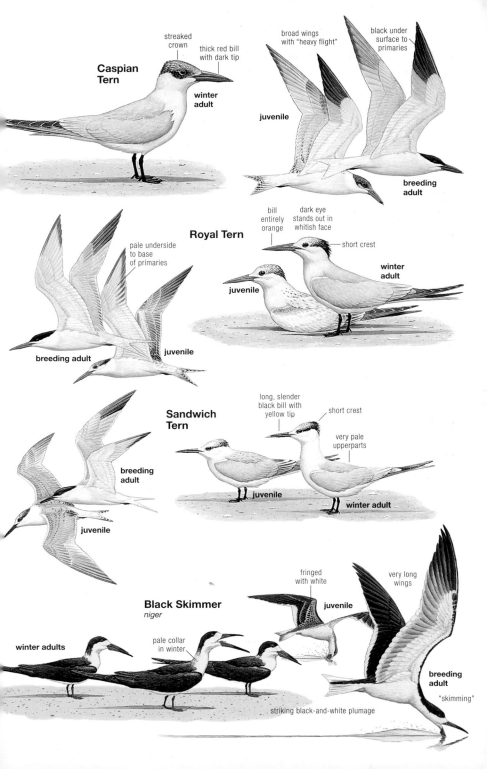

Caspian Tern

streaked crown

thick red bill with dark tip

winter adult

broad wings with "heavy flight"

black under surface to primaries

juvenile

breeding adult

Royal Tern

pale underside to base of primaries

bill entirely orange

dark eye stands out in whitish face

short crest

winter adult

juvenile

breeding adult

juvenile

Sandwich Tern

long, slender black bill with yellow tip

short crest

very pale upperparts

breeding adult

juvenile

juvenile

winter adult

Black Skimmer
niger

fringed with white

juvenile

very long wings

winter adults

pale collar in winter

breeding adult

"skimming"

striking black-and-white plumage

Skuas, Jaegers (Family Stercorariidae)

Formerly placed with the Gulls, Terns, and Skimmers, these have been separated into their own family; recent molecular evidence indicates that they are most closely related to Alcidae. Predatory and piratic seabirds, skuas have broader wings than jaegers. Mostly silent at sea.

Great Skua *Stercorarius skua*
L 22" (56 cm) WS 54" (137 cm) Large, heavy, and barrel-chested; wings broader and more rounded than jaegers (following pages); tail shorter and broader. Shows a distinctly hunchbacked appearance in flight and a conspicuous white bar at base of primaries; bill is heavier than in jaegers. Great Skua is distinguished from South Polar Skua by overall reddish or ginger brown color and heavy streaking on back, wing coverts, and much of underparts; sometimes shows dark brown cap. *Juvenile* and immature show less streaking, especially on underparts. A small number of juvenile dark morphs have much less rufous streaking; resemble juvenile South Polar Skuas. Strong, powerful fliers, skuas pursue gulls and other seabirds and rob them of their prey.
Range: Uncommon; breeds in Iceland and northern Europe; winters in North Atlantic. Seen well offshore from Sept. to Apr.; rare in summer off Canadian coast.

South Polar Skua *Stercorarius maccormicki*
L 21" (53 cm) WS 52" (132 cm) Large, heavy, and barrel-chested; wings broader and more rounded than jaegers (following pages); tail shorter and broader. Like Great Skua, shows a distinctly hunchbacked appearance in flight, a bold white bar at base of primaries, and a heavier bill than in jaegers. In all ages, South Polar Skua shows a uniform mantle coloring and lacks the reddish tones and streaking seen on upperparts of Great Skua. In *light-morph* birds, contrastingly pale gray nape is distinctive; light morph also shows grayish head and underparts. *Dark morph* is uniformly blackish brown across mantle, with golden hackles on nape; distinguished from subadult Pomarine Jaeger by larger size, broader and more rounded wings, more distinct white wing bar. *Juveniles* and immatures of both color morphs are darker than light-morph adults, ranging from dark brown to dark gray. In the field, birds under two years of age are generally indistinguishable from juveniles; birds over two years old are generally indistinguishable from full adults.
Range: South Polar Skua winters (our summer) in the North Atlantic, usually from May to early Nov. Most numerous in late spring. Accidental in North Dakota; a record (photos) from Tennessee after Hurricane Katrina likely this species. Very rarely seen from shore. Difficulty of identification makes range information somewhat speculative for both skua species. Several records (photos) of birds off mid-Atlantic coast could pertain to Brown Skua (*S. antarcticus*) of Southern Hemisphere or possibly to hybrids between that species and South Polar Skua.

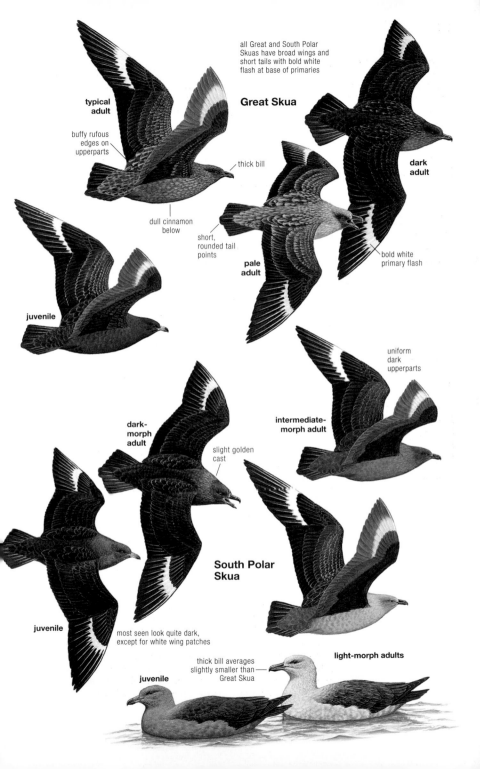

all Great and South Polar Skuas have broad wings and short tails with bold white flash at base of primaries

Great Skua

typical adult

buffy rufous edges on upperparts

thick bill

dull cinnamon below

short, rounded tail points

dark adult

pale adult

bold white primary flash

juvenile

uniform dark upperparts

dark-morph adult

slight golden cast

intermediate-morph adult

South Polar Skua

juvenile

most seen look quite dark, except for white wing patches

thick bill averages slightly smaller than Great Skua

light-morph adults

juvenile

Pomarine Jaeger *Stercorarius pomarinus*

L 21" (53 cm) WS 48" (122 cm)   Body bulkier, bicolored bill longer and thicker, wingbeats slower than Parasitic Jaeger. Most birds show a distinctive second pale underwing patch at base of primaries (fainter or lacking in Parasitic). ***Adult*'**s tail streamers, twisted at ends, form dark blobs when seen from side; length is variable, averages longer in male. Note extensive helmet on sides of head, which extends down to "jowls" area. Compare ***dark-morph adults*** and subadults with South Polar Skuas (preceding page). Some grayish brown ***juveniles*** are dark, some pale, but none shows the rufous tones of most juvenile Parasitics; underwing is paler than body; pale, barred uppertail covert forms a contrasting patch above. Central tail feathers barely project beyond outer tail feathers and have blunt tips. When seen perching, Pomarine's thicker, sharply two-toned bill distinguishes it from Parasitic, which has a thinner bill with a darker tip. Juvenile Pomarine's primaries lack conspicuous pale tips; strongly and evenly barred under tail. Note that juvenile Pomarines are not so obviously bulkier overall as Parasitics—in contrast to the adults, where differences in body heft are more apparent.

Range: Nests on Arctic tundra, where it feeds primarily on lemmings and young birds; otherwise frequents offshore waters, where it may be seen chasing smaller gulls, terns, and shearwaters. Seen much less often from shore than Parasitic. Uncommon in winter. Casual inland away from Great Lakes (where rare), mostly in late fall. Juveniles do not typically begin to arrive well south of the breeding grounds until late September at the earliest, later than for Parasitic and Long-tailed Jaegers; more likely to be found inland in late fall and early winter (mid-Nov. onward) than the other jaegers.

IDENTIFYING: Jaegers Compared to gulls, jaegers invariably appear darker and have longer, more pointed wings. They fly with ease and power, covering a good deal of distance in a very short period of time. Separating the three jaeger species is difficult—especially juveniles and subadults—and has long been a subject of debate. Characteristics to keep in mind include the overall size and shape, the size and shape of the bill, the pattern of white patches and primary shafts on the wing, and the shape and length of the central tail feathers. On adults the color and shape of the black or blackish cap and the coloration of the mantle are also important features.

Pomarine is the largest species, with a broader arm and a heavy, bicolored bill. It has a prominent pale flash at the base of the primaries and a second smaller flash one at the base of the primary coverts, which is usually diagnostic. (This second patch may also be found on a few

thick two-toned bill

Pomarine juvenile

dark

strong bars

slender bill

most have rufous cast

pale tips

fainter bars

Parasitic juvenile

stubby bill

dark

Long-tailed juvenile

strong bars

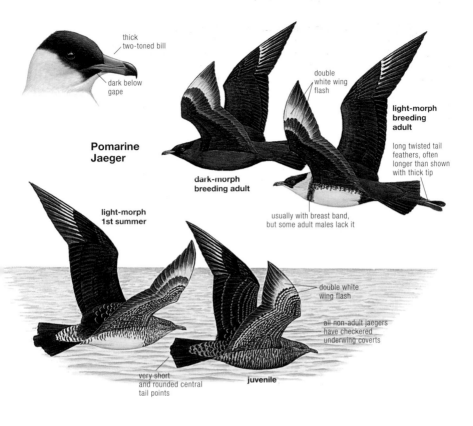

thick
two-toned bill

dark below
gape

**Pomarine
Jaeger**

double
white wing
flash

**light-morph
breeding
adult**

long twisted tail
feathers, often
longer than shown
with thick tip

**dark-morph
breeding adult**

**light-morph
1st summer**

usually with breast band,
but some adult males lack it

double white
wing flash

all non-adult jaegers
have checkered
underwing coverts

very short
and rounded central
tail points

juvenile

juvenile Parasitics.) Adult Pomarines have more extensive black on the sides of the face, and their long, central tail feathers twist near the end, forming a blob at the tip. Juvenile Pomarines have very short, blunt-ended central tail feathers. The nape is faintly vermiculated. From above, the rump contrasts as the palest part of the upperparts. Both juvenile Pomarines and Long-taileds lack pale primary tips.

Parasitics are smaller and narrower winged than Pomarines and chase terns in a falconlike manner. They have rather long but fine bills, a particularly useful distinction in separating the juveniles. The adult's cap is less solidly black than Pomarine, and there is a small light patch just above the bill. Many have a brownish wash across the breast. The extended central tail feathers are sharply pointed in all plumages. Like all juvenile jaegers, the coloration is individually variable: Some are light rufous overall, and some are

blackish with narrow rufous fringes. Juvenile Parasitics have streaked napes and pale rufous-buff fringes on the primaries, unlike Pomarines, and the rump appears darker than that species.

The petite Long-tailed is the smallest jaeger, and its actions of hovering and buoyant flight are often almost ternlike. Its bill is short but appears rather thick; its wings are long and slender, with only two to three white primary shafts. Adults show no white primary patch on the underwing, and the grayish upperparts contrast with the darker flight feathers. The adult has a sharply defined black cap. The long central tail feathers are diagnostic, but many adults seen in migration lack them. Juveniles vary from grayish to dark chocolate overall and are fringed with whitish; paler birds have white bellies, unlike any juvenile Pomarine or Parasitic. Juvenile Long-taileds lack pale primary tips and have strong and even dark-and-white barring under the tail.

Parasitic Jaeger *Stercorarius parasiticus*
L 19" (48 cm) WS 42" (107 cm) Smaller size, more slender body, faster wingbeats than Pomarine Jaeger; also smaller head, thinner bill, pointed tail streamers. ***Adult*** lacks helmeted effect of Pomarine, shows small pale area above base of bill. ***Juvenile*** is highly variable; shows rufous-buff tips on primaries; distinctive rusty tones particularly evident on **light morphs;** both the uppertail coverts and the undertail region have fainter, wavier bars than Pomarine. When close viewing is possible, the slender and less sharply two-toned bill is an excellent distinguishing characteristic from Pomarine. Short central tail feathers are pointed. Also compare with Long-tailed Jaeger.
Range: Nests on Arctic tundra; found at sea during nonbreeding seasons. Fairly common; the jaeger species most often seen from shore in migration, often in pursuit of terns. Casual fall migrant inland; more regular on Great Lakes, where it is an earlier fall migrant than Pomarine, although overlap occurs, especially in late Oct. and early Nov.

Long-tailed Jaeger *Stercorarius longicaudus*
L 22" (56 cm) WS 40" (102 cm) The most lightly built jaeger, with round chest, flat belly, narrow wings, and disproportionately long tail in all ages; bill rather short and thick. Flight is more graceful, ternlike. Note distinctive contrast between grayish mantle and darker flight feathers; usually has only two to three white primary shafts; no pale underwing patch except on juvenile. ***Adult*** has well-defined black cap (most restricted in extent of the three jaeger species), no breast band as in most other jaegers, and usually very long, pointed central tail streamers. Juvenile's central tail feathers have round, often white-edged tips; bill is half dark, half gray and appears stubby, unlike the slender and longer bill of Parasitic. Note too that the dark primaries lack the rufous-buff tips seen on Parasitic. Long-tailed's body is grayer overall than Parasitic except for dark morph; fringing above whitish, never rusty. ***Light-morph juveniles*** show distinctive white belly and strong, even, black barring on upper- and undertail coverts; palest birds may have very pale gray heads. ***Dark-morph juveniles*** often lack barring on uppertail coverts.
Range: Nests commonly on dry, upland tundra; migrating birds rare well off East Coast (mainly in early fall); very rare inland (mainly in early fall); casual off Gulf Coast. Away from the Great Lakes, where Parasitic dominates, Long-tailed is as likely or more likely seen than the other two jaeger species, particularly in early fall. Feeds on small mammals, insects, even berries while on tundra; the most likely jaeger to be seen feeding on insects during migration. Winters in southern hemisphere oceans.

pale at base of forehead

slender bill

Parasitic Jaeger

primaries with variable number of white shafts

light-morph breeding adult

dark-morph breeding adult

dark brown above

most have a diffuse grayish brown breast band

pointed tail feathers of moderate length

light-morph 1st summer

rufous tips to feathers above

light-morph juveniles

pointed tips to central tail feathers

2 to 3 primary shafts in nearly all plumages

breeding adult

no white wing flash

gray upperparts contrast sharply with blackish flight feathers

very long pointed central tail feathers

1st summer

Long-tailed Jaeger

long slender wings

pale tips to feathers above

clean blackish cap

stubby bill

light-morph juvenile

long tail has rounded central tail feathers with pale tips

some with pale belly and dark breast

dark-morph juvenile

Auks, Murres, Puffins (Family Alcidae)

These black-and-white "penguins of the north" have set-back legs that give them an upright stance on land. In flight, wingbeats are rapid and shallow. Mostly silent when at sea.

Razorbill *Alca torda* L 17" *(43 cm)*

A chunky bird, with a big head and thick neck; black above, white below. Rather long, pointed tail; heavy head; and large, arching bill distinguish Razorbill (an auk) from murres. Swimming birds often hold tail cocked up. A white band crosses the bill; in ***breeding*** plumage, a white line runs from bill to eye. ***Immature*** birds lack white band; bill is smaller but still distinctively shaped.

Range: Nests on rocky cliffs and among boulders. Winters offshore in large numbers on the Grand Banks off Newfoundland, regularly south to Long Island and irregularly to North Carolina. Regularly seen from shore at some coastal promontories. Casual south to Florida; accidental inland.

Common Murre *Uria aalge* L 17½" *(45 cm)*

Large, with a long, slender, pointed bill. Upperparts dark sooty gray, head brownish; underparts white. Some Atlantic birds have a ***"bridle,"*** a white eye ring and spur. In ***winter*** plumage, a dark stripe extends from eye across white cheek. ***Juvenile*** has shorter bill. Distinguished from Thick-billed Murre by white facial stripe, browner upperparts, mottled flanks, and thinner bill; from Razorbill by bill shape, browner upperparts, and shorter tail.

Range: Nests in dense colonies on rocky cliffs. Chick accompanies adult at sea. Found well offshore during nonbreeding seasons; only casually seen from land. Rare south of Cape Cod, to mid-Atlantic states.

Thick-billed Murre *Uria lomvia* L 18" *(46 cm)*

Stocky, with a thick, fairly short bill, arched at tip to form a blunt hook. Upperparts and throat of adult are darker than Common Murre; white of underparts usually rises to a sharp point on the foreneck. Most birds show a distinct white line on cutting edge of upper mandible. In immature and ***winter*** adult, face and neck are more extensively dark than in Common. Immature has smaller bill than adult. First-summer bird is browner above than adult; otherwise similar to winter bird.

Range: Common on breeding grounds. Nests in colonies on rocky cliffs. Chick accompanies adult at sea. More regular in winter in New England waters than Common Murre; casual to mid-Atlantic states; recorded to Florida. Winters well offshore, rarely seen from land. Accidental inland, though no recent records.

Razorbill

slightly smaller bill

unique thick bill with white band

whitish

white

immature

winter adult

breeding adult

black hood and upperparts

long pointed tail

thick bill

breeding adult

Common Murre

bridled breeding adult

long, pointed bill

breeding adult

rounded

grayish brown cast to head and upperparts

breeding adult

winter

juvenile

dark postocular spur

flank streaks

Thick-billed Murre
lomvia

short, thick bill

distinct white line

breeding adults

pointed

blacker on head and upperparts than Common

short thick bill with curved culmen

dark face

faint gape stripe

black back

white flanks

winter adult

Long-billed Murrelet *Brachyramphus perdix*
L 11½" (29 cm) Vagrant. In **winter,** lacks conspicuous white collar of similar Marbled Murrelet, which is not recorded inland or from East (not shown); shows small pale oval patches on sides of nape; in **breeding** plumage upperparts are less rufous, throat paler. Another Pacific Ocean alcid, Ancient Murrelet (not shown), also has occurred casually in the East. It shows a distinct contrast between a black cap and gray back.
Range: Native to coastal northeast Asia. Casual throughout North America; most records are in fall of winter-plumaged birds.

Dovekie *Alle alle L 8¼" (21 cm)*
Small and plump with short neck, stubby bill. **Breeding adult** is black above, white below; black upper breast contrasts sharply with white underparts; dark wing linings. Usually swims tilted forward in the water. In **winter** plumage, throat, chin, and lower face are white, with white curving around behind eye.
Range: Abundant on breeding grounds. Winters irregularly at sea in North Atlantic south to off mid-Atlantic coast; very rarely to Florida. Seen rarely from shore away from eastern Newfoundland. Accidental inland; in past, large "wrecks" of many birds blown inland by late-autumn storms, though none recent.

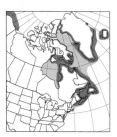

Black Guillemot *Cepphus grylle L 13" (33 cm)*
Breeding adult black overall, with large white patch on upperwing. **Winter adult** white; upperparts heavily mottled with black except on nape; wing patch less distinct. **Juvenile** is sooty above; sides and wing patches mottled. First-summer birds are patchily black-and-white; wing patches mottled. In East Coast race *arcticus,* juveniles and winter birds are darker than in high Arctic race, *mandtii.*
Range: Fairly common; usually seen close to shore. In winter, found regularly south to Massachusetts, rarely to Long Island; casual to Carolinas. Accidental inland.

Atlantic Puffin *Fratercula arctica L 12½" (32 cm)*
The only East Coast puffin. **Breeding adult** is identified by its massive, brightly colored bill; its pale face and underparts contrast with dark upperparts. **Winter adult** has a smaller, darker bill and a dusky face. In **juvenile** and first-winter birds, face is even duskier, bill much duller and smaller. Full adult bill takes about five years to develop. In flight, distinguished from murres and Razorbill (preceding page) by red-orange legs, rounded wings, grayish wing linings, and absence of white trailing edge on wing.
Range: Locally common in breeding season; winters, usually solitary, in deep water, well out at sea, a few south to off Virginia; casual farther south. Accidental inland to eastern Great Lakes region.

Long-billed Murrelet

brownish with pale throat

often with pale spot on back of head

nearly complete whitish eye ring

breeding adult

slender bill

winter

white scapular patch

even line of separation between dark and white

black head

Dovekie

blackish underwings

winter

white tips to secondaries

breeding adult

stubby bill

winter

dark neck band

whitish extends up into ear coverts

overall much paler than *arcticus*

winter adult *mandtii*

pure white wing linings

Black Guillemot *arcticus*

winter adult

juvenile

white wing patch

younger birds have dark tips to coverts

breeding adult

winter adult

bright red legs

uniquely shaped and colored bill

pale gray face

breeding adult

dark collar

breeding adult

dark underwings

darker face

smaller bill

Atlantic Puffin

winter adult

juvenile

red-orange legs

Pigeons, Doves (Family Columbidae)

The larger species of these birds usually are called pigeons, the smaller ones doves. All are strong, fast fliers. Juveniles have pale-tipped feathers and lack the neck markings of adults. Pigeons and doves feed chiefly on grain, other seeds, and fruit.

White-crowned Pigeon *Patagioenas leucocephala*
L 13½" (34 cm) A large, square-tailed pigeon of the Florida Everglades and Keys. Crown patch varies from shining white in **adult males** to grayish white in most **females** and grayish brown in juveniles. Otherwise this species looks all-black; the iridescent collar is visible only in good light.
Voice: Calls include a loud, deep *coo-cura-cooo* or *coo-croo*.
Range: Flocks commute from nest colonies in coastal mangroves to feed inland on fruit. Most winter on Caribbean islands. Accidental to Mississippi.

Red-billed Pigeon *Patagioenas flavirostris* *L 14½" (37 cm)*
Dark overall, with a mainly red bill. Maroon wash to head and breast may be difficult to see.
Voice: Distinctive call, which is heard in early spring and summer, is a long, high-pitched *cooooo* followed by three loud *up-cup-a-coo* notes.
Range: Uncommon, local, and declining in Texas. Most frequently recorded along the Rio Grande from below Falcon Dam to above Zapata, more rarely farther north to southern Maverick County. Accidental on the lower Texas coast (Nueces County) and from the Texas Hill Country (Kerr County). Rare in winter. Perches in tall trees above a brushy understory; forages for seeds, nuts, and figs. Seldom comes to the ground except to drink.

Rock Pigeon *Columba livia* *L 12½" (32 cm)*
The highly variable city pigeon; multicolored birds were developed over centuries of near domestication. The birds most closely resembling their wild ancestors have head and neck darker than back, black bars on inner wing, white rump, and black band at end of tail. Flocks in flight show a variety of plumage patterns.
Voice: Call is a soft *coo-cuk-cuk-cuk-coooo*.
Range: Rock Pigeon was introduced from Europe by early settlers, now widespread and common, particularly in urban settings. Nests and roosts chiefly on high window ledges, bridges, grain elevators, and barns. Feeds during the day in parks and fields. Some groups have reverted back to nesting on rocky cliffs, the species' ancestral native habitat.

white crown
pale eye
red bill with pale tip
♀
dark slaty gray body

White-crowned Pigeon

♂

pale eye with orange orbital ring

red bill with pale yellow tip

maroon head, neck, and wing coverts; otherwise slate gray

Red-billed Pigeon
flavirostrsis

ancestral natural coloration

white rump

Rock Pigeon

many other color variations are seen

color variations

Eurasian Collared-Dove *Streptopelia decaocto*
L 12½" (32 cm) Slightly larger than Mourning Dove. Very pale gray-buff; black collar. Escapes of domesticated *African Collared-Dove* (*S. roseogrisea*), formerly named Ringed Turtle-Dove (*S. risoria*), an Old World species, may form small populations, but do not do well in the wild. African Collared Dove is smaller, paler; has whitish undertail coverts, gray primaries; tail shorter, less black from below. Believed to derive from African Collared-Dove, *S. roseogrisea.* Such paler birds are found scattered within many populations of typical-looking Eurasian Collared-Doves.
Voice: Three-syllable call, *coo-coo-cup;* most similar domestics give a two-syllable call.
Range: Eurasian species; introduced to Bahamas, spread to Florida. Common; now nearly throughout U.S. Some populations are the result of local releases.

White-winged Dove *Zenaida asiatica L 11½" (29 cm)*
Large white wing patches and shorter, rounded tail distinguish this species from Mourning Dove. On sitting bird, wing patch shows only as a thin white line. Note also the slightly longer bill and orange-red eye.
Voice: Loud, drawn-out, cooing call, *who-cooks-for-you,* with many variations is heard mainly during breeding season.
Range: Nests singly or in large colonies in dense mesquite, mature citrus groves, riparian woodlands, and towns. Has recently become well established in Florida and locally along the central Gulf Coast. Range on Great Plains expanding northward. Very rare visitor north to southern Canada.

Mourning Dove *Zenaida macroura L 12" (31 cm)*
Trim body; long tail tapers to a point. Black spots on upperwing; pinkish wash below. In flight, shows white tips on outer tail feathers. *Juvenile* has heavy spotting; scaled effect on wings; compare with Common Ground-Dove and Inca Dove.
Voice: Call is a mournful *oowoo-woo-woo-woo.* Wings produce a fluttering whistle as the bird takes flight.
Range: Our most abundant and widespread dove, found in a wide variety of habitats.

White-tipped Dove *Leptotila verreauxi L 11½" (29 cm)*
This large, plump dove has a whitish forehead and throat and dark back. Most easily seen at or near woodland feeding stations. In flight, white tips show plainly on fanned tail.
Voice: Low-pitched call is like the sound produced by blowing across the top of a bottle.
Range: Feeds on or near the ground, keeping close to woodlands with dense understory. Accidental to Dry Tortugas, Florida.

Eurasian Collared-Dove

black collar

grayish

Eurasian Collared

African Collared

Mourning

grayish

whitish

African Collared-Dove

three-toned wing

red eye with blue orbital ring

White-winged Dove

rounded tail with white tips

white leading edge to wing

crescent-shaped white patch

Mourning Dove

♂

♀

black spotting

long, pointed tail

juvenile

White-tipped Dove
angelica

pale yellow eye

chunky body shape

white forehead and throat

short, broad slightly rounded tail

whitish belly

white tail tips

Common Ground-Dove *Columbina passerina*
L 6½" (17 cm) Very small, with pink at base of bill; scaled effect on head and breast; short tail, often raised. Plain scapulars; bright chestnut primaries and wing linings visible in flight. *Male* has a slate gray crown, pinkish gray underparts. *Female* is grayer, more uniformly colored.
Voice: Call is a repeated soft, ascending *wah-up.*
Range: Declining in Southeast region, where primarily found in sandy brushy areas; accidental as far north as Massachusetts in fall and winter.

Inca Dove *Columbina inca* L 8¼" (21 cm)
Plumage conspicuously scalloped. In flight, shows chestnut on wings like Common Ground-Dove, but note the Inca Dove's longer, white-edged tail.
Voice: Call, a double *cooo-coo.*
Range: Found usually near human habitations, often in parks and gardens. Range on Great Plains slowly spreading northward. Casual wanderer north to North Dakota, Ontario, and Maryland.

Lories, Parakeets, Macaws, Parrots (Family Psittacidae)

Most parrots in the wild in North America are descendants of escaped cage birds. Shown are those with established populations, mostly from southern parts of California, Texas, and Florida. ABA accepts White-winged, Monk, and Green Parakeets; Red-crowned Parrot; and Budgerigar. Calls are mostly fairly loud and raspy, grating, or shrill.

Budgerigar *Melopsittacus undulatus* L 7" (18 cm)
Australian species. Native birds green, as were populations established in southwest Florida in early 1960s; reached tens of thousands before 1980s. Only a few now present in Hernando and Pasco Counties, maybe due to competition for nest cavities with European Starling. Note barred upperparts and white wing stripe visible in flight. Escapes may be blue, white, or yellow.

Monk Parakeet *Myiopsitta monachus* L 11½" (29 cm)
Species of temperate South America. The most widespread parrot in south Florida. Also found very locally in several cities of the Northeast, the Midwest, and Texas. Note extensive gray on face and underparts.
Voice: Call a loud, grating *krii.*

White-winged Parakeet *Brotogeris versicolurus*
L 8¾" (22 cm) From northern Amazon area. Small numbers established in southern Florida and California by 1960s, but have declined in recent years. Note white outer secondaries and inner primaries; yellow greater coverts; unfeathered lores.

Yellow-chevroned Parakeet *Brotogeris chiriri*
L 8¾" (22 cm) Native of southern Amazon to northern Argentina. Found in southern California and Florida. Lacks white on flight feathers; body yellow-green.

Common Ground-Dove

grayish cap

pink-based bill ♀

scaly breast and nape ♂

rufous outer wing

short tail

♂

pinkish breast

Inca Dove

dark scales on head and body

long tail with white edges

rufous primary patches

Budgerigar variants

gray forehead

gray throat and breast

bluish remiges

yellow face

barred above

green

long, pointed tail

natural coloration

Budgerigar

Monk Parakeet

White-winged Parakeet

white secondaries and inner primaries

unfeathered gray lores

yellow greater coverts

green secondaries

slightly brighter yellow-green head

yellow greater coverts

Yellow-chevroned Parakeet

Dusky-headed Parakeet *Aratinga weddellii L 11" (28 cm)*
From western Amazon Basin. Some established in Miami area.
Gray head with white around eye and black bill.

Black-hooded Parakeet *Nandayus nenday*
L 13¾" (35 cm) Native of southwest Brazil to north Argentina.
Found Los Angeles area; widely established Pinellas County,
Florida. Black on head, black bill, blue wash on breast, red thighs.

Green Parakeet *Aratinga holochlora L 13" (33 cm)*
Mexican species; populations in towns in extreme southern Texas
may include Mexican strays. Large, nearly all-green.
Voice: A loud, grating chatter.

Blue-crowned Parakeet *Aratinga acuticaudata*
L 14" (36 cm) South American species. Small numbers established
on Key Biscayne and Key Largo, Florida, and in Los Angeles area.
Blue face; bicolored bill; base of tail reddish below.

Mitred Parakeet *Aratinga mitrata L 15" (38 cm)*
South American species. Numerous in Los Angeles area, a few in
south Florida. Large, green, with white eye ring; red face, forehead,
variable elsewhere on head; underwings yellow-olive.

Red-masked Parakeet *Aratinga erythrogenys*
L 13" (33 cm) From Ecuador and Peru. In Los Angeles area and
in Dade County, Florida. Similar to Mitred, but note red on leading edge of wing and underwing coverts, more red on head.

IDENTIFYING: Flight Silhouettes The flight
patterns of psittacid genera differ.

Brotogeris. These small parakeets have moderately long, pointed tails. In flight several rapid
wingbeats are followed by brief closure of bowed
wings. Flight is rapid but seems halting and undulating from wing closures and side-to-side twisting of body.

Psittacula. Rose-ringed Parakeet is of medium
size and has a markedly long, slender tail. It
appears relatively small headed and thus does not
seem "front-heavy." Its wingbeats are deeper and
more sweeping than those of other parakeets.

Aratinga, Nandayus, and *Myiopsitta.* These
medium-size parakeets have long, pointed tails.
Their bills are moderate to large in size, giving
them a more front-heavy look. Flight is rapid and
constant; wingbeats are fairly shallow, with wings
bowed slightly below the body plane. There is
some side-to-side body twisting.

Amazona. These medium- to large-size parrots seem large headed and markedly front-
heavy in flight. The tail is squared and moderately
short. Wings are bowed down; wingbeats are
stiff, continuous, and fast, but flight is slower than
in parakeets.

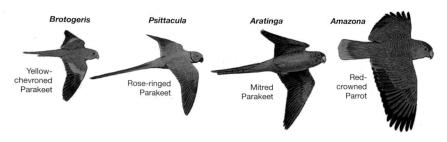

Brotogeris
Yellow-
chevroned
Parakeet

Psittacula
Rose-ringed
Parakeet

Aratinga
Mitred
Parakeet

Amazona
Red-
crowned
Parrot

black
remiges

gray head
with white
around eye

black
bill

black
remiges

black head

black
bill

bluish
chest

red

some with a
few scattered
red feathers

mainly
green
coloration

**Black-hooded
Parakeet**

**Green
Parakeet**
holochlora

**Dusky-headed
Parakeet**

limited red on head
and leading edge of wing

scattered red
head feathers

extensive
red on head

partly
bluish
head

bicolored
bill

rod on
leading
edge
of wing

reddish
tail
base

**Mitred
Parakeet**

long, pointed tail

**Blue-crowned
Parakeet**

**Red-masked
Parakeet**

Rose-ringed Parakeet *Psittacula krameri*

L 15¾" (40 cm) Small numbers of this Asian and African species are established in Miami and Los Angeles and Bakersfield areas of southern California. Appear to be of Indian race, *manillensis*. Slender tail with very long central feathers; bright red upper mandible. ***Adult males*** show black, rose-edged collar.
Voice: Call is a loud, flickerlike *kew.*

Red-crowned Parrot *Amazona viridigenalis*

L 13" (33 cm) Endemic native of northeast Mexico. Established in towns of southernmost Texas; some may be visitors from Mexico, but most or all are probably descendants of escaped cage birds. Began to appear in south Texas in the early 1970s. Outside of south Texas, scattered reports north to Austin and Corpus Christi likely involve local escapees rather than dispersal from southernmost Texas. Also found in Fort Lauderdale and widespread in the Los Angeles metropolitan area. Pale blue on sides of head, yellow eyes, yellowish band across tip of tail. ***Adult male*** has red crown; ***female*** and juvenile show less red. Most easily found when leaving and returning to communal roosts early and late in the day.
Voice: Calls are generally raucous but they include a mellow, rolling *rreeoo.*

Orange-winged Parrot *Amazona amazonica*

L 12¼" (31 cm) South American species, found mostly east of the Andes from Colombia to southeast Brazil. Small numbers established in Miami area. Note blue stripe and nape on yellow head; orange at base of outer tail feathers.

Lilac-crowned Parrot *Amazona finschi L 13" (33 cm)*

West Mexican species. Small numbers established in Los Angeles area; a few have been seen in south Texas and Florida. Like Red-crowned, but has lilac wash on crown and nape; maroon band across forehead; orange eye; a dusky or dark gray rather than a pinkish flesh cere; longer tail has entirely green central tail feathers. Likely has hybridized with Red-crowned Parrot in southern California.
Voice: Calls include a distinctive upslurred whistle.

Yellow-headed Parrot *Amazona oratrix L 14½" (37 cm)*

Drastically declining species from Mexico and Belize. Small but declining numbers established in Los Angeles area; a few also in south Texas and Florida. Large, with yellow head; immature shows less yellow. Some escapes are of closely related Yellow-naped (*A. auropalliata*) and Yellow-crowned (*A. ochrocephala*) Parrots, formerly treated as subspecies of Yellow-headed.
Voice: Calls include a resonant *haa-haa-haa.*

Red-crowned Parrot

red bill

black neck ring

adult ♂

♀

red forehead

red crown

♀

adult ♂

Rose-ringed Parakeet

adult ♂

yellowish terminal tail band

very long and thin pointed tail

bluish on head and nape

orange base to outer tail feathers

Orange-winged Parrot

lilac crown and nape

maroon forehead

yellow head

adults

pale bill

Lilac-crowned Parrot

Yellow-headed Parrot

Cuckoos, Roadrunners, Anis (Family Cuculidae)

Of this large family, widespread in the Old World, only a few species are seen in North America. Most are slender with long tails; two toes point forward, two back.

Mangrove Cuckoo *Coccyzus minor* L 12" (31 cm)

Black mask and buffy underparts distinguish this species from other cuckoos. Upperparts grayish brown; lacks rufous primaries of Yellow-billed Cuckoo. Black tail feathers are broadly tipped with white. Species is usually considered monotypic, but Mexican birds average brighter below; two variations shown. In all juveniles, mask is paler, tail pattern muted.
Voice: Call is a slow, guttural *gaw gaw gaw*.
Range: Found chiefly in mangrove swamps. Like other cuckoos, perches quietly near center of tree. An accidental vagrant along our Gulf Coast from Mexico to Texas and northwest Florida.

Yellow-billed Cuckoo *Coccyzus americanus*

L 12" (31 cm) Grayish brown above, white below; rufous primaries; lower mandible yellow. Under tail patterned in bold black and white. In *juvenal* plumage, held well into fall, tail has a much paler pattern and bill may show little or no yellow; may be confused with Black-billed Cuckoo.
Voice: One song sounds hollow and wooden, a rapid staccato *kuk-kuk-kuk* that usually slows and descends to a *kakakowlp-kowlp* ending. Also a series of *coo* notes and a slowly repeated single *koop*.
Range: Common in open woods, orchards, and streamside willow and alder groves. Rare vagrant to Atlantic Canada during fall.

Black-billed Cuckoo *Coccyzus erythropthalmus*

L 12" (31 cm) Grayish brown above, pale grayish below. Bill is usually all-dark. Lacks the rufous primaries of Yellow-billed Cuckoo. Note also *adult*'s reddish orbital ring. Under tail patterned in gray with white tipping; compare juvenile Yellow-billed. *Juvenile* Black-billed has a buffy orbital ring; under tail is paler; underparts may have yellowish tinge, especially on undertail coverts; primaries may show a little rusty brown.
Voice: Song usually consists of monotonous *cu-cu-cu* or *cu-cu-cu-cu* phrases.
Range: Uncommon to fairly common; found in woodlands, scrub, and along streams. Very rare in Southeast.

Greater Roadrunner *Geococcyx californianus*

L 23" (58 cm) A large, ground-dwelling cuckoo streaked with brown and white. Note the long, heavy bill, conspicuous bushy crest, and long, white-edged tail. Short, rounded wings show a white crescent on the primaries.
Voice: Song is a dovelike cooing, descending in pitch.
Range: Uncommon in scrub desert, brushland, and open woodland. Eats insects, lizards, snakes, rodents, and small birds.

adults

thick bill; lower mandible
has yellow base

**Mangrove
Cuckoo**

uniform
brown
wings

buffy underparts

large white
spots on
black tail

yellow
orbital ring

thick,
extensively
yellow bill

**Yellow-billed
Cuckoo**

adult

juvenile

spots less bold
than adult

adult

rufous primaries
striking in flight

large white spots
on black tail

**Black-billed
Cuckoo**

slender,
dark bill

red
orbital ring

adult

slight buff tint
to throat

buffy
orbital ring

juvenile

adult

uniform
brown
wings

small white
spots on
grayish tail

crest can
be raised or
flattened

indistinct
tips

**Greater
Roadrunner**

very long, graduated
tail with white tips

Smooth-billed Ani *Crotophaga ani* L 14½" (37 cm)

Bill size variable, but shape distinguishes both ani species from grackles (page 382). Black overall with iridescent bronze overtones. Long tail is often dipped and wagged. Found in brushy fields, scrublands; often feeds on insects stirred up by cattle. Both ani species are gregarious; several pairs usually share a nest and take turns incubating the eggs.

Voice: Call is a whining, rising *quee-lick.*

Range: Has declined greatly in Florida and is on verge of being extirpated. Still numerous in the West Indies, including the Bahamas and Cuba. Accidental north along Atlantic coast to North Carolina; also to Ohio.

Groove-billed Ani *Crotophaga sulcirostris* L 13½" (34 cm)

Groove-billed is smaller in overall size and has a smaller bill than Smooth-billed Ani. Bill does not extend above crown; lower mandible is straighter. Plumage is black overall with iridescent purple and green overtones; long tail is often dipped and wagged. Grooves in bill, which are visible only at close range, are distinctive. Groove-billeds skulk for much of the time, but they will perch in the open occasionally and are conspicuous in flight.

Voice: Call is a liquid *tee-ho,* accented on the first syllable. Call is distinctive.

Range: Common in summer in woodlands. Rare primarily in fall and winter along the Gulf Coast east to Florida. Casual north to Minnesota and east to New Jersey, mostly in fall.

Barn Owls (Family Tytonidae)

Owls are distinctive birds of prey, divided by structural differences into two families, Barn Owls and Typical Owls. All have immobile eyes in large heads. Fluffy plumage makes their flight nearly soundless. To help locate prey at night, they have a round facial disc and very acute hearing. Barn Owls are strictly nocturnal. They hunt small mammals from a perch or in low, quartering flights, sometimes hovering in place. They differ from other owls by their heart-shaped face, short, squared tail, and relatively smaller eyes.

Barn Owl *Tyto alba* L 16" (41 cm)

A pale owl with dark eyes in a heart-shaped face. Rusty brown above; underparts vary from white to cinnamon. Darkest birds are always ***females,*** palest birds ***males.*** Compare with Snowy Owl (page 226). The Barn Owl roosts and nests in dark cavities in city and farm buildings, cliffs, and trees. Flies with shallow, slow wingbeats, often with long legs dangling.

Voice: Typical call is a raspy, hissing screech.

Range: Frequents open country, including grasslands, farmland, and marshes. Rare to uncommon, local, and declining in the East, especially in the upper Midwest, and is now extirpated as a breeder from the northern tier of states and southern Ontario. Some northerly populations are migratory.

long tail

grooves visible
at close range

**Groove-billed
Ani**
sulcirostris

some show raised base
to culmen, but many others do not

bill has
no distinct
grooves

**Smooth-billed
Ani**

slightly larger than very similar
Groove-billed; most birds
best distinguished by voice

dark eyes with
whitish heart-
shaped face

underparts vary
from whitish
to cinnamon-buff;
males average paler

♂

♀

Barn Owl
pratincola

long legs

looks pale in flight with
rounded wings and no
dark carpal patches as
in Short-eared Owl

Typical Owls (Family Strigidae)

Many species hunt at night and roost during the day. To find owls, search the ground for regurgitated pellets of fur and bone below a nest or roost. Listen for flocks of small songbirds noisily mobbing a roosting owl. Although several species give familiar hooting calls, others make a variety of different sounds, including whistles, chattering, and barking.

Short-eared Owl *Asio flammeus* L 15" (38 cm)

Tawny; boldly streaked on breast; belly paler, more lightly streaked. Ear tufts are barely visible. In flight, long wings show buffy patch above, black "wrist" mark below; these markings are usually more prominent than in Long-eared Owl, which also has less distinct but more individual bars on primaries. Flight is wavering, wingbeats erratic. During the day it roosts on the ground or on open, low perches: short poles, muskrat houses, and duck blinds.

Voice: Typical call, heard in breeding season and sometimes in winter, is a raspy, high barking.

Range: A bird of open country, marshes, tundra, and weedy fields; nests on the ground. Uncommon. Somewhat irregular and gregarious in winter; groups may gather where prey is abundant. Short-eared Owls sighted on Florida Keys and Dry Tortugas are thought to have originated from West Indian populations, likely *domingensis* from Cuba.

Long-eared Owl *Asio otus* L 15" (38 cm)

A slender owl with long, close-set ear tufts. Boldly streaked and barred on breast and belly. Wings generally have a less prominent buffy patch with more dark barring and a smaller black "wrist" mark than Short-eared Owl; facial disk is rusty. Lives in thick woods; hunts at night over open fields, marshes. By day it roosts in a tree, close to the trunk.

Voice: Generally silent except in breeding season. Common call is one or more long *hooo* notes.

Range: Uncommon. More gregarious in winter, when often forms roosting groups.

Great Horned Owl *Bubo virginianus* L 22" (56 cm)

Size, bulky shape, and white throat separate this owl from the Long-eared Owl; ear tufts distinguish it from other large species. Nests in trees, caves, or on the ground. Chiefly nocturnal.

Voice: Call is a series of three to eight loud, deep hoots; the second and third hoots are often short and rapid.

Range: Common; habitats vary from forest to city. Takes prey as large as skunks and grouse. Widespread interior race, *subarcticus,* is paler.

slow, floppy wingbeats

dark primary covert patch on underwing

buffy and blackish wing patches

Short-eared Owl
flammeus

very short ear tufts

blackish around eyes

heavily spotted above

streaked below

long ear tufts that are close together

rufous facial disk

blackish around eyes

Long-eared Owl

overall slender body

heavily streaked and barred below

prominent broad ear tufts on side of head

Great Horned Owl

color of facial disk varies geographically

white

bulky body shape

overall pale

barred below

subarcticus

Great Gray Owl *Strix nebulosa L 27" (69 cm)*

This is our largest but not our heaviest owl. Heavily ringed facial disks make the yellow eyes look small. Lacks ear tufts. Hunts over forest clearings and nearby open country, chiefly by night but also at dawn and dusk; hunts by day during summer in northern part of range, as well as sometimes during overcast days in winter.

Voice: Call, given on the breeding grounds, is a series of deep, resonant *whoo* notes.

Range: Inhabits boreal forests and wooded bogs in the far north. Generally uncommon; rare and irregular winter visitor to limit of dashed line on map. Accidental farther south, to Nebraska, Iowa, Ohio, Pennsylvania, and Long Island. Preys on small mammals.

Barred Owl *Strix varia L 21" (53 cm)*

This chunky owl has dark eyes, dark barring on upper breast, and dark streaking below. Its is chiefly nocturnal; its daytime roost is well hidden. Easily flushed, it does not generally tolerate close approach.

Voice: Distinctive call is a rhythmic series of loud hoots: *who-cooks-for-you, who-cooks-for-you-all;* also a drawn-out *hoo-ah,* sometimes preceded by an ascending agitated barking. Much more likely than other owls to be heard in daytime. Often a chorus of two or more owls will call back and forth.

Range: Common resident in dense coniferous or mixed woods of river bottoms and swamps; also in upland woods. Preys primarily on mammals and amphibians.

Snowy Owl *Bubo scandiacus L 23" (58 cm)*

Large white owl, with rounded head and yellow eyes. Dark bars and spots are heavier on females, heaviest on ***immatures;*** old males may be pure white. Sometimes Barn Owls, particularly when seen flying through artificially lit areas, are mistaken for Snowy Owls.

Voice: Mostly silent away from breeding site.

Range: An owl of open tundra; nests on the ground; preys chiefly on lemmings and other small mammals, hunting by day as well as at night. Retreats from northernmost part of range in winter; at least a few are seen annually to limit indicated by dashed line on map. In years when the lemming population plummets, many move south into northern tier of states, and some may wander in winter as far south as Oklahoma and Virginia, exceptionally to Gulf Coast states. These irruptives, usually heavily barred younger birds, often perch conspicuously on the ground or on low stumps, fence posts, and buildings. Winter diet includes both mammals and a variety of birds, including waterfowl.

huge size

Great Gray Owl
nebulosa

dark rings
on facial disk

black and white
at bottom of
facial disk gives
"bow tie" effect

**Barred
Owl**

dark eyes

barred
breast

vertical
streaks

**Snowy
Owl**

immature

round head

color varies from all-white
to heavily barred
depending on age and sex

Eastern Screech-Owl *Megascops asio L 8½" (22 cm)*

All three owl species shown on this page are small, with yellow eyes. Ear tufts prominent if raised; when flattened, bird has a round-headed look. Underparts on all three are marked by vertical streaks crossed by dark bars: These markings are less distinct on the Eastern ***rufous morph;*** the latter predominates in the South, the ***gray morph*** on the Great Plains and in southernmost Texas. Lightest and whitest, the *maxwelliae* race is found in the northwestern part of the range.

Voice: Nocturnal; best located and identified by voice. Two typical calls: a series of quavering whistles, descending in pitch; and a long single trill, all on one pitch. Sometimes may be heard calling from inside roost hole after dawn.

Range: Eastern Screech-Owls are common in a wide variety of habitats: woodlots, forests, swamps, orchards, parks, and suburban gardens. Formerly classified with Western Screech-Owl as one species; range separation is not yet fully known.

Elf Owl *Micrathene whitneyi L 5¾" (15 cm)*

Our smallest owl. Yellow eyes; very short tail. Lacks ear tufts. Upperparts brownish gray; *idonea* of south Texas is grayish above and has little or no cinnamon below, including the face; more westerly *whitneyi* of west Texas and the Southwest is tinged cinnamon below.

Voice: Call is an irregular series of high *churp* notes and chattering notes.

Range: Strictly nocturnal; roosts and nests in cavities in trees. Uncommon in woodlands and mesquite. Eats mostly large insects. Casual in winter in southernmost Texas.

Ferruginous Pygmy-Owl *Glaucidium brasilianum*

L 6¾" (17 cm) Long tail, reddish with dark or dusky bars. Upperparts gray-brown; crown faintly streaked. Eyes yellow; black nape spots look like eyes on the back of the head. White underparts streaked with reddish brown. Unlike other North American owls, pygmy-owls fly with quick, unmuffled wingbeats. Elf Owl differs by its even smaller size, shorter tail, and lack of false eyes.

Voice: Most common call is a series of rapid, repeated whistled *took* notes, varying from about ten to more than a hundred notes, and are repeated for minutes at a time with pauses of five to ten seconds between phrases. The female's call is higher pitched and wheezier.

Range: Uncommon. Chiefly diurnal; active any time of day. Roosts in crevices and cavities. The brownish *ridgwayi* is resident in south Texas woodlands north to near Kingsville. The largest numbers are in and near the King Ranch, where extensive habitat remains. A few are found in woodlands along the Rio Grande from about Bentsen–Rio Grande Valley State Park to Falcon Dam.

rufous morph more numerous in Southeast

Eastern Screech-Owl

ear tufts

yellow eyes

pale greenish bill

rufous morph

gray morph

strong vertical and horizontal bars on underparts

gray-morph juvenile

overall pale

maxwelliae

rounded head with no ear tufts

yellow eyes

Elf Owl
western
whitneyi

tiny size

very short tail

streaked crown

"false eyes"

Ferruginous Pygmy-Owl
ridgwayi

long tail with rusty bars

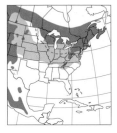

Northern Saw-whet Owl *Aegolius acadicus* L 8" (20 cm)
Reddish brown above; white below with reddish streaks; bill dark; facial disks reddish, without dark border. **Juvenile** dark brown above, tawny rust below. Strictly nocturnal. In winter, preferred roost is in dense evergreens. Concentrations of regurgitated pellets and "whitewash" excrement build up below favored roosts. Once found, this species can be closely approached.
Voice: Call, heard primarily in breeding season from late winter to late spring, is a monotonously repeated single-note whistle; another, raspy call sounds like a saw being sharpened. Also gives a rising screech.
Range: Uncommon. Inhabits coniferous or mixed forests, wooded swamps, and tamarack bogs. The number of migrants that move southward in fall and winter vary substantially from year to year.

Northern Hawk Owl *Surnia ulula* L 16" (41 cm)
Long tail, falconlike profile, and black-bordered facial disks identify this owl of the northern forests. Underparts are barred with brown. Flight is low and swift; sometimes hunts during daylight as well as at night. Is most often seen, however, perched high in a spruce tree. Usually can be closely approached.
Voice: Mostly silent away from nesting sites.
Range: Mostly nonmigratory, but retreats slightly in winter from northernmost part of range. Periodic winter irruptions bring a few birds even farther south. Casual south of mapped range.

Boreal Owl *Aegolius funereus* L 10" (25 cm)
White underparts streaked with chocolate brown. Whitish facial disk has a distinct black border; bill is pale. Darker above than Northern Saw-whet Owl. **Juvenile** is chocolate brown below. Boreal Owls are strictly nocturnal; roost during daylight in dense cover, usually close to tree trunk.
Voice: Call, heard primarily in breeding season from late winter to midspring, is a short, rapid series of hollow *hoo* notes.
Range: Inhabit dense northern forests and muskeg. Irruptive, usually in small numbers; otherwise seldom seen south of mapped range, but this may be due to difficulty of locating them.

Burrowing Owl *Athene cunicularia* L 9½" (24 cm)
Long legs separate this ground dweller from all other small owls. Adult boldly spotted, barred. **Juvenile** buffy below. Nocturnal; flight low, undulating; often hovers like a kestrel. Florida birds (*floridana*) are darker above with more whitish spotting; less buffy below. Perches conspicuously during daylight at entrance to burrow nest or on low post.
Voice: Calls include a soft *coo-coooo* and a chattering series of *chack* notes. Disturbed in its nest, the Burrowing Owl often gives an alarm call that imitates the sound of a rattlesnake.
Range: An owl of open country, golf courses, and airports. Nests in single pairs or small colonies. Declining in much of range; may be partly due to destruction of prairie dog towns, and by agricultural growth. Rare on eastern Great Plains. Casual vagrant (both North American subspecies) to East Coast, north to Maine.

Northern Saw-whet Owl
acadicus

no dark border
to facial disk

dark bill

rufous overall
coloration

juvenile

**Northern
Hawk Owl**
caparoch

black border
to facial disk

prominent
black border to
facial disk

pale bill

**Boreal
Owl**
richardsoni

dark barring
on underparts

long tail

juvenile

darker body
coloration
than juvenile
Northern
Saw-whet

round head

Burrowing Owl
western *hypugaea*

heavily spotted
with white above

no dark
barring below

juvenile

232

Goatsuckers (Family Caprimulgidae)

Wide mouths help these night hunters snare flying insects. Most are located and identified by their distinctive calls.

Lesser Nighthawk *Chordeiles acutipennis* L 8½" (22 cm)
Resembles Common Nighthawk but wings shorter and usually more rounded; whitish bar across primaries slightly closer to tip. Upperparts paler and more uniformly mottled; in Common paler wing coverts contrast more with back. Throat is white in *males,* usually buffy in *females* and juveniles. Underparts buffy, with faint barring. Male has white tail band. Female lacks tail band; note buffy wing bar and markings at base of primaries, often indistinct in juvenile female. Seen chiefly around dusk.
Voice: Distinctive call is a rapid, tremulous trill, heard only on breeding grounds.
Range: Fairly common; found in dry, open country. Very rare migrant on Gulf Coast, and in winter in Texas, Florida.

Antillean Nighthawk *Chordeiles gundlachii* L 8" (20 cm)
Wings long and pointed; tail slightly forked. Females and juveniles lack white tail band. Very difficult to distinguish from variable but longer-winged and larger Common Nighthawk.
Voice: Call is a varying *pity-pit-pit,* best identifies Antillean.
Range: Uncommon in late spring and summer on Florida Keys east to Marathon; also seen on Dry Tortugas and southeastern Florida mainland. Accidental to Louisiana and North Carolina.

Common Nighthawk *Chordeiles minor* L 9½" (24 cm)
Wings long and pointed; tail slightly forked. Bold white bar across primaries slightly farther from wing tip than in Lesser. Subspecies range from dark brown in eastern birds to more grayish in the northern Great Plains race, *sennetti;* color variations are subtle in adults, distinct in juveniles. Throat white in *male,* buffy in *female;* underparts whitish, with bold dusky bars. Female lacks white tail band. *Juvenile* shows less white on throat.
Voice: In courtship display, male's wings make a hollow booming sound. Nasal *peent* call distinctive.
Range: Seen over dry woodlands, plains, cities, and towns; more active in daylight than other goatsuckers. Roosts on the ground, on branches, posts, and roofs. Declining in East.

IDENTIFYING: Nighthawks Across a large part of North America, Common Nighthawk is the only nighthawk species found. Lesser Nighthawk is normally restricted to the Southwest region from southern Texas west to northern California. It has a knack for wandering out of range, however, particularly eastward along the Gulf Coast. A few birds even have been found wintering in south Florida. With far-flung vagrants having turned up at such places as at sea off British Columbia, in northwest Alaska, and in West Virginia, observers should be on the lookout for this species almost continent-wide, particularly when they encounter a nighthawk out of season. The third species found in the East—Antillean Nighthawk—is restricted to the

Lesser Nighthawk
texensis

rounder wing tip than Common

white bar closer to wing tip

♂

buffy primary markings

♀

markings and wing shape much like Common

Antillean Nighthawk

♂

♂

long pointed wings

white bar on inner primaries

♂

♀

males with white bar

Common Nighthawk
minor

♂

juvenile
sennetti

Florida Keys in late spring and summer, but one individual wandered well north to the Outer Banks of North Carolina.

Characteristics to emphasize in differentiating Lesser from Common Nighthawks include the location and color of the pale bar on the wing (farther out the wing—and buffy in the female—in Lesser), wing shape (slightly rounder in Lesser), vent color (slightly buffier and less strongly barred in Lesser), and the presence or absence of spotting at the base of the primaries (present in Lesser). On perched birds, note the relative location of the pale primary patch versus the tips of the tertials: In Common the patch is forward of the tertial tips, whereas it is nearly directly below the tertial tips in Lesser.

Common Poorwill *Phalaenoptilus nuttallii L 7¾" (20 cm)*

Our smallest nightjar, distinguished by short, rounded tail and short, rounded wings. Outer tail feathers are tipped with white, more boldly in *males* than in females. Plumage is variable; upperparts range from brownish gray to pale gray. Broad white band crosses dark throat and breast.
Voice: Song is a whistled *poor-will,* with a final *ip* note audible at close range.
Range: Fairly common in sagebrush and on rocky slopes; often seen on roads or roadsides after dusk or before dawn. Roosts on the ground; flies up a short distance to catch an insect, then returns to the same or a nearby location.

Common Pauraque *Nyctidromus albicollis L 11" (28 cm)*

In flight, long, rounded tail separates it from nighthawks; also shorter, rounder wings. Broad white bands on wings distinguish it from other nightjars. White tail patches conspicuous on *male,* smaller and often buffy on *female.* In close view, note chestnut ear patch.
Voice: Distinctive song, one or more low *pur* notes followed by a higher, descending *wheeer.*
Range: Common in woodland clearings and scrub. Seen just before dawn and after dusk. Flies close to the ground; often lands on roads or roadsides.

Whip-poor-will *Caprimulgus vociferus L 9¾" (25 cm)*

Mottled gray-brown overall; wings rounded; tail long, rounded. Whip-poor-will is smaller and grayer than Chuck-will's-widow; dark throat contrasts with white or buffy necklace and pale underparts. *Male*'s tail shows much more white than in male Chuck-will's-widow, especially with eastern nominate race. *Female*'s tail has contrasting pale tip on dark outer feathers.
Voice: Song is a loud *whip-poor-will,* clear and mellow in eastern birds, with accent on first and last syllables.
Range: Uncommon to fairly common but local and declining in open coniferous and mixed woodlands in the East, particularly those with a drier substrate.

Chuck-will's-widow *Caprimulgus carolinensis*

L 12" (31 cm) Our largest nightjar. Mottled buff-brown overall; wings rounded; tail long, rounded. Larger and warmer-colored than smaller-headed Whip-poor-will; buff-brown throat and whitish necklace contrast with dark breast. *Male*'s tail has less white than in male Whip-poor-will; tips of outer feathers are buff. *Female*'s tail lacks white. Rather shy; not usually approachable even when roosting during the day. Unlike eastern Whip-poor-will, birds will flush when disturbed.
Voice: Loud, whistling song sounds like *chuck-will's-widow,* the first note often inaudible.
Range: Fairly common but local in oak-pine woodlands and live oak groves. Casual north to southern Canada, west to western Great Plains.

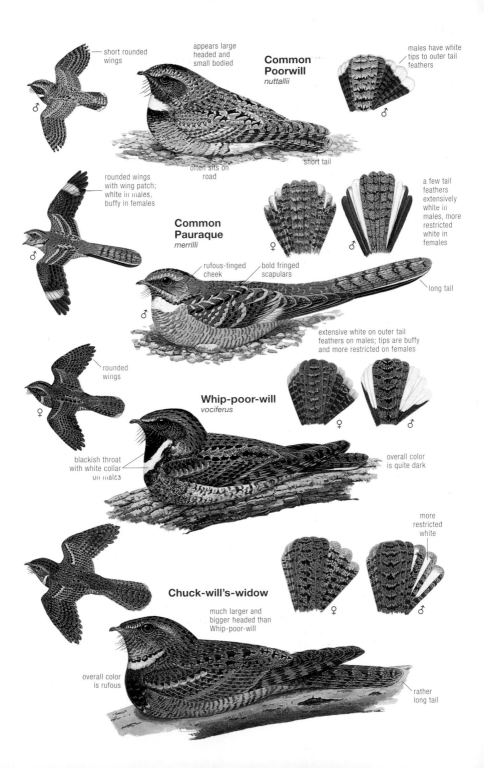

short rounded wings

appears large headed and small bodied

Common Poorwill
nuttallii

males have white tips to outer tail feathers

often sits on road

short tail

♂

rounded wings with wing patch; white in males, buffy in females

Common Pauraque
merrilli

♀ ♂

a few tail feathers extensively white in males, more restricted white in females

♂

rufous-tinged cheek

bold fringed scapulars

long tail

♂

extensive white on outer tail feathers on males; tips are buffy and more restricted on females

rounded wings

Whip-poor-will
vociferus

♀ ♂

♀

blackish throat with white collar on males

overall color is quite dark

more restricted white

Chuck-will's-widow

♀ ♂

much larger and bigger headed than Whip-poor-will

overall color is rufous

rather long tail

236

Swifts (Family Apodidae)

These fast-flying birds spend the day aloft. Long wings bend closer to the body than on similar swallows.

Chimney Swift *Chaetura pelagica L 5¼" (13 cm)*
Cigar-shaped body; short, stubby tail. Chimney Swift is largely dark, with paler throat and upper breast, slightly paler rump.
Voice: Gives a loud, chattering call. Gives a rocking display: Wings upraised, bird rocks from side to side.
Range: Nests in chimneys, barns, and hollow trees. Casual north to Newfoundland. No winter records in the U.S.

White-throated Swift *Aeronautes saxatalis*
L 6½" (17 cm) Black above, black-and-white below, with long, forked tail. In poor light, may be mistaken for Chimney Swift but is substantially larger.
Voice: Call is a descending harsh chatter.
Range: Uncommon and local in canyons, cliffs. Nests in crevices.

Hummingbirds (Family Trochilidae)

These birds hover at flowers to sip nectar with needlelike bills. Often identified by their calls. Males' throat feathers (gorget) look black in poor light.

Green Violet-ear *Colibri thalassinus L 4¾" (12 cm)*
Range: Tropical species. Green overall with dark subterminal tail band; bill slightly downcurved. ***Adult male*** has blue-violet patches on face and breast. Female and ***immature*** slightly duller, immature grayer on belly.
Voice: Song is a repeated *tsip-tsup.*
Range: Most records in summer in Texas's Hill Country, where nearly annual; casual in remainder of eastern North America.

Green-breasted Mango *Anthracothorax prevostii*
L 4¾" (12 cm) Vagrant from Mexico. Has curved bill and purplish color in outer tail feathers. ***Adult male*** is deep green overall. ***Female*** shows broad blackish green stripe on underparts bordered in white. ***Immature*** is similar to female but shows cinnamon border to sides of underparts.
Voice: Gives hard *chip* notes, sometimes in a series; often silent.
Range: Found from eastern Mexico to northern South America. Casual, mostly in fall and winter, to southern Texas; accidental to North Carolina and Wisconsin.

Buff-bellied Hummingbird *Amazilia yucatanensis*
L 4¼" (11 cm) Green overall with buff belly and chestnut tail; bill pinkish red with black tip.
Voice: Calls are shrill and squeaky.
Range: Fairly common in lower Rio Grande Valley. Rare in winter along Gulf Coast to northwest Florida; accidental to Georgia.

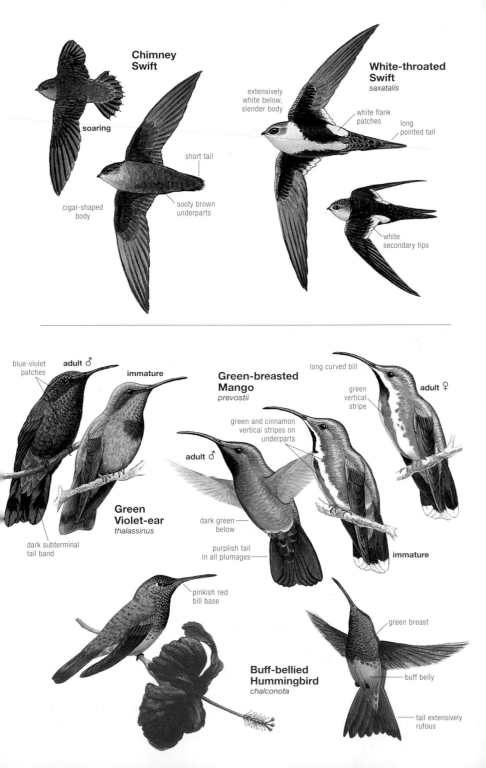

Chimney Swift

soaring

cigar-shaped body

short tail

sooty brown underparts

White-throated Swift
saxatalis

extensively white below, slender body

white flank patches

long pointed tail

white secondary tips

blue-violet patches

adult ♂

immature

Green-breasted Mango
prevostii

long curved bill

green vertical stripe

adult ♀

green and cinnamon vertical stripes on underparts

adult ♂

Green Violet-ear
thalassinus

dark green below

purplish tail in all plumages

immature

dark subterminal tail band

pinkish red bill base

Buff-bellied Hummingbird
chalconota

green breast

buff belly

tail extensively rufous

Ruby-throated Hummingbird *Archilochus colubris*
L 3¾" (10 cm) The only hummingbird regularly seen through-out most of the East. Metallic green above. *Adult male* has a brilliant red throat and black chin, but the throat may appear entirely black in poor light; underparts are whitish; sides and flanks dusky green; tail forked. *Female*'s throat is whitish; underparts grayish white, with buffy wash on sides; tail is similar to female Black-chinned Hummingbird. Immatures resemble adult female. Some *immature males* begin to show red spotting on throat by early fall. As with all hummingbirds, adult males migrate earlier than females and immatures. *Archilochus* hummingbirds seen in the Southeast in winter may be Black-chinned, but females and immatures of these two species are extremely difficult to separate. Ruby-throated generally has a greener crown, shorter bill; note darker face and more pointed shape of darker primaries, especially outermost.
Voice: Calls very similar to Black-chinned (see below).
Range: Ruby-throated Hummingbirds are fairly common in parts of range; found in gardens and woodland edges. Small numbers are found in winter at feeders from North Carolina to Texas.

Black-chinned Hummingbird *Archilochus alexandri*
L 3¾" (10 cm) Metallic green above. In good light, *adult male* shows violet band at lower border of black throat. Underparts whitish; sides and flanks dusky green. *Female*'s throat can be all-white or show faint dusky or greenish streaks. Immatures resemble adult female; *immature male* may begin to show violet on lower throat in the fall. Twitches tail more than Ruby-throated while feeding.
Voice: Call is a soft *tchew;* chase note combines high squeals and *tchew* notes.
Range: A few winter at feeders in Southeast. Casual in late fall and winter north to Atlantic Canada.

Anna's Hummingbird *Calypte anna L 4" (10 cm)*
Adult male's head and throat are deep rose red, the color extending a short distance onto sides of neck. *Female*'s throat usually shows red flecks, often forming a patch of color. In both sexes, underparts are grayish, washed with a varying amount of green. Bill is disproportionately short. Immatures resemble female; *immature male* usually shows some red on crown. *Juveniles* lack red on throat; compare with smaller female Black-chinned and Ruby-throated Hummingbirds.
Voice: Common call note, a sharp *chick;* chase call is a rapid dry rattling. Male's song is a jumble of high squeaks and raspy notes.
Range: Very rare to Texas and the Gulf Coast states, mostly in fall and winter; casual elsewhere in the East.

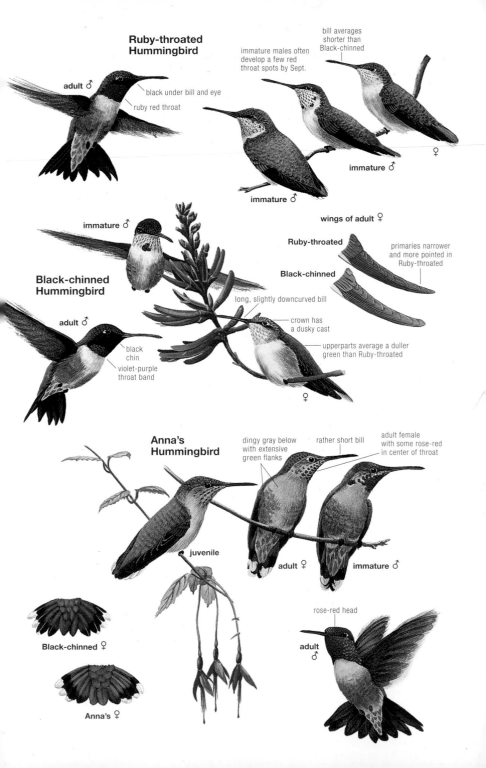

Ruby-throated Hummingbird

adult ♂

black under bill and eye

ruby red throat

immature males often
develop a few red
throat spots by Sept.

bill averages
shorter than
Black-chinned

immature ♂

immature ♂

♀

Black-chinned Hummingbird

immature ♂

wings of adult ♀

Ruby-throated

Black-chinned

primaries narrower
and more pointed in
Ruby-throated

adult ♂

black
chin

violet-purple
throat band

long, slightly downcurved bill

crown has
a dusky cast

upperparts average a duller
green than Ruby-throated

♀

Anna's Hummingbird

dingy gray below
with extensive
green flanks

rather short bill

adult female
with some rose-red
in center of throat

juvenile

adult ♀

immature ♂

Black-chinned ♀

Anna's ♀

rose-red head

adult
♂

Broad-tailed Hummingbird Selasphorus platycercus
L 4" (10 cm) **Adult male** has rose red throat. **Female** has blended buff on underparts; similar to smaller and shorter-billed female Calliope, but note tail tip extends well past primaries. Also compare to Rufous and Allen's, which show more rufous in tail.
Voice: Except during winter molt, all *Selasphorus* adult males' wingbeats produce a loud whistle, harsh and trilling in Broad-tailed. Calls include a metallic *chip*, often given in a short series.
Range: Rare migrant through western Great Plains. Very rare to casual in fall and winter at feeders and gardens in Southeast.

Calliope Hummingbird Stellula calliope L 3¼" (8 cm)
Smallest North American bird; very short bill (smallest in adult male) and tail; primary tips extend well past end of tail. Carmine streaks on **adult male**'s throat form a V-shaped gorget. **Female**'s and immature's underparts similar to female Broad-tailed. Show dark and light spots in front of eye and, usually, a faint pale line running from below to in front of eye.
Voice: Gives soft *chip* notes, but often silent.
Range: Very rare in Southeast at feeders in fall and winter; casual north to Great Lakes and New England in late fall.

Rufous Hummingbird Selasphorus rufus L 3¾" (10 cm)
Tail mainly rufous. **Adult male** has rufous back, sometimes marked with green, very rarely entirely green; orange-red gorget. **Immatures** resemble **adult female**; immature male may show reddish brown back by winter before acquiring full gorget.
Voice: Calls include a sibilant *chip*, often given in a series; chase note, *zeee-chuppity-chup*.
Range: Rare in fall in the East; winters regularly in Southeast.

Allen's Hummingbird Selasphorus sasin L 3¾" (10 cm)
Adult male has full, orange-red gorget; usually distinguishable from Rufous by solid green back. Adult female and immatures inseparable in the field from female Rufous, though tail feathers are comparatively narrower for each sex and age class.
Voice: Similar to Rufous Hummingbird.
Range: Allen's migrates earlier in fall and spring than Rufous. Casual vagrant to eastern U.S. in fall and winter.

IDENTIFYING: Western Hummingbirds in the East Since the 1980s there has been a veritable explosion both in the popularity of hummingbird feeding and gardening and in the occurrence of western species of hummingbirds in the East. This watershed began in Louisiana and bordering states, where there may be well over 300 such individual hummingbirds found in a single late autumn and winter. The most numerous winter species is Rufous, followed by Black-chinned and late-lingering eastern Ruby-throated.

The nonadult male Rufous can be distinguished from the exceedingly similar Allen's by taking in-hand measurements, particularly of the tail feathers, during bird-banding captures. The growth of hummingbird feeding in towns along the western edge of the Great Plains has resulted in an increase in the reports of western hummingbirds there, primarily in late summer and early autumn; species most often encountered include Rufous, Broad-tailed, Calliope, and Black-chinned.

Broad-tailed Hummingbird

pale whitish eye ring in all plumages

rose-red throat

adult ♂

bluish green above

♀

long broad tail

blended buffy underparts

Calliope Hummingbird

purplish red throat streaks

adult ♂

very short bill

whitish in supraloral region

♀

overall females and immatures are very similar to Broad-tailed but with shorter tail and bill

Rufous Hummingbird

rufous back

adult ♂

slight golden cast above

white collar

adult ♀

immature ♂

Allen's Hummingbird
sasin

solid green back (a few adult male Rufous Hummingbirds also have green backs)

green-flecked ♂

adult ♂

Broad-tailed ♀
longer than Rufous or Allen's and has more restricted rufous

Rufous ♀
Rufous and Allen's have extensive rufous

Allen's ♀
feathers narrower in each sex and age class than Rufous

Calliope ♀
shorter than Rufous or Allen's and lacks rufous

There are also regular appearances in the Gulf Coast and Southeast regions of small numbers of Buff-bellied, Calliope, Broad-tailed, and Allen's. And since the 1990s, observers in the Mid-Atlantic, the Great Lakes, and the Northeast have been documenting regular autumn and early winter occurrences of Rufous; multiple records of Black-chinned, Calliope, and Allen's; and more and more late-lingering Ruby-throateds. Rarer still have been Broad-billeds (north to the Great Lakes and Maritimes), White-eareds (Mississippi),

Blue-throateds (east to South Carolina), Magnificents (east to Virginia), Anna's (east to New York), and Costa's (north to Minnesota, east to Alabama). Many of the more southerly birds survive the winter in the semi-mild climes and some may return in subsequent years.

When identifying hummingbirds, pay attention to plumage, overall size and structure (e.g., bill and tail length) and, especially, vocalizations.

In sum, any late-season hummingbird in the East should be closely scrutinized!

Kingfishers (Family Alcedinidae)

Stocky and short-legged, with a large head, a large bill, and, in two North American species, a ragged crest. Look for kingfishers near woodland streams and ponds and in coastal areas. They hover over water or watch from low perches, then plunge headfirst to catch a fish. With strong bill and feet, they dig nest burrows in stream banks.

Belted Kingfisher *Megaceryle alcyon L 13" (33 cm)*

The only kingfisher in most of North America. Both ***male*** and ***female*** have slate blue breast band; white belly and undertail coverts. Female has rust belly band and flanks; may be confused with female Ringed Kingfisher, note white belly and smaller size. Juvenile resembles adult but has rust spotting in breast band.
Voice: Call is a loud, dry rattle.
Range: Common and conspicuous along rivers and brooks, ponds and lakes, and estuaries but much more local during the breeding season. Generally solitary. Rare in winter north to border states.

Ringed Kingfisher *Megaceryle torquatus L 16" (41 cm)*

Larger than Belted Kingfisher; generally frequents larger rivers and ponds, perches on higher branches than Belted. Rufous underwing coverts of ***female*** distinctive in flight; white in ***male.*** Male is rust below with white undertail coverts. Female has slate blue breast, narrow white band, rust belly and undertail coverts. Juveniles resemble adult female, but juvenile male's breast is largely rust.
Voice: Calls include a harsh rattle, lower and slower than in Belted Kingfisher, and single *chack* notes, given chiefly in flight.
Range: Resident in lower Rio Grande Valley; very rare visitor elsewhere in southern and central Texas. Accidental to Oklahoma and Louisiana.

Green Kingfisher *Chloroceryle americana L 8¾" (22 cm)*

Smallest of our kingfishers with a very long bill; crest inconspicuous. ***Male*** is green above, with white collar; white below, with rufous breast and dark green spotting. ***Female*** has a band of green spots across breast. Juvenile resembles adult female. Flight is direct, low over the water, and very fast; white outer tail feathers conspicuous in flight. Often perches on low, sheltered branches. More retiring than the other kingfishers; it is often first detected by its call.
Voice: One call, a faint but sharp *tick tick,* often ends in a short rattle; another, a squeaky *cheep,* is given in flight.
Range: Uncommon and often hard to see. Resident of lower Rio Grande Valley; rarer on Edwards Plateau. Casual wanderer along the Texas coast.

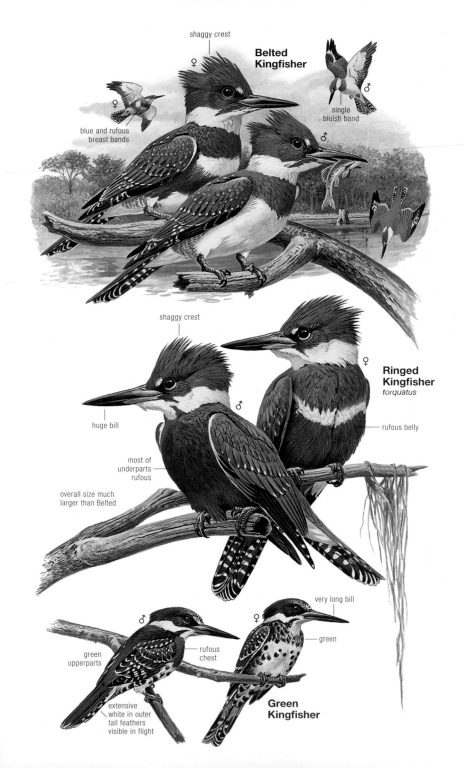

shaggy crest

Belted Kingfisher

♀

blue and rufous breast bands

single bluish band

♂

shaggy crest

Ringed Kingfisher
torquatus

huge bill

♂

♀

rufous belly

most of underparts rufous

overall size much larger than Belted

very long bill

♂

green

♀

green upperparts

rufous chest

extensive white in outer tail feathers visible in flight

Green Kingfisher

244

Woodpeckers, Allies (Family Picidae)

Strong claws, short legs, and stiff tail feathers enable woodpeckers to climb tree trunks. Sharp bill is used to chisel out insect food and nest holes and to drum a territorial signal.

Red-headed Woodpecker *Melanerpes erythrocephalus*
L 9¼" (24 cm) Entire head, neck, and throat are bright red in *adults,* contrasting with blue-black back and snowy white underparts. *Juvenile* is brownish; acquires red head during gradual winter molt. Distinctive white inner wing patches and white rump are visible in all ages in perched and flying birds. Wing patch mottled in young birds. By spring they closely resemble adults, but most retain dark barring on the secondaries.
Voice: In breeding season utters a loud *queark,* similar to Red-bellied Woodpecker (next page) but harsher and sharper; call heard year-round is a rather soft guttural rattle.
Range: Uncommon to fairly common and declining. Inhabits a variety of open and densely wooded habitats; often seen catching flies. Now rare in the Northeast, chiefly in fall; no longer breeds there regularly, due in part to habitat loss and competition with European Starlings for nest holes. Very rare to Maritime Provinces.

Acorn Woodpecker *Melanerpes formicivorus*
L 9" (23 cm) A western species. Black chin, yellowish throat, white cheeks and forehead, red cap. *Female* has smaller bill than *male;* smaller red crown patch is separated by black bar. In flight, white rump and small white patches on outer wings are conspicuous.
Voice: Most frequent call, *waka,* usually repeated several times.
Range: A small, very local population is resident in oak woods on Edwards Plateau, Texas. Casual visitor on western Great Plains. Sociable; generally found in small, noisy colonies. Eats chiefly acorns and other nuts in winter, which they store in granaries on thick tree trunks; telephone poles are also favored where available. Also eats insects in summer.

Lewis's Woodpecker *Melanerpes lewis* *L 10¾" (27 cm)*
A western species. Greenish black head and back; gray collar and breast; dark red face, pinkish belly. In flight, darkness, large size, and slow, steady wingbeats give it a crowlike appearance. *Juvenile* lacks collar and red face; belly may be only faintly pink; acquires more adultlike plumage from late fall through winter.
Voice: Generally silent.
Range: Fall and winter movements unpredictable. Very rare from western Great Plains to central Texas. Accidental elsewhere in the East, occurring at a variety of seasons. Main food, insects, mostly caught in the air; also eats fruit and nuts. Stores acorns, which it first shells, in tree bark crevices. Often perches on telephone poles.

pure white
secondaries

adult

white primary
patches

♂

**Red-headed
Woodpecker**

brownish head

juvenile

red head

female has black
forecrown bar

♀

barring on
secondaries

clown head
pattern

♂

adult

**Acorn
Woodpecker**

dark red face

browner head
and no collar

juvenile

gray collar

oily green
upperparts

**Lewis's
Woodpecker**

pink belly

adults

slow crowlike
wingbeats

Red-bellied Woodpecker *Melanerpes carolinus*

L 9¼" (24 cm) Black-and-white barred back; white uppertail coverts; barred central tail feathers. Crown and nape are red in **males. Females** have red nape only; small reddish patch or tinge on belly, usually difficult to see.

Voice: Call, a rolling *churr* or *chiv-chiv,* is slightly softer than that of Golden-fronted Woodpecker, slightly less harsh than Red-headed.

Range: Red-bellied Woodpeckers are common in open deciduous woodlands, suburbs, parks. Regularly come to feeders, particularly suet. Breeding range extending northward. Rare to Maine and Maritimes, mostly in fall and winter.

Golden-fronted Woodpecker *Melanerpes aurifrons*

L 9¾" (25 cm) Black-and-white barred back, white rump, usually an all-black tail; golden orange nape, paler in **females;** yellow feathering above bill. **Male** has a small red cap. Yellow tinge on belly not easily seen. Juvenile has streaked breast, brownish crown. In flight, all plumages show white wing patches, white rump as in Red-bellied Woodpecker; but Golden-fronted shows black, not barred, tail.

Voice: Calls are a rolling *churr-churr* and cackling *kek-kek,* are slightly louder and raspier than in Red-bellied.

Range: Fairly common in woodlands and mesquite brushlands.

Northern Flicker *Colaptes auratus* L 12½" *(32 cm)*

Two distinct groups occur: *"Yellow-shafted Flicker"* in the East and far north, and *"Red-shafted Flicker"* in the West. These flickers have a brown, barred back; spotted underparts, with black crescent bib. White rump is conspicuous in flight; no white wing patches. "Yellow-shafted Flicker" has yellow wing lining, yellow under tail, gray crown, and tan face with red crescent on nape. "Red-shafted Flicker" has brown crown and gray face, with no red crescent. "Yellow-shafted" male has a black moustachial stripe (red stripe in "Red-shafted" male); **females** lack these stripes. Intergrades are regularly seen in the Great Plains. These birds may show a mix of head colorations and patterns typical of the two "pure" groups, and the color of the wing linings and under tail may approach one or the other, or may be an intermediate, salmon color.

Voice: Call, which is heard on the breeding grounds, is a long, loud series of *wick-er* notes; a single, loud *klee-yer* is also given year-round.

Range: Common in open woodlands and suburban areas. "Red-shafted" is casual in the East in fall and winter, though many such birds are likely intergrades.

red nape

♀

pink on
lower belly

**Red-bellied
Woodpecker**

solid red crown
and nape

♂

male with red
crown

**Golden-fronted
Woodpecker**
aurifrons

♂

gold forehead

♀

gold
nape

speckled
white rump

barred

whitish primary
patch in both
Red-bellied and
Golden-fronted

♂

red nape and pale
brown face

"Yellow-shafted" ♂

male has
black whisker

pure white
rump area

dark

male has
red whisker

"Red-
shafted" ♂

brown
nape and
gray face

all North American
flickers have
white rumps

"Yellow-
shafted" ♀

**Northern
Flicker**

yellow
underwing

pinkish red
underwing

"Red-shafted" ♀

Red-cockaded Woodpecker *Picoides borealis* **E**

L 8½" (22 cm) Black-and-white barred back, black cap, and large white cheek patch identify this woodpecker; red tufts, seldom visible, on the *male*'s head. Similar Hairy and Downy Woodpeckers (next page) have solid white down backs.

Voice: Distinctive calls, a raspy *sripp* and high-pitched *tsick,* are buzzy; recall a loud Brown-headed Nuthatch.

Range: Red-cockaded inhabits open, mature pine or pine-oak woodlands. Bores nest hole only in a large living pine afflicted with heartwood disease, then drills small holes around the nest opening. Pine pitch oozing down the trunk from these holes may repel predators; also makes the tree a distinctive signpost. Populations continue to decline. Almost eliminated from Virginia, and has disappeared from Kentucky and Tennessee in the last 15 years. Accidental to northeast Illinois and Ohio.

Ladder-backed Woodpecker *Picoides scalaris*

L 7¼" (18 cm) Black-and-white barred back, spotted sides; face and underparts slightly buffy or grayish; face marked with black lines. *Male* has red crown.

Voice: Call is a crisp *pik,* very similar to Downy Woodpecker's call; also gives a descending whinny.

Range: Common in dry brushlands, mesquite and cactus country; also towns and rural areas. Feeds on beetle larvae from small trees; also eats cactus fruits and forages on the ground for insects.

Sapsuckers

These woodpeckers drill evenly spaced rows of holes in trees and then visit these "wells" for sap and the insects it attracts. Red-naped Sapsucker was formerly considered a subspecies of Yellow-bellied.

Yellow-bellied Sapsucker *Sphyrapicus varius*

L 8½" (22 cm) Red forecrown on black-and-white head; chin and throat red in *male,* white in *female.* Back is blackish, with white rump and large white wing patch. Underparts yellowish, paler in female. *Juvenile* retains largely brownish plumage until late in the winter.

Voice: Calls include nasal mewing and squeals. As with other sapsuckers, drumming starts fast and then slows.

Range: Fairly common in deciduous and mixed forests. Highly migratory.

Red-naped Sapsucker *Sphyrapicus nuchalis*

L 8½" (22 cm) A western species. Very similar to Yellow-bellied, but has variable red patch on back of head (although rare Yellow-bellied may also have red); spotting on back more clearly organized into two rows. On *male,* extensive red on throat penetrates the surrounding black "frame"; on *female,* throat is partly red to almost entirely red on some birds. Juvenile is brownish overall; resembles adult by first fall except for lack of black chest.

Voice: Similar to Yellow-bellied Sapsucker.

Range: Very rare to casual visitor to western Great Plains.

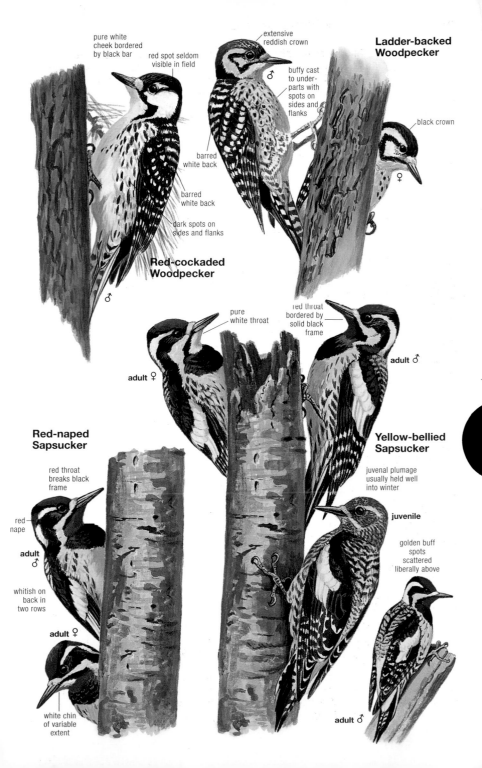

pure white cheek bordered by black bar

red spot seldom visible in field

extensive reddish crown

Ladder-backed Woodpecker

buffy cast to under-parts with spots on sides and flanks

♂

black crown

barred white back

barred white back

dark spots on sides and flanks

Red-cockaded Woodpecker

♂

pure white throat

red throat bordered by solid black frame

adult ♂

adult ♀

Red-naped Sapsucker

red throat breaks black frame

red nape

adult ♂

whitish on back in two rows

adult ♀

white chin of variable extent

Yellow-bellied Sapsucker

juvenal plumage usually held well into winter

juvenile

golden buff spots scattered liberally above

adult ♂

Downy Woodpecker *Picoides pubescens* L 6¾" (17 cm)
White back generally identifies both Downy and similar Hairy Woodpecker. Downy is smaller, with a smaller bill; outer tail feathers generally have faint dark bars or spots.
Voice: Downy's call, *pik,* and whinny are softer and higher pitched than Hairy Woodpecker's.
Range: Common; active, and somewhat unwary; often seen in suburbs, parklands, and orchards, as well as in forests. A familiar visitor to feeders.

Hairy Woodpecker *Picoides villosus* L 9¼" (24 cm)
White back generally identifies both Hairy and similar Downy Woodpecker. Hairy is larger, with a larger bill; outer tail feathers are entirely white. ***Juveniles,*** particularly in the Maritime Provinces, have some barring on back and flanks; sides may be streaked. In young males, the forehead is spotted with white; crown streaked with red or orange.
Voice: Hairy's calls include a loud, sharp *peek* and a slurred whinny.
Range: Fairly common; inhabits both open and dense forests. Also visits feeders. Uncommon to rare in the South and in Florida.

American Three-toed Woodpecker *Picoides dorsalis*
L 8¾" (22 cm) Black-and-white barring down center of back distinguishes most races of American Three-toed Woodpecker from similar Black-backed. Both have heavily barred sides. ***Male***'s yellow cap is usually more extensive in Three-toed but less solid. New English and scientific names reflect a recent split: The eight Old World subspecies are now considered their own species, *P. tridactylus.* In East *bacatus* found over much of range; westerly *fasciatus* is resident from northern and western Northwest Territories to western Saskatchewan.
Voice: Call a soft *pik* or *kimp.* Drum becomes slightly faster and weaker toward end.
Range: American Three-toed is found in coniferous forests, especially in burned-over areas. Scarcer than Black-backed in the East. Accidental south to Rhode Island in winter; Rocky Mountain subspecies *dorsalis* east to southwest Kansas—in summer.

Black-backed Woodpecker *Picoides arcticus*
L 9½" (24 cm) Solid black back, heavily barred sides. ***Male*** has a solid yellow cap. Compare especially with eastern race of Three-toed Woodpecker, *bacatus,* which has a darker back than other Three-toeds. Black-backed Woodpecker is larger; has longer, stouter bill; and lacks white streak behind the eye.
Voice: Call note is a single, sharp *pik* or flat *kuk,* lower pitched than call of Three-toed.
Range: Black-backed inhabits coniferous forests; often found in burned-over areas. Forages on dead conifers, flaking away large patches of loose bark rather than drilling into it, in search of larvae and insects. Casual south of mapped range in the East; fewer records in recent decades.

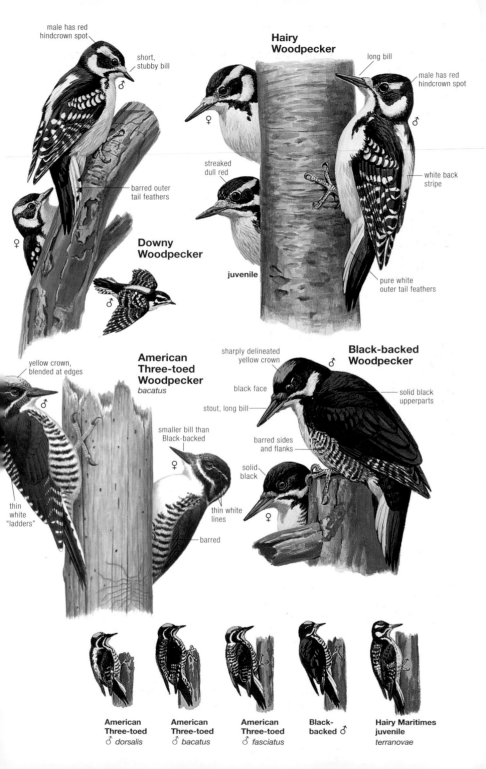

male has red
hindcrown spot

short,
stubby bill

♂

barred outer
tail feathers

♀

**Downy
Woodpecker**

♂

**Hairy
Woodpecker**

long bill

male has red
hindcrown spot

♀

♂

streaked
dull red

white back
stripe

juvenile

pure white
outer tail feathers

yellow crown,
blended at edges

♂

**American
Three-toed
Woodpecker**
bacatus

sharply delineated
yellow crown

black face

stout, long bill

smaller bill than
Black-backed

♀

♂

**Black-backed
Woodpecker**

solid black
upperparts

barred sides
and flanks

thin white
"ladders"

thin white
lines

barred

solid
black

♀

**American
Three-toed
♂ *dorsalis***

**American
Three-toed
♂ *bacatus***

**American
Three-toed
♂ *fasciatus***

**Black-
backed ♂**

**Hairy Maritimes
juvenile**
terranovae

Ivory-billed Woodpecker *Campephilus principalis* **E**
L 19½" (50 cm) In Apr. 2005 came the much publicized announcement that this species had been rediscovered more than a year earlier in the Big Woods of the White River-Cache River system of eastern Arkansas. Documentation was provided in the form of sound recordings and videotape. However, intense subsequent searching has yet to produce more documentation; some authorities now question the conclusions reached from the original evidence. Recent unconfirmed reports from north Florida. For identification note Ivory-billed's black chin, striking ivory bill, and the extensive white wing patches and scapular lines, visible in perched birds; tail longer than Pileated, especially visible in flight. *Female* has black rather than red crest. Compare also the black-and-white wing patterns of Ivory-billeds and Pileateds in flight; in Ivory-billed from below, white leading edge and white secondaries are divided by a black bar; viewed from above, white secondaries are diagnostic; flight of Ivory-billed is more direct and swift.
Voice: Distinctive call note sounds like a toy trumpet, a high-pitched, nasal *yank,* given singly or in short series, like a loud version of the call of eastern White-breasted Nuthatch, but beware of Blue Jays giving similar calls; double-rap drum is characteristic of genus *Campephilus.*
Range: Formerly found north to the Ohio River, near its confluence with the Mississippi. Ivory-billed required large tracts of old-growth river forest; dead and dying trees supplied nesting sites and food: the larvae of wood-boring beetles. Destruction of habitat at the end of the 19th century and early in the 20th century led to the disappearance of this never-common species. Last definite records from U.S. were in 1944 in the Singer Tract, near Tallulah in northeastern Louisiana. Possibly valid sightings recorded into the 1950s in Florida; from 1948, perhaps into the 1980s in Cuba (subspecies *bairdii*), but now probably extinct there. Additional unconfirmed sightings over the last 50 years include those from eastern Texas, Louisiana, Georgia, and Florida.

Pileated Woodpecker *Dryocopus pileatus*

L 16½" (42 cm) Perched bird is almost entirely black on back and wings. White chin and dark bill also distinguish Pileated Woodpecker, along with smaller size. Compare also the wing patterns of the two species in flight; also note Pileated's deep, slow, crowlike wingbeats. This is the largest woodpecker now generally seen in North America. *Female*'s red cap is less extensive than in *male.* Juvenal plumage, held briefly, resembles adult's but is duller and browner overall. Generally shy.
Voice: Call is a loud *wuck* note or series of notes, given all year, often in flight; similar call of Northern Flicker is given only in the breeding season. Listen for its loud, resonant, territorial drumming, given by both sexes but less frequently by females.
Range: Prefers dense, mature forest as well as woodlots and parklands. Look for the long rectangular or oval holes it excavates. Carpenter ants in fallen trees and stumps are its major food. Common in Southeast; uncommon elsewhere.

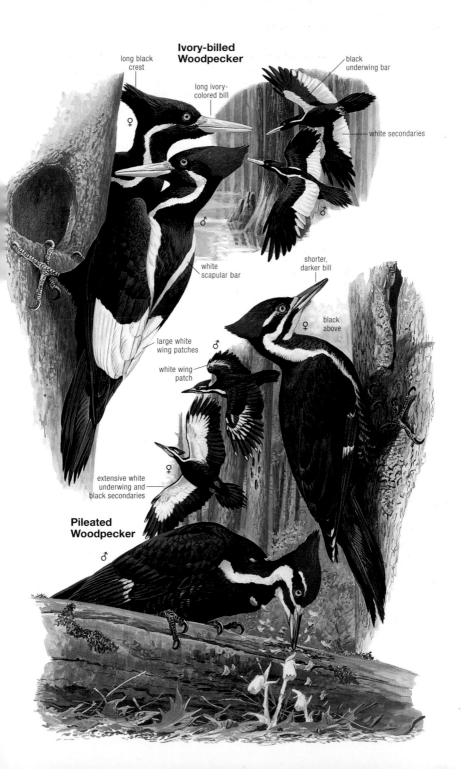

Ivory-billed Woodpecker

long black crest

long ivory-colored bill

black underwing bar

white secondaries

♀

♂

white scapular bar

♂

large white wing patches

white wing patch

♀

extensive white underwing and black secondaries

shorter, darker bill

♀

black above

Pileated Woodpecker

♂

Tyrant Flycatchers (Family Tyrannidae)

A typical flycatcher darts out from a fixed perch to catch insects. Most have a large head, bristly "whiskers," and a broad-based, flat bill.

Olive-sided Flycatcher *Contopus cooperi* L 7½" (19 cm)
Large, with rather short tail. Brownish olive above; white tufts on sides of rump distinctive but often not visible. Throat, center of breast, and belly dull white. Sides and flanks brownish olive and streaked. Bill is mostly dark; center and sometimes base of lower mandible dull orange.
Voice: Distinctive song, a clear *quick-three-beers*, the second note higher; typical call, a repeated *pip*.
Range: Uncommon and declining; breeds in coniferous forests and bogs. Often perches on high, dead branches, including in migration. Very rare in coastal Southeast.

Eastern Wood-Pewee *Contopus virens* L 6¼" (16 cm)
Plumage generally dark grayish olive above, with dull white throat, darker breast; underparts whitish or pale yellow. Bill of **adult** has dark upper mandible, dull orange lower mandible. **Juvenile** and immature may have all-dark bill.
Voice: Distinctive song is a clear, slow, plaintive *pee-a-wee*, the second note lower; this phrase often alternates with a downslurred *pee-yer*. Calls include a loud *chip* and clear, whistled, rising *pweee* notes; often given together, *chip pweee*.
Range: Common in a variety of woodland habitats. No winter records in U.S.

Western Wood-Pewee *Contopus sordidulus*
L 6¼" (16 cm) Plumage variable; slightly darker and less greenish than Eastern Wood-Pewee; base of lower mandible usually shows some yellow-orange. Identification very difficult; best done by range and voice.
Voice: Calls include a harsh, slightly descending *peeer* and clear whistles suggestive of Eastern's *pee-yer*. Song, heard chiefly on breeding grounds, has three-note *tswee-tee-teet* phrases mixed with the *peeer* note.
Range: Uncommon migrant (possible breeder) on western Great Plains; casual elsewhere in East. No midwinter records in U.S.

Northern Beardless-Tyrannulet *Camptostoma imberbe* L 4½" (11 cm)
Grayish olive above and on breast; dull white or pale yellow below. Indistinct whitish eyebrow; small, slightly curved bill. Crown is darker than nape in many birds and often raised in a bushy crest. Distinguished from similar Ruby-crowned Kinglet (page 300) by buffy wing bars and lack of bold eye ring. Most easily located by voice.
Voice: Song on breeding grounds is a descending series of loud, clear *peer* notes; call, an innocuous, whistled *pee-yerp*.
Range: Rather uncommon in U.S. Often found in mesquite woodland and oak mottes.

mostly
dark bill

chunky body shape

dark breast
sides with
diffuse
streaking

white extends up
through center

white flank
patches show
periodically
from above

Olive-sided
Flycatcher

adults

long
wings

short
tail

usually adults
have orange
lower mandible

juveniles
can have
all-dark bill

slightly paler
nape than
Western

Eastern
Wood-
Pewee

variations

fresh
spring
adult

worn
late-summer
adult

long primary
projection

juvenile

Western
Wood-Pewee

short, pale
supercilium

variations

Northern
Beardless-
Tyrannulet

can raise crest

rounded bill tip
with orange base

faint wing bars

worn
adult

paler
adult

darker
adult

fresh

averages darker plumage with darker lower
mandible than Eastern, but identification
safely done only by voice

Flycatchers

Empidonax Flycatchers

Empids are drab, with pale eye rings and wing bars. From spring to summer, plumages grow duller from wear. Some species molt before fall migration, acquiring fresh plumage in late summer. Identification depends on voice, nesting habitat, behavior, and subtle differences in size, bill shape, primary projection, and tail length. Most flip tails up.

Acadian Flycatcher *Empidonax virescens* L 5¾" (15 cm)
Olive above, with thin yellowish eye ring, two buffy or whitish wing bars; very long primary projection. Long, broad-based bill, with mostly yellowish lower mandible. Most birds show pale grayish throat, pale olive wash across upper breast, white lower breast, and yellow belly and undertail coverts. Molts before migration; *fall* birds have buffy wing bars. Juvenile is brownish olive above, edged with buff.
Voice: Call is a soft *peace,* extended in song to an emphatic *pee-tsup,* accented on first syllable. On breeding grounds, also gives a flickerlike *ti ti ti ti ti.*
Range: Found in woodlands and swamps.

Yellow-bellied Flycatcher *Empidonax flaviventris*
L 5½" (14 cm) Has rather short tail and big head. Olive above, yellow below. Broad yellow eye ring. Lower mandible entirely pale orange. Shows a more extensive olive wash across breast than Acadian Flycatcher; lacks pale area between olive and yellow belly. Also, throat is yellow, rather than whitish; bill smaller. Molts after migration; *worn fall* migrants slightly grayer above, duller below.
Voice: Song is a liquid *je-bunk;* also a plaintive, rising *per-wee.* Call, a sharp, whistled *chiu* that sounds somewhat like Acadian.
Range: Nests in bogs, swamps, and damp coniferous woods. Very rare migrant in coastal Southeast, mostly in fall.

IDENTIFYING: Flycatchers Many of our most difficult identification challenges can be found within the tyrant flycatcher family. As with other difficult groups, it's best to start with determining the genus before identifying the species. Each genus has its own structural and behavior clues for identification. For instance, the *Contopus* (Pewees) are long winged and rather short tailed; they take long flights from a perch and sit still upon returning. The similarly colored *Empidonax* take shorter flights in pursuit of prey and often work within the canopy. Nearly all species flip their tail up when they return to a perch. *Empidonax* have much shorter primary projection and longer tails than *Contopus*. *Myiarchus* flycatchers (only Great Crested is regular in the East), which are also long tailed and short winged, tend to feed within the canopy, whereas most species of *Tyrannus* (kingbirds) are longer winged and shorter tailed and feed out in the open. The three species of *Sayornis* (Phoebes) and the closely related genus *Pyrocephalus* (Vermilion Flycatcher) all bob their tails downward. The species within *Empidonax* are notoriously difficult to identify. They are best separated by song, but even contact calls are in some cases diagnostic, and unlike the song, these calls are given year-round. Individuals will often be silent for long periods of time, so it is best to follow one around until it calls. Before identifying any *Empidonax* by sight, it is always essential to eliminate a pewee first. In addition to noting structural differences, watch for tail movement—or the lack of it. Once the bird is sorted with certainty to *Empidonax*, there are several general features to look for. These

Acadian Flycatcher

thin yellowish eye ring

fall

long primary projection

longer, stout bill

worn summer adult

greenish above

spring

Yellow-bellied Flycatcher

conspicuous circular yellow eye ring

short bill

1st fall

yellow throat and belly

olive breast

worn fall adult

spring

include the length and shape of the bill, the extent of color on the lower mandible, the shape and strength of the eye ring, and the overall coloration, both above and below. Also keep in mind the distributional patterns of each species. Of the five species that occur in the East, only Acadian is a trans-Gulf migrant, the others— along with most flycatchers—take a circum-Gulf route through south Texas. This means that migrants seen on or near the Gulf Coast from eastern Texas to Florida, especially in spring, are overwhelmingly Acadian. In spring, Leasts along with some Acadians are the earliest arrivals while Yellow-bellieds and Alders are the latest. Finally, at the western edge of the region, several western species are regular migrants, and a number of them have occurred casually in the East. Most of these are duller in coloration and

have paler wings with less contrasting wingbars and tertial edges.

Eastern Wood-Pewee
Contopus

Least Flycatcher
Empidonax

Willow Flycatcher *Empidonax traillii L 5¾" (15 cm)*

Lacks prominent eye ring. Nominate eastern race has pale gray head and greenish back. Slightly larger and longer billed than Least. Distinguished from pewees (page 254) by shorter wings, upward flicks of tail, and voice. Formerly considered conspecific with Alder Flycatcher and collectively known as "Traill's" Flycatcher; given the very similar appearance mostly silent birds seen in the field are best referred to as simply "Traill's."

Voice: Call is a liquid *wit.* Songs are a sneezy *fitz-bew,* and, on breeding grounds, also a rising *brreet;* Willow Flycatcher often sings in spring migration.

Range: Found in brushy habitats in wet areas. Quite local in southern portion of breeding range. Casual migrant in coastal Southeast. Most eastern birds winter in northern South America.

Alder Flycatcher *Empidonax alnorum L 5¾" (15 cm)*

Very similar to Willow Flycatcher, but bill is slightly shorter, eye ring usually more prominent, back greener. Distinguished from eastern race of Willow by darker head; from western races (not yet recorded from East) by well defined tertial edges, bolder wing bars, long primary projection. Also compare carefully to Least Flycatcher, which is browner above, has a shorter bill with a dark tip to lower mandible, and has a very different call note. Best identified by voice.

Voice: Call is a loud *pip* or *pep.* Song is a falling, wheezy *weebee-a* or *weeb-ew.* On breeding grounds, Alder Flycatcher also gives a descending *wheer.*

Range: Common in brushy habitats in and near bogs and swamps and in birch and alder thickets. Arrives in spring a bit later than Willow Flycatcher. Very rare migrant in coastal Southeast, mostly in fall. Winters in South America.

Least Flycatcher *Empidonax minimus L 5¼" (13 cm)*

Smallest eastern empid. Large-headed; bold but variable white eye ring; rather short primary projection. Throat whitish; breast washed with gray; belly and undertail coverts pale yellow or whitish. Bill short, triangular; lower mandible mostly pale. Molt occurs after fall migration. ***First-fall*** has buffier wing bars.

Voice: Song, a dry *che-bek* accented on the second syllable, is usually delivered in a rapid series; call, a sharp *whit,* is sometimes also given in a series. Of the eastern *Empidonax,* Least Flycatcher tends to vocalize most in migration.

Range: Inhabits deciduous woods, orchards, and parks. Fairly common. Least is the first *Empidonax* to arrive in spring in the East. Rare migrant in coastal Southeast. Most birds winter in Mexico and Central America, a few in Florida; casual in winter elsewhere along Gulf Coast.

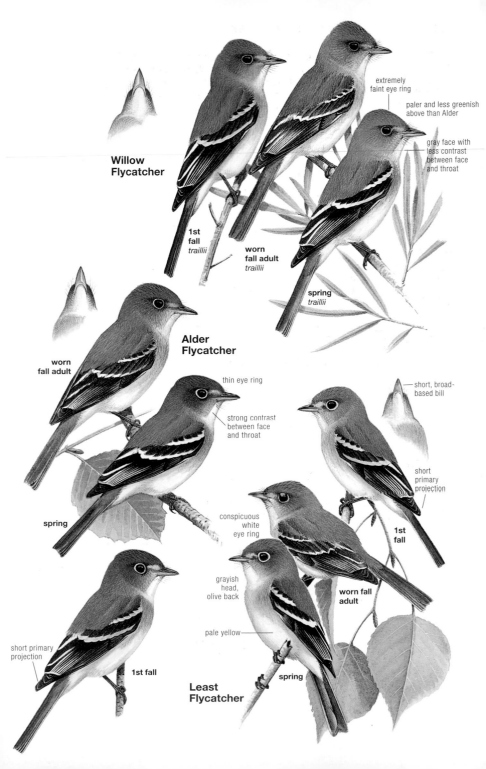

Willow Flycatcher

1st fall
traillii

worn
fall adult
traillii

extremely
faint eye ring

paler and less greenish
above than Alder

gray face with
less contrast
between face
and throat

spring
traillii

**Alder
Flycatcher**

worn
fall adult

thin eye ring

strong contrast
between face
and throat

short, broad-
based bill

short
primary
projection

spring

1st
fall

conspicuous
white
eye ring

grayish
head,
olive back

worn fall
adult

short primary
projection

1st fall

pale yellow

spring

**Least
Flycatcher**

Hammond's Flycatcher   *Empidonax hammondii*
L 5½" (14 cm) A small empid, with a fairly large head and short tail. White eye ring, usually expanded in a "teardrop" at rear. Grayish head and throat; grayish olive back; gray or olive wash on breast and sides; belly tinged with pale yellow. Molt occurs before migration; *fall* birds are much brighter olive above and on sides of breast, yellower below. Medium-length, slightly notched tail is edged with gray. Bill is slightly shorter, thinner, and usually somewhat darker than in similar Dusky and Least Flycatchers; primary projection is longer.
Voice: Call note is a sharp *peek*. Song resembles Dusky's but is hoarser and lower pitched, especially on the second note.
Range: Very rare migrant on the western Great Plains. Casual fall and winter vagrant in the East.

Gray Flycatcher   *Empidonax wrightii* L 6" (15 cm)
Gray above, with a slight olive tinge in fresh fall plumage; whitish below, belly washed with pale yellow by late fall. Head is disproportionately small and rounded; white eye ring inconspicuous on pale gray face. Long bill; on most birds, lower mandible mostly pinkish orange at base, sharply divided from dark tip; on a few, entire lower mandible is pinkish orange. Short primary projection. Long tail, with thin whitish outer edge. Perched bird dips its tail down, like a phoebe.
Voice: Song is a vigorous *chi-wip* or *chi-bit,* followed by a liquid *whilp,* trailing off in a gurgle. Call, a loud *wit.*
Range: Very rare to casual fall migrant on the western Great Plains. Accidental fall and winter vagrant in the East.

Dusky Flycatcher   *Empidonax oberholseri* L 5¾" (15 cm)
Grayish olive above; yellowish below, with whitish throat, pale olive wash on upper breast. White eye ring. Bill partly dark, orange at base of lower mandible blending into dark tip. Bill and tail slightly longer than Hammond's Flycatcher. Short primary projection. Molt occurs after fall migration; fresh late-fall birds are quite yellow below.
Voice: Calls include a *wit* note, softer than Gray Flycatcher. Song has several phrases: A clear *sillit;* an upslurred *ggrrreep;* another high *sillit,* often omitted; and a clear, high *pweet.*
Range: Rare migrant on the western Great Plains. Accidental fall and winter vagrant in the East.

Cordilleran Flycatcher   *Empidonax occidentalis*
L 5¾" (15 cm) Formerly considered same species as Pacific-slope Flycatcher and together known as the "Western Flycatcher." Nearly identical but slightly larger, darker, and greener above; more olive and yellow below.
Voice: Separable in field only by male's call, a two-note *pit peet;* also a *seet* note, perhaps slightly sharper in Cordilleran than in Pacific-slope Flycatcher.
Range: Rare to casual migrant on the western Great Plains. Several late fall records of "Western Flycatcher" in the East probably or definitely pertain to Pacific-slope.

short, thin-based bill

western species of *Empidonax* have slightly browner wings (less blackish) than eastern species

Hammond's Flycatcher

fall

spring

bill longer than Hammond's and has extensive pale base with dark tip

Gray Flycatcher

short primary projection

winter

spring

long tail, often bobbed down like a phoebe unlike all other *Empidonax*

Dusky Flycatcher

1st fall

fall birds are dull; compare to Gray

worn fall adult

mainly yellow below in fresh plumage; throat paler

moderately long but thin-based bill

winter

spring

short primary projection

long tail

eye ring extends slightly beyond eye

all-orange lower mandible

usually slight break to eye ring

olive sides to breast have slight brownish tint

spring

Cordilleran Flycatcher

longer tail projection than Yellow-bellied

Eastern Phoebe *Sayornis phoebe L 7" (18 cm)*

Brownish gray above, darkest on head, wings, and tail. Under-parts mostly white with pale olive wash on sides and breast; *fresh fall* birds are washed with yellow below. Molts before migration. All phoebes are distinguished from pewees (page 254) by their habit of pumping down and spreading their tails; Eastern Phoebe also by all-dark bill and lack of distinct wing bars. Also compare lack of eye rings and wing bars with *Empidonax* flycatchers (preceding pages).

Voice: Distinctive song, a harsh, emphatic *fee-be,* accented on first syllable. Typical call note is a sharp *chip.*

Range: Common in woodlands, farmlands, and suburbs; often nests under bridges, in eaves and rafters. An early spring and late fall migrant, especially for a flycatcher.

Black Phoebe *Sayornis nigricans L 6¾" (17 cm)*

Black head, upperparts, and breast; white belly and undertail coverts. *Juvenal* plumage, held briefly, is browner, with two cinnamon wing bars, cinnamon rump.

Voice: Four-syllable song, a rising *pee-wee* followed by a descending *pee-wee.* Calls include a loud *tseee* and a sharper *tsip,* slightly more plaintive than Eastern Phoebe's call.

Range: Uncommon; found near water; casual to Oklahoma, accidental Minnesota, Florida.

Say's Phoebe *Sayornis saya L 7½" (19 cm)*

Grayish brown above, darkest on head, wings, and tail; breast and throat pale grayish brown; belly and undertail coverts tawny.

Voice: Song is a fast *pit-tse-ar,* often given in fluttering flight. Typical call, a plaintive, whistled *pee-ee,* slightly downslurred.

Range: Fairly common in dry, open areas, canyons, cliffs; perches on bushes, boulders, fences. Highly migratory; casual in eastern North America.

Vermilion Flycatcher *Pyrocephalus rubinus L 6" (15 cm)*

Adult male strikingly red and brown. *Adult female* grayish brown above, with blackish tail; throat and breast white, with dusky streaking; belly and undertail coverts are peach; note also whitish eyebrow and forehead. *Juvenile* resembles adult female but is spotted rather than streaked below; belly white, often with yellowish tinge. *Immature male* begins to resemble adult by midwinter.

Voice: Male in breeding season sings during fluttery display flight. Song, a soft, tinkling *pit-a-see pit-a-see;* also sings while perched. Typical call note is a sharp, thin *pseep.* Frequently pumps and spreads its tail down.

Range: Found along streamsides, and near small wooded ponds. Rare winter visitor to the Gulf Coast states. Casual elsewhere in eastern North America, primarily in fall.

Eastern Phoebe

worn summer adult

dark cap and face

fresh fall

pale yellow belly in fresh plumage

Black Phoebe

blackish

phoebes drop their tail down

sharply contrasting white belly

juvenile

Say's Phoebe

grayish back

tawny belly

blackish tail

Vermilion Flycatcher

dark face

immature ♀

streaked breast

pale supercilium

immature ♂

adult ♂

adult ♀

pale pinkish

juvenile

spotted breast

Great Crested Flycatcher *Myiarchus crinitus*

L 8½" (21 cm) Dark olive above. Gray throat and breast; bright lemon yellow belly and undertail coverts. Note broad, sharply contrasting edge to inner tertial. Outer tail feathers show entirely reddish inner webs.
Voice: Distinctive call, a loud whistled *wheep;* sometimes given in a quick series. Song is a clear, loud *queeleep, queelur, queeleep.*
Range: Common in a wide variety of open woods; feeds high in the canopy.

Ash-throated Flycatcher *Myiarchus cinerascens*

L 7¾" (19 cm) Grayish brown above; throat and breast pale gray; underparts paler than in Brown-crested. Tail shows rufous on inner webs with dark tips. As in all *Myiarchus* flycatchers, brief *juvenal* plumage shows mostly reddish tail.
Voice: Distinctive call, heard year-round, is a rough *prrrt.* Song, heard on breeding grounds, is a series of burry *ka-brick* notes.
Range: Common in a wide variety of habitats. Casual to very rare late fall and winter visitor to East.

Brown-crested Flycatcher *Myiarchus tyrannulus*

L 8¾" (22 cm) Brownish olive above; as in all *Myiarchus* flycatchers, shows a bushy crest, rufous in primaries; bill longer, thicker, broader than Ash-throated Flycatcher. Throat and breast are pale gray; belly slightly paler yellow than in Great Crested Flycatcher. Tail feathers show reddish on outer two-thirds of inner webs. Texas race, *cooperi,* is smaller than southwestern *magister.*
Voice: Song is a clear musical whistle, a rolling *whit-will-do.* Call is a sharp *whit.*
Range: Fairly common in woodlands, river groves, and well-vegetated residential areas. Very rare in Louisiana (specimens of both *cooperi* and *magister*) and Florida, mostly in winter.

Great Kiskadee *Pitangus sulphuratus* *L 9¾" (25 cm)*

Yellow crown patch on black-and-white head often concealed. Brown above, with reddish brown wings and tail. Found chiefly in wet woodlands or near watercourses; in addition to flycatching, dives for fish.
Voice: Calls include a slow, deliberate *kis-ka-dee* and a loud *kreah,* given all year.
Range: Common. Casual vagrant north to Kansas and along Gulf Coast to Louisiana. Introduced to Bermuda.

La Sagra's Flycatcher *Myiarchus sagrae* *L 7½" (19 cm)*

Vagrant from West Indies. Grayish brown upperparts, mainly white underparts suggestive of Ash-throated Flycatcher, but bill longer; inner tertial edge stronger; rufous on outer tail less extensive. Often appears somewhat dopey looking, hunched forward.
Voice: Distinctive call is a rather high-pitched *wink,* which is often doubled.
Range: Native to woodlands of Bahamas, Cuba, and Caymans. Casual visitor, mainly in winter and spring, to south Florida; accidental to Alabama.

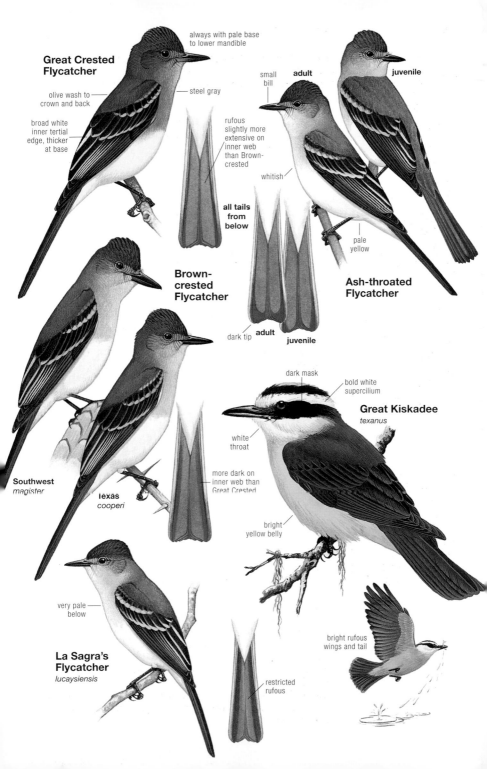

Great Crested Flycatcher

always with pale base to lower mandible

steel gray

olive wash to crown and back

broad white inner tertial edge, thicker at base

rufous slightly more extensive on inner web than Brown-crested

all tails from below

Brown-crested Flycatcher

dark tip   **adult**

juvenile

Ash-throated Flycatcher

small bill

adult

juvenile

whitish

pale yellow

Southwest
magister

Texas
cooperi

more dark on inner web than Great Crested

dark mask

bold white supercilium

Great Kiskadee
texanus

white throat

bright yellow belly

La Sagra's Flycatcher
lucaysiensis

very pale below

restricted rufous

bright rufous wings and tail

Cassin's Kingbird *Tyrannus vociferans* L 9" (23 cm)

Dark brown tail; narrow buffy tips and lack of white edges on outer tail feathers help distinguish this species from Western Kingbird. Bill is much shorter than in Tropical and Couch's Kingbirds. Upperparts darker gray than in Western, washed with olive on back; paler wings contrast with darker back. White chin contrasts with dark gray head and breast. Belly dull yellow. *Juvenile* is duller, slightly browner above, with bold buffy edges on wing coverts; paler below.

Voice: Most common call, given year-round, is a short, loud *chi-bew*, accented on second syllable.

Range: Uncommon and local along western edge of Great Plains; casual to Florida; accidental elsewhere in East.

Western Kingbird *Tyrannus verticalis* L 8¾" (22 cm)

Black tail, with white edges on outer feathers. Bill much shorter than in Tropical and Couch's Kingbirds. Upperparts ashy gray, paler than in Cassin's Kingbird, tinged with olive on back; dark wings contrast with paler back. Throat and breast pale gray; belly bright lemon yellow. *Juvenile* has slightly more olive on back and buffy edges on wing coverts, brownish tinge on breast, paler yellow belly.

Voice: Common call is a sharp *whit*.

Range: Common in open country; perches on fences, telephone lines. Some pairs breed east to Mississippi River Valley and beyond. Regular straggler in fall and early winter along the East Coast from the Maritime Provinces south; winters in small numbers in central and southern Florida.

Couch's Kingbird *Tyrannus couchii* L 9¼" (24 cm)

Almost identical to Tropical Kingbird, with thicker, broader-based bill; back slightly greener and less gray; at close range, tips of individual primaries are evenly spaced on *adult*. Distinguished from Western and Cassin's Kingbirds by larger bill, darker ear patch, and slightly notched brown tail. Juvenile is duller overall, with buffy edges on wing coverts.

Voice: Distinctive calls, a shrill, rolling *breeeer;* and a more common *kip*, similar to call of Western Kingbird, given singly or in a series.

Range: Common in the lower Rio Grande Valley in summer; uncommon in winter. Found in groves and shrubs. Casual on Gulf Coast in fall and winter. Accidental to Michigan and East Coast.

Tropical Kingbird *Tyrannus melancholicus* L 9¼" (24 cm)

Almost identical to Couch's Kingbird. Bill is thinner and longer; back slightly grayer, less green; at close range, tips of individual primaries are unevenly staggered on *adult*. Distinguished from Western and Cassin's Kingbirds by larger bill, darker ear patch, and slightly notched brown tail.

Voice: Distinctive call is a rapid, twittering *pip-pip-pip-pip*.

Range: Uncommon in Rio Grande Valley, Texas; usually found near water. Accidental to Great Lakes region and East Coast, mostly in fall.

Cassin's adult ♂

Western adult ♂

Tropical adult ♂

Couch's adult ♂

Cassin's Kingbird

juvenile

dark gray head, back, and breast

adults

brownish gray wings — usually paler than back

spring adult ♂

worn fall adult

usually pale tip

Western Kingbird

darker wings contrast with gray back

pale gray head and back

juvenile

adults

spring adult ♂

worn fall adult

black tail with white edge

Couch's Kingbird

broad-based bill

spring adult ♂

adults

Tropical Kingbird

longer, thinner-based bill

yellow more extensive below than Western

best identified by calls

even spacing of tips

primary tips adult ♂

spring adult ♂

uneven spacing of tips

adult ♂ primary tips

Gray Kingbird *Tyrannus dominicensis L 9" (23 cm)*
Pale gray above, with blackish mask. Red crown patch seldom visible. Bill long and thick. Underparts mostly white, with pale yellowish wash on belly and undertail coverts when in fresh plumage. Deeply notched tail is slightly longer than Eastern's and lacks white terminal band. Juvenal plumage, held well into fall, is browner above.
Voice: Song is a buzzy, twittering *pecheer-ry,* accented on second syllable.
Range: Common on the Florida Keys, local in mangroves on the mainland. Casual spring and fall wanderer north along the Atlantic coast to the Maritimes, inland to Michigan and Ontario, and along the Gulf Coast to Texas.

Eastern Kingbird *Tyrannus tyrannus L 8½" (22 cm)*
Black head, slate gray back; tail has a broad white terminal band. Underparts are white, with a pale gray wash across the breast. Orange-red crown patch is seldom visible. **Juvenile** brownish gray above, darker on breast.
Voice: Call is a harsh *dzeet* note, also given in a series.
Range: Common and conspicuous in woodland clearings, farms, and orchards; often seen perched on fence lines and near water. Winters in South America.

Fork-tailed Flycatcher *Tyrannus savana L 14½" (37 cm)*
Widespread tropical species; vagrant to U.S. and Canada. Extremely long black tail flutters in flight. Black cap, white underparts, white wing linings distinguish it from Scissor-tailed Flycatcher. Many sightings are of **immatures,** which resemble **adult** but have a much shorter tail.
Voice: Mostly silent in U.S. and Canada.
Range: Casual vagrant on Atlantic coast and in Texas; accidental elsewhere: recorded north to southern Canada, mostly in fall but also in spring; a few winter records in Texas and Florida.

Scissor-tailed Flycatcher *Tyrannus forficatus*
L 13" (33 cm) Pearl gray above; whitish below with orange-buff flanks and salmon pink underwing, which is best viewed in flight. Has very long outer tail feathers, white with black tips. **Male**'s tail is longer than female's; **juvenile** is paler overall, with shorter tail. Tail remains largely rigid in flight.
Voice: Song and calls similar to Western Kingbird.
Range: Common; found in semi-open country. Scissor-tailed is an early spring and late fall migrant. Very rare to casual wanderer in much of North America outside normal range; also very rarely nests east to Virginia and North Carolina. Winters in small numbers in southern Texas and Florida.

Gray Kingbird

dark mask

long, stout bill

gray on head and back

Eastern Kingbird

blackish

small bill

juvenile

black cap

gray back

adult

white tail tip

immature

Fork-tailed Flycatcher

very long, forked black tail

shorter tail

Scissor-tailed Flycatcher

juvenile

pale gray head and back

juvenile

reddish pink

adult ♂

long forked tail with extensive white; female has shorter tail

orange buff

adult ♂

Becards

Becards are possibly related to the tyrannid flycatchers. Tropical in distribution, just one species barely reaches the southern U.S.

Rose-throated Becard *Pachyramphus aglaiae*
L 7¼" (18 cm) Rosy throat distinctive in male; **adult male** of eastern Mexico, *gravis,* has blackish cap, pale gray underparts. **Female** has slate gray crown, rufous back. First-fall male shows partially pink throat; acquires full adult plumage after second summer. Foot-long nest is suspended from a tree limb.
Voice: Call, thin, mournful *seeoo*, sometimes preceded by chatter.
Range: Very rare (mostly in winter, but has bred) along lower Rio Grande, Texas.

Shrikes (Family Laniidae)

These masked hunters scan the countryside from lookout perches, then swoop down on insects, rodents, snakes, and small birds. Known as butcher-birds, they often impale their prey on thorns. Recent research indicates that this is to mark territory and attract mates.

Loggerhead Shrike *Lanius ludovicianus* L 9" (23 cm)
Slightly smaller and darker than Northern Shrike. Head and back medium gray; underparts white, clean or very faintly barred. Broad black mask extends above eye and thinly across top of bill. All-dark bill, shorter than in Northern Shrike, with smaller hook. Rump varies from gray to whitish. **Juvenile** is paler and barred overall, with brownish gray upperparts; acquires **adult** plumage by first fall. Seen in flight, wings and tail are darker and white wing patches smaller than in Northern Mockingbird (page 310).
Voice: Song is a medley of low warbles and harsh, squeaky notes; calls include a harsh *shack-shack*.
Range: Loggerheads hunt in open or brushy areas, diving from a low perch, then rising swiftly to the next lookout. Uncommon to fairly common but declining over much of range; rare to very rare in the eastern Midwest; has disappeared from the Northeast, where now a casual visitor.

Northern Shrike *Lanius excubitor* L 10" (25 cm)
Larger than Loggerhead Shrike, with paler head and back, lightly barred underparts; rump whitish. Mask is narrower than in Loggerhead, does not extend above eye; feathering above bill is white. Bill longer, with a more distinct hook. Often bobs its tail. **Juvenile** is brownish above and more heavily barred below than adult. **Immature** is grayer; retains barring on underparts until first spring.
Voice: Song and calls are similar to those of Loggerhead.
Range: Uncommon; often perches high in tall trees. Southern range limit and numbers on wintering grounds vary unpredictably from year to year.

slaty head

rose throat

blackish cap

adult ♂

Rose-throated Becard
gravis

buffy cinnamon body

♀

Northern Mockingbird for comparison

Loggerhead Shrike

black extends across forehead

darker gray

adults

stubby black bill

juvenile

gray forehead

paler gray

Northern Shrike

longer bill with distinct hook

faint mask with white eye ring

brownish on head and upperparts

adult

immature

barred underparts

juvenile

Vireos (Family Vireonidae)

Short, sturdy bills slightly hooked at the tip characterize these small songbirds. Vireos are closely related to shrikes. Some have "spectacles" and wing bars. Others have eyebrow stripes and no wing bars. They are generally chunkier and less active than warblers.

White-eyed Vireo *Vireo griseus* L 5" (13 cm)

Grayish olive above; white below, with pale yellow sides and flanks; two whitish wing bars; yellow spectacles. Distinctive white iris visible at close range. Juvenile is duller, with gray or brown iris. Subspecies on the Florida Keys, *maynardi,* is grayer above, with less yellow below; bill larger. Southern Texas race, *micrus,* is colored like *maynardi,* but smaller.

Voice: Typical song is a loud, variable five- to seven-note phrase usually beginning and ending with a sharp *chick;* also gives a chatter call suggestive of House Wren.

Range: Casual vagrant north across southern Canada.

Black-capped Vireo *Vireo atricapilla* **E**

L 4½" (11 cm) Olive above, white below, with yellow flanks and yellowish wing bars. Hard to see, stays hidden in oak scrub, thickets. *Male*'s glossy black cap contrasts with broken white spectacles. Spectacles, smaller size, and secretive behavior distinguish *female;* immature males similar; *immature females* are more buffy.

Voice: Best located by song, a persistent string of varied, twittering, two- or three-note phrases. Common call note, *tsidik,* almost identical to Ruby-crowned Kinglet.

Range: Endangered. Extirpated from Kansas by 1930s. Major factors are habitat destruction and brood parasitism by Brown-headed Cowbird. Accidental to Ontario.

Yellow-throated Vireo *Vireo flavifrons* L 5½" (14 cm)

Bright yellow spectacles, throat, and breast; white belly; two white wing bars. Upperparts olive, with contrasting gray rump. Compare with Pine Warbler (page 332), which has greenish yellow rump, blurry streaked sides, thinner bill, and less complete and distinct spectacles.

Voice: Song, a slow repetition of burry, low-pitched two- or three-note phrases separated by long pauses, often contains a rising *three-eight.* Calls include a rapid, harsh series of *cheh* notes.

Range: Frequents deciduous woodlands, particularly those with oaks. Fairly common in most of breeding range. Rare or casual in southernmost Florida in winter. Most reports are misidentified Pine Warblers (page 332) or Yellow-breasted Chats (page 342).

Bell's Vireo *Vireo bellii* L 4¾" (12 cm)

Plumage variable. Indistinct white spectacles; one or two whitish wing bars. More easterly nominate race is greenish above, yellowish below; often bobs tail. Active, rather secretive.

Voice: Song, a series of harsh, scolding notes.

Range: Uncommon in bottomlands, mesquite, and in eastern part of range in shrubby areas.

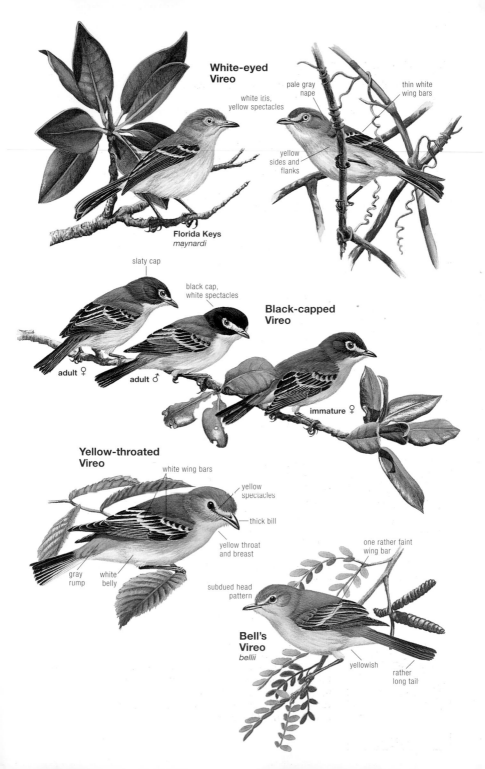

White-eyed Vireo

white iris, yellow spectacles

pale gray nape

thin white wing bars

yellow sides and flanks

Florida Keys
maynardi

slaty cap

black cap, white spectacles

Black-capped Vireo

adult ♀

adult ♂

immature ♀

Yellow-throated Vireo

white wing bars

yellow spectacles

thick bill

yellow throat and breast

gray rump

white belly

one rather faint wing bar

subdued head pattern

Bell's Vireo
bellii

yellowish

rather long tail

Hutton's Vireo *Vireo huttoni L 5" (13 cm)*

Grayish olive above, with pale area in lores; white eye ring broken above eye. Southwestern *stephensi* and more easterly *carolinae* are grayish. Separated from Ruby-crowned Kinglet by larger size, thicker bill, lack of dark area below lower wing bar, and voice.
Voice: Song is a repeated or mixed rising *zu-wee* and descending *zoe zoo;* also a flat *chew.* Calls include a low *chit* and whining chatter; birds from interior Southwest give a harsh *tchurr-ree.*
Range: A western species. Scarce and local but increasing in woodlands on Edwards Plateau, Texas (*carolinae*).

Gray Vireo *Vireo vicinior L 5½" (14 cm)*

White eye ring; wings brownish, with faint wing bars, the lower more prominent; short primary projection; long tail. Compare with Bell's Vireos and Plumbeous.
Voice: Song is a series of musical *chu-wee chu-weet* notes, faster and sweeter than Plumbeous. Calls include shrill, descending musical notes.
Range: Found in semiarid habitat. Sticks to undergrowth; flicks tail as it forages. Only casually seen during migration. There is a remarkable early Oct. specimen record from Wisconsin.

Blue-headed Vireo *Vireo solitarius L 5" (13 cm)*

Adult male's solid blue-gray hood contrasts with white spectacles and throat; hood of female and immatures partly gray. All ages have bright olive back; yellow-tinged wing bars and tertials; greenish yellow edges to dark secondaries. White on outer tail; bright yellow sides and flanks, sometimes mixed with green. Larger Appalachian *alticola* has more slaty back; only flanks are yellow.
Voice: Song similar to Red-eyed, but slower. Call a harsh chatter.
Range: Fairly common in mixed woodlands.

Plumbeous Vireo *Vireo plumbeus L 5¼" (13 cm)*

Larger, with bigger bill than Cassin's Vireo; has sharper head and throat contrast; gray upperparts. Pattern of tail feathers similar to Blue-headed Vireo. White wing bars and flight feather edges; pale yellow, if present, only on flanks. Sides of breast gray, sometimes tinged olive. Compare worn summer birds to shorter-winged Gray.
Voice: Song hoarser than Blue-headed; call similar.
Range: Rare migrant on western Great Plains; accidental farther east.

Cassin's Vireo *Vireo cassinii L 5" (13 cm)*

Similar to Blue-headed, but slightly smaller and duller. Less contrast between head and throat; duller, whitish wing bars and tertial edges; less white in tail. Immature female can have entirely green head; compare to Hutton's Vireo.
Voice: Song is hoarser than Blue-headed Vireo; call similar.
Range: Scarce fall migrant on western Great Plains; accidental farther east.

Hutton's Vireo

Southwest *stephensi*

broken eye ring

pale lores

thick bill

white edgings connect to lower wing bar

Ruby-crowned Kinglet for comparison

tiny bill

black panel at base of secondaries

Gray Vireo

whitish eye ring but no spectacled effect

short primary projection

long tail, which is flipped about

Blue-headed Vireo *solitarius*

white spectacles, bluish gray head

sharp contrast between auricular and throat

yellow sides with some olive

♂

Plumbeous Vireo *plumbeus*

white spectacles

gray above with two white wing bars

long primary projection

slaty gray

shorter tail than Gray

Cassin's Vireo

more blended border than Blue-headed

duller sides

♀

Yellow-green Vireo *Vireo flavoviridis* L 6" (15 cm)
Similar to Red-eyed Vireo, but bill longer; head pattern more blended. Strong yellow-green wash above extends onto sides of face; extensive yellow on sides, flanks, under tail; brightest in fall.
Voice: Song, a hesitant series of notes, suggests House Sparrow.
Range: Rare in summer in southern Texas. Casual in spring in central Texas and on the upper Gulf Coast.

Red-eyed Vireo *Vireo olivaceus* L 6" (15 cm)
Blue-gray crown; white eyebrow bordered above and below with black. Olive back, darker wings and tail; white underparts. Lacks wing bars. Ruby red iris visible at close range. *First-fall* bird has brown iris. Immatures and some fall adults have pale yellow on flanks and undertail coverts.
Voice: Persistent song, sung all day, a variable series of deliberate, short phrases. Calls include a nasal, whining *quee.*
Range: Common in eastern woodlands; winters in South America.

Black-whiskered Vireo *Vireo altiloquus* L 6¼" (16 cm)
Variable dark malar stripe, often hard to see. Bill larger and longer than in Red-eyed Vireo. Grayish brown crown; pattern more diffuse than Red-eyed. Dull green above; whitish below, with variable pale yellowish wash on sides and flanks.
Voice: Song, deliberate one- to four-note phrases, less varied and more emphatic than Red-eyed.
Range: Fairly common in hardwoods and mangroves of Florida Keys and along Florida coasts. Casual along rest of Gulf Coast and north to Carolinas.

Philadelphia Vireo *Vireo philadelphicus* L 5¼" (13 cm)
Adult variably yellow below, palest on belly. Greenish above, with contrasting grayish cap, dull grayish olive wing bar, dull white eyebrow, and dark eye line. First-fall birds and most *fall* adults are often brighter yellow below. Distinguished from Warbling Vireo by dark eye line extending through lores, darker cap, dark primary coverts, and yellow at center of throat and breast. Similar Tennessee Warbler (page 320) has a thinner bill, white undertail coverts.
Voice: Song resembles Red-eyed Vireo but is generally slower, thinner, and higher pitched.
Range: Uncommon; found in open woodlands, streamside willows and alders. Rare migrant in coastal Southeast.

Warbling Vireo *Vireo gilvus* L 5½" (14 cm)
Gray or olive-gray above. Underparts white. Dusky postocular stripe; white eyebrow, without dark upper border; brown eye. Lacks wing bars. Smaller and paler than Red-eyed Vireo; crown does not contrast strongly with back. Birds in fresh *fall* plumage tend to be greener above, pale yellow on sides of flanks.
Voice: Song of eastern *gilvus* is delivered in long, melodious, warbling phrases.
Range: Fairly common in deciduous woods, especially near water. Very rare migrant in coastal Southeast.

Yellow-green Vireo

duller gray cap than
Red-eyed with less-evident
lateral crown stripe

yellowish olive above

often cocks tail

large bill

yellow sides and flanks,
some yellowish into face

black lateral
crown stripe

**Red-eyed
Vireo**

breeding

olive above, white below

1st fall

pale yellow

less evident
dark lateral
crown stripe

longer bill than Red-eyed

black
whisker

**Black-whiskered
Vireo**

Florida
barbatulus

pale lores

**Warbling
Vireo**
gilvus

spring

dark eye line
extends
through lores

**Philadelphia
Vireo**

fall

shorter tail

fall birds
often quite
bright yellow

dark primary
coverts

fall

yellow
brightest
on sides

paler primary
coverts

spring

yellow of equal
intensity extends
across breast

eastern Warbling distinctly
larger than Philadelphia

Crows, Jays (Family Corvidae)

Harsh voice and aggressive manner draw attention to these large, often gregarious birds. In most species, bristles cover nostrils. Powerful, all-purpose bill efficiently handles a varied diet.

Blue Jay *Cyanocitta cristata L 11" (28 cm)*
Crested jay with black barring and white patches on blue wings and tail, black necklace on whitish underparts.
Voice: Most common of varied calls is a piercing *jay jay jay;* also gives a musical *weedle-eedle* and mimics the call of Red-shouldered Hawk. Generally very noisy and bold.
Range: Common in suburbs, parks, and woodlands. Often migrates in large flocks.

Gray Jay *Perisoreus canadensis L 11½" (29 cm)*
A fluffy, long-tailed jay with small bill and no crest. Widespread nominate *canadensis,* one of several races common in northern boreal forests, has a white collar and forehead, with dark gray crown and nape. *Juveniles* are sooty gray overall, with a faint white moustachial streak. Gray Jays are familiar camp and cabin visitors, but in general they are more retiring than most other jays.
Voice: Call notes include a whistled *wheeoo* and a low *chuck.*
Range: Largely resident. Casual visitor in winter even slightly south of normal, resident range.

Western Scrub-Jay *Aphelocoma californica*
L 11" (28 cm) Long tail; blue above; variable bluish band on chest. Interior races include stouter-billed *texana* and slender-billed *woodhouseii.* Interior races rather shy.
Voice: Calls include raspy *shreep,* often in a short series.
Range: Uncommon in canyon and hill-country woodlands. Race *texana* is resident in Texas Hill Country; *woodhouseii* is a casual fall and winter irruptive to western Great Plains. Accidental to Indiana.

Florida Scrub-Jay *Aphelocoma coerulescens* **T**
L 10½" (27 cm) Distinguished from other scrub-jays by whitish forehead and eyebrow; shorter, broader bill; paler back; distinct collar; indistinct streaking below; disproportionately longer tail; and range.
Voice: Varied calls include raspy, hoarse notes. Has cooperative breeding system: Fledged young remain on territory and help rear nestlings.
Range: Restricted to Florida scrub region where population has declined some 90 percent in 20th century due to habitat destruction. Optimum habitat is transitional, produced by fire: consists of scrub, mainly oak, about ten feet high with small openings.

bluish crest

Blue Jay

blackish throat band

extensive white in wings

white tail tips

dark rear to head

whitish forehead

small bill

pale gray underparts

boreal adult *canadensis*

pale tail tips

Gray Jay

sooty overall

Western Scrub-Jay *texana*

heavier bill

deeper blue than *woodhouseii* with more contrasty back

underparts paler than *woodhouseii*

long tail

juvenile

pale tail tips

woodhouseii

darker underparts

whitish forehead

grayish back

Florida Scrub-Jay

long tail

Green Jay *Cyanocorax yncas* L 10½" *(27 cm)*
Green and blue plumage blends with dappled sun and shade in woodland habitat.
Voice: Somewhat inquisitive. Gregarious and noisy; most common call is a series of raspy *cheh-cheh-cheh* notes.
Range: Resident and locally common in woodland and brushy areas of the lower Rio Grande Valley; locally farther north.

Black-billed Magpie *Pica hudsonia* L 19" *(48 cm)*
Readily identified as a magpie by black and white markings and unusually long tail with iridescent green highlights. White wing patches flash in flight.
Voice: Gregarious and noisy; typical calls include a whining *mag* and a series of loud, harsh *chuck* notes. Calls and many behavioral traits resulted in North American Black-billed Magpie being split from Old World populations of magpie, whose calls are faster and lower pitched.
Range: Uncommon inhabitant of open woodlands and thickets in rangelands and foothills, especially along watercourses. Casually stray south and east of normal range in winter. Some birds seen well east may be escaped cage birds.

Brown Jay *Cyanocorax morio* L 16½" *(42 cm)*
Very large jay with long, broad tail. Dark, sooty brown overall except for pale belly. ***Adult*** has black bill. Juvenile has yellow bill and eye ring, turning black by second winter; in transition, many have blotchy yellow-and-black bills.
Voice: A noisy species; its harsh scream is similar to the call of a Red-shouldered Hawk. Another call sounds like a hiccup.
Range: Tropical species; range barely extends to Texas, where it is resident but rare in woodlands and mesquite along the Rio Grande in vicinity of Falcon Dam.

Chihuahuan Raven *Corvus cryptoleucus* L 19½" *(50 cm)*
Heavier bill and wedge-shaped tail distinguish both raven species from crows. Distinguished from Common Raven by shorter wings and shorter, less wedge-shaped tail; bristles extend farther out on shorter, thicker-appearing bill. Neck feathers white rather than grayish at base, but usually obscured.
Voice: Frequent call, a drawn-out croak, usually slightly higher pitched than call of Common Raven.
Range: Fairly common in desert areas and scrubby grasslands, also farms, towns, dumps.

Common Raven *Corvus corax* L 24" *(61 cm)*
Large, with long, heavy bill and long, wedge-shaped tail. Larger than Chihuahuan Raven; note thicker, shaggier throat feathers and nasal bristles that do not extend as far out on larger bill.
Voice: Most common call is a low, drawn-out croak.
Range: Found in a variety of habitats, including mountains, deserts, and woodlands. Numerous in northern part of range; uncommon and local, but slowly spreading, in Appalachians, New England, and northern Great Plains.

blue and
black head

**Green
Jay**
glaucescens

body largely
greenish

yellow outer
tail feathers

heavy black bill

**Black-billed
Magpie**

very
large size

adult

Brown Jay
palliatus

pale belly

thin yellow
orbital ring

yellow bill

black-and-white
coloration

juvenile

long tail

shorter,
thicker bill

**Chihuahuan
Raven**

shorter,
more
rounded tail

overall
smaller size

long,
heavy bill

**Common
Raven**

long wings

long, wedge-
shaped tail

Tamaulipas Crow *Corvus imparatus L 14½" (37 cm)*

A rare, irregular resident in southernmost Texas. Smaller, glossier than American Crow. Compare with larger Chihuahuan Raven.
Voice: Call, a low, froglike croak.
Range: First appeared in U.S. in late 1960s near Brownsville, Texas, where it has nested. Present mostly in winter in varying numbers, sharply declining over last two decades.

American Crow *Corvus brachyrhynchos L 17½" (45 cm)*

Long, heavy bill is noticeably smaller than that of raven. Fan-shaped tail distinguishes all crows from ravens in flight.
Voice: Adult American Crow is readily identified by familiar *caw* call, but juvenile's higher-pitched, nasal *cah* begging call resembles the call of the similar Fish Crow.
Range: Generally common throughout most of its range in a wide variety of habitats. May form large foraging flocks and nighttime roosts in fall and winter.

Fish Crow *Corvus ossifragus L 15½" (39 cm)*

Slightly smaller than American Crow with smaller bill and feet; wings more pointed; wingbeats faster.
Voice: Best distinguished by voice: Call, a high, nasal *uh uh,* the second note lower; also short, nasal *car* notes.
Range: Found in tidewater marshes and inland locally at lakes and in low valleys along eastern river systems. Interior range expanding. Often seen in winter in flocks with American Crows, when also found on farmland, in towns, and in dumps.

IDENTIFYING: Crows and Ravens Most people do not study crows and ravens very closely. In fact, a lot of people just don't like crows in particular. These birds are basically all-black, making them not only "boring" but also lacking in obvious plumage features to use in separating them! Several species are showing range expansions, such as the Fish Crow up major river and lake systems in the interior and Common Raven moving south and out of the mountains in New England and parts of the mid-Atlantic region, as well as in the northern Great Plains. Many populations of American Crows have been significantly reduced recently, however, as a result of the West Nile Virus, although some are already showing signs of recovery.

Over most of eastern North America, the primary identification pitfall lies with distinguishing American Crow from Fish Crow and American Crow from Common Raven. While American Crows are most numerous in farm country, residential areas, and upland areas, Fish Crows are most numerous in tidewater areas and at lakes and along river systems. But there is substantial overlap in habitats used, particularly during the nonbreeding season, when large single- or mixed-species flocks may form in agricultural land, at dumps, and at night-time roosts. Fish Crow is slightly smaller than American Crow, with slightly smaller bill and feet. But such differences are often hard to appreciate when only a single species is present. Fish Crow also has slightly more pointed wings and a quicker wingbeat, but, again, such differences are subtle. In excellent light, some Fish Crows appear to have a glossy bluish sheen to their plumage, which is less obvious in American Crow.

The best field mark by far is the call. Fish Crow gives both a single nasal *ca* and a doubled nasal *ca-hah* (second note lower), versus the familiar, raspier *cah, caw,* or *caaw-caaw* of American Crow (which also gives a rattling call). Note, however, that juvenile American Crows, particularly those that are begging, may give a more nasal call, quite like that of a Fish Crow, but such a call is typically given singly, not doubled.

small bill

only crow in south Texas

Tamaulipas Crow

small with glossy blue plumage

American Crow

square cut tail

smaller bill than ravens

smaller bill than American Crow

Fish Crow

long legs

shorter legs

Common Ravens are distinguished from similar American Crows by their larger size; larger bill; wedge-shaped tail; longer, more swept-back wings; shaggier neck feathers; and low, croaking call. Ravens are far more likely than crows to soar on thermals. In the East, Common Ravens are usually seen only singly, in pairs, or in family groups, but larger groupings may sometimes accumulate, particularly at northern disposal sites.

Tamaulipas Crow is a very rare visitor to southernmost Texas. It first appeared in the late 1960s and early 1970s and quickly became a common winter visitor and rare summer resident in the vicinity of the Brownsville Sanitary Landfill. But during the 1990s it rapidly declined and now barely maintains an irregular presence there, with one or two pairs continuing on a sporadic basis at the nearby port, airport, or surrounding residential areas. It is the only species of crow in that area and differs from an American by its smaller size, glossier plumage, and odd-sounding, frog-croaking call. It is perhaps more likely to be con-

fused with the locally resident Chihuahuan Raven, which in turn is very difficult to separate from the Common Raven where both species potentially overlap on the western Great Plains and in central Texas (Edwards Plateau).

One of the most underrated field identification problems in North America is the separation of these two species. Chihuahuan Raven is slightly smaller and has slightly shorter wings and tail, a proportionately thicker bill, longer nasal bristles on the upper mandible, and a slightly higher-pitched call. It is also more gregarious than Common Raven, often congregating in large flocks during the nonbreeding season, and is more apt to move long distances seasonally. It prefers flatter agricultural and grassland areas, whereas Common frequents more rocky desert areas, canyons, and hill country. But as with Fish and American Crows, there may be some overlap in habitat, particularly outside the breeding season (e.g., both species frequent dumps), and even the odd, lone Common Raven may wander well outside its normal range.

284

Larks (Family Alaudidae)

Ground dwellers of open fields, larks are slender-billed seed- and insect-eaters. They seldom alight on trees or bushes. On the ground, they walk rather than hop.

Horned Lark *Eremophila alpestris* L 6¾-7¾" *(17-20 cm)*
Head pattern distinctive in all subspecies: black "horns"; white or yellowish face and throat with broad black stripe under eye; black bib. *Female* duller overall than *male*, horns less prominent. Conspicuous in flight is the mostly black tail with white outer feathers, brown central feathers. Brief *juvenal* plumage has whitish markings above, streaks below; can be confused with Sprague's Pipit (page 316). Three widespread races are found in the East: *"Prairie Horned Lark,"* *praticola*, which breeds in southern Canada and the eastern U.S., is pale, with white eyebrows and throat. *"Northern Horned Lark,"alpestris,* is much darker, with a yellow throat. The central Arctic coast race, *hoyti,* is pale like *praticola*, but larger; *giraudi* from western Gulf Coast is quite yellow below. Western subspecies vary widely in overall color; selected extremes are shown here: *enthymia* (Plains, not illustrated) is very pale. Some subspecies are highly migratory, others are largely resident.
Voice: Horned Lark's calls include a high *tsee-ee* or *tsee-titi.* Song is a weak twittering, delivered from the ground or in flight.
Range: Common on Great Plains, less numerous and more local farther to the east. Horned Lark prefers dirt fields, gravel ridges, airports, sod farms, and shores. The flocks in midwinter in the eastern U.S. are mainly *alpestris.* Horned Larks are relatively late fall migrants and very early spring migrants. By late winter, pairs of *praticola* have already established their breeding territories.

Swallows (Family Hirundinidae)

Slender bodies with long, pointed wings resemble swifts, but "wrist" angle is sharper and farther from the body; flight is more fluid. Adept aerialists, swallows dart to catch flying insects. Flocks perch in long rows on branches and wires.

Purple Martin *Progne subis* L 8" *(20 cm)*
Male is dark, glossy purplish blue. *Female* and juvenile are gray below. *First-spring males* have some purple below. In flight, male especially resembles European Starling (page 314); but note forked tail, longer wings, and typical swallow flight, short glides alternating with rapid flapping.
Voice: Rich, liquid gurgling and whistles; also a low *churr.*
Range: Locally common where suitable nest sites are available. Very early spring migrant in South; winters in South America.

black tail with white outer tail feathers

alpestris

"Northern Horned Lark"
alpestris

giraudi

hoyti

winter ♂

♂

♀ except juveniles, all have dark breast band

Horned Lark

Lapland Longspur for comparison

spotted with white

juvenile
alpestris

juvenile often mistaken for Sprague's Pipit

arcticola

small "horns"

"Prairie Horned Lark"
praticola

♀

Purple Martin

often soars; wingbeats are slow and deep

adult ♂

broad wings

dark purple overall

adult ♂

1st spring ♂

whitish belly

♀

Tree Swallow *Tachycineta bicolor* L 5¾" *(15 cm)*

Dark, glossy greenish blue above, slightly duller in female, greener in fall plumage; white below. White cheek patch does not extend above eye. *Juvenile* gray-brown above; usually has more diffuse breast band than Bank Swallow. *First-spring female* shows varying amount of adult color on crown, back.

Voice: Calls and song include whistles and liquid gurgles or chirps.
Range: Common in wooded habitat near water, and where dead trees provide nest holes. Also nests in fence posts, barn eaves, nest boxes. Migrates in huge flocks; goes north earlier in spring and lingers farther north in fall than other swallows.

Bank Swallow *Riparia riparia* L 4¾" *(12 cm)*

Our smallest swallow. Distinct brownish gray breast band, often extending in a line down center of breast. Throat is white; white curves around rear border of ear patch. *Juvenile* has thin buffy wing bars; compare with juvenile Northern Rough-winged Swallow and juvenile Tree Swallow. Locally common throughout most of range. Unlike Northern Rough-winged, wingbeats are shallow and rapid; also paler rump contrasts with wings.

Voice: Call, a series of buzzy, short *dzrrt* notes.
Range: Nests in colonies, excavating nest burrows in riverbank cliffs, gravel pits, and highway cuts. Winters chiefly in South America.

Northern Rough-winged Swallow

Stelgidopteryx serripennis L 5" *(13 cm)* Brown above, whitish below, with gray-brown wash on chin, throat, and upper breast. Lacks Bank Swallow's distinct breast band; wings are longer, wingbeats deeper and slower. *Juvenile* has cinnamon wing bars.
Voice: Call a distinct low, buzzy *zzrtt*.
Range: Nests in single pairs in riverbanks, cliffs, culverts, and under bridges. Migrates singly or in small flocks.

IDENTIFYING: Brown Swallows Separating the brown swallows—Bank and Northern Rough-winged—is not particularly difficult given adequate views. Juvenile Tree Swallows need to be considered as well, as they are also brownish in color. Swallows are most numerous and are best studied over water, especially on cloudy inclement days, or while perched on wires or on the bare branches of a dead tree.

Of the three species, Bank Swallow is easily the smallest and is also the slimmest. It often looks tiny in the field and flies with rapid flaps. Its back and rump are grayish sandy brown and contrast with the darker brown wings. The breast band can be hard to see at times in flight. When Bank is perched, its breast band is obvious; note also the downward dark spur in the middle. Also note the pale coloring that wraps around up the sides of the neck, isolating the dark auricular.

Northern Rough-winged Swallow is larger and flies with a slow and relaxed, floppy flight. It is more uniformly brown above and has a dusky wash across the breast. Juveniles show distinct cinnamon wing bars.

Tree is the largest species, and in juveniles the brown above is darker—more of a chocolate brown. Tree has distinct white edges on the tertials and often shows a broad and blended dusky band across the chest, never as distinct as Bank Swallow. Look for isolated bluish feathers in the otherwise brown upperparts. Its flight is somewhat intermediate between Northern Rough-winged and Bank.

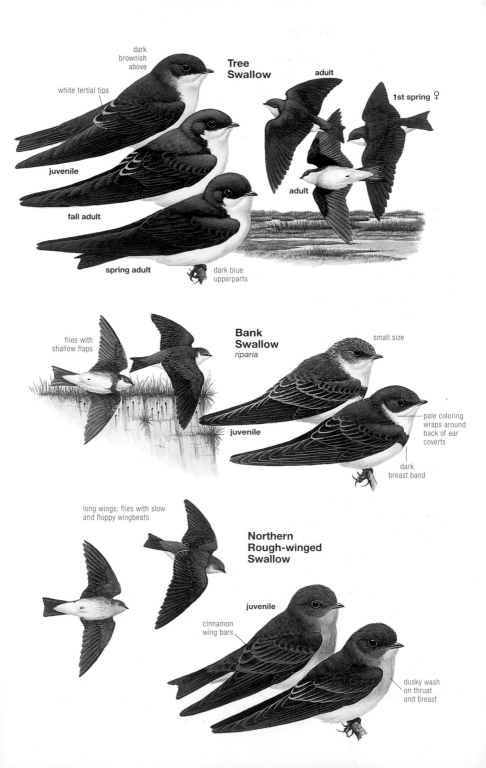

Tree Swallow

dark brownish above

white tertial tips

juvenile

fall adult

spring adult

dark blue upperparts

adult

1st spring ♀

adult

Bank Swallow
riparia

flies with shallow flaps

juvenile

small size

pale coloring wraps around back of ear coverts

dark breast band

Northern Rough-winged Swallow

long wings; flies with slow and floppy wingbeats

juvenile

cinnamon wing bars

dusky wash on throat and breast

Cave Swallow *Petrochelidon fulva* L 5½" (14 cm)

Squarish tail; distinguished from Cliff by buffy throat color extending through auriculars and around nape setting off dark cap and giving the bird a somewhat masked look; rump averages a richer color; cinnamon forehead; juvenile much paler and lacks white stripes on back; compare with southwestern subspecies of Cliff also with cinnamon forehead.

Voice: Call a rising *pweih,* much sweeter than Cliff Swallow.

Range: Mexican and West Indian species: West Indies race, *fulva,* a local breeder in south Florida, is smaller than Mexican *pelodoma,* which is widespread in the Southwest; *fulva* also has more buff below and darker rump. Nests in colonies in limestone caves, sinkholes, culverts, and under bridges, sometimes with Barn and Cliff Swallows. Very rare to Great Lakes and on East Coast, mainly in late fall; most such records involve *pelodoma,* but *fulva* has occurred as well (in spring).

Cliff Swallow *Petrochelidon pyrrhonota* L 5½" (14 cm)

Squarish tail and buffy rump distinguish this swallow from all others except Cave Swallow. Most Cliff Swallows have dark chestnut and blackish throat, pale forehead. A primarily southwestern race, *melanogaster,* has cinnamon forehead like Cave Swallow, but throat is dark chestnut. It has been recorded as far east as southern Florida. All **juveniles** are much duller and grayer than adults; throat is paler, and forehead is darker.

Voice: Cliff's calls include a rough, squeaky *chri, a* nasal *trrr,* and a rattle.

Range: Uncommon to locally common around bridges, rural settlements, and in open country on cliffs. Range has expanded in last two decades. Nests in colonies, building gourd-shaped mud nests. Winters in South America.

Barn Swallow *Hirundo rustica* L 6¾" (17 cm)

Long, deeply forked tail. Throat is reddish brown; upperparts blue-black; underparts are usually cinnamon or buffy. In all **juveniles,** tail is shorter but still noticeably forked; underparts are pale. The flight of Barn Swallow is similar to Northern Rough-winged, with slow, floppy wingflaps and with glides. Over most of the East, indeed over much of North America, this is the most numerous and widespread swallow. It has interbred with both Cliff and Cave Swallows.

Voice: Call a short, sweet, single or double *vit* or *veet;* song a series of squeaky notes.

Range: Common; generally nests on or inside farm buildings, under eaves, bridges, and docks, and inside culverts; nests in pairs or small colonies. Winters from Mexico south to southern South America.

juvenile

Southwest
pelodoma

rump slightly
more cinnamon
than Cliff

cinnamon forehead

buffy throat wraps
around sides of neck,
contrasts with dark cap

Cliff and Cave Swallows
both have fairly square-ended
tails and buffy rumps

side and flanks more
cinnamon tinged than
pelodoma

has cinnamon
forehead
like Cave

**Cave
Swallow**

West Indies
fulva

Southwest
melanogaster

buffy rump

pale collar

darker
cinnamon
than
pelodoma

capped
appearance

**Cliff
Swallow**

dusky throat and
forehead on juvenile,
often with some
whitish feathers

adult
pelodoma

juvenile

white forehead

buffy rump

dark throat

**Barn
Swallow**
erythrogaster

paler below
than adult

long,
forked tail
with white
at base

juvenile

shorter tail

bluish above

290

Chickadees, Titmice (Family Paridae)

Often found in mixed-species flocks, actively searching for food; several species are well-known visitors at feeders.

Black-capped Chickadee *Poecile atricapillus*
L 5¼" (13 cm) Black cap and bib; cheeks more extensively and purer white than similar Carolina Chickadee. Note that Black-capped Chickadee's greater wing coverts and secondaries are broadly edged in white; tertials more boldly edged, with darker centers than Carolina's; flanks buffier, lower edge of black bib a bit more ragged. These differences are obscured in **worn summer** birds. More northerly Black-cappeds tend to be larger and frostier, more distinct from Carolina.
Voice: Best distinction is voice. Black-capped's call is a lower, slower *chick-a-dee-dee-dee* than Carolina's; typical song, a clear, whistled *fee-bee* or *fee-bee-ee*, the first note higher in pitch; vocalizations show some geographic variation.
Range: Common in open woodlands, clearings, and suburbs. Usually forages in thickets and low branches of trees. The usual ranges of Black-capped and Carolina barely overlap, but periodic fall irruptions especially in eastern portion of region push Black-capped's range south of mapped range; most frequently recorded from eastern Kentucky to eastern Maryland. Where breeding ranges overlap, the two species hybridize. In the Appalachians, Black-capped inhabits higher elevations.

Carolina Chickadee *Poecile carolinensis* *L 4¾" (12 cm)*
Very similar to Black-capped Chickadee: black cap and bib, whitish cheeks. Note that Carolina lacks broad white edgings on greater wing coverts; lower edge of black bib is usually neater, has less buff on flanks than Black-capped and feathers of rear of cheek are tipped with gray. Westernmost race, *atricapilloides*, is grayer than nominate.
Voice: Best distinction for separating the two species is voice. Carolina's call is a higher, faster version of *chick-a-dee-dee-dee* than Black-capped; typical song is a four-note whistle, *fee-bee fee-bay*.
Range: Common in open deciduous and mixed forests, woodland clearings and edges, suburban areas. Feeds in trees and thickets; seldom descends to ground. At northern edge, especially the northeastern edge, its range in some winters is invaded by Black-capped. In the Appalachians, Carolina prefers valleys and foothills.

Boreal Chickadee *Poecile hudsonica* *L 5½" (14 cm)*
Grayish brown on crown and back, with pinkish brown flanks. Note that rear portion of cheeks is heavily washed with gray.
Voice: Call is a nasal, wheezy *tseek-a-day-day*.
Range: Uncommon in coniferous forests. In some winters, small numbers wander up to hundreds of miles south of normal range. Recorded casually south to Iowa, Illinois, Ohio, northern Virginia, Maryland, and Delaware, but most records are not recent.

cheeks uniformly white

prominent
white-edged
secondaries

worn
summer

**Black-capped
Chickadee**
atricapillus

**fresh
fall**

atricapilloides

**Carolina
Chickadee**
extimus

grayish
tinge to
rear cheek

worn
summer

slightly shorter tail
than Black-capped

**fresh
fall**

extimus

slightly duller
flanks than
Black-capped

brownish cap

grayish rear
cheek

fresh fall

juvenile

**Boreal
Chickadee**
hudsonica

pinkish
buff flanks

worn
summer

Tufted Titmouse *Baeolophus bicolor* L 6¼" (16 cm)

Note gray crest and distinct blackish forehead. *Juvenile* has brownish forehead and pale crest. In overlap zone in Texas, Tufted x Black-crested Titmouse hybrids show variable brown foreheads and dark gray crests. Active and noisy.
Voice: Typical song is loud, whistled *peter peter peter;* but less vocal than Black-crested; calls softer and less nasal.
Range: Deciduous woodlands, parks, and suburbs. Regularly comes to feeders. Range has recently expanded northward.

Black-crested Titmouse *Baeolophus atricristatus*

L 5¾" (15 cm) Resplit from Tufted Titmouse. *Adult* has black crest and pale forehead. In *juvenile,* crown is darker than upperparts; forehead is dirty white.
Voice: Calls louder, sharper than Tufted Titmouse. Song is similar but given more rapidly.
Range: Fairly common in a variety of woodland and scrub habitats.

Penduline Tits, Verdins (Family Remizidae)

Small, spritely birds with finely pointed bills. They inhabit arid scrub country, feed in brush chickadee-style, and build spherical nests.

Verdin *Auriparus flaviceps* L 4½" (11 cm)

Adult has dull gray plumage, chestnut shoulder patches, yellow head and throat. *Juvenile* is brown-gray overall; shorter tail helps separate it from Bushtit.
Voice: Song is a plaintive three-note whistle, the second note higher. Calls include rapid, hard *chip* notes.
Range: Common in mesquite and other dense thorny shrubs of drier regions.

Long-tailed Tits, Bushtits (Family Aegithalidae)

A longer tail distinguishes these tiny birds from other chickadee-like species. Except during nesting, they usually feed in large, busy, twittering flocks. Their nests are elaborate hanging structures.

Bushtit *Psaltriparus minimus* L 4½" (11 cm)

Note very small size. Gray above, paler below; *female* has pale eyes; *male* has dark eyes . Away from Pacific states, all birds show brown ear patch and gray cap.
Voice: Gives sharp, twittering calls.
Range: Uncommon in a variety of woodlands and brushy areas. Casual in fall and winter to western Kansas.

Tufted Titmouse

juvenile

tall crest

dark forehead

pinkish flank patch

adult

Black-crested Titmouse

juvenile

black crest

white forehead

adult

Verdin

yellow head, black eye line

sharply pointed bill

chestnut lesser coverts

very plain, lacks yellow head

juvenile

Bushtit
interior
plumbeus

gray crown

pinkish buff face

♂

female with pale eye

long tail

♀

294

Creepers (Family Certhiidae)

With curved bills, these little tree-climbers dig insects and larvae from bark. Stiff tail feathers serve as props.

Brown Creeper *Certhia americana* L 5¼" (13 cm)
Camouflaged by streaked brown plumage, Creepers spiral upward from base of a tree, then fly to a lower place on another tree.
Voice: Call is a soft, sibilant *see;* song, a high-pitched, variable *see see see titi see.* Fairly common but hard to spot.
Range: Nests in coniferous, mixed, or swampy forests. Generally solitary, but sometimes seen in winter flocks of titmice and nuthatches. Rather rare at southern end of mapped winter range; casual to south Florida.

Nuthatches (Family Sittidae)

These short-tailed acrobats climb up, down, and around tree trunks and branches.

White-breasted Nuthatch *Sitta carolinensis*
L 5¾" (15 cm) Black cap tops all-white face and breast; extent of rust below is variable. *Females* in the Northeast have gray crowns more consistently than in the South.
Voice: Typical song is a rapid series of nasal whistles on one pitch. Call is usually a low-pitched, repeated, nasal *yank* in eastern birds.
Range: Common; found in deciduous and mixed woods. The Rocky Mountain subspecies, *nelsoni,* with somewhat different appearance from eastern birds and very different vocalizations, has been collected in southwest Kansas and should be looked for elsewhere on the Great Plains at the west edge of the region in fall and winter.

Red-breasted Nuthatch *Sitta canadensis* L 4½" (11 cm)
Black cap and eye line, white eyebrow, rust underparts; *female* and juveniles have duller head, paler underparts.
Voice: High-pitched, nasal call sounds like a toy tin horn.
Range: Resident in northern and montane conifers; gleans small branches, outer twigs. Irruptive migrant; numbers and winter range vary yearly. Resident range is expanding slightly southward.

Brown-headed Nuthatch *Sitta pusilla* L 4½" (11 cm)
Brown cap; dull buff underparts. Pale nape spot usually visible at close range. Narrow dark eye line borders cap.
Voice: Call is a repeated double note like the squeak of a rubber duck. Feeding flocks also give twittering, chirping, and talky *bit bit bit* calls.
Range: Fairly common; found in pine woodlands. Accidental north to Wisconsin, Northern Illinois, Ohio, southeastern Kentucky, and New Jersey.

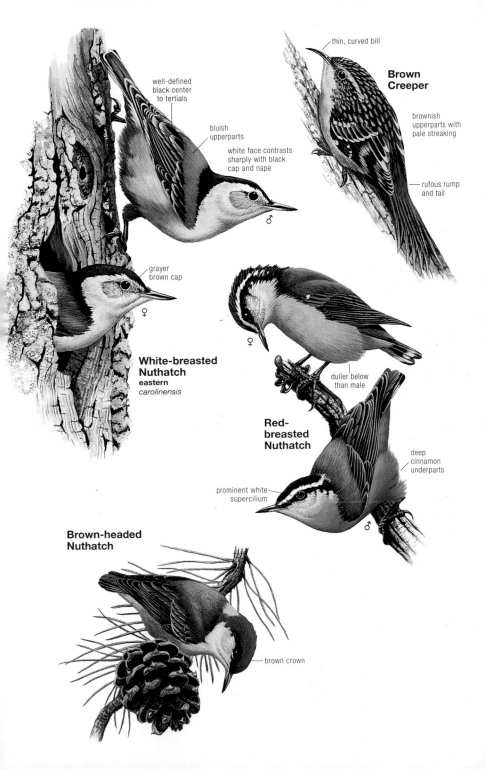

thin, curved bill

Brown Creeper

brownish upperparts with pale streaking

rufous rump and tail

well-defined black center to tertials

bluish upperparts

white face contrasts sharply with black cap and nape

♂

grayer brown cap

♀

White-breasted Nuthatch
eastern
carolinensis

♀

duller below than male

Red-breasted Nuthatch

deep cinnamon underparts

prominent white supercilium

♂

Brown-headed Nuthatch

brown crown

296

Wrens (Family Troglodytidae)

Found throughout most of North America, wrens are chunky birds with slender, slightly curved bills. Tails are often uptilted. Loud song and vigorous territorial defense belie the small size of most species.

House Wren *Troglodytes aedon* L 4¾" *(12 cm)*
Brown above with faint eyebrow. Separated from Winter Wren by longer tail, less prominent barring on belly, and larger overall size. By current classification, western *parkmanii* breeds east to central Ontario and western Kentucky; is grayer above and paler below.
Voice: Exuberant song is a cascade of bubbling whistled notes. Calls include a soft *chek* and a harsh scold.
Range: Common in shrubs, gardens, parks. Winters rarely north into summer range.

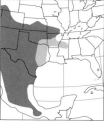

Winter Wren *Troglodytes troglodytes* L 4" *(10 cm)*
Very small size; stubby tail; dark barring on belly. Widespread eastern subspecies *hiemalis* breeds across the north; similar *pullus* (not shown) breeds in the Appalachians.
Voice: Eastern subspecies give a *kelp-kelp* call like Song Sparrow. Song is a long, rapid series of melodious trills.
Range: Rather secretive, nests in dense brush, ferns, and tree-falls, especially along stream banks, in moist coniferous woods; in winter may be found in any type of dense woodland understory.

Bewick's Wren *Thryomanes bewickii* L 5¼" *(13 cm)*
Long, sideways-flitting tail, edged with white spots; long white eyebrow. Eastern *bewickii* reddish brown above; south Texas *cryptus* (not shown) duller, still tinged red. May be confused with juvenile, which has pale underparts, and worn adult Carolina Wrens.
Voice: Song variable, a high, thin buzz and warble, similar to Song Sparrow. Calls include a flat, hollow *jip*.
Range: Found in brushland, hedgerows, stream edges, open woods, and clear-cuts. Sharply declining east of the Rocky Mountains, especially east of the Mississippi, where extirpated over most of range.

Carolina Wren *Thryothorus ludovicianus* L 5½" *(14 cm)*
Deep rusty brown above, variably warm buff below; white throat and prominent white eye stripe.
Voice: Vivacious, melodious song, a loud, clear *teakettle tea-kettle teakettle* or *cheery cheery cheery.* Sings any time of day or year. Calls include loud, rich scolding.
Range: Common in the concealing underbrush of woodlands and swamps, wooded suburbs. Nonmigratory, but after mild winters resident populations expand north of mapped range. After harsh winters, range limits retract.

tail of moderate length

juvenile

**House
Wren**

western
parkmanii

indistinct
head pattern

eastern
aedon

Winter Wren
eastern *hiemalis*

very short tail

blackish flank
barring

buffy breast

bold white
supercilium

**Carolina
Wren**

rufous-brown
upperparts

Bewick's Wren
eastern *bewickii*

extensively rich
buffy underparts

warm ruddy
brown above

bold white
supercilium

white bars
in long tail

grayish white
underparts

Cactus Wren *Campylorhynchus brunneicapillus*
L 8½" (22 cm) Large; dark crown, streaked back, heavily barred wings and tail, broad white eyebrow. Breast is densely spotted with black.
Voice: Song is a low-pitched, harsh, rapid *cha cha cha cha cha.* Call is a variety of low, croaking notes, sometimes in a series.
Range: Common in cactus country and arid hillsides and valleys. Bulky nests are tucked into the protective spines of cacti or thorny bushes.

Rock Wren *Salpinctes obsoletus L 6" (15 cm)*
Dull gray-brown above with contrasting cinnamon rump, buffy flanks and tail tips, broad blackish tail band. Breast finely streaked. Frequently bobs its body, especially when alarmed.
Voice: Song is a variable mix of buzzes and trills; call, a buzzy *tick-ear* or *dzeeee.*
Range: Fairly common in arid and semiarid habitats, scrublands, and dry washes. Casual especially in fall and winter to the East.

Canyon Wren *Catherpes mexicanus L 5¾" (15 cm)*
White throat and breast, chestnut belly. Long bill aids in extracting insects from deep crevices.
Voice: Loud, silvery song, a decelerating, descending series of liquid *tee* and *tew* notes. Typical call is a sharp, buzzy *jeet.*
Range: Uncommon in canyons and cliffs; may also build its cup nest in stone buildings and chimneys.

Marsh Wren *Cistothorus palustris L 5" (13 cm)*
Somewhat secretive. Much plumage variation in eastern and western races. Where ranges overlap on western and central Great Plains, eastern birds darker, more richly colored, with black-and-white speckled neck; western birds duller, with brownish smudges on neck.
Voice: Songs are a mechanical-sounding mix of bubbling and trilling notes, more liquid in the East; harsher and much more variable in the West. Alarm call, a sharp *tsuk,* often doubled.
Range: Common in reedy marshes and cattail swamps. Football-shaped nest attached to reeds above water.

Sedge Wren *Cistothorus platensis L 4½" (11 cm)*
Often difficult to see. Crown and back streaked; eyebrow whitish or buffy and indistinct; underparts largely buff.
Voice: Song begins with a few single notes followed by a weak staccato trill or chatter; call note, a rich *chip,* often doubled. Globular nest similar to that of Marsh Wren.
Range: Nests in wet meadows and sedge marshes. Generally common but local on Great Plains; uncommon to rare in the East. Winters also in upper saltmarshes; most numerous along western Gulf Coast.

bold white supercilium

Rock Wren

buffy tail tips

cinnamon rump

Cactus Wren

densely spotted

faintly streaked

very large size

banded tail

very long bill

spotted grayish crown

Canyon Wren

rufous tail

white throat

extensively chestnut belly

white streaks on back

solid crown, whitish supercilium

Marsh Wren

streaked crown with indistinct supercilium

extensively buff below

Sedge Wren

300

Kinglets (Family Regulidae)

Small, active birds that often hover to feed. They regularly join mixed-species feeding flocks with chickadees and warblers during the nonbreeding season.

Golden-crowned Kinglet *Regulus satrapa* L 4" (10 cm)
Orange crown patch of **male** is bordered in yellow and black; **female**'s crown is yellow. Head pattern and paler underparts are unlike Ruby-crowned Kinglet.
Voice: Call is a series of high, thin *tsee* notes. Song, almost inaudibly high, is a series of *tsee* notes accelerating into a trill.
Range: Fairly common in coniferous woodlands; also in deciduous woods during nonbreeding season.

Ruby-crowned Kinglet *Regulus calendula* L 4¼" (11 cm)
Male's red crown patch seldom visible except when bird is agitated; dusky underparts. Compare carefully with Golden-crowned Kinglet. Active; flicks wings rapidly.
Voice: Calls include a scolding *je-ditt*. Song, several high, thin *tsee* notes followed by descending *tew* notes, ends with warbled three-note phrases.
Range: Common. Nests in coniferous forests; winters in a variety of woodlands, thickets.

Old World Warblers, Gnatcatchers
(Family Sylviidae)

Gnatcatchers are the only representatives in the East of this large, primarily Old World family. They are small, slender birds with long tails that are often cocked in a wrenlike fashion.

Black-tailed Gnatcatcher *Polioptila melanura*
L 4" (10 cm) White terminal spots on graduated tail feathers; short bill. **Breeding male** has glossy black cap, contrasting with eye ring. **Female** washed with brown above.
Voice: Calls include rasping *cheeh* and hissing *ssheh;* song is a rapid series of *jee* notes; all harsher than Blue-gray Gnatcatcher vocalizations.
Range: Resident in arid scrub.

Blue-gray Gnatcatcher *Polioptila caerulea*
L 4¼" (11 cm) Active. Long tail with white outer tail feathers is not graduated. **Male** is bluish above, in **breeding** plumage has black line on sides of crown. **Female** is grayer.
Voice: Call is a querulous *pwee.*
Range: Favors woodlands, thickets. May join mixed-species feeding flocks with kinglets and warblers.

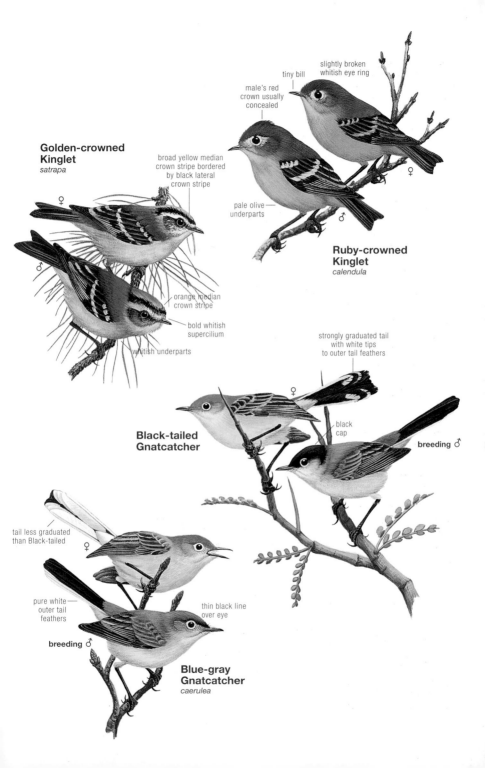

Golden-crowned Kinglet
satrapa

broad yellow median crown stripe bordered by black lateral crown stripe

orange median crown stripe

bold whitish supercilium

whitish underparts

male's red crown usually concealed

tiny bill

slightly broken whitish eye ring

pale olive underparts

Ruby-crowned Kinglet
calendula

strongly graduated tail with white tips to outer tail feathers

black cap

breeding ♂

Black-tailed Gnatcatcher

tail less graduated than Black-tailed

pure white outer tail feathers

breeding ♂

thin black line over eye

Blue-gray Gnatcatcher
caerulea

Thrushes (Family Turdidae)

Eloquent songsters of many habitats. With narrow, notched bills, they feed on insects and fruit.

Eastern Bluebird *Sialia sialis* L 7" *(18 cm)*

Chestnut throat, sides of neck, breast, sides and flanks; contrasting white belly, white undertail coverts. **Male** is uniformly deep blue above; *female* grayer. Distinguished from Western Bluebird by chestnut on throat and sides of neck and by white, not grayish, belly and under tail.

Voice: Call note is a musical, rising *chur-lee,* extended in song to *chur chur-lee chur-lee.*

Range: Found in open woodlands, farmlands, and orchards. Nests in holes in trees and posts; also in nest boxes. Serious decline in recent decades was due largely to competition with starling and House Sparrow for nesting sites. The provision of specially designed boxes has resulted in a comeback.

Western Bluebird *Sialia mexicana* L 7" *(18 cm)*

Male's upperparts and throat are deep purple-blue; breast, sides, and flanks chestnut; belly and undertail coverts grayish. Most show some chestnut on shoulders and upper back. *Female* duller, brownish gray above; breast, flanks tinged with chestnut; throat pale gray.

Voice: Call note is a mellow *few,* extended in brief song to *few few fawee.*

Range: Rare and irregular fall and winter visitor to central Texas.

Mountain Bluebird *Sialia currucoides* L 7¼" *(18 cm)*

Male sky blue above, paler below, with whitish belly and undertail coverts. **Female** brownish gray overall, with white belly and undertail coverts; white edges on coverts give folded wing a scalloped look. In fresh fall plumage, female's throat and breast tinged with red-orange; brownish rear flank contrasts with white undertail coverts, unlike female Eastern Bluebird, which has reddish flank. Mountain also has longer, thinner bill and longer primary tip projection. Often hovers above prey, chiefly insects, before dropping to catch them; also catches insects in flight.

Voice: Call is a thin *few;* song, a low, warbled *tru-lee.*

Range: Nests in tree cavities and nest boxes in open rangelands, meadows; in winter, found primarily in open lowlands and desert. Highly migratory; casual east of the Great Plains during migration and winter.

Townsend's Solitaire *Myadestes townsendi*

L 8½" *(22 cm)* Large and slender; gray overall, with bold white eye ring. Buff wing patches and white outer tail feathers are most conspicuous in flight. Often seen on a high perch.

Voice: Call note is a high-pitched *eek;* song, heard all year, a loud, complex, melodious warbling.

Range: In winter, found in valleys, canyons, and shelterbelts where juniper berries are available. Highly migratory; casual in fall and winter in Midwest and Northeast.

rufous in both sexes wraps around sides of neck and includes throat

juvenile

♂

♀

Eastern Bluebird
sialis

white belly and undertail coverts

Western Bluebird

gray sides to neck

♀

all-blue head

some dark rufous scapulars

♂

gray undertail coverts

thin bill

♀

♂

gray flanks

long primary projection

overall sky blue coloration

Mountain Bluebird

boldly spotted plumage

juvenile

overall gray color with prominent white eye ring

buffy wing patches

Townsend's Solitaire

prominent buffy wing stripe

white outer tail feathers

Northern Wheatear *Oenanthe oenanthe* L 5¾" *(15 cm)*
Tail pattern is distinctive: white rump, tail with dark central and terminal band. Greenland and eastern Canada Arctic race, *leucorhoa,* in **breeding** plumage, is buff below. *Males* in fall and winter resemble females. Active; bob their tails.
Voice: Calls include *chak* and whistled *wheet,* often combined. Song, a scratchy warbling mixed with call notes, is often given in flight with tail spread.
Range: Prefers open, stony habitats. Uncommon; very rare along Atlantic coast during fall; casual elsewhere and in late spring. Winters in Africa.

Swainson's Thrush *Catharus ustulatus* L 7" *(18 cm)*
Brownish olive above, with buffy lores and bold buffy eye ring; buffy breast with dark spots; brownish gray sides and flanks. Compare with Gray-cheeked Thrush (next page).
Voice: Song is an ascending spiral of varied whistles; common call, a sharp *quirk;* at night a peeping *queep* is heard.
Range: Fairly common; found in moist woods and swamps. Winters in South America; only a handful of documented early winter records in U.S.

Hermit Thrush *Catharus guttatus* L 6¾" *(17 cm)*
Complete, often whitish eye ring; reddish tail. Upperparts vary from rich brown to gray-brown. Eastern races such as widespread *faxoni* have buff-brown flanks. Larger, paler western mountain races, such as *auduboni,* have grayish flanks. Often flicks wings and slowly raises tail.
Voice: Song is a serene series of clear, flutelike notes with an introductory note followed by several quavering notes; the similar phrases are repeated at different pitches. Calls include a deeper *chuck,* often doubled, and a whiny, upslurred *wee.*
Range: Fairly common; found in coniferous or mixed woodlands, thickets, and gardens.

IDENTIFYING: *Catharus* Thrushes Separating the various *Catharus* thrushes is vexing, particularly when considering geographic variation within North America as a whole. Except for Bicknell's, all are polytypic. The geographic variation in two species (Hermit and Swainson's) is particularly striking, although in much of eastern North America these differences are more muted. This complex includes Veery, Gray-cheeked, Bicknell's, Swainson's, and Hermit Thrushes; the larger and distinctly colored and patterned Wood Thrush is in its own genus, *Hylocichla.*

Always consider the time of year when viewing any *Catharus.* During winter in North America, a *Catharus* is almost certainly a Hermit, there being only a handful of well-documented midwinter records of the other species. Look too for behavioral clues. Only Hermit regularly raises and lowers its tail and also often flicks its wings. The other species occasionally flick their wings.

When noting plumage, look carefully for tail and back contrast: All except Hermit show a uniform tail and back. Hermit has a rufous tail that contrasts with its brownish back. Also look carefully at the face: Veery, Gray-cheeked, and the very closely related (to Gray-cheeked) Bicknell's all have a dark eye that stands out on a blank, somewhat grayish face. There may be a trace of an eye ring around the rear of the eye. Swainson's, on the other hand, has a distinct buffy eye ring and supraloral line; Hermit has a circular whitish eye ring. The pattern and distinctness of the spotting

Northern Wheatear

♀

black inverted T shape on short, white tail

long wings

pale supercilium

pale gray upperparts

blackish mask

rich buffy chest

blackish wings

1st fall
leucorhoa

breeding adult
♂ *leucorhoa*

all juvenile *Catharus* have spotted plumage

juvenile
faxoni

warm brown upperparts with contrasting rufous tail

faxoni

brownish buff flanks

Hermit Thrush

olive brown upperparts

buffy eye ring and supraloral line

thin eye ring

grayish upperparts

auduboni

Alaska
incanus

grayish flanks

compare to Gray-cheeked Thrush

pale rufous tail

Swainson's Thrush

swainsoni

brownish flanks

below and the color of the flanks are also important. Veery is distinctive in that it has gray flanks; the others have grayish brown to buffy flanks, depending on the species and subspecies. The nominate race of Veery is also only faintly marked across a buffy breast, unlike the other species and some more westerly Veeries, which have bolder chest markings. Calls between species are diagnostic and should be learned; each gives multiple calls, though some are mainly known as nocturnal flight calls.

Identifying Bicknell's from Gray-cheekeds away from their breeding grounds is difficult, unless supported by diagnostic vocalizations—and even here the differences are not striking. The plumage features are all very subtle and probably overlap.

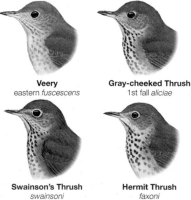

Veery
eastern *fuscescens*

Gray-cheeked Thrush
1st fall *aliciae*

Swainson's Thrush
swainsoni

Hermit Thrush
faxoni

Wood Thrush *Hylocichla mustelina* L 7¾" (20 cm)

Reddish brown above, brightest on crown and nape; rump and tail brownish olive. White eye ring conspicuous on streaked face. Large dark spots on whitish throat, breast, and sides.
Voice: Loud, liquid song of three- to five-note phrases, each phrase usually ending with a complex trill. Calls include a rapid *pit pit pit.*
Range: Fairly common in moist deciduous or mixed woods. Declining in some regions.

Veery *Catharus fuscescens* L 7" (18 cm)

Reddish brown above, white below, with gray flanks, grayish face, incomplete and indistinct gray eye ring. Upperparts duller, breast more spotted in more westerly *salicicola* than in eastern *fuscescens.*
Voice: Song is a descending series of *veer* notes; call, a sharp, descending, whistled *veer.*
Range: Fairly common; found in dense, moist woodlands and streamside thickets. Winters in South America. Only several valid winter records in U.S.

Bicknell's Thrush *Catharus bicknelli* L 6¾" (17 cm)

Identification of Bicknell's Thrush when not singing is very difficult due to variation within Gray-cheeked, of which Bicknell's formerly was considered a subspecies. Bicknell's is slightly smaller, warmer brown above, especially on tail; lower mandible has more yellow. Compare also with Hermit Thrush (preceding page).
Voice: Song similar to Gray-cheeked and usually comes in three parts, but with the first and the last rising. Call very similar to Gray-cheeked.
Range: Nests in stunted conifer—"krummholz"—vegetation at elevations above 3,000 feet and very locally along the coast. Winters in Caribbean montane forests, primarily on Hispaniola. Has disappeared from a number of peripheral breeding sites. Presumed to migrate close to Atlantic seaboard from Appalachians eastward, but rarely detected.

Gray-cheeked Thrush *Catharus minimus* L 7¼" (18 cm)

Cold gray-brown above, with faint, incomplete grayish white eye ring. Dark spots on breast, which is usually less buffy than Swainson's; flanks brownish gray. Breeding *minimus* on Newfoundland can be warmer colored above, more like Bicknell's.
Voice: Thin, nasal song is somewhat like Veery's, but first and last phrases drop, middle one rises; call, a sharp *pheu* similar to Veery's, but higher pitched, not descending.
Range: Uncommon. Somewhat shy. Nests in taiga and stunted vegetation near tree line. In migration found in a variety of woodlands. Winters in South America.

Wood Thrush

rich rufous above, especially on crown and nape

nearly complete bold, white eye ring

speckled cheeks

boldly spotted with black below

Veery

face pattern like Gray-cheeked with faint partial eye ring around rear of eye

faintly spotted chest

gray flanks

western
salicicola

eastern
fuscescens

Bicknell's Thrush

almost identical to Gray-cheeked, but slightly smaller and averages warmer above, especially on tail

grayish brown flanks

faint partial eye ring around rear of eye

Gray-cheeked Thrush

grayish lores

1st fall
aliciae

aliciae

grayish brown flanks

minimus

American Robin *Turdus migratorius L 10" (25 cm)*
Gray-brown above, with darker head and tail; bill yellow; under-parts brick red; lower belly white. Most western birds paler and duller overall than eastern nominate *migratorius* (shown here); in most, tail has white corners, visible in flight. *Juvenile*'s under-parts are tinged with cinnamon, heavily spotted with brown.
Voice: Loud, liquid song, is a variable *cheerily cheer-up cheerio.* Calls include a single *tup* and rapid *tut tut tut;* a high, thin *ssip* in flight.
Range: Common, widespread. Often seen on lawns, head cocked as it searches for earthworms; also eats insects and berries. Nests in shrubs, trees, on sheltered windowsills, and eaves. In winter, found in moist woodlands, swamps, suburbs, and parks. Num-bers vary greatly from winter to winter.

Clay-colored Robin *Turdus grayi L 9" (23 cm)*
Brownish olive above; tawny buff below; pale buffy throat is lightly streaked with olive. Lacks white around eye conspicuous in Amer-ican Robin.
Voice: Calls include a slurred *reeeur-ee,* a clucking note, and, in flight, a high, thin *ssi;* song resembles American Robin's but is slower and more slurred, clearer, much less varied.
Range: Species from east Mexico to north Colombia; rare but increasing and regular visitor and breeder in southernmost Texas. Rather secretive; forages in dense thickets, streamside brush, and woodlands. Will come to feeders.

Redwing *Turdus iliacus L 8¼" (21 cm)*
Vagrant to Northeast from Eurasia and Greenland. Distinctive whitish to buffy eyebrow; boldly streaked below, with rusty red flanks; rusty red wing linings visible in flight.
Voice: Call is a thin, penetrating *seeeh,* usually heard in flight; also a hard *kuk* note.
Range: Casual visitor to Newfoundland, mainly in winter; acci-dental south to New York and Pennsylvania.

Fieldfare *Turdus pilaris L 10" (25 cm)*
Vagrant to Northeast from Greenland and Eurasia. Large thrush with gray head and rump contrast with reddish brown upper back, blackish tail. Below, dark arrowhead-shaped spots pattern the buffy breast and extend along sides. White wing linings flash in flight.
Voice: Song is a noisy twittering; call note is a series of *shack* notes; also gives a thin *seeh.*
Range: Breeds from southern Greenland to Russian Far East. Casual vagrant, mainly in winter, to northeastern North Amer-ica. Most records are from Atlantic Canada. Accidental to Ontario and Minnesota.

juvenile

heavily
spotted

bold white
broken eye ring

yellow bill

♀

♂

**American
Robin**
migratorius

brick red
underparts

unlike American
Robin, no pale
markings around eye

brownish head
and upperparts

greenish
bill

tawny buff
underparts

**Clay-colored
Robin**
tamaulipensis

distinct
whitish buff
supercilium

Redwing

rusty red
wing linings

reaked
erparts

rusty red
flanks

immature

gray head

flashy white
wing linings

Fieldfare

buffy breast with bold
arrow-shaped spots

purplish brown back

gray rump

immature

Varied Thrush *Ixoreus naevius* L 9½" (24 cm)
Male has grayish blue nape and back, orange eyebrow; underparts orange with black breast band; buffy orange bar on underwing prominent in flight. *Female* distinguished from American Robin (preceding page) by orange eyebrow and wing bar, dusky breast band, and unmarked throat. *Juvenile* resembles female but has white belly, scalier-looking throat and breast. In a very rare variant morph, all orange color is replaced by white.
Voice: Call is a soft, low *tschook;* song, a slow series of variously pitched, eerie, whistled notes, rapidly trilled.
Range: Breeds in western coniferous forests. Very rare in winter as far east as Atlantic Canada and south to Virginia, especially at feeders during harsh weather. Typically does not associate with American Robins.

Mockingbirds, Thrashers (Family Mimidae)

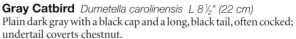

Notable singers, unequaled in North America for the rich variety and volume of their song. Some mimic the songs of other species.

Gray Catbird *Dumetella carolinensis* L 8½" (22 cm)
Plain dark gray with a black cap and a long, black tail, often cocked; undertail coverts chestnut.
Voice: Song is a mixture of melodious, nasal, and squeaky notes interspersed with catlike *mew* notes; some are good mimics. Most readily identified by harsh, downslurred *mew* call; also gives a low *quirt* and a clucking noise.
Range: Generally common but rather secretive in thickets.

Northern Mockingbird *Mimus polyglottos* L 10" (25 cm)
White outer tail feathers and white wing patches flash in flight and in territorial displays.
Voice: Song is a mixture of original and imitative phrases, each repeated several times.Often sings at night. Imitates other species' songs and calls. Both sexes sing in fall, claiming feeding territories. Call is a loud, sharp *check.*
Range: Found in a variety of habitats, including towns. Casual well north of mapped range.

Bahama Mockingbird *Mimus gundlachii* L 11" (28 cm)
Vagrant from Caribbean. Larger and browner than Northern Mockingbird, with streaking on neck and flanks; white only on tail tip. Lacks white patches on wings; flight more direct. Behaves more thrasher-like, skulking.
Voice: Song is varied but not known to include imitations; call slightly harsher, more downslurred than Northern.
Range: Casual in south Florida. Prefers dense cover.

Varied Thrush
meruloides

juvenile

orange wing bars and markings on wing

orange supercilium

♀

♂

black breast band

blackish cap

dark chestnut undertail coverts

short, slender dark bill

Gray Catbird

steel gray coloration

whitish wing patch

juvenile

white outer tail feathers

Northern Mockingbird
polyglottos

Bahama Mockingbird
gundlachii

distinct streaks on lower sides, flanks, and undertail coverts

darker tail than Northern Mockingbird

lacks white wing patch of Northern Mockingbird

whitish tail tips

Sage Thrasher *Oreoscoptes montanus L 8½" (22 cm)*
Yellow eye, white wing bars, and white-cornered tail. Grayish above, boldly streaked below. *Worn* late-summer birds show much less streaking. Juvenile has streaked head and back. Juvenile Northern Mockingbird also shows some dark streaking or spotting below.
Voice: Song is a long series of warbled phrases. Calls include a *chuck* and a high *churr.*
Range: Found in sagebrush plains. Casual vagrant to eastern North America.

Curve-billed Thrasher *Toxostoma curvirostre*
L 11" (28 cm) Breast mottled; bill all-dark, long, heavy, and strongly curved. Race from extreme southeastern Arizona to south Texas, *oberholseri,* shows clear spotting below; has pale wing bars; conspicuous white tips on tail. Juvenile has shorter bill.
Voice: Distinctive calls; *oberholseri* gives a sharp, even-pitched *whit-whit.* Song is elaborate and melodic, and includes low trills and warbles.
Range: Uncommon in canyons, brushlands. Casual east to the Great Plains, upper Midwest, and Florida panhandle.

Crissal Thrasher *Toxostoma crissale L 11½" (29 cm)*
Large and slender, with a distinctive chestnut undertail patch and a dark malar streak.
Voice: Song is varied and musical, its cadence more leisurely than in Curve-billed Thrasher. Calls include a repeated *chideery* and a whistled *toit-toit-toit.*
Range: Secretive, hiding in underbrush. Found mainly in dense mesquite and willows along streams and washes.

Brown Thrasher *Toxostoma rufum L 11½" (29 cm)*
Reddish brown above, heavily streaked below. Immature's eyes darker. Compare to Wood Thrush (page 306).
Voice: Sings a series of varied melodious phrases, each phrase usually given only two or three times. Seldom imitates other birds. Calls include a sharp *spuck* and a low *churr.*
Range: Uncommon to fairly common in hedgerows and woodland edges. Rare to Maritimes; casual to Newfoundland.

Long-billed Thrasher *Toxostoma longirostre*
L 11½" (29 cm) Closely resembles Brown Thrasher but grayer above and on cheek, with longer, more strongly curved bill; also has darker malar stripe, blacker streaking on whiter upperparts, shorter primary projection.
Voice: Song similar to Brown Thrasher. Gives *tsuck* call like Brown; other calls, a mellow *kleak,* and a loud, whistled *cheeooep.*
Range: Inhabits dense thickets in woodlands.

Sage Thrasher

small size
short bill
streaked underparts

worn

Curve-billed Thrasher *oberholseri*

striking orange iris
thick, curved bill
whitish wing bars
round spots below
white tail tips

Crissal Thrasher

thin, long, strongly downcurved bill
grayish overall
thin, dark malar stripe bordered by thin, whitish submoustachial
very long tail
chestnut undertail coverts

Brown Thrasher *rufum*

rufous upperparts
long rufous tail
shorter bill than Long-billed

Long-billed Thrasher *sennetti*

shorter primary projection than Brown
grayish brown upperparts
long curved bill
gray face

Bulbuls (Family Pycnonotidae)

Noisy, active Old World family of the tropics and subtropics.

Red-whiskered Bulbul *Pycnonotus jocosus* L 7" (18 cm)
Asian and African species. Red ear spot and undertail coverts distinctive but usually inconspicuous in behavior. *Juvenile* lacks ear patch; undertail coverts are paler.
Voice: Utters a chattering series of notes.
Range: Escaped cage birds first noted in early 1960s in Miami, Florida; now established as a small population in suburbs and parklands south of Miami. Some also in Los Angeles area.

Starlings (Family Sturnidae)

Widespread Old World family. Chunky and glossy birds; most species are gregarious and bold.

Common Myna *Acridotheres tristis* L 10" (25 cm)
Southern Asian species. Dark brown, with black head and white undertail coverts; yellow bill and skin around eye; white tail tip, patch at base of primaries, and wing linings distinctive in flight. Juveniles have more brownish heads.
Voice: Calls include gurglings, whistles, and screeches.
Range: Established in south Florida, where it is spreading. Found in urban and suburban areas; also open country in native range. Introduced elsewhere, including Hawaii, where it is common.

Hill Myna *Gracula religiosa* L 10½" (27 cm)
Asian species, fine mimic, popular as a cage bird. Glossy black; orange-red bill; yellow wattles and legs; white wing patch.
Voice: Calls include whistles and squawks.
Range: A small number of escaped birds, first noted in 1960s, persists but is very local in Miami.

European Starling *Sturnus vulgaris* L 8½" (22 cm)
Adult in **breeding** plumage is iridescent black, with a yellow bill with blue base in male, pink in female. In fresh **fall** plumage, feathers are tipped with white and buff, giving a speckled appearance; bill brownish. In flight, note short, square tail, stocky body, and short, broad-based, pointed wings that appear pale gray from below. *Juvenile* is gray-brown, with brown bill.
Voice: Call notes include squeaks, gurgles, warbles, chirps, and twittering; also imitates songs of other species.
Range: A Eurasian species introduced in New York in 1890-91, it soon spread across the continent and is found in a wide variety of human-altered habitats. Abundant, bold, aggressive, it often competes successfully with native species for nest holes. Outside nesting season, usually seen in large flocks, sometimes mixed with blackbirds.

Red-whiskered Bulbul

long black crest

small red auricular spot

black breast mark

red undertail coverts

juvenile

white tail tips

Common Myna
tristis

yellow skin around eye

blackish head

yellow bill

brown

white wing patch

white

white tail tip

Brown-headed Cowbird for comparison

yellow wattle

thick orange bill

white wing patch

Hill Myna
intermedia

triangular wings

fall

plumage heavily spotted with whitish

European Starling
vulgaris

winter

slender dark bill

short tail

yellow bill

glossy plumage

breeding ♂

overall grayish brown

dull, blurred streaks

juvenile

Wagtails, Pipits (Family Motacillidae)

Slender-billed birds. Most species pump their tails as they walk.

American Pipit *Anthus rubescens* L 6½" (17 cm)
Breeding birds grayish above, faintly streaked below. Becomes browner above and more streaked below in **winter**. Bill mostly dark; legs dark or tinged with pink. Tail has white outer feathers.
Voice: Call, given in flight, is a sharp *pip-pit;* song, a rapid series of *chee* or *cheedle* notes.
Range: Fairly common; nests on tundra in the far north, mountaintops farther south. Winter flocks are found in fields, other shortgrass environments, and on upper beaches.

Sprague's Pipit *Anthus spragueii* L 6½" (17 cm)
Dark eye prominent in pale buff face. Pale edges on back feathers give a scaly look. Underparts whitish, with a buffy wash and short, dark streaks on the breast. Legs pinkish. Uncommon, secretive, and somewhat solitary. Does not pump tail. Compare also with juvenile Horned Lark (page 284).
Voice: Call is a loud, squeaky *squeet,* usually given two or more times. Song, given continuously in high flight, is a descending series of musical *tzee* and *tzee-a* notes.
Range: Nests in prairies; winters in grassy fields. Accidental in eastern North America.

Waxwings (Family Bombycillidae)

All waxwings have sleek crests, silky plumage, and yellow-tipped tails. Red, waxy tips on secondary wing feathers may be indistinct or absent altogether.

Bohemian Waxwing *Bombycilla garrulus* L 8¼" (21 cm)
Larger, grayer than Cedar Waxwing; undertail coverts cinnamon. White and yellow wing spots. In flight, white wing patch is conspicuous. **Juvenile** browner above, streaked below, with pale throat.
Voice: Distinctive call, a buzzy twittering, lower and harsher than call of Cedar Waxwing.
Range: Nests in open coniferous or mixed woodlands. Winter range varies widely and unpredictably; large flocks visit scattered locations, feeding on berries and small fruits; also eats insects. Irregular winter wanderer to the Northeast, most often to Maine, Atlantic Canada. Individuals sometimes seen in flocks of Cedars.

Cedar Waxwing *Bombycilla cedrorum* L 7¼" (18 cm)
Smaller and browner than Bohemian Waxwing; belly pale yellow; undertail coverts white. Lacks yellow spots on wings. **Juvenile**'s streaked plumage seen well into fall. Usually nests late in summer.
Voice: Call is a soft, high-pitched, trilled whistle.
Range: Found in open habitats where berries are available; also eats insects. Highly gregarious in migration and winter.

American Pipit
rubescens

slender bill

breeding

dark malar stripe broadens at bottom

streaked underparts

winter

dark eye stands out in blank face

Sprague's Pipit

extensively pink at base of lower mandible

streaked back

faint necklace

pinkish legs

juvenile

crest

Cedar Waxwing

yellowish belly

yellow tail tip

juvenile

Bohemian Waxwing
pallidiceps

gray belly

gray belly

cinnamon undertail coverts

white base to primaries conspicuous in flight

318

Wood-Warblers (Family Parulidae)

A New World family. About half of its numerous species occur in North America.

Blue-winged Warbler *Vermivora pinus* L 4¾" (12 cm)
Male has bright yellow crown and underparts, white or yellowish white undertail coverts, black eye line, blue-gray wings with two white wing bars. **Female** duller overall. In both sexes, bill is long and slender; extensive white on tail is visible from below. Hybridizes with Golden-winged where ranges overlap. Hybrids may vary considerably from parent species in amount of black on head and throat, amount of yellow below, and size and color of wing bars. Some variations are shown here of the two main types, the more frequent *"Brewster's Warbler"* and the rare *"Lawrence's Warbler"* backcross. The latter is most often produced by crossing a first-generation hybrid with one of the parent species, which can result in the recessive traits showing, thus a "Lawrence's Warbler."
Voice: Main song is a wheezy *beee-bzzz,* the second note lower; alternate song is longer and more complex. Call a dry, sharp *chip;* in flight, a thin *zit.*
Range: Locally common; inhabits brushy meadows, second-growth woodlands, power-line cuts; nests on the ground. Rare to Atlantic Canada in fall. Blue-winged prefers a greater diversity of habitat than Golden-winged Warbler. Range is expanding at northern edge; gradually replacing Golden-winged. Winters in Mexico and Central America.

Golden-winged Warbler *Vermivora chrysoptera*
L 4¾" (12 cm) **Male** has black throat and yellow crown and wing patch; black ear patch is bordered in white. **Female** is similar but duller. In both sexes, extensive white on tail is conspicuous from below; underparts are grayish white; and bill is long and slender.
Voice: Main song is a high, soft *bee-bz-bz-bz,* the first note higher; also gives an alternate song similar to Blue-winged Warbler. Calls similar to Blue-winged Warbler. Songs of hybrids of these two species (see above) usually sound like one of the parent species.
Range: Prefers overgrown pastures, power-line cuts, second-growth and briary woodland borders and bogs; overall prefers early successional habitats more than Blue-winged does; nests on the ground. Uncommon to rare and declining. Very rare in fall to Maritimes. Found farther north and at higher elevations in the Appalachians than Blue-winged. Winters in southern Mexico and Central America.

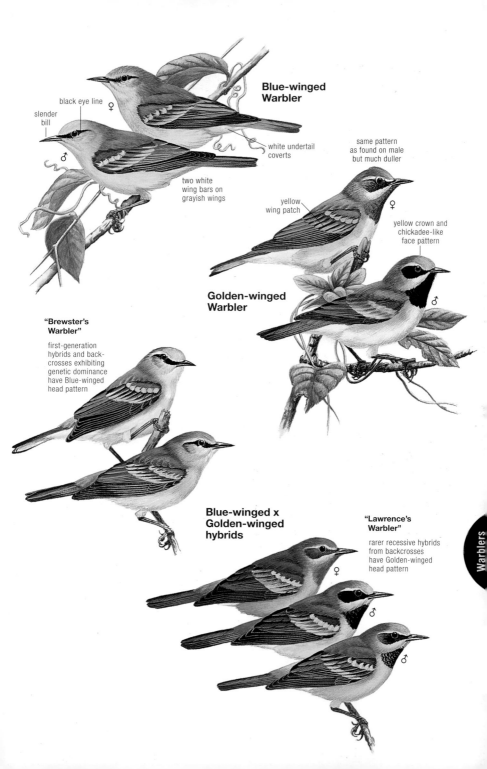

Blue-winged Warbler

slender bill

black eye line ♀

♂

white undertail coverts

two white wing bars on grayish wings

same pattern as found on male but much duller

yellow wing patch

♀

yellow crown and chickadee-like face pattern

♂

Golden-winged Warbler

"Brewster's Warbler"

first-generation hybrids and back-crosses exhibiting genetic dominance have Blue-winged head pattern

Blue-winged x Golden-winged hybrids

"Lawrence's Warbler"

rarer recessive hybrids from backcrosses have Golden-winged head pattern

♀

♂

♂

Warblers

Tennessee Warbler *Vermivora peregrina* L 4¾" (12 cm)

Plump, with short tail and long, straight bill. *Male* in spring is green above with gray crown, bold white eyebrow; white below. *Female* is tinged with yellow or olive overall, especially in fresh fall plumage. Adult male in fall resembles spring adult female but shows more yellow below. Immature also yellowish below; resembles young Orange-crowned, but is greener above and has a shorter tail and usually white undertail coverts. Spring birds may be confused with Warbling and Red-eyed Vireos (page 276); note especially Tennessee Warbler's slimmer bill, greener back.
Voice: Distinctive two- or three-part song; in three-part version, several rapid two-syllable notes are followed by a few higher single notes, ending with a staccato trill. Call a sharp *chip;* flight call a thin *seet.*
Range: Fairly common in interior, uncommon along East Coast. Found in coniferous and mixed woodlands in summer, mixed open woodlands and brushy areas during fall migration. Nests on the ground.

Orange-crowned Warbler *Vermivora celata*

L 5" (13 cm) Olive above, paler below. Yellow undertail coverts and faint, blurred streaks on sides of breast distinguish this species from the similar Tennessee Warbler. Note also that Orange-crowned's bill is thinner and slightly downcurved; tail is longer. Plumage varies among subspecies; the dullest, *celata,* breeds across Alaska and Canada and winters primarily in southeastern U.S.; *celata* is one of the latest fall migrant warblers. Tawny orange crown, absent in some *females* and *immatures,* is seldom discernible in the field. Immature *celata* can be particularly drab. Young birds are similar to immature Tennessees but show yellow undertail coverts and grayer upperparts.
Voice: Song is a high-pitched staccato trill with slight change of pitch; call note, a sharp, somewhat metallic *chip;* also a thin *seet.*
Range: Inhabits open, brushy woodlands, forest edges, and thickets. Nests on the ground; generally feeds in low branches, often in dead leaf clumps. Scarce along the East Coast.

Bachman's Warbler *Vermivora bachmanii* E

L 4¾" (12 cm) Probably extinct; the last definite record was in 1962 near Charleston, South Carolina. Bill is very thin, long, somewhat downcurved; undertail coverts white in both sexes. *Male* has yellow forehead, chin, and shoulders; black crown and bib. Immature male has less black on crown and throat, less yellow on shoulders, and more white on lower belly. *Female* drabber, crown gray, throat and breast gray or yellow.
Voice: Distinctive song, typically a rapid series of buzzes on one pitch; similar to Blue-winged Warbler's alternate song.
Range: Bachman's once bred in canebrakes and wet woodlands; was known very locally in the southeastern U.S., from southeastern Missouri and Logan County in southern Kentucky east to South Carolina, but was probably never numerous. Wintered in Cuba and on Isle of Pines.

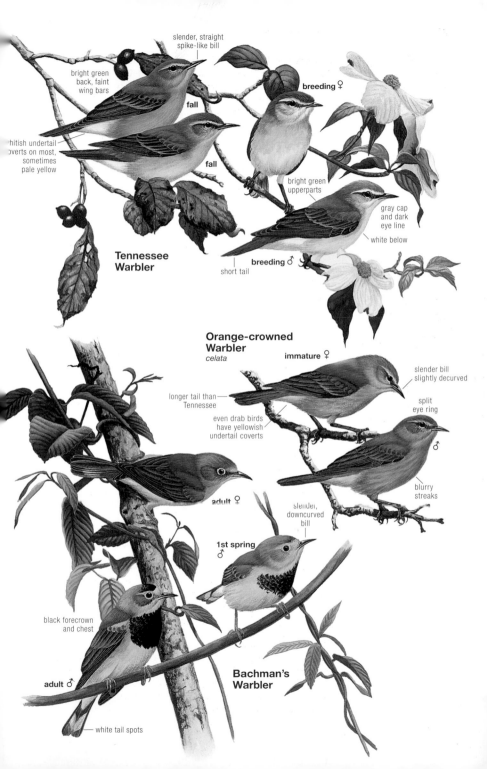

slender, straight
spike-like bill

bright green
back, faint
wing bars

fall

breeding ♀

hitish undertail
overts on most,
sometimes
pale yellow

fall

bright green
upperparts

gray cap
and dark
eye line

white below

**Tennessee
Warbler**

short tail

breeding ♂

**Orange-crowned
Warbler**
celata

immature ♀

slender bill
slightly decurved

longer tail than
Tennessee

split
eye ring

even drab birds
have yellowish
undertail coverts

♂

blurry
streaks

adult ♀

slender,
downcurved
bill

1st spring
♂

black forecrown
and chest

**Bachman's
Warbler**

adult ♂

white tail spots

Nashville Warbler *Vermivora ruficapilla L 4¾" (12 cm)*
Bold white eye ring, gray head, olive upperparts, white area below legs, and short tail. ***Female*** is duller than ***male.*** Eastern birds, *ruficapilla,* may wag their tail slightly.
Voice: Song of eastern *ruficapilla* is a series of high *see-weet* notes and a lower short trill; call, a dull metallic *pink.*
Range: Common; found in second-growth woodlands, brushy areas, and spruce bogs.

Virginia's Warbler *Vermivora virginiae L 4¾" (12 cm)*
Bold white eye ring on gray head; upperparts gray. Yellow patch on breast, yellow undertail coverts. Female is duller overall. Fall ***immature*** is slightly browner; little or no yellow on breast.
Voice: Song is a rapid series of thin notes, often ending with lower notes; call is a sharp *pink.* Often wags its long tail.
Range: Very rare migrant along western Great Plains. Casual in the East.

Northern Parula *Parula americana L 4½" (11 cm)*
Short-tailed warbler, gray-blue above with yellowish green upper back, two bold white wing bars. Throat and breast bright yellow, belly white. In ***adult male,*** reddish and black bands cross breast. In female and immature male, bands are fainter or absent.
Voice: One song is a rising buzzy trill, ending with an abrupt *zip* in eastern birds; no clear final note in more westerly birds. Calls include a clear *chip.*
Range: Nests in coniferous or mixed woods, especially near water and where Spanish moss (in South) and "old man's beard" lichen (in North) grow. These are used in building nests.

Tropical Parula *Parula pitiayumi L 4½" (11 cm)*
Dark mask and lack of distinct white eye ring distinguish Tropical from Northern Parula. Also yellow of throat extends farther onto sides of face and yellow below is more extensive; ***male*** has more blended orange breast band.
Voice: Song like Northern Parula.
Range: Rare in south Texas. Inhabits woodlands.

Yellow Warbler *Dendroica petechia L 5" (13 cm)*
Plump, yellow overall, with short tail; dark eye prominent in uniformly yellow face; reddish streaks below are distinct in ***male,*** faint or absent in ***female; immatures*** are duller. Much geographic variation. Northern races are more greenish above. Resident *gundlachi* of southernmost Florida is of the "Golden" group of the West Indian races. Note green crown and short primary projection. Resident subspecies in extreme south Texas and farther south are known as "Mangrove Warbler"; adult males of most subspecies have chestnut heads; immatures of this race and "Golden" are dull.
Voice: Song, rapid, variable, is sometimes written *sweet sweet sweet I'm so sweet.* Call a sweet, rich *chip.*
Range: Favors wet habitats, especially willows and alders; open woodlands, orchards. "Golden" and "Mangrove" Warblers resident in mangroves.

Nashville Warbler
ruficapilla

overall brownish gray with yellow undertail coverts

immature ♀

olive upperparts

grayish head with complete white eye ring

♂

dull whitish eye ring

immature

♂

extensively yellow underparts

yellow breast patch

short tail

pale vent

olive-edged remiges

tail longer than Nashville, frequently bobbed

yellow undertail coverts

Virginia's Warbler

gray-edged remiges

Northern Parula

bluish above with bronze-green back

immature ♀

broken white eye ring

banded chest

no eye ring

yellow extends into partly bluish face

♀

adult ♂

thick white wing bars

adult ♂

blended orange breast

extensively yellow on underparts

olive crown, sometimes with orange tinge

rufous head

"Mangrove" adult ♂
oraria

Tropical Parula
nigrilora

"Golden" adult ♂
gundlachi

dark eye stands out in blank face

adult ♂

immature ♀
aestiva

pale tertial edges

red streaks on underparts

Yellow Warbler
aestiva

immature ♀
gundlachi

♀

faint streaks

whitish underparts

short tail with yellow tail spots

immature ♀
amnicola

overall duller and darker than *aestiva*

Chestnut-sided Warbler *Dendroica pensylvanica*

L 5" (13 cm) ***Breeding male*** has yellow crown, black eye line, black whisker stripe; extensive chestnut on sides; ***female*** has greenish crown, less chestnut. Fall adults and ***immatures*** are lime green above, with white eye ring, whitish underparts, yellowish wing bars. Chestnut-sided often cocks its tail.

Voice: Song is a whistled *please please pleased to meetcha;* call, a rich *chip* note like Yellow Warbler.

Range: Fairly common in second-growth deciduous woodlands.

Cape May Warbler *Dendroica tigrina* *L 5" (13 cm)*

Most plumages have yellow on face, the color usually extending to sides of neck. Note also short tail; yellow or greenish rump; thin bill, slightly downcurved. ***Breeding male***'s chestnut ear patch and striped underparts distinctive; wing patch white. ***Female*** drabber, grayer, with two narrow white wing bars. ***Immature male***'s ear patch is less distinct. ***Immature female*** can be extremely drab, with gray face and only a tinge of yellow below and on rump; always has greenish edges on flight feathers. Cape May Warbler often shows aggressive behavior.

Voice: One song is a high, thin *seet seet seet seet;* call, a very high, thin *sip.*

Range: Breeds in black spruce forests, where often uncommon except during spruce budworm outbreaks. Rare west to Texas in migration. Winters chiefly in the West Indies, a few in southernmost Florida.

Magnolia Warbler *Dendroica magnolia* *L 5" (13 cm)*

Male is blackish above, with white eyebrow, white wing patch; broad white tail patches. Underparts yellow, streaked on breast and sides; undertail coverts white; under tail white except for black band at tip. Female has two wing bars; some ***first-spring females*** have dull white eye ring; often confused with rare Kirtland's Warbler (page 330). ***Fall adults*** and ***immatures*** are drabber, with grayish olive upperparts; white eye ring; faint gray band across breast. Compare immature Prairie Warbler (page 330). Does not bob tail.

Voice: Song is a short, whistled *weety-weety-weeteo.* Call, given rather infrequently, a unique, weak *tchif* or *wenk.*

Range: Fairly common to common; nests in moist coniferous forests. Very rare in winter in southern Florida.

Yellow-rumped Warbler *Dendroica coronata*

L 5½" (14 cm) Yellow rump, yellow patch on side, yellow crown patch, white tail patches. In northern and eastern birds, ***"Myrtle Warbler,"*** note white eyebrow, white throat and sides of neck, contrasting cheek patch. Western birds, ***"Audubon's Warbler,"*** have yellow throat, except for a few immature females. ***Females*** and fall males duller than ***breeding males*** but show same basic pattern.

Voice: Song, a soft warble, usually trailing off at the end. Call note of "Myrtle" is lower, flatter.

Range: Common in coniferous or mixed woodlands, also thickets during migration and winter. "Audubon's" is uncommon to Great Plains, central Texas; casual in the East.

usually cocks tail

greenish crown

Chestnut-sided Warbler

lime green upperparts

gray face with white eye ring

yellowish wing bars

grayish white underparts

breeding adult ♀

immature

yellow crown

chestnut sides

breeding adult ♂

all Cape Mays have greenish edges to remiges

breeding adult ♀

very slender, slightly decurved bill

yellow surrounds chestnut cheeks

breeding adult ♂

white wing patch

Magnolia Warbler

silver gray crown with bold supercilium

yellow rump in all plumages

1st spring ♀

yellow throat with extensive black streaking below

breeding adult ♂

Cape May Warbler

greenish rump

black back, white wing patch

gray head, white eye ring

immature ♀

grayish breast band

immature

immature ♂

all plumages with streaked underparts

extensive white vent and undertail coverts

white wing bars

fall adult ♂

"Myrtle Warbler" *coronata*

yellow crown patch

white throat

yellow patches on sides of breast

breeding ♀

most have pale yellow in rounded throat patch

"Audubon's Warbler" *auduboni*

breeding ♂

overall browner above than "Audubon's"

whitish supercilium, dark auriculars

angled whitish throat

fall ♀

yellow rump

yellow throat

Yellow-rumped Warbler

fall ♀

breeding ♂

Black-throated Blue Warbler *Dendroica caerulescens*
L 5¼" (13 cm) ***Male***'s black throat, cheeks, and sides separate blue upperparts, white underparts. Bold white patch at base of primaries. Appalachian males south of Susquehanna River drainage average darker above; back largely black in the case of *cairnsi* in southern Appalachians. ***Female***'s pale eyebrow is distinct on dark face; upperparts brownish olive; underparts buffy; wing patch smaller, occasionally absent on immature females.
Voice: Typical song is a slow series of four or five wheezy notes, the last note higher: *zwee zwee zwee zweeee* or a slower *zur zurr zreee.* Call is a single sharp *dit,* like the call of a Dark-eyed Junco.
Range: Inhabits deciduous forests; usually seen in lower or mid-level branches. A few birds winter in south Florida; most migrate to the West Indies. Very rare migrant west of Mississippi River, to Texas and Great Plains.

Cerulean Warbler *Dendroica cerulea* L 4¾" (12 cm)
Small, with short tail and two wide white wing bars. ***Adult male*** is bluish above with dark streaks; white below, with dark breast band and dark blue-gray streaking on sides. ***Female*** has greenish mantle, blue-green or bluish crown; pale eyebrow broadens behind the eye; breast and throat are pale yellowish. Immature male is like female, but shows some bluish and dark streaks above. Compare with immature female Blackburnian Warbler (below).
Voice: Song is a short, fast, accelerating series of buzzy notes on one pitch, ending with a long, single buzz note. Call includes a somewhat buzzy *tzzt.*
Range: Declining in the heart of its range. Found in tall trees in swamps, bottomlands, mixed woodlands near water. Fall migration begins from the second week of July. Range is expanding slightly in Northeast. Casual migrant north to Atlantic Provinces, west to Great Plains.

Blackburnian Warbler *Dendroica fusca* L 5" (13 cm)
Fiery orange throat, broad white wing patch, triangular ear patch, conspicuous in ***adult male. Female*** and immature male have paler throat, ***immature female*** paler still; note also the two white wing bars, streaked back, and bold yellow or buffy eyebrow, broader behind the eye, that curls around onto side of neck. Orange or yellow forehead stripe and white in outer tail feathers are distinct in all males, less so in females.
Voice: One song, a short series of high notes followed by a squeaky, ascending trill, ends on a very high note. Call includes a sharp *tckik.*
Range: Fairly common in coniferous or mixed forests of northern breeding range; pine-oak woodlands in the Appalachians. Generally stays in the upper branches.

whitish supercilium
with dark cheek

whitish
eye arc

buffy
underparts

most females
show whitish patch at
base of primaries

♀

dark blue

black

**Black-throated
Blue Warbler**

black stippling
on back

caerulescens ♂

white patch
larger in
adult males

Appalachians ♂
cairnsi

bold, broad supercilium
does not connect
to sides of neck

unstreaked
greenish back

bold, whitish
wing bars

**Cerulean
Warbler**

cerulean blue head
and upperparts

pale blue above,
brightest on crown

immature ♀

short tail

adult ♂

blackish
breast band

adult ♀

**Blackburnian
Warbler**

breeding ♀

bold white
wing patch

fiery
orange
throat

adult males have
a buffy belly

all Blackburnians
have pale mantle lines

fall adult ♂

**breeding
adult** ♂

dark triangular
auricular patch

immature ♀

bold, broad supercilium
connects to pale
sides of neck

Black-throated Gray Warbler *Dendroica nigrescens*

L 5" (13 cm) **Adult** plumage is basically the same year-round: black-and-white head; gray back streaked with black; white underparts, sides streaked with black; small yellow spot between eye and bill. Lacks central crown stripe of the Black-and-white Warbler (page 334); undertail coverts are white. Immature male resembles adult male; immature female is brownish gray above, throat white.

Voice: Varied songs include a buzzy *weezy weezy weezy weezy-weet.* Call is a sharp, flat *tchip.*

Range: Inhabits woodlands, brushlands, chaparral. Rare in winter in lower Rio Grande Valley, Texas; very rare during migration on western Great Plains; casual otherwise in eastern North America.

Golden-cheeked Warbler *Dendroica chrysoparia* **E**

L 5½" (14 cm) Dark eye line, unmarked yellow ear patches, and lack of any yellow on underparts distinguish this species from similar Black-throated Green Warbler. **Male** black above, with black crown, black bib, black-streaked sides. **Female** and immature male duller, upperparts olive with dark streaks; chin yellowish or white; sides of throat streaked. **Immature female** shows less black on underparts.

Voice: Song, *bzzzz layzee dayzee,* ends on a high note.

Range: Endangered; local in mixed cedar-oak woodland of the Edwards Plateau in central Texas. Casual migrant elsewhere in Texas.

Townsend's Warbler *Dendroica townsendi L 5" (13 cm)*

Dark crown, dark ear patch bordered in yellow. Olive above, streaked with black; yellow breast, white belly, yellowish black-streaked sides. **Adult male**'s throat and upper breast are black; **female** and immature male have streaked lower throat. **Immature female** is duller, lacks streaking on back; streaking on underparts is diffuse. Hybridizes with Hermit Warbler (not shown); hybrids usually have yellowish, streaked underparts of Townsend's, yellow head of Hermit.

Voice: Variable song, a series of hoarse *zee* notes. Call is a flat, sharp *tip,* similar to Black-throated Green.

Range: Rare fall migrant on western Great Plains. Casual in the East.

Black-throated Green Warbler *Dendroica virens*

L 5" (13 cm) Bright olive green upperparts; yellow face with greenish ear patch. Underparts are white, tinged with yellow on sides of vent and often on breast. **Male** has black throat and upper breast and black-streaked sides. **Female** and **immatures** show much less black below; **immature female** generally has dark streaking only on sides.

Voice: One song is a hoarse *zeee zeee zee-zo-zee;* the other, often written as *trees, trees, whispering trees.* Call is a sharp but flat *tip* or *tsik.*

Range: Fairly common in coniferous or mixed forests in summer.

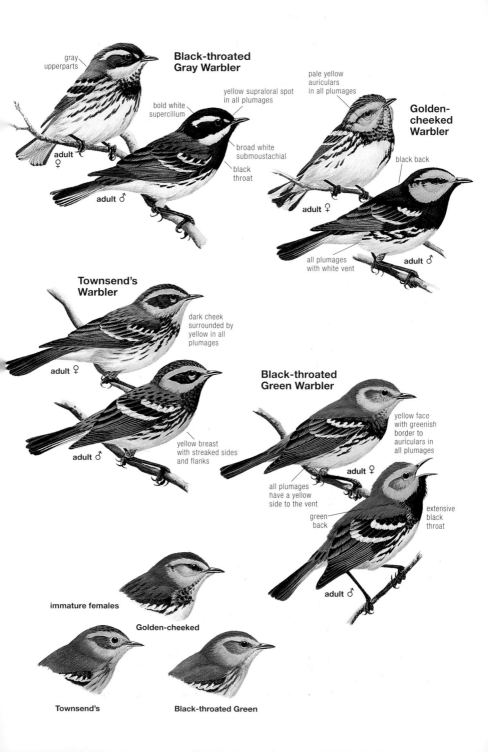

gray
upperparts

**Black-throated
Gray Warbler**

pale yellow
auriculars
in all plumages

**Golden-
cheeked
Warbler**

bold white
supercilium

yellow supraloral spot
in all plumages

broad white
submoustachial

black
throat

black back

adult ♀

adult ♀

broad white
submoustachial

adult ♂

all plumages
with white vent

adult ♂

**Townsend's
Warbler**

dark cheek
surrounded by
yellow in all
plumages

adult ♀

**Black-throated
Green Warbler**

yellow face
with greenish
border to
auriculars in
all plumages

yellow breast
with streaked sides
and flanks

adult ♂

all plumages
have a yellow
side to the vent

green
back

adult ♀

extensive
black
throat

immature females

Golden-cheeked

adult ♂

Townsend's

Black-throated Green

Kirtland's Warbler *Dendroica kirtlandii* **E**

L 5¾" (15 cm) Blue-gray above, strongly black-streaked on back; yellow below, streaked on sides; white eye ring, broken at front and rear; two whitish wing bars, thin and indistinct. Often confused with first-spring female Magnolia Warbler (page 324). **Adult female** is slightly duller; **immature female** brownish above. Kirtland's Warbler constantly wags its tail.

Voice: Song is loud and lively, a variable series of low, sharp notes followed by slurred whistles.

Range: The annual breeding census counted 1,420 singing males in 2005, up from the historic low of 167 in 1987. Controlled plantings and fires help produce the required habitat: thickets of young jack pines. Very rare in summer in Ontario and especially Wisconsin. Very rarely seen in migration. Winters in the Bahamas.

Yellow-throated Warbler *Dendroica dominica*

L 5½" (14 cm) Plain gray back; large, white patch on each side of head. *Male* has black crown and face; in female, black is less extensive. Throat and upper breast bright yellow; rest of underparts white, with black streaks on sides; bold white eyebrow. Eastern races *dominica* and *stoddardi* (of eastern Gulf Coast, not shown) have yellow supraloral area, unlike more westerly *albilora; stoddardi* and birds from Delmarva Peninsula have very long bills.

Voice: Song is a series of clear, downslurred whistles ending with a rising note. Call is a rich *chip.*

Range: Fairly common in live oak and pine woodlands (especially *dominica*), cypress, sycamores (especially *albilora*). Usually forages high in the trees, creeping methodically along the branches.Very rare northward to southern Canada.

Prairie Warbler *Dendroica discolor* *L 4¾" (12 cm)*

Adult male olive above, with faint chestnut streaks on back; bright yellow eyebrow, yellow patch below eye; bright yellow below (duller on undertail coverts), streaked with black on sides of neck and body. Two indistinct wing bars. *Female* and immature male are slightly duller. *Immature female* is duller still, grayish olive above; lack of complete eye ring or gray breast band distinguish her from fall Magnolia Warbler (page 324). Wags or flicks tail.

Voice: Song, a rising series of buzzy *zee* notes. Call is a flat *tsuk.*

Range: Fairly common in open woodlands, overgrown fields, mangroves. Rare in fall to Atlantic Canada. Declining in the upper Midwest.

Palm Warbler *Dendroica palmarum* *L 5½" (14 cm)*

Breeding adult of eastern race, *hypochrysea,* has chestnut cap, yellow eyebrow, and entirely yellow underparts, with chestnut streaking on sides of breast. Fall adults and immatures lack chestnut cap and streaking; yellow is duller. Western nominate race, *palmarum,* has whitish belly and darker streaks on sides of breast; less chestnut. *Fall adults* and immatures are drab. Habitually wags its tail.

Voice: Song is a rapid, buzzy trill. Call is a sharp *tsik.*

Range: Fairly common; nests in bogs. During migration and winter, found in woodland borders, open brushy areas.

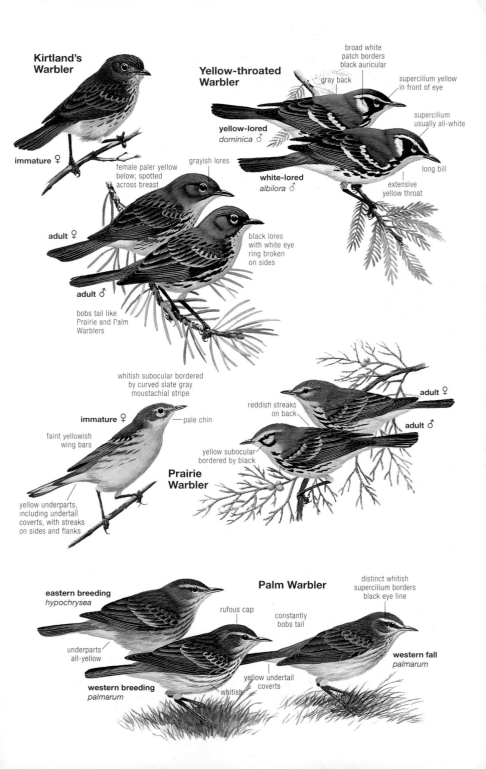

Kirtland's Warbler

immature ♀

Yellow-throated Warbler

broad white patch borders black auricular

gray back

supercilium yellow in front of eye

yellow-lored
dominica ♂

supercilium usually all-white

long bill

white-lored
albilora ♂

extensive yellow throat

female paler yellow below; spotted across breast

grayish lores

adult ♀

black lores with white eye ring broken on sides

adult ♂

bobs tail like Prairie and Palm Warblers

whitish subocular bordered by curved slate gray moustachial stripe

immature ♀ — pale chin

faint yellowish wing bars

reddish streaks on back

adult ♀

adult ♂

yellow subocular bordered by black

Prairie Warbler

yellow underparts, including undertail coverts, with streaks on sides and flanks

Palm Warbler

distinct whitish supercilium borders black eye line

eastern breeding
hypochrysea

rufous cap

constantly bobs tail

underparts all-yellow

western fall
palmarum

western breeding
palmarum

whitish

yellow undertail coverts

Bay-breasted Warbler *Dendroica castanea L 5½" (14 cm)*

Breeding male has chestnut crown, throat, and sides; black face; creamy patch at each side of neck; two white wing bars. *Female* is duller. *Fall adults* and *immatures* resemble Blackpoll Warbler and Pine Warbler. Bay-breasted is brighter green above, wing bars are thicker; underparts show little or no streaking and little yellow; flanks usually show some buff or bay color; legs usually entirely dark; undertail coverts are buffy or whitish. Short tail projection past undertail coverts for both Bay-breasted and Blackpoll.

Voice: Song consists of high-pitched double notes. Calls include a sharp *chip.*

Range: Uncommon; nests in coniferous forests. Migrates earlier in fall than Blackpoll.

Blackpoll Warbler *Dendroica striata L 5½" (14 cm)*

Solid black cap, white cheeks, and white underparts identify *breeding male;* back and sides boldly streaked with black. Compare with Black-and-white Warbler (next page). *Female* is duller overall, variably greenish above and pale yellow below; some are gray; note streaking. *Fall adults* and immatures resemble Bay-breasted and Pine Warblers. Blackpoll is mostly pale greenish yellow below, with dusky streaking on sides; legs pale on front and back, dark on sides; undertail coverts long and usually white.

Voice: Song is a series of high *tseet* notes. Calls include a sharp *chip.*

Range: Common; nests in coniferous forests. Migrates later in fall than Bay-breasted Warbler. Very rare in fall in most of South because much migration is off East Coast.

Pine Warbler *Dendroica pinus L 5½" (14 cm)*

Relatively large bill; long tail projection past undertail coverts; throat color extends onto sides of neck, setting off dark cheek patch. *Male* is greenish olive above, without streaking; throat and breast yellow, with dark streaks on sides of breast; belly and undertail coverts white. *Female* is duller. *Immatures* are brownish or brownish olive above, with whitish wing bars and brownish tertial edges; male is dull yellow below, female largely white; both have brown wash on flanks.

Voice: Song is a twittering musical trill, varying in speed. Calls include a flat, sweet *chip.*

Range: Common in pines in summer; also in mixed woodlands in winter. Rare to Atlantic Canada in fall and early winter.

IDENTIFYING: Blackpoll, Bay-breasted, and Pine Warblers Blackpoll and Bay-breasted Warblers are structurally similar in that they are chunky with only short tail projection past the undertail coverts. Pine Warblers, on the other hand, show very long tail projection past the undertail coverts. Both fall Blackpolls and Bay-breasteds show blended auriculars to the throat, while Pine in all plumages always shows sharp contrast between the throat and the auriculars. Pines are variable in color depending on age and sex; immature females are essentially brown above and whitish below. They are unstreaked above. Fall Blackpolls show distinct but somewhat narrow white wing bars and white edges to the tertials (Pines lack

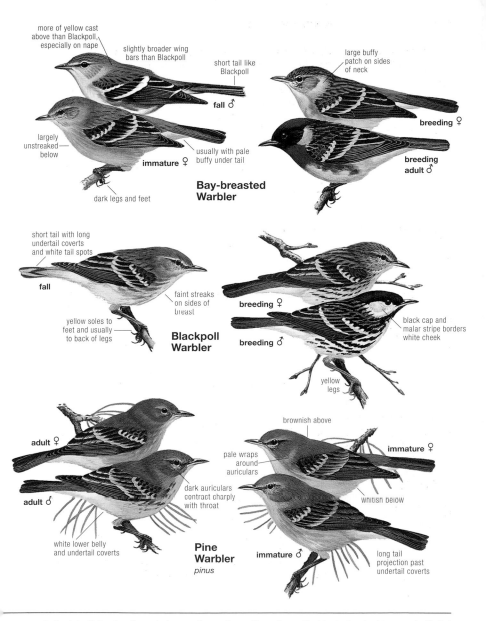

Bay-breasted Warbler

more of yellow cast above than Blackpoll, especially on nape

slightly broader wing bars than Blackpoll

short tail like Blackpoll

fall ♂

large buffy patch on sides of neck

breeding ♀

breeding adult ♂

largely unstreaked below

immature ♀

usually with pale buffy under tail

dark legs and feet

Blackpoll Warbler

short tail with long undertail coverts and white tail spots

fall

faint streaks on sides of breast

yellow soles to feet and usually to back of legs

breeding ♀

breeding ♂

black cap and malar stripe borders white cheek

yellow legs

Pine Warbler
pinus

adult ♀

adult ♂

pale wraps around auriculars

dark auriculars contrast sharply with throat

white lower belly and undertail coverts

brownish above

immature ♀

immature ♂

whitish below

long tail projection past undertail coverts

distinct tertial edges), a dark eye line, olive upperparts with darker streaks, and some indication of streaking on the sides of the breast. Fall Bay-breasteds are brighter, more of a yellow-green above, especially on the nape; they are clearer below; and they have thicker white wing bars and less of an eye line. Many, especially males, show some chestnut on the flank.

Even those that lack chestnut have a buffy tint to the rear flank and vent region. This region is snowy white—and sometimes washed with pale yellow—on Blackpoll. Bay-breasteds and Pines have dark legs and feet. Fall Blackpolls have largely dark legs, but look for the pale soles to the feet as well as pale along the back of the leg.

Prothonotary Warbler *Protonotaria citrea*

L 5½" (14 cm) Plump, short tailed, and long billed. Eyes are large, dark, and prominent. **Male**'s head and underparts golden yellow, fading to white undertail coverts; wings blue-gray, without wing bars; blue-gray tail has large white patches. **Female** duller.
Voice: Song is a series of loud, ringing *zweet* notes; gives a dry *chip* note and buzzy flight call.
Range: Fairly common. The only eastern warbler that nests in cavities and crannies, usually surrounded by sluggish or stagnant water. Casual to rare vagrant west and north of normal range.

Worm-eating Warbler *Helmitheros vermivorum*

L 5¼" (13 cm) Bold, dark stripes on buffy head; upperparts brownish olive; breast buffy; long, spikelike bill.
Voice: Song is a series of sharp, dry *chip* notes, like Chipping Sparrow's song but faster. Common call, *zeep-zeep*.
Range: Found chiefly in dense undergrowth on wooded slopes. Often feeds in clusters of dead leaves. Casual vagrant to Atlantic Canada and western Great Plains.

Swainson's Warbler *Limnothlypis swainsonii*

L 5½" (14 cm) Pale eyebrow, conspicuous between brown crown and dark eye line. Brown-olive above, grayish below. Bill very long and spiky. Walks or shuffles on the ground and shivers while picking up dead leaves.
Voice: Song is a series of thin, slurred whistles like beginning of song of Louisiana Waterthrush; often ends with a rising *tee-oh*. Calls include a loud, dry *chip*.
Range: Uncommon and secretive. Found in undergrowth in swamps and canebrakes; local in mountain laurel and rhododendron. Casual north to southern Canada.

Black-and-white Warbler *Mniotilta varia* *L 5¼" (13 cm)*

The only warbler that regularly creeps along branches and up and down tree trunks like a nuthatch. Boldly striped on head, most of body, and undertail coverts. **Male**'s throat and cheeks are black in breeding plumage; in winter, chin is white. **Female** and **immatures** have pale cheeks; female diffusely streaked on buffy flanks; buffy wash particularly bright on immatures.
Voice: Song is a long series of high, thin *wee-see* notes. Calls include a sharp *chip* and high *seep-seep*.
Range: Common in mixed woodlands.

American Redstart *Setophaga ruticilla* *L 5¼" (13 cm)*

Male glossy black, with bright orange patches on sides, wings, and tail; belly and undertail coverts white. **Female** is gray-olive above, white below with yellow patches. Immature male resembles female; by **first spring,** lores are usually black, breast has some black spotting; adult male plumage is acquired by second fall. Often fans its tail and spreads its wings when perched.
Voice: Variable song, a series of high, thin notes usually followed by a wheezy, downslurred note. Call is a rich, sweet *chip*.
Range: Common in second-growth woodlands.

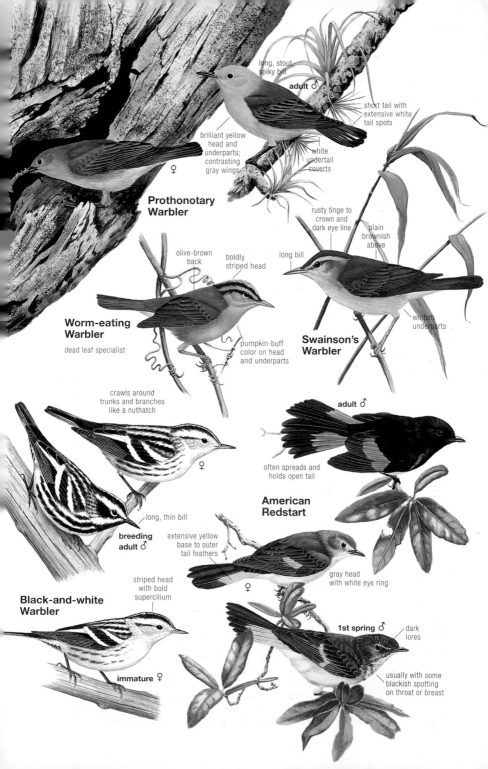

long, stout, spiky bill

adult ♂

short tail with extensive white tail spots

brilliant yellow head and underparts; contrasting gray wings

white undertail coverts

♀

Prothonotary Warbler

rusty tinge to crown and dark eye line

plain brownish above

long bill

whitish underparts

Swainson's Warbler

olive-brown back

boldly striped head

Worm-eating Warbler

dead leaf specialist

pumpkin-buff color on head and underparts

crawls around trunks and branches like a nuthatch

adult ♂

often spreads and holds open tail

♀

American Redstart

long, thin bill

breeding adult ♂

extensive yellow base to outer tail feathers

♀

gray head with white eye ring

Black-and-white Warbler

striped head with bold supercilium

immature ♀

1st spring ♂

dark lores

usually with some blackish spotting on throat or breast

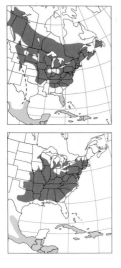

Ovenbird *Seiurus aurocapilla L 6" (15 cm)*

Russet crown bordered by dark stripes; bold white eye ring. Olive above; white below, with bold streaks of dark spots; pinkish legs. Plump body. Generally seen on the ground; walks, with tail cocked, rather than hops.

Voice: Typical song, a loud *teacher teacher teacher,* rising in volume. Calls include a sharp, dry *chip.*

Range: Common in mature forests. Rare in winter along Gulf and Atlantic coasts to North Carolina.

Louisiana Waterthrush *Seiurus motacilla L 6" (15 cm)*

Distinguished from Northern Waterthrush by contrast between white underparts and salmon-buff flanks; bicolored eyebrow, pale buff in front of eye, white and much broader behind eye; larger bill; bubblegum pink legs. A ground dweller; walks, rather than hops, bobbing its tail constantly but usually slowly.

Voice: Call note, a sharp *chink,* is slightly flatter than that of Northern Waterthrush. Song begins with three or four shrill, slurred notes followed by a brief, rapid jumble.

Range: Uncommon; found along flowing streams in woodlands, also near ponds and in swamps. Returns early in spring; many depart south already in midsummer. Casual to Great Plains, Maritimes.

Northern Waterthrush *Seiurus noveboracensis*

L 5¾" (15 cm) Distinguished from Louisiana Waterthrush by lack of contrast in color between flanks and rest of underparts; buffy eyebrow, of even width throughout or slightly narrowing behind eye; smaller bill; drabber leg color. Some birds are washed with pale yellow below, whereas others are whiter below, with whiter eyebrow. A ground dweller; walks, rather than hops, bobbing its tail constantly and usually rapidly.

Voice: Call note, a metallic *chink,* is slightly sharper than that of Louisiana Waterthrush. Song begins with loud, emphatic notes and ends in lower notes, delivered more rapidly.

Range: Found chiefly in woodland bogs, swamps, puddles, and thickets. Wintering birds also found in mangroves.

IDENTIFYING: Waterthrushes The two species of waterthrush differ in their choices of breeding habitats: Louisiana prefers clear tumbling streams in the foothills and mountains, while Northern prefers more stagnant bogs in northern boreal regions and in the central and northern Appalachians. Louisiana also breeds on the eastern coastal plain along slow-moving streams. In migration, both species can use the same pools and streams. Louisiana is an earlier migrant in both spring and fall. The first Louisiana can appear in the South by early March, whereas Northern doesn't arrive until a month later. In fall, any waterthrush seen after about 20 August is almost certainly a Northern, especially on into September. Northern, which is a bit smaller and longer tailed than Louisiana, has a more petite bill. The ground color of the underparts and the supercilium is usually buffy yellow, sometimes strongly so, but some are paler, almost whitish. This variation is individual, not geographic, although some populations average more yellowish overall (e.g., in the Northeast and Atlantic Canada). Still, the coloration of these areas is uniform. Northern is heavily streaked below, including across the

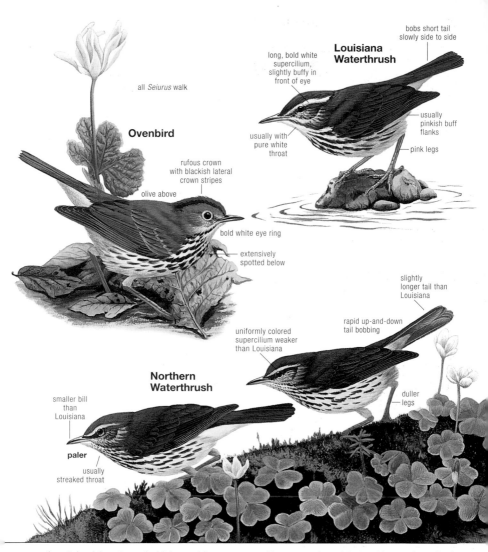

all *Seiurus* walk

Ovenbird

rufous crown
with blackish lateral
crown stripes

olive above

bold white eye ring

extensively
spotted below

**Louisiana
Waterthrush**

bobs short tail
slowly side to side

long, bold white
supercilium,
slightly buffy in
front of eye

usually
pinkish buff
flanks

pink legs

usually with
pure white
throat

slightly
longer tail than
Louisiana

rapid up-and-down
tail bobbing

uniformly colored
supercilium weaker
than Louisiana

**Northern
Waterthrush**

smaller bill
than
Louisiana

duller
legs

paler

usually
streaked throat

throat. Louisiana has a bold, long white supercilium that is tinged with buff in front of the eye.
The streaking below is less strong, and the
throat is usually pure white, although some
show dark spots. Usually a patch of pinkish buff
contrasts with the rest of the underparts. In
fresh plumage it extends across the vent region.
Louisiana has a bigger bill and a shorter tail, and
it averages a little grayer above. Louisiana's legs
are usually a purer pink.

Both species bob their tails. In Northern, bobbing is a rather rapid up-and-down movement;
in Louisiana, it is slower and more deliberate

with more of a side-to-side motion. Both
species give a loud sharp call. Northern's call
is a sharp *chink,* but Louisiana's has more of an
itch sound at the end. Experienced observers
with a good ear can usually tell the difference.
The songs of the two strongly differ: The opening of Louisiana's is quite suggestive of Swainson's Warbler, though the sputtering notes at
the end are quite different. The loud ringing song
of Northern can be confused with both Connecticut and Kirtland's Warbler, especially if
heard at a distance. Louisiana is a little shyer
on average and hard to approach.

Mourning Warbler *Oporornis philadelphia* L 5¼" (13 cm)
Lack of bold white eye ring distinguishes *adult male* from Connecticut Warbler. *Adult female* and especially *immatures* may show a thin, nearly complete eye ring, but compare with Connecticut. Immatures generally have more yellow on throat than MacGillivray's; compare also with female Common Yellowthroat (page 342). Immature males often show a little black on breast. Mourning Warblers hop rather than walk.
Voice: Call is a flat, hollow *chip.* Song is a series of slurred two-note phrases followed by two or more lower phrases.
Range: Uncommon in dense undergrowth, thickets, moist woods; nests on the ground. Most spring migration is west of the Appalachians.

MacGillivray's Warbler *Oporornis tolmiei* L 5¼" (13 cm)
Bold white crescents above and below eye distinguish all plumages from male Mourning and all Connecticut Warblers. Crescents may be very hard to distinguish from the thin, nearly complete eye ring found on female and immature Mourning Warblers. *Immature* MacGillivray's Warblers generally have grayer throat than immature Mournings and a fairly distinct breast band above yellow belly. Field identification is often difficult. MacGillivray's hops rather than walks.
Voice: Call is a sharp, harsh *tsik.* Song has two parts: a buzzy trill ending in a downslur.
Range: Rare migrant along western Great Plains. Casual to East.

Connecticut Warbler *Oporornis agilis* L 5¾" (15 cm)
Large eye with bold white eye ring conspicuous on *male*'s gray hood and *female*'s brown or gray-brown hood. Eye ring is sometimes slightly broken on one side only. *Immature* has a brownish hood and brownish breast band. A large, stocky warbler, noticeably larger than Mourning and MacGillivray's Warblers. Like Mourning, long undertail coverts give Connecticut a short-tailed, plump appearance. Walks rather than hops.
Voice: Loud, accelerating song repeats a brief series of explosive *beech-er* or *whip-ity* notes. *Chip* note rarely heard.
Range: Uncommon; found in spruce bogs, moist woodlands; nests on the ground; generally feeds on the ground or on low limbs. Spring migration is almost entirely west of the Appalachians. Fall migrants uncommon in the East.

IDENTIFYING: *Oporornis* **Warblers** This largely terrestrial genus comprises four species of rather large and chunky warblers with short tails, hefty bills, and long legs. All occur in the East, though MacGillivray's occurs regularly only along the western edge; it is casual through the remainder of the region. With its uniformly bright yellow underparts, bright olive-green upperparts, and distinctive head pattern, Kentucky is easily

separated. Over much of the East, Mourning and Connecticut Warblers are often confused with each other. Both arrive late in the spring; Connecticut is our latest arriving warbler, with very few migrants noted before early May, even from south Florida, their point of entry. Their fall migrations overlap, though Connecticut averages later.

Behavior is the best distinguishing feature. Mourning, like the other *Oporornis* species, hop,

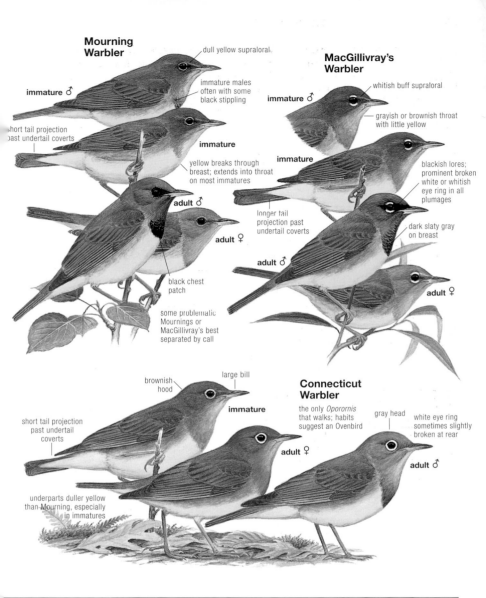

Mourning Warbler

dull yellow supraloral

immature ♂

immature males often with some black stippling

short tail projection past undertail coverts

immature

yellow breaks through breast; extends into throat on most immatures

adult ♂

adult ♀

black chest patch

some problematic Mournings or MacGillivray's best separated by call

MacGillivray's Warbler

whitish buff supraloral

immature ♂

grayish or brownish throat with little yellow

immature

blackish lores; prominent broken white or whitish eye ring in all plumages

longer tail projection past undertail coverts

dark slaty gray on breast

adult ♂

adult ♀

Connecticut Warbler

brownish hood

large bill

immature

the only *Oporornis* that walks; habits suggest an Ovenbird

gray head

white eye ring sometimes slightly broken at rear

adult ♀

adult ♂

short tail projection past undertail coverts

underparts duller yellow than Mourning, especially in immatures

whereas Connecticut walks. Connecticut Warblers have a more hooded look, with a fuller and complete eye ring (often with a break at the rear), and duller yellow underparts. Mourning gives a loud hollow *chip* frequently; Connecticut seldom gives its *chip* note, and its flight call is a buzzy *zeet*. Mourning and MacGillivray's give a thin *seep* for a flight note. MacGillivray's can usually be separated from Mourning by plumage, but some problematical birds are nearly identical in appearance and are best identified by their very different *chip* calls.

Although not an *Oporornis*, Nashville Warbler—with its olive upperparts, mostly yellow underparts, gray head, and circular whitish eye ring—is sometimes misidentified as a Connecticut Warbler. However, Nashville is smaller, has a distinct yellow throat, and is much more active.

Kentucky Warbler *Oporornis formosus* L 5¼" (13 cm)

A short-tailed, long-legged warbler. Bold yellow spectacles separate black crown from black on face and sides of neck; underparts are entirely yellow, upperparts bright olive. Black areas are duller on *female,* olive on immature female.

Voice: Song is a series of rolling musical notes, *churry churry churry,* much like the song of the Carolina Wren. Call is a low, sharp *chuck.*

Range: Fairly common in rich, moist woodlands; nests and feeds on the ground in dense undergrowth. Very rare to Maritimes; casual to Newfoundland. Rare to southern Ontario, mainly in spring; very rare to Maritimes, casual to Newfoundland.

Canada Warbler *Wilsonia canadensis* L 5¼" (13 cm)

Black necklace on bright yellow breast identifies *male;* note also spectacles composed of bold white eye ring and yellow supraloral. In *females,* necklace is dusky and indistinct. Male is blue-gray above, females duller. All birds have white undertail coverts.

Voice: Song begins with one or more short, sharp *chip* notes and continues as a rich and highly variable warble. Call is a sharp *tick.*

Range: Uncommon in dense woodlands and brush. Usually forages in undergrowth or low branches, but also seen fly-catching. Winters in South America. Rather rare in eastern Gulf region and Florida, mostly recorded in fall.

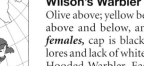

Wilson's Warbler *Wilsonia pusilla* L 4¾" (12 cm)

Olive above; yellow below, with yellow lores. Long tail is all-dark above and below, and often cocked. *Male* has black cap; in *females,* cap is blackish or absent, forehead yellowish. Yellow lores and lack of white in tail help distinguish female from female Hooded Warbler. Eastern race, *pusilla,* is duller than the two western subspecies; is also scarcer.

Voice: Song is a rapid, variable series of *chee* notes, often trailing off into a trill; common call, a sharp *chimp.*

Range: Fairly common; nests in dense, moist woodlands, bogs, willow thickets, and streamside tangles.

Hooded Warbler *Wilsonia citrina* L 5¼" (13 cm)

All ages have dark lores, unlike Wilson's Warbler; also bigger bill and larger eye. Extensive black hood identifies *male. Adult female* shows blackish or olive crown and sides of neck; sometimes has black throat or black spots on breast; *immature female* lacks black. Note that in both sexes tail is white below; seen from above, white outer tail feathers are conspicuous as the bird flicks its tail open.

Voice: Song is loud, musical, whistled variations of *ta-wit ta-wit ta-wit tee-yo.* Call is a flat, metallic *chink.*

Range: Fairly common in swamps, moist woodlands; generally stays hidden in dense undergrowth and low branches. Very rare north to northern Great Plains and Atlantic Canada.

Kentucky Warbler

uniformly green above

black stippled with gray

yellow supercilium wraps around under eye

short tail

uniformly bright yellow below

mostly black face

♀

♂

dark olive under eye with limited or no black on immature females

Canada Warbler

immature ♀

necklace can be very faint on immature females

bold eye ring and yellow supraloral line

plain gray upperparts

adult ♂

white undertail coverts

bold, black necklace

smaller black cap; absent in immature

olive

adult ♀

Wilson's Warbler
pusilla

long dark tail

black cap

dark eye stands out in plain face

♂

rapidly opens and closes tail

black hood

all Hoodeds have dusky lores

Hooded Warbler

adult ♂

large dark eye and blank face

adult ♀

older females have some black to extensive black in hood and necklace

extensive white

immature ♀

Common Yellowthroat *Geothlypis trichas* L 5" (13 cm)

Adult male's broad black mask is bordered above by gray or white, below by bright yellow throat and breast; undertail coverts yellow. ***Female*** lacks black mask; has whitish eye ring. Races vary geographically in color of mask border and extent of yellow below. ***Immatures*** are duller and browner overall. Often cocks tail.
Voice: Variable song; one version is a loud, rolling *wichity wichity wichity wich.* Calls include a raspy *chuck.*
Range: Common; stays low in grassy fields, shrubs, and marshes.

Yellow-breasted Chat *Icteria virens* L 7½" (19 cm)

Our largest warbler, with long tail, thick bill, and white spectacles. Lores black in ***males,*** gray in ***females.*** Rather shy.
Voice: Unmusical song, a jumble of harsh, chattering clucks, rattles, clear whistles, squawks; sometimes given in hovering flight.
Range: Inhabits dense thickets. Regular straggler in fall to Maritimes and Newfoundland; rare in winter on the East Coast.

Golden-crowned Warbler *Basileuterus culicivorus*

L 5" (13 cm) Tropical species. Resembles Orange-crowned Warbler (page 320) but crown shows a distinct yellow or buffy orange central stripe, bordered in black; note yellowish green eyebrow.
Voice: Call, a rapidly repeated *tuck.*
Range: Casual in southern Texas; occurs chiefly in winter.

Gray-crowned Yellowthroat *Geothlypis poliocephala*

L 5½" (13 cm) Tropical species. Long tail; thick, curved bicolored bill; split white eye ring; lores blackish in ***males,*** gray in ***females.***
Voice: Song, a rich, varied warble; call, a rising *chee dee.*
Range: Former resident of the Brownsville area in southern Texas; population eliminated in early 20th century. Recently, several certain records in the lower Rio Grande Valley; other reports uncertain. Favors grassland with scattered bushes.

Rufous-capped Warbler *Basileuterus rufifrons*

L 5¼" (13 cm) Mexican species. Rufous crown, bold white eyebrow, throat extensively bright yellow. Long tail, often cocked.
Voice: Song begins with musical *chip* notes, accelerates into a series of dry, whistled warbles; call, a *tik,* often doubled or in a rapid series.
Range: Casual to Texas. Inhabits brush, usually staying low in the undergrowth.

Bananaquit *(Incertae sedis)*

Family affiliation of this species is uncertain. Prefers nectar.

Bananaquit *Coereba flaveola* L 4½" (11 cm)

Vagrant from West Indies. Note thin, downcurved bill. ***Adult*** has conspicuous white eyebrow, yellow rump; underparts white, with yellow breast; small white wing patch. ***Juvenile*** is duller.
Voice: Call is a high-pitched *sint.*
Range: Casual visitor from the Bahamas to southern Florida.

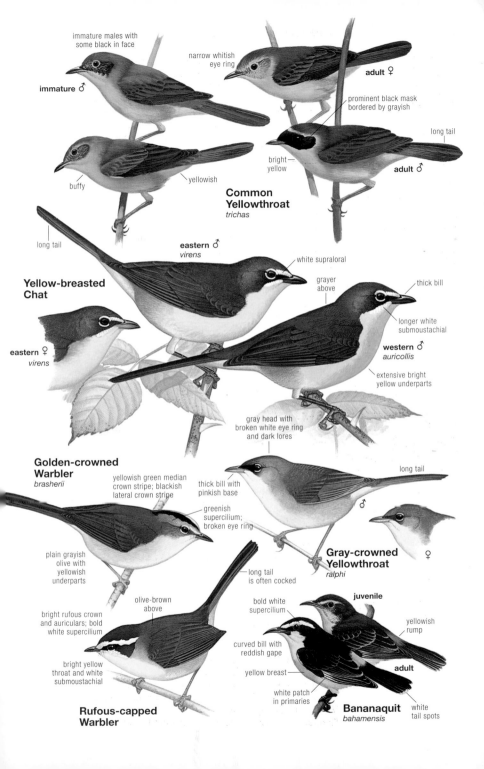

immature males with some black in face

narrow whitish eye ring

immature ♂

adult ♀

prominent black mask bordered by grayish

long tail

buffy

yellowish

bright yellow

adult ♂

Common Yellowthroat
trichas

long tail

eastern ♂
virens

white supraloral

grayer above

thick bill

Yellow-breasted Chat

eastern ♀
virens

longer white submoustachial

western ♂
auricollis

extensive bright yellow underparts

gray head with broken white eye ring and dark lores

Golden-crowned Warbler
brasherii

yellowish green median crown stripe; blackish lateral crown stripe

thick bill with pinkish base

long tail

greenish supercilium; broken eye ring

♂

plain grayish olive with yellowish underparts

Gray-crowned Yellowthroat
ralphi

♀

long tail is often cocked

olive-brown above

bold white supercilium

juvenile

yellowish rump

bright rufous crown and auriculars; bold white supercilium

curved bill with reddish gape

yellow breast

adult

bright yellow throat and white submoustachial

white patch in primaries

Rufous-capped Warbler

Bananaquit
bahamensis

white tail spots

Tanagers (Family Thraupidae)

These brightly colored, mostly fruit-eating, tropical birds are related to warblers.

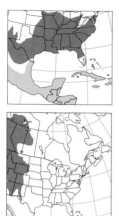

Summer Tanager *Piranga rubra* L 7¾" (20 cm)

Adult male is rosy red year-round. **First-spring male** usually has red head. Some **females** show overall reddish wash; most have a mustard tone, lack olive of female Scarlet Tanager; bill larger.
Voice: Song is robinlike; call, a staccato *ki-ti-tuck.*
Range: Common in pine-oak woods. Very rare visitor north to southern Canada.

Western Tanager *Piranga ludoviciana* L 7¼" (18 cm)

Conspicuous wing bars, often paler and thinner in **female,** upper bar yellow in **male.** Male's red head becomes more yellowish and finely streaked in **winter,** with some orange restricted to face. Female's grayish back contrasts with greenish yellow nape and rump. Some females are duller below, grayer above. Compare with female orioles (page 387).
Voice: Song is like Scarlet Tanager's; call, *pit-er-ick.*
Range: Breeds in western coniferous forests. Rare on western Gulf Coast in migration, casual in the East, mostly in late fall and at winter feeders.

Scarlet Tanager *Piranga olivacea* L 7" (18 cm)

Breeding male bright red and black. In late summer, becomes splotchy green-and-red as he molts to yellow-green winter plumage. **Female** has uniformly olive head, back, and rump; whitish wing linings; bill smaller than in Summer Tanager. Immature **male** resembles adult male, but note brownish primaries and secondaries. Some immatures show faint wing bars.
Voice: Robinlike song (hoarser than Summer Tanager) of raspy notes, *querit queer query querit queer.* Call is a hoarse *chip-burr.*
Range: Found in deciduous forests. Winters in South America.

Western Spindalis *Spindalis zena* L 6¾" (17 cm)

Formerly known as Stripe-headed Tanager. Vagrant from West Indies. **Males** are strikingly patterned: Most are black-backed (*zena*); a few unconfirmed sightings of *townsendi*, restricted to Grand Bahama and Abaco, show greenish orange back; occasionally black with dull orange edgings. Recent winter record in Key West of male *pretrei* from Cuba. **Females** of all races are grayish olive, with pale eyebrow, pale greater covert patch, and distinct white spot at base of primaries.
Voice: Call is a thin, high *tsee,* given singly or in a series.
Range: West Indian species; very rare visitor, from Bahamas to southeast Florida and Florida Keys.

Summer Tanager
rubra

some females with patchy dull red

red morph ♀

large bill

overall rosy red

red head and patches elsewhere; greenish remiges

overall ochre plumage

♀

1st spring ♂

adult ♂

gray saddle; white wing bars and tertial edges

1st fall ♂

larger bill than Scarlet

gray morph ♀

Scarlet Tanager

1st spring ♂

small bill

wings contrast darker to olive-green back

♀

some very dull

winter adult ♂

reddish head

Western Tanager

black contrasts with greenish remiges

1st fall ♂

shorter tail than Summer

breeding adult ♂

black back and yellow rump

fall adult ♂

breeding adult ♂

striking head pattern

Western Spindalis

nearly all males seen in Florida have blackish backs

♂ *zena*

orange breast

prominent buffy white supercilium borders dark auricular

green

green and black

solid black wings and tail

♀ *townsendi*

white spot at base of primaries

♂ *townsendi*

♂ *townsendi*

Emberizids (Family Emberizidae)

All have conical bills. This large family includes the towhees, sparrows, longspurs, and *Emberiza* buntings. Many species eat mostly seeds in winter but more insects in summer.

White-collared Seedeater *Sporophila torqueola*
L 4½" (11 cm) Tiny, with thick, short, strongly curved bill; rounded tail. *Adult male* has black cap; white crescent below eye; incomplete buffy collar; white wing bars; white patch at base of primaries. *Females* are paler, lack cap and collar; wing bars duller.
Voice: Song is pitched high, then low, a variable *sweet sweet sweet sweet cheer cheer cheer.* Calls include a distinct, high *wink.*
Range: In U.S., favors canebrakes and other riverside vegetation.

Olive Sparrow *Arremonops rufivirgatus* L 6¼" (16 cm)
Dull olive above, with brown stripe on each side of crown. Lacks reddish cap of similar Green-tailed Towhee. *Juveniles* are buffier, with pale wing bars; faintly streaked on neck and breast.
Voice: Calls include a dry *chip* and a buzzy *speeee.* Song is an accelerating series of *chip* notes.
Range: Frequents dense undergrowth, brushy areas, live oak.

Genus *Pipilo*

Towhees are the largest of the sparrows. They are often seen foraging on the ground. kicking both feet back to expose food.

Canyon Towhee *Pipilo fuscus L 8" (20 cm)* Grayish brown,
with reddish crown, which gives a capped appearance; crown is sometimes raised as short crest. Whitish belly patch with diffuse dark spot at junction with breast; pale throat bordered by fine streaks; distinct buffy eye ring. Juveniles are streaked below.
Voice: Call is a shrill *chee-yep* or *chedep.* Song opens with a call note, followed by sweet slurred notes. Also gives a duet of lisping and squealing notes.
Range: Favors arid, hilly country; desert canyons. Largely resident within range. Casual to southwest Kansas.

Green-tailed Towhee *Pipilo chlorurus L 7¼" (18 cm)*
Olive above with reddish crown, distinct white throat bordered by dark stripe and white stripe. Juvenile has two faint olive wing bars; plumage is streaked overall; upperparts tinged with olive; lacks reddish crown.
Voice: Clear, whistled song begins with *weet-chur,* ends in raspy trill. Calls include a catlike *mew.*
Range: Western species, rare migrant through western Great Plains. Casual in fall and winter throughout the East.

short, stubby bill with strongly curved culmen

tiny size

buffy below

thin, pale wing bars

blackish head

White-collared Seedeater
sharpei

♀

pale buffy white collar

1st winter ♂

adult ♂

distinctly patterned wings

prominently streaked head

olive upperparts

Olive Sparrow
rufivirgatus

juvenile

blurred breast streaks

pale underparts

pale rufous crown

Canyon Towhee

buffy throat

whitish belly with inconspicuous breast spot

olive wings and tail

dull rufous crown

white throat, submoustachial, and supraloral

gray

Green-tailed Towhee

Sparrows

Eastern Towhee *Pipilo erythrophthalmus* L 7½" (19 cm)

Male's black upperparts and hood contrast with rufous sides and white underparts. Distinct white patch at base of primaries and distinct white tertial edges. White in outer tail feathers is conspicuous in flight. Most have red eyes. *Females* are similarly patterned, but black areas are replaced by brown. *Juveniles* are brownish and show distinct streaks below. The nominate race is largest and shows most extensive white in tail. Wing length, and the extent of white in wings and tail, declines from the northern part of the range to the Gulf Coast, while the size of bill, legs, and feet increases. The subspecies from the Florida peninsula, *alleni,* is paler, and duller; has straw-colored eyes. The *rileyi* race (not shown), from northernmost Florida to North Carolina, shows intermediate characteristics, eyes being either red or straw colored.
Voice: Full song has three parts, often rendered as *drink your tea,* or shortened to two, *drink tea.* Northeastern birds' call is a slightly upslurred *chwee;* in *alleni,* clearer, even-pitched or upslurred *swee.*
Range: Partial to second growth with dense shrubs and extensive leaf litter; southern races, especially *alleni,* favor coastal scrub or sand dune ridges and pinelands. Has declined in the northeastern part of its range by as much as 90 percent in recent decades. Eastern and Spotted Towhee formerly considered one species, Rufous-sided Towhee. The two interbreed along rivers in the Great Plains.

Spotted Towhee *Pipilo maculatus* L 7½" (19 cm)

Distinguished from similar Eastern Towhee by white spotting on back and scapulars; also on tips of median and greater coverts, which forms white wing bars. In general, *females* differ less from *males* than in Eastern, with *arcticus* from Great Plains showing the greatest difference. In both sexes the amount of white spotting above and white in tail shows marked geographical variation, with *arcticus* displaying the most white.
Voice: Interior races give introductory notes, then a trill. Call of Great Plains *arcticus* is an upslurred, questioning *queee.*
Range: Some populations largely resident, others migratory; *arcticus* is the most migratory and is casual in eastern North America.

Genus *Aimophila*

Aimophila sparrows are fairly large, long tailed, and somewhat shy; some are difficult to identify.

Rufous-crowned Sparrow *Aimophila ruficeps*

L 6" (15 cm) Gray head with dark reddish crown, distinct whitish eye ring, rufous line extending back from eye, dark malar stripe. Gray-brown above, with reddish streaks; gray below; tail long, rounded. Subspecies range in overall color; paler, grayer *eremoeca* is the one that reaches the East. *Juvenile* is buffier above; breast and crown streaked; may show two pale wing bars.
Voice: Call, a sharp *dear,* usually given in a series; song, a bubbling series of *chip* notes.
Range: Uncommon and local on rocky hillsides and on steep brushy slopes.

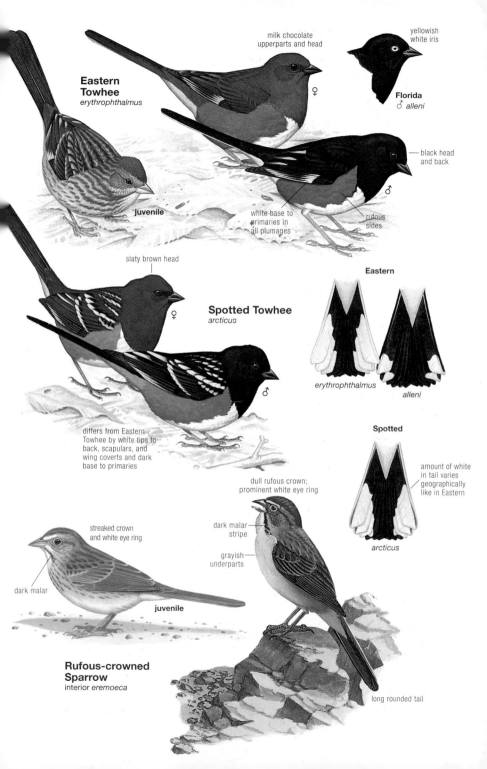

milk chocolate
upperparts and head

yellowish
white iris

**Eastern
Towhee**
erythrophthalmus

♀

Florida
♂ *alleni*

— black head
and back

white base to
primaries in
all plumages

rufous
sides

♂

juvenile

slaty brown head

Eastern

♀

Spotted Towhee
arcticus

♂

erythrophthalmus

alleni

differs from Eastern
Towhee by white tips to
back, scapulars, and
wing coverts and dark
base to primaries

Spotted

amount of white
in tail varies
geographically
like in Eastern

arcticus

dull rufous crown;
prominent white eye ring

dark malar
stripe

streaked crown
and white eye ring

grayish
underparts

dark malar

juvenile

**Rufous-crowned
Sparrow**
interior *eremoeca*

long rounded tail

Bachman's Sparrow *Aimophila aestivalis* L 6" (15 cm)

A large sparrow with large bill, fairly flat forehead, and long, rounded, dark tail. Adult is gray above, heavily streaked with chestnut or dark brown; sides of head buffy gray; a thin dark line extends back from eye. Breast and sides buff or gray; belly whitish. Subspecies range in overall brightness from the reddish *illinoensis* of the western part of range to the grayer and darker *aestivalis* of Florida. Birds from northeastern part of range (*bachmani,* not shown) are intermediate. *Juvenile* has a distinct eye ring; throat, breast, and sides are streaked. First-winter plumage usually retains some streaking. Quite secretive outside breeding season.
Voice: Best located and identified by song: one clear, whistled introductory note, followed by a variable trill or warble on a different pitch. Male sings from open perch and is often heard in late summer.
Range: Inhabits dry, open woods, especially pines; also scrub palmetto. Northern range has markedly declined over last several decades.

Cassin's Sparrow *Aimophila cassinii* L 6" (15 cm)

A large, drab sparrow, with large bill, fairly flat forehead. Long, rounded tail is dark gray-brown; distinctive white tips on outer feathers are most conspicuous in flight. Gray upperparts are streaked with dull black, brown, and variable amount of rust; blackish marks form anchor marks; underparts are grayish white, usually with a few short streaks on the flanks. *Juvenile* is streaked below; paler overall than juvenile Botteri's. In fresh fall plumage, shows bolder white wing bars than similar Botteri's Sparrow, and black-centered, white-fringed tertials.
Voice: Best located and identified by song, often given in brief, fluttery song flight: typically a soft double whistle, a loud, sweet trill, a low whistle, and a final, slightly higher note; or a series of *chip* notes ending in a trill or warbles. Also gives a trill of *pit* notes.
Range: Secretive; inhabits arid grasslands with scattered shrubs, cactus, and mesquite. Casual vagrant to the East.

Botteri's Sparrow *Aimophila botterii* L 6" (15 cm)

A large, plain sparrow with large bill, fairly flat forehead; tail long, rounded, dusky brown, lacking white tips and central barring of the very similar Cassin's Sparrow. Upperparts streaked with dull black, rust or brown, and gray; underparts unstreaked; throat and belly whitish, breast and sides grayish buff. Subspecies *texana* of extreme southern Texas is slightly grayer than southwestern subspecies. *Juvenile*'s belly is buffy; breast broadly streaked, sides narrowly streaked.
Voice: Best located and identified by song: several high sharp *tsip* or *che-lik* notes, often followed by a short, accelerating, rattly trill.
Range: Generally secretive; inhabits grasslands dotted with brush. The *texana* race is declining because of habitat loss; now uncommon and local.

Aimophila sparrows have large bills and long, rounded tails. They are generally secretive except for singing territorial males.

brighter rufous above than nominate race

prominent head and back streaks

buffy breast, sides, and flanks

illinoensis

Bachman's Sparrow
aestivalis

juvenile

whitish eye ring

overall appears like a large Brewer's

dark "anchors" on upperpart feathers

whitish tertial fringes

faint flank streaks

Cassin's Sparrow

whitish tail corners

juvenile

head pattern more poorly defined than Bachman's

streaked upperparts

slightly larger bill than Cassin's

Botteri's Sparrow
texana

juvenile

buffy, unstreaked rear flanks

Genus *Spizella*

Spizella sparrows are small and slim, and they have long, notched tails. Immatures and winter birds of some species may be difficult to separate.

Chipping Sparrow *Spizella passerina* L 5½" (14 cm)

Breeding adult identified by bright chestnut crown, distinct white eyebrow, and black line extending from bill through eye to ear; note also the gray nape and cheek with no dark moustachial stripe; gray unstreaked rump; and two white wing bars. ***Winter adult*** has browner cheek, dark lores, and streaked crown showing some rufous color. ***First-winter*** bird is similar but averages little or no rufous on the crown; breast and sides are tinged with buff. In ***juvenal*** plumage, often held into October, especially in the West, underparts are prominently streaked; crown usually lacks rufous; rump may show slight streaking.

Voice: Song, rapid trill of dry *chip* notes, all on one pitch. Flight call, also given perched, is a high, hard *seep* or *tsik*.

Range: Widespread and common, Chipping Sparrows are found on lawns and in fields, woodland edges, and pine-oak forests.

Clay-colored Sparrow *Spizella pallida* L 5½" (14 cm)

Brown crown with black streaks and a distinct buffy white or whitish median crown stripe. Broad, whitish eyebrow; pale lores; brown cheek outlined by dark postocular and moustachial stripes; conspicuous pale submoustachial stripe. Nape gray; back and scapulars are buffy brown, with dark streaks; rump is not streaked but color does not contrast with back as in Chipping Sparrow. Adult in fall and winter is buffier overall. ***Juvenile*** and ***immature*** birds are much buffier; gray nape and pale stripe on sides of throat stand out more; in juvenile, breast and sides are streaked.

Voice: Song is a brief series of insectlike buzzes. Flight call is a thin *sip*.

Range: Fairly common in brushy fields. Winters primarily from Mexico south, uncommonly in southern Texas. Rare but regular in fall, very rare in winter and spring to East. Breeders have recently spread very locally to Northeast.

Brewer's Sparrow *Spizella breweri* L 5½" (14 cm)

Brown crown with fine black streaks, without clearly defined, pale median crown stripe of Clay-colored; head pattern lacks Clay-colored's strong contrast. Distinct whitish eye ring; grayish white eyebrow; ear patch pale brown with darker borders; pale lores; dark malar stripe. Upperparts buffy brown and streaked; rump buffy brown, may be lightly streaked. ***Juvenile*** is buffier overall, lightly streaked on breast and sides. Fall and winter adults and immatures are somewhat buffy below.

Voice: Song is a series of varied bubbling notes and buzzy trills at different pitches. Call is a thin *sip*, like call of Clay-colored.

Range: Breeds in sagebrush flats. Scarce migrant along western Great Plains; accidental farther east.

white
supercilium

dark eye line
in all plumages

breeding

**Chipping
Sparrow**
passerina

contrasty gray rump,
but often hidden
by folded wings

**winter
adult**

no dark
moustachial
stripe

juvenile

streaky juvenal
plumage seen
into October

buffy breast

1st winter

all have pale lores
unlike Chipping

bold head pattern, including
strong median crown stripe and
buffy cast to plumage

contrasty
grayish
nape

dark
moustachial
stripe

breeding

immature

juvenile

brownish rump

**Clay-colored
Sparrow**

head pattern like Clay-colored,
but more muted and without contrastingly
pale median crown stripe

white
eye ring

brownish
rump

juvenile

**Brewer's
Sparrow**
breweri

American Tree Sparrow *Spizella arborea* L 6¼" *(16 cm)*

Gray head and nape; rufous crown; rufous stripe behind eye. Gray throat and breast, with dark central spot, rufous patches at sides of breast. Back and scapulars streaked with black and rufous. Tail notched; outer feathers thinly edged in white on outer webs. Underparts grayish white with buffy sides. **Winter** birds are buffier; rufous color on crown sometimes forms a central stripe. *Juvenile* is streaked on head and underparts. Western *ochracea* is paler overall.

Voice: American Tree Sparrow gives a musical *teedle-eet* call and also gives a thin *seet.* Song usually begins with several clear notes followed by a variable, rapid warble.

Range: Fairly common. Breeds along edge of tundra, in open areas with scattered trees and brush. Winters in weedy fields, marshes, and groves of small trees.

Field Sparrow *Spizella pusilla* L 5¾" *(15 cm)*

Gray face with reddish crown, distinct whitish eye ring, bright pink bill. Back is streaked except on gray-brown rump. Breast and sides are buffy red; belly grayish white; legs pink. *Juvenile* streaked below; wing bars buffy. Birds in westernmost part of range, *arenacea*, are paler and grayer; extremes are shown here.

Voice: Song is a series of clear, plaintive whistles accelerating into a trill; *chip* note hard but sweet.

Range: Fairly common in open, brushy woodlands, fields. Rare in Maritimes.

Black-throated Sparrow *Amphispiza bilineata*

L 5½" *(14 cm)* Black lores and triangular black patch on throat and breast contrast with white eyebrow, white submoustachial stripe, white underparts. Upperparts plain brownish gray. *Juvenal* plumage, often held well into fall, lacks black on throat, but note bold white eyebrow; breast and back finely streaked.

Voice: Song is rapid, pitched high: two clear notes followed by a trill; calls are faint, tinkling notes.

Range: Fairly common in desert, especially on rocky slopes; casual to eastern U.S. in fall and winter.

Lark Sparrow *Chondestes grammacus* L 6½" *(17 cm)*

Head pattern distinctive in adults; note dark central breast spot. *Juvenile*'s colors are duller; breast, sides, and crown streaked. In all ages, white-cornered tail is conspicuous in flight.

Voice: Song begins with two loud, clear notes, followed by a series of rich, melodious notes and trills and unmusical buzzes. Call is a sharp *tsip*, often a rapid series.

Range: Found in various types of open country, often along roads. Formerly bred as far east as New York and Maryland; now rare in the East, mostly in fall.

American Tree Sparrow

largest *Spizella*

bicolored bill

breeding
arborea

winter
ochracea

rufous patch at breast sides and buffy flanks

spot

juvenile
ochracea

Field Sparrow

western
arenacea

grayish median crown stripe and white eye ring

eastern juvenile
pusilla

grayer overall than nominate race

pink bill

buffy breast

eastern
pusilla

bold white supercilium and submoustachial stripe

Black-throated Sparrow
deserticola

large black throat

bold white supercilium

white throat

white edge to outer tail feathers and small white tail tip

white

Lark Sparrow
grammacus

distinctive head pattern

confiding behavior

whitish at base of primaries

dark breast spot

juvenile

juvenile

subdued head pattern and streaked below

extensive white in tail

Genus *Ammodramus*

Sparrows of the genus *Ammodramus* tend to be large headed and large billed; they are also usually secretive.

Grasshopper Sparrow *Ammodramus savannarum*
L 5" *(13 cm)* Buffy breast and sides, usually without obvious streaking. Small and chunky, with short tail and flat head. Dark crown has a pale central stripe; note also white eye ring and, on most birds, a yellow-orange spot in front of eye. Lacks broad buffy orange eyebrow and pale blue-gray ear patch of Le Conte's Sparrow (next page). Compare also with Savannah Sparrow (page 360). *Juvenile*'s breast and sides are streaked with brown. *Fall* birds are buffier below but never as bright as Le Conte's. Subspecies vary in overall color, with Florida race, *floridanus* (**E**), the darkest; eastern *pratensis* is slightly more richly colored than western *perpallidus*, which spreads east through the Great Plains.
Voice: Typical song is one or two high chip notes followed by a brief, grasshopperlike *buzz;* also sings a series of varied squeaky and buzzy notes.
Range: Found in pastures, grasslands, palmetto scrub, and old fields. Declining in East.

Baird's Sparrow *Ammodramus bairdii* L 5½" *(14 cm)*
Orange tinge to head (duller on worn summer birds), usually with less distinct median crown stripe than Savannah Sparrow (page 360); note especially the two isolated dark spots behind ear patch and lack of postocular line. Widely spaced, short dark streaks on breast form a distinct necklace; also shows chestnut on scapulars. *Juvenile*'s head is paler and creamier; central crown stripe is finely streaked; white fringes give a scaly appearance to upperparts; underparts are more extensively streaked. Very secretive, especially away from breeding grounds.
Voice: Song consists of two or three high, thin notes, followed by a single warbled note and a low trill.
Range: Uncommon, local, and declining. Found in grasslands and weedy fields. Accidental in East.

Henslow's Sparrow *Ammodramus henslowii*
L 5" *(13 cm)* Large flat head; large gray bill. Resembles Baird's Sparrow but head, nape, and most of central crown stripe are greenish; wings are extensively dark chestnut. *Juvenile* is paler, yellower, with less streaking below; compare with adult Grasshopper Sparrow. Secretive, but after being flushed several times may perch in the open for a few minutes before dropping back into cover.
Voice: Distinctive song is a short *se-lick,* which is accented on second syllable.
Range: Uncommon, local; in Northeast declining and now occurs only rarely. Found in wet shrubby fields, weedy meadows, and reclaimed strip mines. In winter, found also in the understory of pine woods.

summer
perpallidus

more blackish
above than
nominate race

floridanus

juvenile *pratensis*

streaked
breast

**Grasshopper
Sparrow**

full eye ring and strong
median crown
stripe

rich yellow-buff
supraloral spot; rest
of supercilium gray

large bill

fall *pratensis*

buffy breast

spiky tail as in
other *Ammodramus*

no postocular stripe as
in Savannah Sparrow; median
crown stripe inconspicuous

two dark spots near
auricular stand out on
orangish buff head

short necklace

pea-soup green head
with blackish lateral crown
and postocular stripes

rich dark
chestnut on
upperparts

large
bill

necklace

**Baird's
Sparrow**

juvenile

**Henslow's
Sparrow**

juvenile

largely
unstreaked
breast

Saltmarsh Sharp-tailed Sparrow

Ammodramus caudacutus L 5" (13 cm) Similar to Nelson's, but bill longer and head flatter; orange-buff face triangle contrasts strongly with paler, crisply streaked, whiter underparts. Eyebrow streaked with black behind eye. *Juvenile*'s crown is blacker than juvenile Nelson's; cheek darker; streaks below more widespread and distinct. With Nelson's Sharp-tailed Sparrow, formerly treated as one species, Sharp-tailed Sparrow.
Voice: Song softer, more complex than Nelson's.
Range: Found in grassy tidal marshes. Accidental inland.

Le Conte's Sparrow *Ammodramus leconteii L 5" (13 cm)*

White central crown stripe, becoming orange on forehead, chestnut streaks on nape, and straw-colored back streaks distinguish Le Conte's from sharp-tailed sparrows. Bright, broad, buffy orange eyebrow, grayish ear patch, thinner bill, and orange-buff breast and sides separate it from Grasshopper Sparrow (preceding page). Sides of breast and flanks have dark streaks. Buffy *juvenal* plumage seen in fall migration; crown stripe tawny; breast heavily streaked.
Voice: Song is a short, high, insectlike buzz.
Range: A bird of wet grassy fields, marsh edges. Fairly common but secretive; scurries through matted grasses like a mouse. Casual migrant in the Northeast.

Nelson's Sharp-tailed Sparrow *Ammodramus nelsoni*

4¾" (12 cm) Distinguished from Le Conte's by gray median crown stripe; whitish or gray streaks on scapulars; gray, streakless nape. *Juvenile* has fainter median crown stripe; duller nape; variably thicker eye line; less contrast above; lacks streaking across breast. Plumage variable: *nelsoni,* of interior, has orange-buff triangle on face; streaked buffy breast contrasts with white belly; back strongly marked with black and white stripes; *subvirgatus,* of the Maritimes south to New Hampshire, is duller overall; has diffuse streaking below; grayer upperparts. In *alterus* (not shown) from James and Hudson Bays, brightness is intermediate, streaks blurred.
Voice: Song, a wheezy *p-tssssshh-uk,* ends on a lower note.
Range: Only rarely detected in interior during migration.

Seaside Sparrow *Ammodramus maritimus L 6" (15 cm)*

Long bill; pointed tail. Yellow supraloral patch. Dark malar stripe separates whitish throat and pale stripe below cheek. Breast is white or buffy, with at least some streaking. *Juveniles* are browner than adults; compare with sharp-tailed sparrows. Seaside Sparrows vary in overall color. Most races, like the widespread *maritimus,* are grayish above. The greener *mirabilis* (**E**), formerly called "Cape Sable Sparrow," inhabits a small area in southwestern Florida. Gulf Coast races such as *fisheri* have buffier breasts. The darkest race, *nigrescens,* formerly "Dusky Seaside Sparrow," was found only near Titusville, Florida, and became extinct in 1987.
Voice: Seaside Sparrow's song resembles that of Red-winged Blackbird but is buzzier.
Range: Fairly common in grassy tidal marshes; accidental inland. Rare in Maine; casual to the Maritimes.

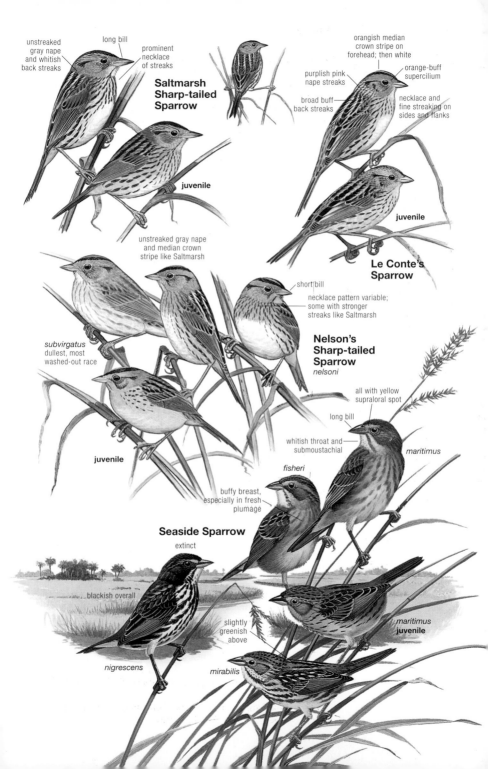

unstreaked gray nape and whitish back streaks

long bill

prominent necklace of streaks

Saltmarsh Sharp-tailed Sparrow

orangish median crown stripe on forehead; then white

purplish pink nape streaks

orange-buff supercilium

broad buff back streaks

necklace and fine streaking on sides and flanks

juvenile

juvenile

unstreaked gray nape and median crown stripe like Saltmarsh

short bill

necklace pattern variable; some with stronger streaks like Saltmarsh

Le Conte's Sparrow

Nelson's Sharp-tailed Sparrow
nelsoni

subvirgatus dullest, most washed-out race

all with yellow supraloral spot

long bill

whitish throat and submoustachial

maritimus

juvenile

fisheri

buffy breast, especially in fresh plumage

Seaside Sparrow

extinct

blackish overall

slightly greenish above

maritimus **juvenile**

nigrescens

mirabilis

Lark Bunting *Calamospiza melanocorys* L 7" (18 cm)

Stocky, with short tail and whitish wing patches; bill bluish gray; whitish tips or corners to tail visible in flight. **Breeding male** is mostly black. **Female** is streaked below, with buffy sides and brown primaries. **Winter male** is similar to female, but has black primaries and throat. In flight, looks short and round winged, with shallow wingbeats.

Voice: Distinctive call is a soft *hoo-ee*. Song is a varied series of rich whistles and trills.

Range: Common; nests in dry plains and prairies, especially in sagebrush. Breeding range may expand or contract in response to varying rainfall. Gregarious in migration and winter. Casual in the East, mostly in fall.

Vesper Sparrow *Pooecetes gramineus* L 6¼" (16 cm)

White eye ring; dark ear patch is bordered in white along lower and rear edges; white outer tail feathers. Lacks bold eyebrow of the slightly smaller Savannah Sparrow (below). Distinctive chestnut lesser coverts not easily seen. Eastern nominate race is slightly darker overall than the widespread subspecies, *confinis*.

Voice: Song is rich and melodious: two long, slurred notes followed by two higher notes, and then a series of short, descending trills. Call a sharp *tip*.

Range: Uncommon to fairly common in dry grasslands, farmlands, forest clearings, and sagebrush; declining in the East.

Savannah Sparrow *Passerculus sandwichensis*

L 5½" (14 cm) Variable. Eyebrow yellow to whitish; pale median crown stripe; strong postocular stripe. Paler, tail shorter and more notched, and bill smaller than in Song Sparrow. In the East, the degree of darkness is somewhat reversed: Northeastern Arctic races *oblitus* and *labradorius* (illustrated) are darker than the more southerly continental breeding *savanna* (illustrated) of the East and similarly pale *nevadensis,* which is widespread in the West and is found east to the Plains. Large, pale *princeps* race, **"Ipswich Sparrow,"** breeds on Sable Island, Nova Scotia. Savannahs are somewhat gregarious, While they can skulk, they usually flush when approached, often as a small group, and perch up on a bush, tree, or fenceline. This behavior is very unlike the more solitary, much more secretive sparrows in the genus *Ammodramus.*

Voice: Song begins with two or three chip notes, followed by two buzzy trills. Flight call, a thin *seep.* More infrequently heard *chip* note is like a soft Lincoln's Sparrow *chip* note.

Range: Common in a variety of open habitats, including farmlands, marshes, upper beaches, and grasslands. "Ipswich" winters on East Coast grassy dunes, upper beaches, and marsh edges from Maine to Florida; accidental inland to Ontario (17-27 Dec. 2005, Port Stanley).

early spring ♂

on winter males, black surrounds bill

streaking below darker than on females

winter ♂

indistinct face pattern

all with thick, bluish bill ♀

Lark Bunting

all with white or buffy white (females) wing patches

breeding ♂

short tail with white terminal spots

bold white eye ring; no strong eye line as in Savannah

pale wraps around dark-bordered auricular

streaking less extensive than in smaller Savannah

Vesper Sparrow

chestnut coverts usually concealed

white outer tail feathers

eastern
gramineus

western
confinus

variably yellow supercilium

dark eye line

savanna

extensive streaks

Savannah Sparrow

large and pale overall

pale secondary panel

whitish supercilium

"Ipswich"
princeps

fainter streaks

short tail

labradorius

strongly yellow supercilium

darkest eastern race

Genus *Melospiza*

Members of the genus *Melospiza* have relatively long, rounded tails and are found in brushy habitats.

Song Sparrow *Melospiza melodia* L 5½" (14 cm)

All subspecies have long, rounded tail, pumped in flight. All show broad grayish eyebrow and broad, dark malar stripe bordering whitish throat. Upperparts are usually streaked. Underparts whitish, with streaking on sides and breast that often converges to a central spot. Legs and feet are pinkish. **Juvenile** is buffier overall, with finer streaking. Eastern races typified by *melodia*.
Voice: Typical song, three or four short clear notes followed by a buzzy *tow-wee*, then a trill. Call note is a nasal, hollow *chimp*.
Range: Generally common, especially in streamside thickets.

Fox Sparrow *Passerella iliaca* L 7" (18 cm)

Highly variable. Most subspecies have reddish rump, tail; reddish in wings; underparts heavily marked with triangular spots merging into a larger spot on central breast. The many subspecies are divided into four subspecies groups; may represent distinct species. The brightest, *iliaca,* and slightly duller *zaboria* (**"Red"** group) breed in the far north, from western Alaska to Newfoundland; winter in eastern U.S. Great Basin and Rockies western mountain races ("Slate-colored" group) have gray head, back; grayish olive base to bill.
Voice: Songs are sweet, melodic in northern, "Red" group. Call, a *tschup,* like Lincoln's Sparrow but louder.
Range: Uncommon; found in undergrowth in woodlands and in hedgerows. "Slate-colored" group casual east of Rockies.

Lincoln's Sparrow *Melospiza lincolnii* L 5¾" (15 cm)

Buffy wash and fine streaks on breast and sides, contrasting with whitish, unstreaked belly. Note broad gray eyebrow, whitish chin and eye ring. Briefly held **juvenal** plumage is paler overall than juvenile Swamp Sparrow. Distinguished from juvenile Song Sparrow by shorter tail, slimmer bill, and thinner malar stripe, often broken. Often raises slight crest when disturbed.
Voice: Two call notes: a flat *tschup,* repeated in a series as an alarm call; a sharp, buzzy *zeee.* Rich, loud song, a rapid, bubbling trill.
Range: Found in brushy bogs; in winter prefers thickets. Uncommon east of Mississippi River.

Swamp Sparrow *Melospiza georgiana* L 5¾" (15 cm)

Gray face; rufous upperparts and wings; black streaks on back; white throat. **Breeding adult** has reddish crown, gray breast. **Winter adult** buffier overall; streaked crown, shows gray central stripe; sides are rich buff. Briefly held **juvenal** plumage usually even buffier. **Immature** resembles winter adult.
Voice: Song is a trill, all on one pitch. Two call notes: a prolonged *zeee,* softer than Lincoln's, and an Eastern Phoebe-like *chip.*
Range: Nests in dense, tall vegetation in marshes and bogs. Winters in marshes and brushy fields.

Song Sparrow
melodia

juvenile

all *Melospiza* have long rounded tails

blurry streaks often with central spot

Fox Sparrow

rufous tail

rufous streaking on gray back

rufous in cheek

"Red" *iliaca*

rufous streaking below

Lincoln's Sparrow

juvenile

gray supercilium

well-outlined buffy submoustachial stripe

finer streaking than Song against buffy breast

ruddy rufous wings in all plumages

breeding

grayish

Swamp Sparrow

dark back streaks

juvenile

winter adult

dull, blurry streaks confined to sides

immature

Genus *Zonotrichia*

The genus *Zonotrichia* includes some of the largest sparrows, which form flocks in brushy areas during the nonbreeding season.

Harris's Sparrow *Zonotrichia querula* L 7½" (19 cm)
A large sparrow with black crown, face, and bib; pink bill. *Winter adult*'s crown is blackish; cheeks buffy; throat may be all-black or show white flecks or partial white band. *Immature* resembles winter adult but shows less black; white throat is bordered by dark malar stripe.
Voice: Song is a series of long, clear, quavering whistles, often beginning with two notes on one pitch followed by two notes on another pitch. Calls include a loud *wink* as well as a drawn-out *tseep*.
Range: Fairly common but local; nests in stunted boreal forest bordering tundra; winters in open woodlands, brushlands, and hedgerows. Rare to casual in fall and winter in rest of North America outside mapped range.

White-throated Sparrow *Zonotrichia albicollis*
L 6¾" (17 cm) Conspicuous and strongly outlined white throat; mostly dark bill; dark crown stripes and eye line. Broad eyebrow is yellow in front of eye; remainder is either white or tan. Upperparts rusty brown; underparts grayish, sometimes with diffuse streaking. *Juvenile*'s eyebrow and throat are grayish, breast and sides heavily streaked and with faint central spot.
Voice: Song is a thin whistle, generally two single notes followed by three triple notes: *pure sweet Canada Canada Canada,* often heard in winter. Calls include a sharp *pink* and a drawn-out, lisping *tseep*.
Range: Common. Nests in brushy coniferous and mixed woodlands. Winters in woodland undergrowth, brush, and gardens.

White-crowned Sparrow *Zonotrichia leucophrys*
L 7" (18 cm) Black-and-white striped crown; pink or orange bill; whitish throat; underparts mostly gray. *Juvenile*'s head is brown and buff, underparts streaked. *Immature* has tan and brownish head stripes and is clean grayish white below. Nominate race *leucophrys,* mainly found in the east Canadian tundra has a black supraloral area and larger, dark pink bill; *gambelii,* found from Alaska to Hudson Bay, has whitish supraloral and a smaller, orange-yellow bill. Over much of East, *leucophrys* dominates in migration and winter, but *gambelii* is numerous on the Great Plains, occurring rarely farther east.
Voice: Song is usually one or more thin, whistled notes followed by a twittering trill. Calls include a loud *pink* and sharp *tseep*.
Range: Nests in stunted trees and thickets; winters in woodlands, brushlands, and hedgerows. Generally uncommon in much of East; much more numerous farther west.

black crown
and bib

breeding

large
pink bill

**winter
adults**

dark postocular spot
in all plumages

**Harris's
Sparrow**

dark chest
patch

immature

brownish flank
streaking

yellow
supraloral
spot; dark bill

**White-
throated
Sparrow**

tan-striped morph

juvenile

white throat;
richly colored back

white-striped morph

full whitish
supercilium

whitish
supraloral

black-and-white
head stripes;
blackish supraloral
pinches off white
supercilium at eye

grayer back than
White-throated

pinkish
orange bill

juvenile
gambelii

adult
gambelii

adult
leucophrys

reddish
pink bill

rufous-brown lateral
crown stripes

**White-crowned
Sparrow**

immature
leucophrys

Dark-eyed Junco *Junco hyemalis* L 6¼" (16 cm)

Variable; most races have a gray or brown head and breast sharply set off from white belly. White outer tail feathers are conspicuous in flight. *Male* of the widespread *"Slate-colored Junco"* group of subspecies has a dark gray hood; upperparts are entirely gray or have varying amount of brown at center of back. *Female* is brownish gray overall; some individuals particularly brownish (compare with *"Oregon Junco"*). *Juveniles* of all races are streaked. "Slate-colored" winters mostly in eastern North America; uncommon in the West. Male "Oregon Junco" of the West has slaty to blackish hood, rufous-brown to buffy brown back and sides; females have duller hood color. Lower border of hood typically more convex than in "Slate-colored Junco." "Oregon" types winter east to the central Great Plains; very rare to casual farther east. *"Pink-sided Junco,"* *mearnsi* (considered within "Oregon" group)—which winters east to the central Great Plains, accidental farther east—has very broad, bright pinkish cinnamon sides that sometimes meet across the breast, blue-gray hood, and blackish lores. The *"White-winged Junco"* race, *aikeni*—breeding in the Black Hills area and wintering rarely on the western Great Plains—is mostly pale gray above, usually with two thin, white wing bars; also larger, with a bigger bill and more white on tail. In the *"Gray-headed Junco"* of the southern Rockies, the pale gray hood is barely darker than the underparts; back is rufous. It winters to the western Great Plains; accidental in Midwest. Intergrades between some races are frequent.
Voice: Dark-eyed Junco's song is a musical trill on one pitch, often heard in winter. Varied calls include a sharp *dit* and, in flight, a rapid twittering.
Range: Breeds in coniferous or mixed woodlands. In migration and winter, found in a wide variety of habitats, usually in flocks. Several subspecies may be found in a single flock on the western and central Great Plains.

Snow Bunting *Plectrophenax nivalis* L 6¾" (17 cm)

Black-and-white **breeding** plumage acquired by end of spring by wear instead of molt. Bill is black in summer, orange-yellow in winter. In all seasons, note long black-and-white wings. *Males* usually show more white overall than *females,* especially in the wings. *Juvenile* is grayish and streaked, with buffy eye ring. *First-winter* plumage, acquired before migration, is darker overall than adult plumage.
Voice: Calls include a sharp, whistled *tew;* a short buzz; and a musical rattle or twitter. Song, heard only on the breeding grounds, is a loud, high-pitched musical warbling.
Range: Fairly common; breeds on tundra, rocky shores, and talus slopes. During migration and winter, found on shores, especially sand dunes and beaches, in weedy fields and grain stubble, and along roadsides, often in large flocks that may include Lapland Longspurs and Horned Larks.

all subspecies have
white outer tail feathers

"Slate-colored" ♂

grayish hood

buffy
rufous
sides

blackish hood

"Slate-colored"
hyemalis
♀

♂

"Oregon"
♀ *montana*

**Dark-eyed
Junco**

"Oregon"
♂ *montana*

larger and paler gray
than "Slate-colored"

juvenile

"White-winged"
aikeni
♂

faint white
tips to coverts

bluish gray hood
and dark lores

dark lores

pale gray head and underparts

pale bill

rufous back

♂

broad pinkish
buff sides and
flanks

"Gray-headed"
caniceps

pinkish buff
meets across
lower breast
on some

"Pink-sided"
mearnsi

black back

white
head and
underparts

breeding ♂

**Snow
Bunting**
nivalis

breeding ♂

breeding ♀

prominent white
in spread wing

juvenile

winter ♂

1st winter ♂

warm buffy brown
tones in winter

1st winter ♂

winter ♂

long primary
projection

Genus *Calcarius*

Longspurs are open-country, ground-loving birds. Plumages may vary greatly between male and female, breeding versus nonbreeding.

Smith's Longspur *Calcarius pictus* L 6¼" (16 cm)
Outer two feathers on each side of tail are almost entirely white. Bill is thinner than in other longspurs. Note long primary projection, a bit shorter than Lapland, but much longer than Chestnut-collared or McCown's (next page); shows rusty edges to greater coverts and tertials. ***Breeding adult male*** has black-and-white head, rich buff nape and underparts; white patch on shoulder, often obscured. ***Breeding adult female*** and all **winter** plumages are duller, crown streaked, chin paler. Dusky ear patch bordered by pale buff eyebrow; pale area on side of neck often breaks through dark rear edge of ear patch. Underparts are pale buff with thin reddish brown streaks on breast and sides. Females have much less white on lesser coverts than males.
Voice: Typical call is a dry, ticking rattle, harder and sharper than call of Lapland and McCown's Longspurs. Song, heard in spring migration and on the breeding grounds, is delivered only from the ground or a perch. It consists of rapid, melodious warbles, ending with a vigorous *wee-chew.*
Range: Generally uncommon and secretive, especially in migration and winter. Nests on open tundra and damp, tussocky meadows. Winters in open, grassy areas; sometimes seen with Lapland Longspurs. Regular spring migrant in the Midwest, east to western Indiana. Casual vagrant to East Coast.

Lapland Longspur *Calcarius lapponicus* L 6¼" (16 cm)
Outer two feathers on each side of tail are partly white, partly dark. Note also, especially in winter plumages, the reddish edges on the greater coverts and on the tertials. The reddish edges of the tertials form an indented, or notched, shape. ***Breeding adult male***'s head and breast are black and well outlined: a broad white or buffy stripe extends back from eye and down to sides of breast; nape is reddish brown. ***Breeding adult female*** and all **winter** plumages are duller; note bold dark triangle outlining plain buffy ear patch; dark streaks (female) or patch (male) on upper breast; dark streaks on side. On all winter birds, note broad buffy eyebrow and buffier underparts; white on belly and under tail, unlike Smith's Longspur; also compare head and wing patterns. ***Juvenile*** is yellowish and heavily streaked above and on breast and sides.
Voice: Song, heard only on the breeding grounds, is a rapid warbling, frequently given in short flights. Calls include a musical *tee-lee-oo* or *tee-dle* and, in flight, a dry rattle distinctively mixed with whistled *tew* notes.
Range: Breed on Arctic tundra, winter in grassy fields, grain stubble, and on shores. May be common on Great Plains; uncommon farther east. Often found amid flocks of Horned Larks and Snow Buntings; look for Lapland's darker overall coloring and smaller size.

distinctive black-and-white head pattern

Smith's Longspur

fine streaks on buffy underparts

breeding ♂

long primary projection, but shorter than Lapland

breeding ♀

white lesser coverts often best noted in flight

more white in outer tail than Lapland

winter ♂

chestnut nape

extensive black head bordered by white

breeding ♂

Lapland Longspur

well-defined dark border to auriculars

breeding ♀

dark chest band

very long primary projection

restricted white

winter ♂

dark lateral crown stripes surround paler center to crown

winter ♀

juvenile

rufous-edged greater coverts and tertials

whitish belly

buffy fall ♀

Chestnut-collared Longspur *Calcarius ornatus*

L 6" (15 cm) White tail marked with blackish triangle. Short primary projection; primary tips barely extend to base of tail. ***Breeding adult male***'s black-and-white head, buffy face, and black underparts are distinctive; a few have chestnut on underparts. Lower belly and undertail coverts whitish. Upperparts black, buff, and brown, with chestnut collar, whitish wing bars. ***Winter males*** are paler; feathers edged in buff and brown, obscuring black underparts. Male has small white patch on shoulder, often hidden; compare with Smith's Longspur (preceding page). Breeding adult female resembles ***winter female*** but is darker, usually shows some chestnut on nape. Juvenile's pale feather fringes give upperparts a scaled look; tail pattern and bill shape distinguish juvenile from juvenile McCown's Longspur. Fall and winter birds have smaller, grayer bills than McCown's.

Voice: Song, heard only on breeding grounds, is a pleasant rapid warble, given in song flight or from a low perch. Distinctive call, a two-syllable *kittle,* repeated one or more times. Also gives a soft, high-pitched rattle and a short *buzz* call.

Range: Fairly common; nests in moist upland prairies. Somewhat shy; generally found in dense grass; gregarious in fall and winter. Casual during migration to eastern North America.

McCown's Longspur *Calcarius mccownii* L 6" (15 cm)

White tail marked by dark inverted-T shape. Note also stouter, thicker-based bill than bills of other longspurs. Primary projection slightly longer than in Chestnut-collared Longspur; in perched bird, wings extend almost to tip of short tail. ***Breeding adult male*** has black crown, black malar stripe, black crescent on breast; gray sides. Upperparts streaked with buff and brown, with gray nape, gray rump; chestnut median coverts form contrasting crescent. ***Breeding adult female*** has streaked crown; may lack black on breast and show less chestnut on wing. In ***winter adults,*** bill is pinkish with dark tip; feathers are edged with buff and brown. Winter adult female is paler than female Chestnut-collared, with fewer streaks on underparts and a broader buffy eyebrow. Plain appearance suggestive of female House Sparrow. Some winter males have gray on rump; variable blackish on breast; retain chestnut median coverts. ***Juvenile*** is streaked below; pale fringes on feathers give upperparts a scaled look; paler overall than juvenile Chestnut-collared. In winter, often found amid flocks of Horned Larks. Look for McCown's chunkier, shorter-tailed shape, slightly darker plumage, mostly white tail, thicker bill, and undulating flight.

Voice: Song, heard only on breeding grounds, is a series of exuberant warbles and twitters, generally given in song flight. Calls include a dry rattle, a little softer and more abrupt than Lapland Longspur, interspersed with occasional *pink* notes; also gives single finchlike notes.

Range: Locally fairly common but range has shrunk substantially since the 19th century. Nests in dry shortgrass plains; in winter, also found in plowed fields. Accidental to the East Coast.

chestnut collar

breeding males

short primary projection

black breast and belly

Chestnut-collared Longspur

winter ♂

veiled black breast and belly

small darkish bill

winter ♀

faint streaks

dark triangle on white tail

black crown

black chest patch

McCown's Longspur

breeding ♂

breeding ♀

black inverted-T on white tail

plainer face than Chestnut-collared with buffy supercilium

unstreaked buffy breast

thick pinkish bill

short tail

winter ♀

veiled blackish chest patch

chestnut median coverts

juvenile

slightly longer primary projection than Chestnut-collared

winter ♂

Cardinals, Saltators, Allies (Family Cardinalidae)

In North America, these seedeaters include Northern Cardinal, certain grosbeaks, the *Passerina* and other buntings, and Dickcissel.

Northern Cardinal *Cardinalis cardinalis* L 8¾" (22 cm)
Conspicuous crest; cone-shaped reddish orange bill. *Male* is red overall, with black face. *Female* is buffy brown or buffy olive, tinged with red on wings, crest, and tail. *Juvenile* browner overall, dusky bill; juvenile female lacks red tones. Bill shape and color help distinguish female and juveniles from similar Pyrrhuloxia.
Voice: Song is a loud, liquid whistling with many variations, including *cue cue cue* and *cheer cheer cheer* and *purty purty purty*. Both sexes sing almost year-round. Common call is a sharp *chip*.
Range: Abundant throughout the East, inhabits woodland edges, swamps, streamside thickets, and suburban gardens. Nonmigratory, but this species has expanded its range northward during the 20th century.

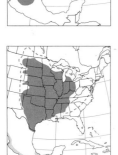

Pyrrhuloxia *Cardinalis sinuatus* L 8¾" (22 cm)
Thick, strongly curved, pale bill helps distinguish this species from female and juvenile Northern Cardinal. *Male* is gray overall, with red on face, crest, wings, tail, and underparts. *Female* shows little or no red.
Voice: Song is a liquid whistle, thinner and shorter than Northern Cardinal's; call is a sharper *chink*.
Range: Fairly common in thorny brush, mesquite thickets, desert, woodland edges, and ranchlands. Casual to central Great Plains.

Dickcissel *Spiza americana* L 6¼" (16 cm)
Yellowish eyebrow, thick bill, and chestnut wing coverts are distinctive. *Breeding male* has black bib under white chin, bright yellow breast. *Female* lacks black bib, but has some yellow on breast; chestnut wing patch muted. *Winter adult male*'s bib is less distinct. *Immatures* are duller overall than adults, breast and flanks lightly streaked; female may show almost no yellow or chestnut. Compare with female House Sparrow (page 396).
Voice: Common call, often given in flight, is a distinctive electric-buzzer *bzrrrrt*. Song, a variable *dick dick dickcissel*.
Range: Breeds in open weedy meadows, grainfields, and prairies. Abundant and gregarious, especially in migration, but numbers and distribution vary locally from year to year outside core breeding range. Irregular east of the Appalachians; occasional breeding is reported outside mapped range. Uncommon to rare migrant on East Coast, mostly in fall, where a few also winter, often at feeders with House Sparrows.

long crest

black surrounds red bill; straight culmen

dark bill

Northern Cardinal
cardinalis

♂

♀

juvenile ♂

overall buffy brown and dull red

yellowish bill; strongly curved culmen

grayish overall with pale buffy breast

♀

♂

overall gray with patchy bright red

Pyrrhuloxia
fulvescens

breeding ♀

winter adult ♂

Dickcissel

chestnut lesser and median coverts

black bib and yellow breast

breeding ♂

pale supercilium

large bill

immature ♀

immature ♂

broad, pale yellow submoustachial

chestnut median coverts

longish wings

Rose-breasted Grosbeak *Pheucticus ludovicianus*
L 8" (20 cm) Large size; has a very large, triangular bill; upper mandible paler than Black-headed Grosbeak. *Breeding male* has rose red breast, white underparts, white wing bars, white rump. Rose red wing linings show in flight. Brown-tipped *winter* plumage is acquired before migration. *Female*'s streaked plumage and yellow wing linings resemble female Black-headed, but underparts are more heavily and extensively streaked. Compare also with female and immature Purple Finch (page 390). Similar *first-fall male* is buffier above, with buffy wash across breast; often has a few red feathers on breast; red wing linings are distinctive.
Voice: Rich, warbled songs of both species are nearly identical. Rose-breasted's call, a sharp *eek,* is squeakier than Black-headed's.
Range: Common in deciduous and mixed woodland habitats.

Black-headed Grosbeak *Pheucticus melanocephalus*
L 8¼" (21 cm) Large, with a very large, triangular bill, upper mandible darker than in Rose-breasted Grosbeak. *Male* has cinnamon or burnt orange underparts, all-black head. In flight, both sexes show yellow wing linings. *Female* plumage is generally buffier above and below than female Rose-breasted, with the streaking below being both finer and more restricted to sides. *First-fall male* Black-headed is rich buff or butterscotch below, with little or no streaking.
Voice: Songs and calls of the two species are nearly identical, but Black-headed's *ik* call is lower in pitch.
Range: Common in open deciduous woodlands and forest edges. Casual during migration and winter to the Midwest and East, often at feeders. Black-headed hybridizes occasionally with Rose-breasted in range of overlap on the Great Plains.

Blue Grosbeak *Passerina caerulea L 6¾" (17 cm)*
Wide chestnut wing bars, large heavy bill, and larger overall size distinguish *male* from male Indigo Bunting (next page). *Females* of these two species also similar; compare bill shape, wing bars, and overall size. Juvenile resembles female; in first fall, some *immatures* are richer brown than female. *First-spring male* shows some blue above and below; resembles adult male by second winter. In poor light, Blue Grosbeak resembles Brown-headed Cowbird (page 384); note Blue Grosbeak's bill shape and wing bars; also the habit of twitching and spreading its tail.
Voice: Listen for distinctive call, a loud, explosive *chink.* Song is a series of rich, rising and falling warbles.
Range: Fairly common; found in low, overgrown fields, streamsides, woodland edges, and hedgerows. Rare in spring and fall north to New England and the Maritime Provinces.

winter
adult ♂

breeding
adult ♂

rose red

**Rose-breasted
Grosbeak**

rich buff chest,
often with a few pink
feathers; reddish
pink underwings

1st fall ♂

breeding
adult ♂

1st spring ♂

♀

strong
streaking
across
breast

darker upper
mandible than
Rose-breasted

**Black-headed
Grosbeak**

buffy breast;
streaking largely
limited to sides
and flanks

♀

**Blue
Grosbeak**
caerulea

breeding
adult ♂

chestnut
wing bars

♀

burnt orange

breeding adult ♂

thick bill

deep buffy color
with rusty buff
wing bars

immature

rich
orange-buff

amount of
blue on head
variable

1st fall ♂

1st spring ♂

frequently
twitches tail

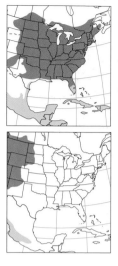

Indigo Bunting *Passerina cyanea* L 5½" (14 cm)

Breeding male deep blue. Smaller than Blue Grosbeak (preceding page); bill much smaller; lacks wing bars. In **winter** plumage, blue is obscured by brown and buff edges. Female is brownish, with diffuse streaking on breast and flanks. Young birds resemble female.
Voice: Song, a series of varied phrases, usually paired. Calls include a sharp *pit* or *spik*.
Range: Common in woodland clearings and brushy borders. Rare but regular to Atlantic Canada.

Lazuli Bunting *Passerina amoena* L 5½" (14 cm)

Adult male bright turquoise above and on throat; cinnamon across breast; thick white median covert wing bar. **Female** grayish brown above, rump grayish blue; has whitish underparts with buffy wash across breast. Juvenile resembles female but has distinct fine streaks across breast; immature male is mostly blue by **first spring.** Winter adult male's blue color is obscured by brown and buff edges.
Voice: Song is a series of varied phrases, sometimes paired; faster and less strident than Indigo Bunting's song. Calls are similar.
Range: Found in open woodlands, especially in brushy areas. Casual visitor in East. Occasionally hybridizes with Indigo.

Painted Bunting *Passerina ciris* L 5½" (14 cm)

Adult male's gaudy colors are retained year-round. **Female** bright green above, paler yellow-green below. **Juvenile** much drabber; telltale hints of green above, yellow below. Fall molt in eastern nominate race takes place on breeding grounds; western *pallidior* molts on winter grounds. First-winter male resembles adult female; by spring, may show tinge of blue on head, red on breast.
Voice: Song is a rapid series of varied phrases, thinner and sweeter than song of Indigo Bunting. Call is a loud, rich *chip*.
Range: Uncommon in low thickets, streamside brush, and woodland borders. Casual vagrant north to Midwest and Northeast. Declining in Southeast.

Varied Bunting *Passerina versicolor* L 5½" (14 cm)

Breeding male's plumage is colorful in good light; otherwise appears black. In **winter,** colors are edged with brown. **Female** is plain gray-brown or buffy brown above, slightly paler below; resembles female Indigo Bunting but lacks streaks and all wing markings; Varied Bunting's culmen is slightly more curved.
Voice: Song is similar to song of Painted Bunting.
Range: Uncommon in thorny thickets in washes and canyons.

Blue Bunting *Cyanocompsa parellina* L 5½" (14 cm)

Tropical species. **Adult male** is blackish blue overall, paler blue on crown, cheeks, shoulder, and rump. Immature male has brownish cast to wings. Contrasting colors and thick, strongly curved bill distinguish male from male Indigo Bunting; separated by female Blue Bunting's richer, uniform color, and lack of streaking below.
Voice: Call a clear *chip*.
Range: Very rare and irregular winter visitor to southern Texas. Found in woodland edges and at feeders.

faint blurry streaks

♀

fall

winter
adult ♂

**Indigo
Bunting**

patchy blue

1st spring ♂

deep blue

breeding
adult ♂

lazuli blue head
and upperparts

**Lazuli
Bunting**

white
median
coverts

rich buffy
breast

breeding
adult ♂

buffy breast contrasts
with white belly; juveniles
show fine streaks

plain and largely
grayish; some
greenish on back

juvenile

1st spring ♂

♀

unmistakable

**Painted
Bunting**

adult ♂

bright green
upperparts; similar
overall to female
Scarlet Tanager

slightly curved
culmen

**Varied
Bunting**

plain and buffy
brown overall;
can show faint
wing bars

♀

♀

large
dark bill

reddish
nape

♀

overall a rich
cinnamon brown

♀

winter
adult ♂

adult ♂

**Blue
Bunting**

breeding
adult ♂

deep, dark blue
with paler
blue highlights

378

Blackbirds (Family Icteridae)

Strong, direct flight and pointed bills mark this diverse group.

Eastern Meadowlark *Sturnella magna* L 9½" (24 cm)
Black V-shaped breast band on yellow underparts is characteristic of both meadowlark species after post-juvenal molt. In fresh
fall plumage, birds are more richly colored overall, with partly
veiled breast band and rich buffy flanks. On Eastern females, yellow does not reach submoustachial area, and barely does so on
males. In widespread northern nominate race, dark centers are
visible on central tail feathers, uppertail coverts, secondary
coverts, and tertials. Southeastern *argutula* is smaller and darker,
especially those from Florida. South Texas birds, *hoopesi,* are
paler in color.
Voice: Song is a clear, whistled *see-you see-yeeer;* distinctive call
a high, buzzy *drzzt,* given in a rapid series in flight.
Range: Generally fairly common in fields, meadows, and upper
marsh edges; has declined in the East in recent decades. Often
gregarious in winter.

Western Meadowlark *Sturnella neglecta* L 9½" (24 cm)
Plumages similar to those of Eastern Meadowlark, but in *spring*
and summer yellow extends well into the submoustachial area,
especially in males; yellow often veiled in *fall.* Lack of dark centers to feathers of upperparts, as well as duller lateral crown
stripes, help to separate Western from the more easterly races
of Eastern, in areas where ranges overlap. Also, in fresh fall and
winter plumage, upperparts, flanks, and undertail region are
much paler.
Voice: Song is a series of bubbling, flutelike notes of variable
length, usually accelerating toward the end. Sharp *chuck* note;
rattled flight call similar to Eastern, but pitched lower; also
gives a whistled *wheet.*
Range: Westerns are gregarious in winter; flocks often gather
along roadsides, whereas Easterns usually prefer taller cover.
Eastern and Western Meadowlarks hybridize in Midwest, where
Western is uncommon and local. Western is casual along the
East Coast, where most records are of singing birds in late
spring and early summer.

IDENTIFYING: Meadowlarks Both meadowlark species are found in the East, though the
Western is a rarity east of the western portion of
the region. Over most of the region, the nominate race of Eastern, *magna,* is found. In fresh
fall plumage Eastern is darker and much more
richly colored above than Western and is much
buffier along the flanks. Eastern also has a more
contrasty head pattern. The color differences are
less apparent by spring and especially summer,

when birds are more worn, but then the species
are vocalizing much more often. At this season
the more extensive yellow in the face of Western
is apparent. Westerns overall are paler and grayer
above and paler yellow below; their sides and
flanks are more spotted rather than streaked;
and they have a thinner black necklace and more
diffuse head pattern. Western has shorter legs
and tends to be more cooperative during the
winter season, often feeding in flocks in rather

darker above than *magna*

spring
argutula

paler above than *magna*

spring
hoopesi

short, broad triangular wings

stiff, fluttery flight

extensive white in tail

spring
magna

spring
magna

Eastern Meadowlark

more richly colored above than Western with stronger head pattern

fall
magna

strong side and flank streaks against rich buffy ground color when in fresh fall and winter plumage

juvenile
magna

yellow extends into submoustachial unlike Eastern

Western Meadowlark
neglecta

lateral and postocular lines paler than Eastern

mottled cheeks

fall

grayer above than Eastern

juvenile

spring

flanks more spotted and against a whiter background

bare fields along roadsides. They are probably underreported in the southwestern portion of the region at this season. Easterns prefer somewhat taller cover. When flushed, the Eastern flies with very stiff and rapid wingbeats, almost like a Northern Bobwhite. Western flies in a similar manner, but its wingbeats seem a bit more relaxed. The species' songs strongly differ, but since passerines' songs are learned, there is occasional overlap. The calls are absolutely diagnostic.

Eastern Meadowlark
fall *magna*

Western Meadowlark
fall *neglecta*

Bobolink *Dolichonyx oryzivorus L 7" (18 cm)*

Breeding male entirely black below; hindneck is buff, fading to whitish by midsummer; scapulars and rump white. Male in *spring* migration shows pale edgings. *Breeding female* is yellow-buff overall, with dark streaks on back, rump, and sides; head is striped with dark brown. Juvenile resembles female, but lacks streaking below; has indistinct spotting on throat and upper breast. All *fall* birds resemble female, but are rich yellow-buff below—especially, on average, the immatures. In all plumages, note sharply pointed tail feathers.

Voice: Gregarious. The male's loud, bubbling *bob-o-link* song, often given in flight, is heard in spring and summer. Flight call heard year-round is a repeated, whistled *ink.*

Range: Bobolinks nest primarily in hayfields, weedy meadows, and tallgrass prairie. Most birds migrate east of the Great Plains. Winters in South America.

Yellow-headed Blackbird

Xanthocephalus xanthocephalus L 9½" (24 cm) **Adult male**'s yellow head and breast and white wing patch contrast sharply with black body. *Adult female* is smaller, dusky brown, lacks wing patch; eyebrow, lower cheek, and throat are yellow or buffy yellow; belly streaked with white. *Juvenile* is dark brown with buffy edgings on back and wing; head mostly tawny. *Immature male* resembles female but darker; wing coverts tipped with white; acquires adult plumage by following fall.

Voice: Song begins with a harsh, rasping note, ends with a long, descending buzz. Call note is a rich *croak.*

Range: Prefers freshwater marshes or reedy lakes; often seen foraging in nearby farmlands and livestock pens. Uncommon and very local in the Midwest. Rare visitor to the East Coast, often in mixed-species blackbird flocks.

Red-winged Blackbird *Agelaius phoeniceus*

L 8¾" (22 cm) Glossy black *male* has red shoulder patches broadly tipped with buffy yellow. In perched birds, red patch may not be visible; only the buffy or whitish border shows. *Females* are dark brown above, heavily streaked below; sometimes show a red tinge on wing coverts or pinkish wash on chin and throat. *First-year male* plumage is like a very dark female with a red shoulder patch.

Voice: Red-winged Blackbird's song is a liquid, gurgling *konk-la-reee,* ending in a trill. Most common call is a *chack* note; also a higher *teeuw.*

Range: This abundant, aggressive species is often found in immense flocks in fall and winter. Generally nests in thick vegetation of freshwater marshes, sloughs, and fields; forages in surrounding moist fields, orchards, and parks, also at feeders.

Bobolink

buffy nape

black face and underparts

white scapulars

white rump

buffy edges when fresh

early spring ♂

breeding ♂

dark pink bill

strong head pattern

rich yellow-buff overall

strong back streaks

very long primary projection

breeding ♀

spiky tail tips

fall

Yellow-headed Blackbird

deep yellow throat and breast

♀

deep yellow head

white wing patch

juvenile

spring adult ♂

spring adult ♂

immature ♂

pale supercilium

strongly streaked below

immature ♀

adult ♀

1st year ♂

red shoulders most visible when singing

adult ♂

Red-winged Blackbird

Common Grackle *Quiscalus quiscula* L 12½" (32 cm)

Long, keel-shaped tail; pale yellow eyes. Plumage appears all-black at a distance. In good light, *males* show glossy purplish blue head, neck, and breast. Widespread race *versicolor,* called "Bronzed Grackle," occurs in most of New England and west of the Appalachians; it has a bronze back, blue head, and purple tail. Smaller "Purple Grackle," *quiscula* of the Southeast, has a narrow bill, purple head, bottle green back, and blue tail. An intergrade population from the mid-Atlantic (*stonei*) shows variable head color and purplish back with iridescent bands of variable color. Females are smaller and duller than males. *Juveniles* are sooty brown, with brown eyes.

Voice: Common Grackle's song is a short, creaky *koguba-leek;* call note, a loud *chuck.*

Range: Abundant and gregarious, roaming in mixed flocks in open fields, marshes, parks, and suburban areas.

Boat-tailed Grackle *Quiscalus major*

♂L 16½" (42 cm) ♀L 14½" (37 cm)   Large grackle with a very long, keel-shaped tail; slightly smaller overall size, duller eye color, and more rounded crown than Great-tailed Grackle. *Adult male* is iridescent blue-black. *Adult female* is tawny brown with darker wings and tail. Male and female eye color is mostly brown in nominate race of coastal Texas and Louisiana and *westoni* of Florida; *alabamensis* of coastal Mississippi to northwest Florida and the largest race, *torreyi,* on the Atlantic coast, have a yellow iris. *First-fall male* is black but lacks iridescence; *juvenile* shows a hint of spotting or streaking on breast. Immatures resemble respective adults by mid-fall.

Voice: Calls include a quiet chuck and a variety of rough squeaks, rattles, and other chatter. Most common song is a series of harsh *jeeb* notes.

Range: This common, noisy grackle seldom strays beyond coastal saltwater marshes except in Florida, where it also inhabits inland lakes and streams. Nests in small colonies. Range has slowly expanded northward on the Atlantic coast.

Great-tailed Grackle *Quiscalus mexicanus*

♂L 18" (46 cm) ♀L 15" (38 cm)   A large grackle with very long, keel-shaped tail and golden yellow eyes. *Adult male* is iridescent black with purple sheen on head, back, and underparts. *Adult female*'s upperparts are brown; underparts cinnamon buff on breast to grayish brown on belly; shows less iridescence than male. *Juveniles* resemble adult female but are even less glossy and show some streaking on underparts. Immature males are duller, with shorter tails and darker eyes than adults by mid-fall. In narrow zone of range overlap, Great-tailed Grackle is distinguished from Boat-tailed by bright yellow eyes, larger size, and flatter crown.

Voice: Varied calls include clear whistles and loud *clack* notes.

Range: Common, especially in open flatlands with scattered groves of trees and in marshes and wetlands. Casual far north of breeding range, which is expanding north.

Common Grackle

keel-shaped tail

overall blackish; purplish gloss to head

bluish head contrasts with bronze-green back and underparts

sooty brown

purple ♂
quiscula

bronze ♂
versicolor

juvenile

Boat-tailed Grackle
major

juvenile

1st fall ♂

cinnamon buff underparts

♀

rounded head with darker eye than Great-tailed of western Gulf race

western Gulf Coast adult ♂

blue-green gloss

long, keel-shaped tail

Great-tailed Grackle

juvenile

long bill

♀

flatter crown and pale eye

♂

purple gloss

very long, keel-shaped tail

Rusty Blackbird *Euphagus carolinus* L 9" (23 cm)

Adults and fall immatures have yellow eyes. Fall adults and immatures are broadly tipped with rust; tertials and wing coverts edged with rust. **Fall female** has broad, buffy eyebrow, buffy underparts, gray rump. **Fall male** is darker; eyebrow fainter. The rusty feather tips wear off by spring, producing the dark **breeding** plumage. Juveniles have dark eyes.
Voice: Call is a low *tschak;* song, a high, squeaky *koo-a-lee.*
Range: Uncommon, declining in wet woodlands and swamps; nests in shrubs or conifers near water. Gregarious in fall, winter.

Brewer's Blackbird *Euphagus cyanocephalus*

L 9" (23 cm) **Male** has yellow eyes; **female**'s are usually brown. Male is black year-round, with purplish gloss on head and neck, greenish gloss on body and wings. **Immature males** show variable buffy feather edgings, but never on tertials or wing coverts, as in Rusty Blackbird; note also the shorter, thicker bill. Female and juveniles are gray-brown.
Voice: Typical call is a harsh *check;* song, a wheezy *que-ee* or *k-seee.*
Range: Found in open habitats; gregarious. Very local in winter in Southeast, mostly at livestock pens. Casual to East Coast.

Shiny Cowbird *Molothrus bonariensis* L 7½" (19 cm)

Sleeker, with longer tail, flatter head, and more pointed bill than Brown-headed. **Male** blackish with purple gloss on head, breast, back. **Female** and juveniles resemble female Brown-headed except for shape, darker color, and more prominent eyebrow.
Voice: Song, whistled notes followed by trills. Male's high-pitched, sweet flight call is not like other cowbirds' calls.
Range: Arrived in south Florida from West Indies in 1985. Uncommon and local in coastal south Florida; very rare in Southeast; accidental west to Oklahoma, north to Maritimes.

Brown-headed Cowbird *Molothrus ater* L 7½" (19 cm)

Male's brown head contrasts with metallic green-black body. **Female** is gray-brown above, paler below. **Juvenile** is paler above, more heavily streaked below; pale edgings give its back a scaled look. Young males molting to adult plumage in late summer are a patchwork of buff, brown, and black. Feeds with tail cocked up.
Voice: Male's song is a squeaky gurgling. Calls include a harsh rattle and squeaky whistles.
Range: Common; found in woodlands, farmlands, suburbs. Gregarious; often mixes with other blackbirds and starlings during nonbreeding season. All cowbirds lay eggs in nests of other species.

Bronzed Cowbird *Molothrus aeneus* L 8¾" (22 cm)

Red eyes distinctive at close range. Bill larger than Brown-headed. **Adult male** black with bronze gloss; wings, tail blue-black; thick ruff on nape and back gives a hunchbacked look. **Adult female** of Texas race, *aeneus,* duller than the male; **juveniles** dark brown.
Voice: Call is a harsh, guttural *chuck.* Song is wheezy and buzzy.
Range: Locally common; forages in flocks, often with other blackbirds. Rare east to Florida; accidental north to Maritimes.

head pattern distinctive with rusty crown with prominent pale supercilium

Rusty Blackbird

pale eye

contrasting gray rump

fall ♀

breeding ♀

long, thin bill

rusty tips to coverts and tertials

fall ♂

breeding ♂

Brewer's Blackbird

wings uniformly dark

bill slightly thicker than Rusty

dark eye

immature ♂

♂

♀

pale supercilium

black spikelike bill

Shiny Cowbird

♀

Brown-headed Cowbird

♀

juvenile

slightly different bill shape than Shiny

♂

black with purple gloss

♂

brown head

juveniles streaked below, scaly above

red eye

Bronzed Cowbird
aeneus

thick bill

juvenile

♂

♀

dark overall

Orchard Oriole *Icterus spurius* L 7¼" *(18 cm)*

Adult male is chestnut overall, with black hood. **Female** is olive above, yellowish below. Immature male resembles female; acquires black bib and, sometimes, traces of chestnut by first spring. Smaller size, lack of orange tones, and thinner, more curved bill distinguish female and immature male from Baltimore and Bullock's Orioles. Compare also with Hooded Oriole.
Voice: Calls include a sharp *chuck*. Song is a loud, rapid burst of whistled notes, downslurred at the end.
Range: Locally common in suburban shade trees, orchards, and shrubby areas. Very rare vagrant to the Maritimes.

Hooded Oriole *Icterus cucullatus* L 8" *(20 cm)*

Bill long and slightly curved. **Breeding male** is orange or orange-yellow; note black patch on throat. The two Texas races, *sennetti* and *cucullatus*, are orange. All winter adult males have buffy brown tips on back, forming a barred pattern. Hooded **female** and immature male lack pale belly of Bullock's Oriole; bill is more curved; immature male acquires black throat by winter. Southwest *nelsoni* (unrecorded in East and not shown) is much more similar in coloring to the smaller female and immature Orchard Orioles.
Voice: Calls include a whistled, rising *wheet;* song is a series of whistles, trills, and rattles.
Range: Uncommon in south Texas. Accidental well north of normal range to Ontario.

Baltimore Oriole *Icterus galbula* L 8¼" *(21 cm)*

Adult male has black hood and back, bright orange rump and underparts; large orange patches on tail. **Adult females** are brownish olive above and orange below, with varying amounts of black on head and throat; those with maximum black (shown) resemble first-spring males. Extent and intensity of color on underparts of **fall immatures** is highly variable; has distinctly contrasting wing bars and palish lores; no eye line or yellowish eyebrow.
Voice: Common call is a rich *hew-li;* also gives a series of rattles. Song is a musical, irregular sequence of *hew-li* and other notes.
Range: Common breeder in deciduous woodland over much of the East. Some winter at feeders and in the South.

Bullock's Oriole *Icterus bullockii* L 8¼" *(21 cm)*

Formerly considered same species as Baltimore Oriole; some interbreeding on Great Plains. **Adult male** has less black on head: crown, eye line, throat patch; note bold white patch on wing, entirely orange outer tail feathers. **Females** and **immatures** have yellow throat and breast, unlike most Baltimore's extensive orange (although the dullest Baltimores difficult to separate from Bullock's); note Bullock's dark eye line, less contrasting wing bars, plainer back. Most birds show dark "teeth" intruding into white of median covert bar. By **first spring,** males have black lores, throat.
Voice: Song, mix of whistles and harsher notes; call, a harsh *cheh* or series of same.
Range: Breeds where shade trees grow. Casual vagrant to the East, where many reports are of dull, immature Baltimores.

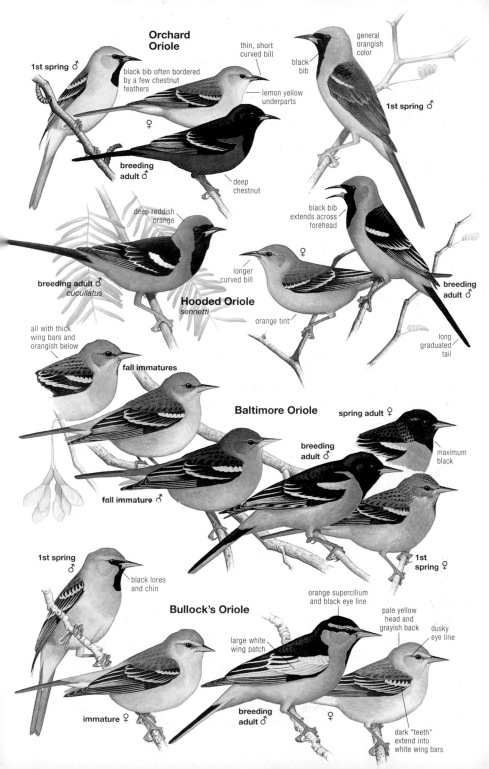

Orchard Oriole

1st spring ♂

thin, short curved bill

black bib often bordered by a few chestnut feathers

lemon yellow underparts

♀

breeding adult ♂

deep chestnut

general orangish color

black bib

1st spring ♂

black bib extends across forehead

deep reddish orange

breeding adult ♂ *cucullatus*

♀

longer curved bill

Hooded Oriole *sennetti*

orange tint

breeding adult ♂

long graduated tail

all with thick wing bars and orangish below

fall immatures

Baltimore Oriole

spring adult ♀

breeding adult ♂

maximum black

fall immature ♂

1st spring ♀

1st spring ♂

black lores and chin

Bullock's Oriole

orange supercilium and black eye line

pale yellow head and grayish back

dusky eye line

large white wing patch

immature ♀

breeding adult ♂

♀

dark "teeth" extend into white wing bars

Altamira Oriole *Icterus gularis* L 10" (25 cm)

Distinguished from Hooded Oriole by larger size, much thicker-based, mostly blackish bill, and, in *adult,* by orange shoulder patch. Lower wing bar whitish. *Immatures* are duller than adults, shoulder patch yellow; like adults by second fall. Found singly or in pairs.

Voice: Calls include a low, raspy *ike ike ike;* song is a series of clear, varied whistles.

Range: Uncommon and possibly declining. Found in southernmost Texas in tall trees and willows.

Audubon's Oriole *Icterus graduacauda* L 9½" (24 cm)

Male has black hood, greenish yellow back, and yellowish collar. Female is slightly duller. Rather secretive; often seen foraging on ground. Found singly or in pairs. Compare with Scott's Oriole (below), whose range typically does not overlap.

Voice: Song is a series of soft, tentative, three-note warbles.

Range: Tropical species, resident but uncommon in south Texas woodlands and brushlands.

Spot-breasted Oriole *Icterus pectoralis* L 9½" (24 cm)

Middle American species. A large oriole with a fairly heavy bill. *Adults* have an orange or yellow-orange patch on shoulders; black lores and throat; dark spots on upper breast; extensive white on wings. *Juveniles* are yellower overall; *immatures* may lack breast spots. Found singly or in pairs.

Voice: Song is a long, loud series of melodic whistles.

Range: Introduced and now established in southern Florida. Prefers suburban gardens. Florida population has declined over past three decades.

Scott's Oriole *Icterus parisorum* L 9" (23 cm)

Adult male's black hood extends to back and breast; rump, wing patch, and underparts bright lemon yellow. Adult female is olive and streaked above, dull greenish yellow below; throat shows variable amount of black. *Immatures* lack any black on head; *first-spring males* show extensive black. *Females* and immatures larger, grayer, more streaked above, and have straighter bill than female Hooded Oriole.

Voice: Common call notes are a harsh *shack* or a flat *chuk;* song is a mixture of rich, whistled phrases reminiscent of Western Meadowlark song.

Range: In eastern region, Scott's Oriole breeds only on the Edwards Plateau of central Texas. Prefers ash-juniper-oak woodlands and oak savannas. Casual east to Pennsylvania, Kentucky, and Louisiana and north to Minnesota, Wisconsin, and Ontario.

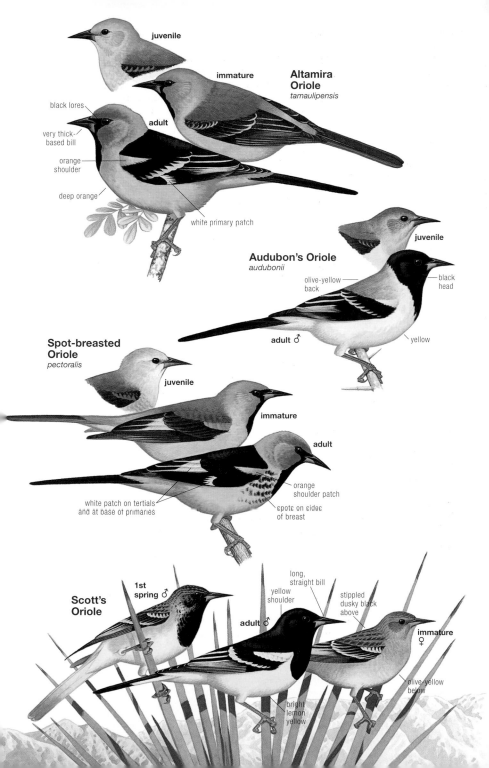

juvenile

immature

Altamira Oriole
tamaulipensis

black lores

very thick-based bill

adult

orange shoulder

deep orange

white primary patch

Audubon's Oriole
audubonii

juvenile

olive-yellow back

black head

adult ♂

yellow

Spot-breasted Oriole
pectoralis

juvenile

immature

adult

orange shoulder patch

white patch on tertials and at base of primaries

spots on sides of breast

Scott's Oriole

1st spring ♂

long, straight bill

yellow shoulder

stippled dusky black above

adult ♂

immature ♀

olive-yellow below

bright lemon yellow

Fringilline and Cardueline Finches, Allies
(Family Fringillidae)

Seedeaters with undulating flight. Many nest in the North; in fall, flocks of "winter finches" may roam south.

Purple Finch *Carpodacus purpureus* L 6" (15 cm)
Not purple, but rose red over most of *adult male*'s body, brightest on head and rump. Rose color is acquired in second fall. Back is streaked; tail notched. *Adult female* and immatures are heavily streaked below; closely resemble Cassin's Finch (see below). Compare also with female House Finch.
Voice: Calls include a musical *chur-lee* and, in flight, a sharp *pit.* Song is a rich warble, lower than House Finch song.
Range: Fairly common; found in coniferous or mixed woodland.

Cassin's Finch *Carpodacus cassinii* L 6¼" (16 cm)
Crimson of *adult male*'s cap ends sharply at brown-streaked nape. Throat and breast paler than Purple Finch; streaks on sides and malar stripe more distinct. Red hues begin to appear late in second summer. Tail strongly notched. Undertail coverts always distinctly streaked, unlike many Purples. *Adult female* and immatures otherwise closely resemble Purple Finch. Cassin's facial pattern is slightly less distinct; culmen is straighter and longer; has longer primary projection.
Voice: Cassin's gives a dry *kee-up* or *tee-dee-yip* call. Warbling song, longer and more complex than song of Purple Finch.
Range: Casual in fall and winter east to Great Plains.

House Finch *Carpodacus mexicanus* L 6" (15 cm)
Male has brown cap; front of head, bib, and rump are typically red but can vary to orange or occasionally yellow. Bib is clearly set off from streaked underparts. Tail is squarish. *Adult female* and juveniles are streaked with brown overall; lack distinct ear patch and eyebrow of Purple and Cassin's Finches. Young males acquire adult coloring by first fall.
Voice: Lively, high-pitched song consists chiefly of varied three-note phrases; includes strident notes, unlike Purple Finch's song; usually ends with a nasal *wheer.* Calls include a whistled *wheat.*
Range: Common; found in a variety of lowland habitats. Introduced in the East in the 1940s, where its range quickly expanded; especially numerous in towns.

Gray-crowned Rosy-Finch *Leucosticte tephrocotis*
L 6½" (17 cm) Dark brown, with gray on head; pink on wings and underparts; underwings silvery. Female less pink, juveniles grayish. All have yellow bill in *winter,* black by spring. Western *littoralis,* "*Hepburn's Rosy-Finch,*" shows more gray on face than widespread nominate race.
Voice: Call, a high, chirping *chew.*
Range: Casual late fall and winter visitor to Great Plains; accidental east to Ohio, Quebec, Maine.

distinct streaks

contrasty pale supercilium

♀

usually unstreaked undertail coverts

Purple Finch
eastern purpureus

stubbier bill than Cassin's; culmen slightly curved

overall deep rose red color

adult ♂

face pattern more blended than female Purple

Cassin's Finch

adult ♀

distinct streaks

crimson red crown

adult ♂

long bill with straight culmen

thick brown malar streak

pale pink

streaked undertail coverts

fine streaks

notched tail

long primary projection

extensive gray face

yellow bill

broad reddish eyebrow

typical ♂

red throat and breast

"Hepburn's" winter ♂
littoralis

House Finch
frontalis

brownish streaked flanks

Gray-crowned Rosy-Finch

gray head band

more square-ended tail

variant ♂

muted brown back

very indistinct face pattern

curved culmen

♀

winter ♂
tephrocotis

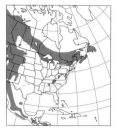

Red Crossbill *Loxia curvirostra* L 5½-7¾" (14-20 cm)

Bill with crossed tips identifies both crossbill species. Red Crossbill's dark brown wings lack the bold white bars of White-winged Crossbill. Plumage highly variable. Most *males* are reddish overall, brightest on crown and rump, but may be pale rose or scarlet or largely yellow; always have red or yellow on throat. Most *females* are yellowish olive; may show patches of red; throat is always gray, except in a small northern subspecies where yellow extends to center, but not sides, of throat. *Juveniles* are boldly streaked; a few juveniles and a very few adult males show white wing bars, the upper bar thinner than the lower. Immatures are like the respective adult but juvenile wing is retained. All birds except adult males have olive edges on wings. Subspecies vary widely in size, including bill size; extremes are shown here. All have their "home range." Distinct differences in vocalizations have led some authorities to believe that there may be a half dozen or more cryptic separate species in the Red Crossbill complex. All have large heads and short, notched tails.

Voice: Calls, given chiefly in flight, vary from one subspecies to another and include *kip* or *chimp*, often repeated. Song begins with several two-note phrases followed by a warbled trill.

Range: Fairly common, Red Crossbills inhabit coniferous woods. May nest at any time of year, especially in southern range. Highly irregular in their wanderings, dependent upon cone crops. Any race may turn up almost anywhere. Irruptive migrant.

White-winged Crossbill *Loxia leucoptera* L 6½" (17 cm)

All ages have black wings with white tips on the tertials; two bold, broad white wing bars. Upper wing bar is often hidden by scapulars. *Adult male* is bright pink overall, paler in winter. *Immature male* is largely yellow, with patches of red or pink. *Adult female* is mottled with yellowish olive or grayish; rump pale yellow; underparts grayish olive, with yellow wash on breast and sides. *Juvenile* is heavily streaked; wing bars thinner than in adults.

Voice: White-winged Crossbill's distinctive flight call is a rapid series of harsh *chet* notes. Variable song, often delivered in display flight, combines harsh rattles and musical warbles.

Range: Inhabits coniferous woods. Highly irregular in its wanderings, dependent upon spruce cone crops. Irruptive migrant.

Pine Grosbeak *Pinicola enucleator* L 9" (23 cm)

Large and plump, with long tail. Bill is dark, stubby, strongly curved. Two white wing bars, sometimes tinged with pink in adult male. *Male*'s gray plumage is tipped with red on head, back, and underparts; pinker in fresh fall plumage. *Female* and immatures are grayer overall; head, rump, and underparts variably yellow or reddish; some females and immature males are *russet.*

Voice: Typical flight call is a whistled *pui pui pui;* alarm call, a musical *chee-vli.* Location call shows considerable geographic variation. Song is a rather short, musical warble.

Range: Uncommon; inhabits open coniferous woods. In winter, found also in orchards and suburban shade trees. Usually unwary and approachable. Irruptive winter migrant.

female typically has olive body with darker wings and gray throat

crossed bill

typical ♀

northern *minor* ♀

Red Crossbill

overall reddish coloration

typical ♂

juvenile

variant ♂

some with faint whitish wing bars

juvenile

White-winged Crossbill
leucoptera

thinner crossed bill

♀

deep pink color

immature ♂

white tertial tips

winter adult ♂

black wings with thick white wing bars

yellow-olive head and back; body otherwise gray

♀

stubby black bill with curved culmen

white wing bars

adult ♂

deep pinkish red

russet variant

Pine Grosbeak
leucura

Common Redpoll *Carduelis flammea* L 5¼" (13 cm)

Red or orange-red cap or "poll," black chin. Closely resembles Hoary Redpoll, but usually has distinct streaks on flanks, rump, undertail coverts; bill is slightly larger. *Male* usually has bright rosy breast and sides. Both sexes paler, buffier in winter. *Juvenile* lacks red cap until late-summer molt; male acquires pinkish breast by end of second summer. Extent of interbreeding between Common and Hoary Redpolls is unknown.

Voice: When perched, Common gives a rising *swee-ee-eet* call; flight call, a dry, scratching single *chit* note or series of *chit* notes. Song combines trills and twittering.

Range: Fairly common; breeds in subarctic forests and tundra scrub. Forms large winter flocks; frequents brushy, weedy areas, also catkin-bearing trees like alder and birch. Irruptive winter migrant.

Hoary Redpoll *Carduelis hornemanni* L 5½" (14 cm)

Closely resembles Common Redpoll but is usually frostier and paler overall, with a slightly smaller bill. Streaking on rump and undertail coverts minimal or absent. *Male*'s breast is usually paler and pinker than on Common; color does not extend to cheeks or sides.

Voice: Calls and song similar to Common.

Range: Uncommon; nests on or near the ground above Arctic tree line. The race *hornemanni,* of Canadian Arctic islands and Greenland, is larger and paler than more widespread *exilipes*. Rare sightings, especially of *exilipes,* occur irregularly south of Canada in winter, almost always with Commons.

Pine Siskin *Carduelis pinus* L 5" (13 cm)

Prominent streaking; yellow at base of tail and in flight feathers conspicuous in flight; bill thinner than in other finches. *Juvenile*'s overall yellow tint is lost by late summer.

Voice: Calls include a whiny, rough, rising *tee-ee* and, in flight, a harsh, descending *chee*. Song is similar to that of American Goldfinch but much huskier.

Range: Gregarious; may flock with goldfinches in winter. Found in coniferous and mixed woods in summer; forests, shrubs, and fields in winter. Winter range is erratic.

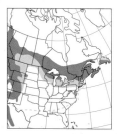

Evening Grosbeak *Coccothraustes vespertinus*

L 8" (20 cm) Stocky, noisy finch. Big bill pale yellow or greenish by spring, whitish by fall; prominent white patch on inner wing. Yellow forehead and eyebrow on *adult male;* dark brown and yellow body. Grayish tan *female* has thin, dark malar stripe, white-tipped tail; second wing patch, on primaries, is conspicuous in flight. *Juvenile* has brown bills; female resembles adult female; male yellower overall, wing and tail like adult male.

Voice: Loud, strident call: *clee-ip* or *peeer.*

Range: Breeds in mixed woods. In winter frequents woodlots, shade trees, and feeders; numbers and range limits vary greatly from year to year, but substantial overall decline during the past two decades.

Common Redpoll
flammea

juvenile

breeding ♀

breeding ♂

extensive pinkish red breast

winter ♀

streaked undertail coverts

winter ♂

Hoary Redpoll

winter ♀
exilipes

slightly smaller bill than Common

paler upperparts than Common

pale rump

very pale pink

winter ♂
exilipes

faint flank streaks

winter ♂
hornemanni

larger and overall paler than *exilipes*

Pine Siskin
pinus

pale wing bars

thin, sharply pointed bill

juvenile

prominent yellow wing stripe and yellow patches at base of tail

streaked underparts

yellow forehead and eyebrow

large bill

white patch on inner wing

Evening Grosbeak
vespertinus

breeding ♂

♂

♀

white primary patch

juvenile ♂

short tail with white tail spots

female with gray on head and back; buffy below

breeding ♀

American Goldfinch *Carduelis tristis* L 5" (13 cm)

Breeding adult male is bright yellow with black cap; black wings have white bars, yellow shoulder patch; uppertail and undertail coverts white. ***Female*** is duller overall, olive above; lacks black cap and yellow shoulder patch. White undertail coverts distinguish female from most Lesser Goldfinches. ***Winter adults*** and immatures are either brownish or grayish above. Bill darker than when breeding. ***Juvenal*** plumage, held into Nov., has buff wing markings and rump.

Voice: Song is a lively series of trills, twitters, and *swee* notes. Distinctive flight call, *per-chik-o-ree.*

Range: Common, and gregarious during nonbreeding season; found in weedy fields, open second-growth woodlands, along roadsides, especially in thistles and sunflowers, and at feeders.

Lesser Goldfinch *Carduelis psaltria* L 4½" (11 cm)

All birds have a white wing patch at base of primaries. Entire crown black on ***adult male;*** back typically black in eastern part of range, greenish in western birds. Most ***adult females*** are dull yellow below; except for a few extremely pale birds, they lack the white undertail coverts typical of American Goldfinch. ***Immature male*** lacks full black cap. Juvenile resembles adult female.

Voice: Call, a plaintive, kittenlike *tee-yee.* Song is somewhat similar to that of American Goldfinch. May imitate other species.

Range: Common in dry, brushy fields, woodland borders, and gardens. Range expanding northward. Accidental in the East.

Old World Sparrows (Family Passeridae)

Old World family. Gregarious; two species have become established in North America.

Eurasian Tree Sparrow *Passer montanus* L 6" (15 cm)

Gregarious all year. Brown crown, black ear patch, black throat distinguish ***adult.*** Compare with House Sparrow's gray crown and more extensively black bib. ***Juvenile*** has dark mottling on crown, dark gray throat and ear patch.

Voice: Similar to House Sparrow, but harder.

Range: Old World species, introduced and now locally common in parks, suburbs, and farmlands around St. Louis, Missouri, and in nearby Illinois north to Iowa. Accidental to Manitoba, Ontario, Kentucky, and Indiana.

House Sparrow *Passer domesticus* L 6¼" (16 cm)

Breeding male has gray crown, chestnut nape, black bib, black bill. Fresh ***fall*** plumage is edged with gray, obscuring these markings; bill becomes brownish. ***Female*** is best identified by the combination of streaked back, buffy eye stripe, and unstreaked breast. Juvenile resembles adult female.

Voice: Calls include a sweet *cheelip* and monotonous chirps.

Range: House Sparrows are common in populated areas. Gregarious in winter. Also known as English Sparrow.

American Goldfinch
tristis

black wings and tail; bright yellow body; white under tail

breeding ♀

breeding ♂

black forehead and forecrown

yellow shoulder; brownish back

winter adult ♂

whitish undertail coverts

prominent wing bars

winter ♀

smaller than American

Lesser Goldfinch
hesperophila

♀

pale yellow underparts

pale ♀

juvenile

black-backed adult ♂
psaltria

blackish cap

green-backed adult ♂

juvenile

chestnut brown cap; whitish collar; bold blackish spot on white cheeks

white patch at base of primaries

immature ♂

Eurasian Tree Sparrow
montanus

adult

gray crown

blackish bill

chestnut brown nape

white wing bar

head pattern more subdued

House Sparrow
domesticus

buffy eyebrow

pale bill

♀

black bib

bill paler

fall ♂

plain underparts; dark streaked back

breeding ♂

Rarities from Latin America, the Caribbean, Europe

This appendix contains casual or accidental species that have been primarily recorded in the East or that are equally rare in both the East and the West. Most originate from Latin America, the Caribbean region (West Indies), or Europe; a few are pelagic species from the eastern or southern Atlantic. Four species that have gone extinct in the past two centuries are also included.

adult
anser

Graylag Goose *Anser anser*

L 29-33" (74-84 cm) WS 59-66" (150-168 cm) Palearctic species that has become widely domesticated (page 44). The European race recently recorded from Greenland. In 2005, one landed and remained on a ship southeast of St. John's, Newfoundland. Largest and bulkiest of gray geese with heavy head, neck, and bill. Pink legs and orange (in nominate *anser*) bill. Head and neck gray, uniform with rest of body, unlike other gray geese, which have a darker head and neck. In flight, striking pale gray forewing and contrasting pale gray underwing coverts.

fall ♂

adult ♂

Garganey *Anas querquedula* *L 15½" (39 cm)*

Old World species. Casual in eastern North America, mostly in spring and early summer. Prominent whitish edge to tertials. *Male's* bold white eyebrows separate dark crown, red-brown face; in flight, shows gray-blue forewing and green speculum bordered fore and aft with white. Female has strong facial pattern: dark crown, pale eyebrow, dark eye line, white lore spot bordered by a second dark line; note also dark bill and legs, dark undertail coverts. Larger and paler than female Green-winged Teal. Female in flight shows gray-brown forewing, dark green speculum bordered in white. Pale gray inner webs of primaries visible in flight from above.

adult ♂

Labrador Duck *Camptorhynchus labradorius* **EX**

L 22½" (57 cm) Extinct. Note the unique bill shape that broadens towards tip. Much of *adult male's* head, neck, and chest white; remainder of body plumage blackish. Adult females, immatures, and eclipse males more grayish brown overall, the throat being whiter than the head. Never common, it was best known from the winter grounds on the mid-Atlantic coast where the last definite record (specimen) was obtained in 1875. Breeding grounds unknown, perhaps Labrador, perhaps farther north.

adult
chlororhynchos

Yellow-nosed Albatross *Thalassarche chlororhynchos*

L 32" (81 cm) WS 80" (203 cm) Casual off Gulf and Atlantic coasts; a few inland sightings in East. Most of nominate subspecies breed in south Atlantic, the probable source of North American records. Confused with Black-browed Albatross (opposite) and with subadult Northern Gannet. *Adult's* bill appears black; at close range, yellow ridge on top and reddish tip are visible. Note light grayish wash on head and blackish triangular patch in front of eye of nominate race. Underwing extensively white with a narrow dark border; some juveniles show more dark on leading edge, which can cause confusion with adult Black-browed. Otherwise juvenile resembles adult, except for all-dark bill, reduced eye patch.

Black-browed Albatross *Thalassarche melanophris*
L 35" (89 cm) WS 88" (224 cm) A circumpolar Southern Hemisphere species. Casual in North Atlantic, most recorded in northeast portion. One certain record of immature photographed off Virginia Beach on 6 Feb. 1999; about 20 other reports (some possibly correct). Potential confusion with subadult Northern Gannets. From similar Yellow-nosed, note larger size with thicker neck and chunkier body. *Adult* has broad dark leading edge to underwing and heavier orange bill with redder tip; black eyebrow. *Juveniles* have darker bills and gray shading about head and neck forming collar; underwing mainly dark. Subadults have more yellowish bill with dark tip and some white in underwings.

Bulwer's Petrel *Bulweria bulwerii*
L 10" (26 cm) WS 26" (66 cm) Bird of tropical and subtropical oceans; accidental summer visitor off Outer Banks, North Carolina (1 Jul. 1992 and 8 Aug. 1998). Sooty brown overall with pale diagonal bar across secondary coverts. Long tail usually held in a point; wedge shape visible only when fanned. Flight is buoyant and erratic, long wings slightly bowed and held forward. Flies within a few feet of the water; flight, when it is windy, is more like gadfly petrels.

Cape Verde Shearwater *Calonectris edwardsii*
L 15½" (39 cm) WS 39½" (101 cm) Breeds Cape Verde archipelago, ranges to West African coast. Accidental off Outer Banks, North Carolina (15 Aug. 2004) and possibly off Ocean City, Maryland (21 Oct. 2006). Smaller, slightly longer tailed than Cory's with darker gray upperparts and more contrasting face; slimmer bill is olive gray, rather than yellowish.

Little Shearwater *Puffinus assimilis*
L 11" (28 cm) WS 25" (64 cm) Casual, two fall specimens from Nova Scotia and South Carolina (*baroli*, breeds Azores); one photographed in Aug. 2007 off Massachusetts; sight records from off North Carolina and Nova Scotia. Similar to larger Audubon's Shearwater (page 74), but has shorter tail, whiter underwings, and grayer two-toned upperwing; white undertail coverts; face whiter. Flies with rapid, stiff, shallow wingbeats. The two North Atlantic subspecies, *baroli* and darker-faced *boydi* (Cape Verde islands), recently treated by some authorities as a separate species from Southern Hemisphere subspecies.

Black-bellied Storm-Petrel *Fregetta tropica*
L 8" (20 cm) WS 18" (46 cm) A widespread southern ocean species; single bird well photographed off Outer Banks, North Carolina, on 31 May 2004 and another 16 Jul. 2006. Black-and-white coloration distinctive on all individuals, but diagnostic black line up through white belly (separating it from another southern oceans species, White-bellied Storm-Petrel, *F. grallaria*) can be hard to see. Note long legs and feet project past tail. Foraging behavior distinctive: splashes breast into water, then springs forward pushing off with long legs.

juvenile

adult

baroli

Great Frigatebird *Fregata minor*
L 37" (95 cm) WS 85" (216 cm) Extensive breeding range in Indian and Pacific Oceans. Closely resembles Magnificent Frigatebird (page 78). Adult male distinguished from Magnificent by russet bar on upperwing coverts and pink feet; often by whitish scallops on axillaries. Note **adult female**'s dark head with pale gray throat, rounder (less tapered) black belly patch, and red orbital ring. When fresh, juvenile has rusty wash to head and chest, and pink feet. Specimen from Perry, Oklahoma (3 Nov. 1975).

Lesser Frigatebird *Fregata ariel*
L 30" (76 cm) WS 73" (185 cm) Widespread in southwest and central Pacific and Indian Ocean; a few colonies in south Atlantic. Our smallest frigatebird, in all plumages a white spur extends from the flanks into the axillaries. Juvenile has pale, rusty head. Recorded at least once from North America, an **adult male** photographed at Deer Island, Maine, on 3 July 1960; a photographed bird from Michigan in fall of 2005 is under review.

Western Reef-Heron *Egretta gularis*
L 23½" (60 cm) WS 37½" (95 cm) Old World species; casual to the West Indies. Single **dark morph** birds recorded in Massachusetts, Newfoundland, Nova Scotia, Maine/New Hampshire, and New Jersey/New York, the latter four possibly involving the same individual. Structurally resembles closely related Little Egret (page 90), but has slightly thicker neck; thicker-based bill is longer and a little more curved. Two color morphs. Much more numerous dark morph is slaty gray overall with white chin and throat; lores and bill dusky yellow; legs black and feet yellow. White morph resembles Little Egret, but note slight structural differences; immatures often have scattered dark feathers.

Gray Heron *Ardea cinerea*
L 33-40" (84-102 cm) WS 61-69" (155-175 cm) Widespread Old World species; one found on Newfoundland coast in Oct. 1999, subsequently died in a rehabilitation center. Similar to Great Blue Heron (page 88), but smaller, with shorter legs and neck. In all plumages lacks rufous thighs of Great Blue; in flight leading edge of wing shows prominent white area, rather than rufous.

Jabiru *Jabiru mycteria L 52" (132 cm) WS 90" (229 cm)*
Huge stork of Central and South America, casual straggler in south Texas; recorded once in Oklahoma and Mississippi. Distinguished from Wood Stork by larger size; large bill, slightly upturned; and all-white wings and tail. Red throat pouch brightens and inflates during **breeding** season. **Juvenile** is patchy brown-gray; head is blackish brown. Usually seen with flocks of Wood Storks.

Crane Hawk *Geranospiza caerulescens*

L 18-21" (46-53 cm) WS 36-41" (91-104 cm) Neotropical species from northeastern and northwestern Mexico to South America. One wintered at Santa Ana National Wildlife Refuge, southern Texas, from 20 Dec. 1987 to 9 Apr. 1988. Distinctive, long profile with small head, long orange legs, and long banded tail; iris reddish. Northeastern subspecies (*nigra*) is darkest. In flight, note white crescent at base of primaries. Juvenile has some whitish in face and under tail, whitish barring below, and duller soft parts.

Collared Forest-Falcon *Micrastur semitorquatus*

L 20" (52 cm) WS 31" (79 cm) Neotropical species found from northeastern and northwestern Mexico to South America. Recorded once in south Texas at Bentsen-Rio Grande Valley State Park, from 22 Jan. to 24 Feb. 1994 (light-morph adult). Distinctive structure: very short, rounded wings (wing tips barely reach base of tail), long graduated tail, and long legs. Three color morphs: more numerous **light morph** is black above, white below; note black crescent on white cheek and thin white bars on tail; juvenile similar but browner above, also barred and more buffy below. In buff morph, white areas replaced with buff; dark morph is rare. Usually seen within forest canopy; often located by loud calls.

Eurasian Kestrel *Falco tinnunculus*

L 13½" (34 cm) WS 29" (74 cm) Casual on western Aleutians and in Bering Sea region; accidental in fall, winter, and spring on the East Coast from New Brunswick and Nova Scotia to New Jersey and Florida. Resembles American Kestrel (page 120), but note larger size and single, not double, dark facial stripe. In flight, distinguished by wedge-shaped tail and two-toned upperwing, with back and inner wing paler. Hovers as it hunts. *Adult male* has russet wings, gray tail; female duller, often with gray rump. *Juvenile* similar to adult female, but dark barring heavier on upperparts and tail.

Red-footed Falcon *Falco vespertinus*

L 11" (27 cm) WS 29" (73 cm) A medium-size falcon that breeds in eastern Europe and western Asia and winters in southern and southwestern Africa. Regular, especially in spring, to northwestern Europe; casual to Iceland. One *first-summer male* was present at Martha's Vineyard, Massachusetts, 8 to 24 Aug. 2004. Adult male slaty gray overall with rufous thighs, rufous undertail coverts. Adult female has buffy crown and underparts, dark moustache, pale sides of neck; adults have red legs and feet. Juvenile similar but browner and more streaked, duller legs and feet. Often hovers.

Corn Crake *Crex crex* *L 10½" (27 cm)*

European species, formerly a very rare vagrant in fall along the East Coast; recently only three fall records: Saint-Pierre, Nova Scotia, and Newfoundland. Found in damp, grassy fields, croplands, not in marshes. Dull buffy yellow overall, with short, thick, brownish bill; distinctive large chestnut wing patch.

adult

light-
morph
adult

juvenile

adult ♂

1st
summer ♂

Paint-billed Crake *Neocrex erythrops* L 7¼-8" (18-20 cm)

Found eastern Panama through South America and Galápagos Islands. Specimens from Brazos County, Texas, on 17 Feb. 1972 (*erythrops*) and near Richmond, Virginia, on 15 Dec. 1978 (*olivascens*). Olive-brown above with gray forecrown and face; throat whitish; sides, flanks, and undertail coverts barred; red legs and yellow-green bill with bright orange base.

adult

Spotted Rail *Pardirallus maculatus* L 10-11¼" (25-28 cm)

Resident on Cuba and Isle of Pines, Hispaniola, and from central Mexico to South America and the Galápagos Islands. Specimens (*insolitus*) from Beaver County, Pennsylvania, on 12 Nov. 1976 and from Brown County, Texas, on 9 Aug. 1977. Rather large, blackish rail. **Adult** is spotted with white on head and upperparts; remainder of underparts banded with white; long, slender greenish yellow bill has red spot at base; iris, legs, and feet red. Juveniles are polymorphic, have duller legs and bill, and brown iris. Dark morph is plain dark brown above, sooty gray below; pale morph has grayish brown throat and breast with fine white bars on breast; barred morph has gray throat with white spots, breast and belly barred with white.

atra

Eurasian Coot *Fulica atra* L 15¾" (40 cm)

Accidental straggler to Newfoundland, Labrador, and Quebec. Slightly larger and darker than American Coot (page 132); undertail coverts all-black. Forehead shield and bill entirely white.

adult

Collared Plover *Charadrius collaris* L 5" (14 cm)

Resident from northern Mexico to South America. Only North America record, 9 to 11 May 1992 at Uvalde, Texas. Small with disproportionately long legs, small thin black bill, pinkish legs; lacks white collar around nape. **Adult** with dark forecrown, often with rusty border; auriculars, nape, and sides of breast often with rusty fringes, especially in males; narrow but complete black breast band, often with distinct rusty fringes at sides, especially in male. Juvenile has incomplete breast band and pale rusty edges above.

Double-striped Thick-knee *Burhinus bistriatus*

L 16½" (42 cm)   Resident from northeastern Mexico to Brazil; recent nesting record from Great Inagua, Bahamas. A specimen record on 5 Dec. 1961 from the King Ranch, Kleberg County, Texas. Crepuscular and terrestrial, with ploverlike gait of runs and abrupt stops. Adults with dark lateral crown stripe and bold white supercilium; dark-tipped yellow bill and yellow legs. Juvenile slightly duller. In flight, two-toned upperwing; prominent broken white bar on primaries.

Eurasian Oystercatcher *Haematopus ostralegus*

L 16½" (42 cm) Palearctic species, breeding west to Iceland; rare migrant to Greenland (over 30 records). Two spring records from Newfoundland: Tors Cove, 22 to 25 May 1994; and Eastport, from 3 Apr. to 2 May 1999. Similar to American Oystercatcher (page 142), but has black back and red iris. In flight white wing bar is bolder and more extensive, and white extends up back. Nonbreeding birds have a white bar across throat.

breeding
adult

juvenile

winter

breeding

Spotted Redshank *Tringa erythropus L 12½" (32 cm)*

Eurasian species, casual on East Coast during migration and winter; accidental elsewhere. Long bill with red-based lower mandible, droops at tip. ***Breeding*** plumage is black overall with white spots above; legs dark red to blackish. Many have underparts variably marked with white. ***Juvenile*** is brownish gray and is heavily barred and spotted below. ***Winter*** birds are pale gray above, spotted with white on coverts and tertials. Both plumages show brighter orange legs. In flight, shows white wedge on back and white wing linings. Distinctive call, a loud rising *chu-weet* closely resembles the call of Semipalmated Plover.

Common Redshank *Tringa totanus L 11" (28 cm)*

Eurasian species; breeds as close as Iceland; numerous records for Greenland. Casual to Newfoundland in spring, once in winter. Bright orange legs, stout bill with reddish orange base, overall brownish plumage with distinct eye ring. ***Breeding*** adults and juveniles are extensively streaked below; winter birds (not illustrated) are diffusely mottled below. In flight, shows white dorsal wedge up back and distinctive broad white trailing edge to secondaries and inner primaries. Calls include a musical *tew* or more mournful *tew-hieu*. Alarm note is a series of *twek* notes.

breeding

Slender-billed Curlew *Numenius tenuirostris* E

L 15" (39 cm) Critically endangered, possibly extinct. Only known nests found in southwestern Siberia, Russia, early in 20th century. Wintered in western Mediterranean region and coastal northwest Africa, where several recorded in Morocco until 1995; last record from Northumberland, United Kingdom, 4 to 7 May 1998, ironically the United Kingdom's first record. In North America a specimen from Crescent Beach, Ontario, from "about 1925." Size of Whimbrel but patterned like Eurasian Curlew (below), but with slender bill and black heart-shaped spots, not chevrons, on sides and flanks.

adult

Eurasian Curlew *Numenius arquata L 22" (56 cm)*

A widespread Eurasian species. Casual on East Coast in fall and winter. The seven records are from Newfoundland to Long Island, New York, except for one at Middle Cheyne Lake, Nunavut. A large curlew that is heavily streaked below. The long bill is strongly decurved. Distinguished from Long-billed Curlew (page 148) by paler overall coloration and by white rump and wing linings; from Eurasian races of Whimbrel by larger size, longer bill, and lack of dark stripes on head.

juvenile

adult

breeding

Little Stint *Calidris minuta L 6" (15 cm)*
Eurasian species; casual on East Coast, accidental elsewhere. *Breeding* birds are brightly fringed with rufous above; throat and underparts white (more suffused with color in later summer adults), with bright buff wash and bold spotting on sides of breast. Redder above than Western and Semipalmated Sandpipers (page 154); compare also with Red-necked Stint. *Juvenile* best distinguished from juvenile Red-necked by extensively black-centered wing coverts and tertials, usually edged with rufous; also note split supercilium and streaking on sides of chest.

juvenile

breeding

Broad-billed Sandpiper *Limicola falcinellus L 7" (18 cm)*
Eurasian species, accidental in fall from coastal New York (Jamaica Bay Wildlife Refuge from 27 Aug. to 4 Sept. 1998). Plump body with short legs and long, broad-based bill with distinctive drooped tip give it a unique profile. Note also the distinctive split supercilium. Call is a dry and high-pitched buzzy trill; also shorter calls.

Jack Snipe *Lymnocryptes minimus L 7" (18 cm)*
Small, chunky Eurasian species. Late fall record for Makkovik Bay, Labrador (24 Dec. 1927). Secretive, reluctant to flush. Flight is low, short, fluttery, on rounded wings. Bobs while feeding. Pale base to short bill, pale split eyebrow stripes with no median crown stripe, broad buffy back stripes, streaked flanks, pale underparts.

Eurasian Woodcock *Scolopax rusticola L 13" (33 cm)*
Widespread Old World species. Casual to North America, where most records are old and from the Northeast; older records are from Newfoundland (1862), Quebec (twice in 1862), Pennsylvania (1886, 1890), New Jersey (1859), and Alabama (1889). The last record, and the only one accepted from the 20th century, was one at Goshen, New Jersey, 2 to 9 Jan. 1956, although one from Ohio (specimen lost) in 1935 may have been this species. All dated records fall between early Nov. and early Mar. Distinctly larger than similar American Woodcock (page 160); also duller and heavily barred below.

breeding adult

Gray-hooded Gull *Larus cirrocephalus*
L 16" (41 cm) WS 43" (109 cm) A native to Africa and South America. One adult was photographed on 26 Dec. 1998 at Apalachicola, Florida. *Breeding adult* has pale gray hood with darker border, long dark red bill, and long red legs; wing pattern distinctive. In winter loses hood and has dark ear spot and smudge around eye and dark tip to bill. First-year has similar outer wing pattern to adult, but a diagonal brown bar across the inner wing and a dark secondary bar, and a dark tail band. The pinkish yellow bill has a dark tip.

Belcher's Gull *Larus belcheri L 20" (51 cm) WS 49" (124 cm)*
Resident on west coast of South America; accidental to Florida.
Medium-size, three-year gull. Plumages and bill color similar to
Black-tailed Gull (page 174), but Belcher's has dark eyes, longer
legs, and thicker bill. ***Winter adults*** and second-winter birds have
dark hood, red only on tip of bill. Adult has yellow orbital ring.
First-winter*'s* head and breast are smoky brown; belly white; mot-
tled above.

breeding
adult

1st winter

winter adult

Large-billed Tern *Phaetusa simplex*
L 14½" (37 cm) WS 36" (92 cm) A South American freshwater
species. Accidental; recorded in late spring and summer from Lake
Calumet, Chicago, Illinois (15 Jul. 1949); Evans Lake, Mahoning
County, Ohio (29 May 1954); and Hudson County, New Jersey
(30 May 1988); additionally from Cuba and Bermuda. Mantle and
short tail dark gray; white below with white forehead and black
cap; legs and stout bill yellow. In flight, shows striking Sabine's Gull-
like pattern (page 186).

breeding
adult

Whiskered Tern *Chlidonias hybridus*
L 9½-10" (24-25 cm) WS 26½-28½" (67-72 cm) Widespread Old
World species. Two North American records, both adults. In 1993
one at Cape May, New Jersey, 12 to 15 July, later moved to Delaware
shore from 19 July to 24 Aug. Another at Cape May, 8 to 12 Aug.
1998. Like congeners, secures food by picking it off surface. ***Adults***
have short stout dark red bill and medium-length red legs; dark
gray underparts set off contrasting white cheeks and under tail. In
winter, head and underparts white with thin black postocular
patch, blackish bill and legs; compare head pattern to "ear muff"
effect of White-winged Tern (page 196).

breeding
adult

Great Auk *Pinguinus impennis* **EX** *L 30" (81 cm)*
Extinct. North Atlantic species known in North America from three
nesting colonies on islands off Quebec and Newfoundland, the
largest on Funk Island off Newfoundland. Wintered within breeding range and south to Massachusetts, casually to South Carolina.
Extirpated from Funk Island about 1800; last definite record was
two clubbed on Eldey Stack, Iceland, on 3 June 1844. Flightless.
Resembled a large Razorbill with similarly shaped bill. Distinct,
white circular patch in lores. Winter plumage imperfectly known.

adult

Scaly-naped Pigeon *Patagioenas squamosa*
L 14" (36 cm) Resident throughout most of the West Indies. Two
old specimen records from Key West: 24 Aug. 1898 and 6 May 1929.
A large dark pigeon; in good light, head and upper breast are dark
maroon; feathers on sides of neck more reddish, tipped black,
forming diagonal lines giving scaled appearance; dark red bill with
yellow tip; orange-red iris; orange orbital ring.

adult ♂

Zenaida Dove *Zenaida aurita* L 10" (25 cm)
Primarily West Indian species; now accidental in southern Florida (where it was reported as breeding by Audubon in 1832). Distinguished from Mourning Dove by white on trailing edge of secondaries that shows as a square white spot on inner secondaries of folded wing; and by shorter, rounded, gray-tipped tail. Generally shy.

Passenger Pigeon *Ectopistes migratorius* **EX**
L 15¾" (40 cm) Extinct. Once possibly the most numerous landbird in North America, this species was hunted to extinction. By 1870s relegated to scattered breeding locations. Last records were a specimen from Ohio in 1900 and a reliable sight record in Missouri in 1902. The last individual died at the Cincinnati Zoo in 1914. Resembled a large Mourning Dove (page 212). ***Adult male*** bluish gray above and pinkish below; female browner above and paler below; juvenile similar to female.

adult ♂

European Turtle-Dove *Streptopelia turtur* L 10" (26 cm)
Widespread in Eurasia and Africa. Records from southern Florida (1990), St. Pierre (2001), and Massachusetts (2001). This species strays annually to Iceland. It is known to ride ships. Scapulars and wing coverts have black centers with bold orange-brown edges. Blue-gray panel in center of wing, black-and-white neck patch, and orange eye.

turtur

Key West Quail-Dove *Geotrygon chrysia* L 12" (31 cm)
West Indian species. Reported as breeding on Key West by Audubon in 1832. Population eliminated by about mid-19th century. Casual in southern Florida. Larger and with longer tail than Ruddy Quail-Dove (below). Whitish below, with a white line under the eye. Upperparts, primaries, and tail are chestnut, glossed with purple and green. ***Male*** is highly iridescent above; female is duller.

♂

Ruddy Quail-Dove *Geotrygon montana* L 9¾" (25 cm)
A chunky tropical dove; five records for Florida and one for southern Texas. ***Male***'s primarily rich rufous upperparts and prominent buffy line under the eye are distinctive. ***Females*** are brown above; have a plainer facial pattern. In both sexes, underparts are cinnamon-buff. Quail-doves are so named because they resemble quail and have a similar terrestrial lifestyle.

♀

♂

Carolina Parakeet *Conuropsis carolinensis* **EX**
L 13½" (34 cm) Extinct. Only native breeding North American psittacid. Formerly resident in Southeast. Last certain records were from Florida and Kansas in 1904; a sight record from Missouri in 1905 and perhaps another in 1912. Last captive died on 21 Feb. 1918. ***Adult*** had green body with yellow patches on shoulder, thighs, and vent, a yellow head, and reddish orange face. Immature entirely green, except for orange patch on forehead.

adult

Stygian Owl *Asio stygius L 17" (43 cm) WS 42" (107 cm)*
A medium-size, forest-dwelling nocturnal owl occurring from northern Mexico to South America; also Hispaniola and Gonâve Island, West Indies. Two winter records of birds found roosting and photographed at Bentsen-Rio Grande Valley State Park: 9 Dec. 1994 and 26 Dec. 1996. Deep chocolate brown overall with close-set ear tufts and blackish facial disk with contrasting white forehead; underparts show distinct dark streaks and crossbars. Compare to Long-eared Owl (page 224), which is browner and has a rufous facial disk.

Mottled Owl *Ciccaba virgata L 14" (36 cm) WS 33" (84 cm)*
A medium-size and very vocal nocturnal owl found in a variety of woodland habitats from northwest and northeast Mexico to South America. A road-killed specimen was salvaged in front of Bentsen-Rio Grande Valley State Park, southern Texas, on 23 Feb. 1983. Note round head with no ear tufts and streaked underparts; brown facial disk with bold white eyebrows and whiskers is distinctive. Larger Barred Owl (page 226) has prominent barring across upper breast and paler facial disk.

White-collared Swift *Streptoprocne zonaris*
L 8½" (22 cm) Tropical species, accidental at scattered Gulf Coast and Great Lakes locations in the U.S. and southern Canada. A very large, black swift; note white collar, more indistinct in *immatures,* and slightly forked tail. Soars with wings bent down. Two specimens (Escambia County, Florida, and Kleberg County, Texas) are of large Middle American race, *zonaris*; one from Broward County, Florida, is of smaller West Indian race, *pallidifrons*.

immature

Common Swift *Apus apus L 6½" (17 cm)*
Breeds in Palearctic; winters in Africa. Accidental at St. Pierre and Miquelon off Newfoundland on 23 Jun. 1986; records also from Bermuda and probably the Northeast. Long, thin-winged, dark, with paler throat, long forked tail. Alaska specimen is of Asian *pekinensis* (illustrated), but record off Newfoundland and other probable sightings likely darker nominate *apus* from Europe on odds. Most likely to be confused with Black Swift (*Cypseloides niger*) of western North America (*C. n. borealis*) and locally in West Indies (*C. n. niger*), which has shallower tail fork and is smaller; juvenal plumage darker.

pekinensis

Antillean Palm-Swift *Tachornis phoenicobia L 4¼" (11 cm)*
A tiny Caribbean swift that is resident in the Greater Antilles (except Puerto Rico). Two were present and photographed at Key West, Florida, from 7 July to 13 Aug. 1972. Distinctive are dark cap, dark sides, and thin line across breast contrasting with white throat, belly, and rump; tail has shallow fork. Batlike flight with rapid wingbeats and short glides and twists; generally flies low, among trees and palms.

adult ♂
evelynae   ♀   immature ♂

adult

Bahama Woodstar *Calliphlox evelynae* L 3¾" (10 cm)

Bahamian endemic. Four records of five birds from southeast Florida, none recent. ***Adult male*** has broad white collar, light purple throat, long, forked tail; mixed olive and rich buff below. In ***female*** note tail projection past primary tips, cinnamon tips to outer tail feathers, slightly curved bill. Calls suggestive of Anna's Hummingbird (page 238).

Greenish Elaenia *Myiopagis viridicata* L 5½" (14 cm)

Resident in Mexico from southern Durango and southern Tamaulipas, south to northern Argentina. Recorded once in North America on upper Texas coast at High Island, 20 to 23 May 1984. Overall greenish above with a contrasting grayish head and dark eye stripe with distinct, pale supercilium. Primaries edged with olive; bright yellowish on secondaries; short primary projection. Grayish throat and olive breast contrast with yellow belly. Distinctive call note, a high, thin, and descending *seei-seeur*.

Caribbean Elaenia *Elaenia martinica* L 5½" (14 cm)

Resident on many Caribbean Islands, including throughout Lesser Antilles, but absent from Greater Antilles, except for Puerto Rico. Recorded once (photographs) from Santa Rosa Island, Escambia County, Florida, on 28 Apr. 1984. The AOU, while accepting the record as an elaenia, does not consider the record definitive to species. Overall plumage plain. Short crest rarely raised to show white-based crown feathers. Indistinct pale gray supercilium; dusky lores; pale yellowish wing bars and edges to secondaries; lower mandible flesh-colored at base. Call, a clear whistled *wheee-u*.

Cuban Pewee *Contopus caribaeus* L 6" (15 cm)

West Indian species; accidental in south Florida (three records): 11-17 Mar. and 1-4 Apr. 1995, Palm Beach County; from 29 Sept. to 1 Oct. 1999, Palm Beach County; 16 Feb. 2001 on Key Largo, Monroe County. Short primary projection makes species look like *Empidonax* (pages 256-261), but Cuban does minimal tail flicking. Note expansion of prominent white partial eye ring behind eye; dull wing bars; faint "vest." Call, a clear, steady *dee-dee-dee*, also a soft *dep* note.

Social Flycatcher *Myiozetetes similis* L 6¾-7¼" (17-18 cm)

Common from northeastern and northwestern Mexico to northeastern Argentina. Only one fully documented record at Bentsen-Rio Grande Valley State Park, Texas, 7 to 14 Jan. 2005. A medium-size, colorful flycatcher vaguely suggestive of the much larger Greater Kiskadee (page 264), but black bill is much smaller. ***Adult*** also lacks rufous in the wings and tail, which eliminates Middle American races of Great Kiskadee, although juvenile Social Flycatcher does show rufous edges. The reddish orange central crown patch is concealed by dark gray. Distinctive call is a loud *che cheechee cheechee cheechee;* also a harsh *cree-yooo*.

Piratic Flycatcher *Legatus leucophaius L 6" (15 cm)*
Widespread tropical species. Accidental in U.S. on Dry Tortugas, Florida; on an oil rig in the Gulf of Mexico (Texas); Big Bend, Texas; and eastern New Mexico. Dark olive-brown above; blurry olive streaking below. Distinct head pattern, dark malar streak, pale throat, stubby black bill. Black tail can show rufous edges. Often perches out in the open.

variegatus

varius

Variegated Flycatcher *Empidonomus varius L 7¼" (18 cm)*
South American species; accidental in North America; three records in East. Similar to Piratic, but larger, longer bill has pale base; less distinct malar streak; more distinct streaking on upperparts, edging on wing coverts, and rufous edge on uppertail coverts and tail. Tends to perch lower than Piratic. Compare both to larger Sulphur-bellied Flycatcher. Call is a high, thin *pseee.*

Loggerhead Kingbird *Tyrannus caudifasciatus L 9" (23 cm)*
Endemic West Indian species, resident in northern Bahamas, Greater Antilles, Cayman Islands. One certain record from Key West, 8-27 Mar. 2007. Other Florida records unsubstantiated; one from Islamorada in early 1970s may have been the larger, rounder headed, bigger billed Giant Kingbird (*T. cubensis*), a now rare endemic of Cuba, but with historical extralimital records (specimens) from Great Inagua and the Caicos Islands. Note Loggerhead's dark crown, slight rear crest, gray upperparts, white edges on wing coverts, white underparts, white tail tip, short primary projection, long and moderately thick bill. Polytypic, seven named subspecies; Key West bird likely of nominate race, described above, or possibly *caymanensis* from the Caymans. Bahama's *bahamensis* more yellow below, more brownish above, with less cap contrast. Eastern Greater Antilles' *gabbii* (Hispaniola) and *taylori* (Puerto Rico) lack pale tail tip, have more cinnamon edges on the coverts. Loggerheads tend to perch low and feed more within the canopy than other kingbirds. Wings produce a muffled sound in flight. Nominate's calls include a loud buzzy *tireet*, often repeated.

caudifasciatus

adult ♂

Masked Tityra *Tityra semifasciata L 9" (23 cm)*
Common from northwestern and northeastern Mexico to Brazil. One record from south Texas at Bentsen-Rio Grande Valley State Park, from 17 Feb. to 10 Mar. 1990. Large and chunky; ***males*** are pale gray above and whitish below with contrasting black on face, most of wings, and thick subterminal tail band. Bare skin on face and base of thick bill is pinkish red. Female is similar, but is darker and duller. Distinctive call is a double, nasal grunt, *zzzr-zzzrt.*

Thick-billed Vireo *Vireo crassirostris L 5½" (14 cm)*
Caribbean species, casual visitor to southeast Florida likely from Bahamas or possibly cays off northern Cuba. Many reports from south Florida are misidentified White-eyed Vireos (page 272). Larger than White-eyed, with larger, slightly stouter, grayer bill. Note overall browner color, lack of gray on nape, broken spectacles. Iris is darker than iris of adult White-eyed; song is similar but harsher; call notes slower and harsher.

crassirostris

Yucatan Vireo *Vireo magister* L 6" *(15 cm)*

Resident on Yucatán Peninsula and its offshore islands; also on Grand Cayman and islands off Honduras. One record from Bolivar Peninsula, Texas, from 28 Apr. to 27 May 1984. Overall brownish above with dark eye line, but no dark lateral crown stripe as in Red-eyed Vireo (page 276). Dull whitish below with grayish brown flanks, short primary projection, and very large, heavy bill. Call a nasal *benk*, often strung together in a series.

Eurasian Jackdaw *Corvus monedula* L 13" *(33 cm)*

Arrived in Northeast in early 1980s, most perhaps ship-assisted. Found from Atlantic Canada to Pennsylvania. Few reports by 1990s, the last one in Apr. 1999 from Newfoundland. Small, black overall, with gray nape and face, pale grayish eyes. Lively and inquisitive. Calls include a metallic *kow* and a softer *jack* note.

adult ♀

Cuban Martin *Progne crytoleuca* L 7½" *(19 cm)*

Breeds Cuba and Isle of Pines; wintering grounds unknown, but presumably South America. Only acceptable record is specimen taken on 9 May 1895 at Key West, Florida. Adult male closely resembles Purple Martin (page 284), but has relatively longer and more deeply forked tail; in hand, note concealed white feathers on belly. *Female* resembles female Purple, but with unmarked white belly and undertail coverts; lacks grayish collar. Separation from Caribbean (*P. dominicensis*) and Sinaloa (*P. sinaloae*) Martins, with which it sometimes is treated as conspecific, is difficult; Cuban is darker overall with dark shaft smudges on the undertail coverts and usually with some shaft streaking on the breast and sides.

adult ♀

Gray-breasted Martin *Progne chalybea* L 6¾" *(17 cm)*

Breeds in Mexico from southern Sinaloa and southern Tamaulipas, south to Argentina. Withdraws from northeastern portion of range in winter. Two old specimen records for south Texas: 25 Apr. 1880 at Rio Grande City; 18 May 1889 from Hidalgo County; all other reports unsubstantiated. Similar to female Purple Martin (page 284), but smaller with a less deeply forked tail; also browner on forehead, a less well-defined collar, and paler underparts.

adult ♀

Southern Martin *Progne elegans* L 7" *(18 cm)*

An austral migrant from South America. One specimen record from Key West, Florida, on 14 Aug. 1890. Adult male resembles Purple Martin (page 284), but smaller with slightly longer and more forked tail, and in hand, lacks concealed white patch on sides and flanks. *Female* is darker below than female Purple Martin.

adult
fusca

Brown-chested Martin *Progne tapera* L 6½" *(16 cm)*

South American species. Southern subspecies, *fusca*, an austral migrant to northern South America. Four North American records, three in the East: a specimen (*fusca*) from Monomoy Is., Massachusetts, 12 June 1983; one photographed at Cape May, 6 to 15 Nov. 1997; a sight record from Bluff Point, Connecticut, 1 July 2006. Smaller than Purple Martin (page 284) with brownish upperparts, white below, brown sides, brown breast band.

Mangrove Swallow *Tachycineta albilinea* L 5¼" (13 cm)
A small swallow found from coastal slopes of central Sonora and southern Tamaulipas, Mexico, south through Panama; isolated population in Peru. An adult was at the Viera Wetlands in Brevard County, Florida, 18 to 25 Nov. 2000. *Adults* have an iridescent greenish crown and back; auriculars and lores black; narrow white line, usually meets across forehead; partial white collar; and distinct white rump. Juvenile is like adult, but brownish above. Compare also to Tree (page 286) and Violet-green (*T. thalassina*) Swallows. Within normal range, seldom found far from water.

adult

Bahama Swallow *Tachycineta cyaneoviridis* L 5¾" (15 cm)
Endemic Bahamian species. Breeds in northern Bahamas and vicinity; casual visitor to the Florida Keys, especially Big Pine Key, and nearby mainland but unrecorded for over a decade. Greenish above. Deeply forked tail and white underwing coverts separate this species from similar Tree Swallow (page 286). Immatures have shorter tail fork, dusky wash on breast and wing linings.

adults

♂

♂

Orange-billed Nightingale-Thrush
Catharus aurantiirostris L 6½" (17 cm) Widespread in Neotropics. Two records from south Texas: one photographed in hand on 8 Apr. 1996 at Laguna Atascosa National Wildlife Refuge, and a specimen from Edinburg on 28 May 2004. Orange-brown above, pale gray and whitish below with distinctive bright orange bill, legs, and orbital ring. In flight, lacks pale underwing bar of northern breeding *Catharus* thrushes.

Black-headed Nightingale-Thrush *Catharus mexicanus*
L 6½" (17 cm) Found from northeastern Mexico to western Panama. Only record was one at Pharr, in south Texas, from 28 May to 29 Oct. 2004. Distinctive, with blackish crown and face, whitish throat and belly; otherwise gray below. Bright orange orbital ring, bill, and legs.

Eurasian Blackbird *Turdus merula* L 10½" (27 cm)
Palearctic species. Only accepted record was a *male* found dead on 16 Nov. 1994 at Bonavista, Newfoundland. Other records, mainly from northeastern Canada, are of uncertain origin. There are a dozen Greenland records. Male is all-black; orange-yellow orbital eye ring and bill (duller on immatures). Female is browner with pale throat and dark-streaked chest; soft parts duller.

♂

Song Thrush *Turdus philomelos* L 8-9¼" (20-23 cm)
Old World species found from Europe and Scandinavia to about Lake Baikal, Russia. Northern and eastern populations migratory. Annual in very small numbers to Iceland, chiefly in fall; one Greenland specimen. One record from Saint Fulgence, eastern Québec 11-17 Nov. 2006. Larger than all *Catharus* Thrushes. Plumage vaguely suggestive of Swainson's Thrush, but much more heavily and extensively marked below with arrow-shaped spots; auricular is strongly patterned. Call, a sharp *tick,* unlike any *Catharus* Thrush.

fall immature

suttoni

White-throated Robin *Turdus assimilis L 9½" (24 cm)*

Tropical species; casual to southernmost Texas in winter. Distinct white collar in front; white throat with dark brown streaking; head and upperparts brownish; often shows yellow orbital ring; underparts mostly gray. Compare to Clay-colored Robin's (page 308) less marked throat; lack of collar; overall tawnier color; more extensively yellow bill. Call is a nasal *rreeuh*, often doubled.

rufopalliatus

Rufous-backed Robin *Turdus rufopalliatus L 9¼" (24 cm)*

West Mexican species, casual to southern Texas. Distinguished from American Robin (page 308) by reddish brown back and wing coverts, uniformly gray head with no white around eye, and more extensively streaked throat. Calls include a plaintive, drawn-out, whistled *teeeuu*, a clucking series of *chuk* notes, and in flight, a high, thin *ssi*. Somewhat secretive; found in treetops and dense shrubbery.

adult

Blue Mockingbird *Melanotis caerulescens L 10" (25 cm)*

Mexican species which moves altitudinally. Casual in southern Texas where of questionable origin (though accepted). **Adult** deep slaty blue with black mask and red eye. Immature slightly duller, brownish tinge to wings, darker eye.

winter adult ♂

Citrine Wagtail *Motacilla citreola L 6½" (17 cm)*

Palearctic species that winters farther north than either Western or Eastern Yellow Wagtail. Only North American record was from Starkville, Mississippi, from 31 Jan. to 1 Feb. 1992. All plumages have gray back and bold, well-defined white wing bars. Breeding adult male has bright yellow head and underparts and a dark nape. Adult female and *winter adult male* have yellow-centered, grayish brown auriculars completely surrounded by yellow. Immatures lack all yellow, have similar, winter-adult face pattern. Call is loud buzzy *tsweep*, like Eastern Yellow Wagtail (*M. tschutschensis*).

breeding ♂
alba

White Wagtail *Motacilla alba L 7¼" (18 cm)*

Northeast Asian *ocularis* breeds sparingly in western Alaska; *lugens* breeds coastal East Asia (south of *ocularis*), has nested and hybridized with *ocularis* in western Alaska, was formerly treated as a separate species, the Black-backed Wagtail. In the East, *ocularis* documented in Michigan, South Carolina; *lugens* photographed in North Carolina. Nominate *alba*, breeding as close as Iceland and Greenland, is accidental in Quebec, North Carolina, and probably Newfoundland. Breeding adult *ocularis* has black nape, gray back; eye line, throat, bib, and usually chin, black. In flight, shows mostly dark wings. In breeding adult male *lugens* upperparts are black, wings mostly white; chin usually white. Breeding adult female *lugens* similar, but duller above; winter adults retain distinct wing pattern. In nominate *alba* face is white in all plumages. Juveniles of all races are brownish above with two faint wing bars. Immature closer to adult but retains most of juvenile wing; immature *ocularis* has darker bases to median coverts than *lugens*, but separation problematic. Calls include a two-note *chizzik* given in flight and a whistled *chee-wee* given from perch.

Gray Silky-flycatcher *Ptilogonys cinereus* L 7½" (20 cm)
Resident (some seasonal movement) from northern Mexico to
Guatemala; largely montane. Accepted Texas record: from 31
Oct. to 11 Nov. 1985 at Laguna Atascosa National Wildlife
Refuge. Structured like Phainopepla. *Adult males* are gray with
orange-yellow flanks and bright yellow undertail coverts; note
white eye ring and white base of tail. Females and juveniles are
similar, but duller.

Yellow-faced Grassquit *Tiaris olivaceus* L 4¼" (11 cm)
Tropical species. Accidental in southern Florida and southernmost Texas. *Adult male* of mainland race, *pusillus*, shows extensive black on head, breast, and upper belly; golden yellow
supraloral, throat, and crescent below eye; olive above. Adult
female and immature male have traces of same head pattern; olive
above. Adult male of West Indian race, *olivaceus*, found in Greater
Antilles and Cayman Islands (absent Bahamas), shows less black.
Female lacks black below. Song is thin, insectlike trills; call, a high-
pitched *sik* or *tsi*.

Black-faced Grassquit *Tiaris bicolor* L 4½" (11 cm)
Found nearly throughout West Indies except Cayman Islands and
largely absent from Cuba; also northern South America. Casual
stray to south Florida. *Adult male* mostly black below, dark olive
above; head is black. *Female* and immatures pale gray below,
gray-olive above. Song is a buzzing *tik-zeee;* call, a lisping *tst*.

Crimson-collared Grosbeak *Rhodothraupis celaeno*
L 8½" (22 cm)   Endemic to northeastern Mexico; casual to
south Texas, mainly in winter. Stubby, mostly black bill; long
tail; black on head variable. *Adult male*'s collar and much of
underparts an intense shade of red; upperparts darker. *Adult
female* is olive above; has thin yellowish wing bars; yellow-
green rear collar; yellowish olive underparts. Immatures show
less black than female; male shows some red and black patches
by first spring. Often skulks on or near ground; often raises rear
crown feathers. Song, a variable warble; call, a penetrating, rising and falling *seeiyu*.

Tawny-shouldered Blackbird *Agelaius humeralis*
L 8" (20 cm)   Resident on Cuba and in Haiti. Only U.S. record
was two secured (specimens) at the Key West Lighthouse on 27
Feb. 1936. Smaller and slimmer than Red-winged Blackbird (page
380) and with a slim, pointed bill; lesser coverts tawny, not red,
and rear border has a narrow blended edge. More arboreal than
Red-winged and buzzy, muffled song is more drawn out; calls
differ somewhat too.

adult ♂

adult ♂
olivaceus

♀ *pusillus*

adult
♂ *pusillus*

♀

adult ♂
bicolor

adult
♀

adult
♂

adult ♂

1st spring

adult

Black-vented Oriole *Icterus wagleri* L 8½" (22 cm)
Resident from central Nicaragua to northern Mexico; accidental to south Texas, one adult at Kingsville from 17 Apr. to 10 Oct. 1989. Long, narrow bill and long, graduated tail. **Adult** has solid black head, back, undertail coverts, tail, and wings, except for yellow shoulders; the border between breast and belly is chestnut. **First-spring** has black lores and chin; streaked back. Juvenile lacks black bib. Black-vented Oriole's call is a nasal *nyeh,* often repeated.

♀

♂

Common Chaffinch *Fringilla coelebs* L 6" (15 cm)
Palearctic species; casual to northeastern North America; reports elsewhere possibly escaped cage birds. Has white patches on lesser coverts, base of primaries, wing bar; outer tail feathers white. **Male**'s crown and nape are blue-gray; shows pinkish below, pinkish brown above. **Female**'s head is mostly gray with brown lateral stripes. Call a metallic *pink-pink;* also a *hweet.*

♀

Eurasian Siskin *Carduelis spinus* L 4¾" (12 cm)
Palearctic species. About six records from northeastern North America, but the origin of these has been questioned; a male photographed at Saint-Pierre and Miquelon on 23 June 1983 is perhaps the most compelling. Unrecorded from Greenland. **Male** is distinctive with black forecrown and chin, olive above, and extensively yellow below. **Female** is much duller, the yellow restricted to sides of breast, and a wash of yellow on face, eyebrow, and rump; juvenile duller still. Some Pine Siskins (page 394) are very similar, but wing coverts of Eurasian average darker.

adult ♂

Rarities from Western North America

This unillustrated appendix contains species that are of casual or accidental occurrence in the East *but are more characteristic of the West*. However, some are widespread Eurasian species that likely come from Europe. Most of the species in this appendix receive full treatment in our companion field guide to the West. For species recorded only once or twice in the East, the records are listed individually; otherwise, they are summarized. If states and provinces are listed, they are given in order from west to east and then south to north.

Taiga Bean-Goose *Anser fabalis* Casual: recorded NE, IA, QC

Tundra Bean-Goose *Anser serrirostris* Accidental: recorded Cap Tormente, QC, 14-15 Oct. 1987

Steller's Eider *Polysticta stelleri* Casual: recorded MA, ME, QC, NU

Smew *Mergellus albellus* Casual: recorded MO, NY, RI

Mottled Petrel *Pterodroma inexpectata* Accidental: specimen Mount Morris, NY, early Apr. 1880

Stejneger's Petrel *Pterodroma longirostris* Accidental: decomposed specimen found Port Aransas, TX, 15 Sep. 1995

Buller's Shearwater *Puffinus buller* Accidental: recorded offshore NJ, 28 Oct. 1984

Short-tailed Shearwater *Puffinus tenuirostris* Accidental: moribund specimen off Sanibel Is., FL, 7 Jul. 2000; sight record off Virginia Beach, VA, 18 Jan. 1998

Blue-footed Booby *Sula nebouxii* Accidental: recorded Burnet, Llano, and Bastrop Cos., TX, 2 Jun. 1993 to 12 Apr. 1995

White-tailed Eagle *Haliaeetus albicilla* Resident: Greenland; casual: MA (no records since 1944), possibly NY

Pacific Golden-Plover *Pluvialis fulva* Casual: recorded TX, DE, NJ, MA, ME

Lesser Sand-Plover *Charadrius mongolus* Casual: widespread records

Terek Sandpiper *Xenus cinereus* Accidental: recorded Plum Is., MA, 23 Jun. 1990

Wandering Tattler *Heteroscelus incanus* Casual: recorded east to TX, MB, ON, MA

Wood Sandpiper *Tringa glareola* Casual: recorded NY (twice), NF

Black Turnstone *Arenaria melanocephala* Accidental: recorded NT; Winnebago Co., WI, 22 May 1971

Surfbird *Aphriza virgata* Casual: records scattered Gulf Coast, FL, PA

Red-necked Stint *Calidris ruficollis* Casual: widespread records

Sharp-tailed Sandpiper *Calidris acuminata* Casual: widespread records

Common Snipe *Gallinago gallinago* Accidental: specimen Jack Lane's (Makkovik) Bay, NL, 24 Dec. 1927

Heermann's Gull *Larus heermanni* Casual: widespread records

Slaty-backed Gull *Larus schistisagus* Casual: widespread records

Glaucous-winged Gull *Larus glaucescens* Casual: widespread records

Western Gull *Larus occidentalis* Casual: recorded s. TX, IL, NY

Elegant Tern *Sterna elegans* Casual: recorded TX, FL, VA

Ancient Murrelet *Synthliboramphus antiquus* Casual: widespread records

Band-tailed Pigeon *Patagioenas fasciata* Casual: widespread records

Ruddy Ground-Dove *Columbina talpacoti* Casual: recorded s. TX; accidental: MS

Common Cuckoo *Cuculus canorus* Accidental: recorded Martha's Vineyard, MA, 3-4 May 1981

Flammulated Owl *Otus flammeolus* Casual: recorded Gulf Coast states and offshore

Western Screech-Owl *Megascops kennicottii* Casual: recorded (possibly resident) sw. KS

Vaux's Swift *Chaetura vauxi* Casual: recorded LA, FL

Broad-billed Hummingbird *Cynanthus latirostris* Casual: widespread records

White-eared Hummingbird *Hylocharis leucotis* Casual: recorded c. and s. TX; accidental: MS

Violet-crowned Hummingbird *Amazilia violiceps* Casual: recorded c., s., and e. TX

Blue-throated Hummingbird *Lampornis clemenciae* Casual: widespread records

Magnificent Hummingbird *Eugenes fulgens* Casual: widespread records

Costa's Hummingbird *Calypte costae* Casual: recorded east to s. TX, AL, MN

Elegant Trogon *Trogon elegans* Casual: recorded s. TX

Williamson's Sapsucker *Sphyrapicus thyroideus* Casual: recorded east to LA, IL, NY

Red-breasted Sapsucker *Sphyrapicus ruber* Accidental: recorded McLennan Co., TX, 27 Feb. 1996

Greater Pewee *Contopus pertinax* Casual: recorded c. and s. TX

Pacific-slope Flycatcher *Empidonax difficilis* Casual: widespread records (additional reports of "Western" Flycatchers)

Dusky-capped Flycatcher *Myiarchus tuberculifer* Casual: recorded s. TX

Sulphur-bellied Flycatcher *Myiodynastes luteiventris* Casual: recorded Gulf Coast; accidental: NJ, MA, ON, NB, NF

Thick-billed Kingbird *Tyrannus crassirostris* Accidental: recorded Palo Duro Canyon, TX, 30 Oct. 1998; Matagorda Co., TX, 16 Dec. 2002, again 15 Dec. 2003 to 29 Mar. 2004, and again 20-31 Dec. 2004

Brown Shrike *Lanius cristatus* Accidental: recorded Halifax, NS, 22 Nov. to 1 Dec. 1997

Steller's Jay *Cyanocitta stelleri* Casual irruptive: recorded Great Plains; accidental: IL

Pinyon Jay *Gymnorhinus cyanocephalus* Casual irruptive: recorded Great Plains

Clark's Nutcracker *Nucifraga columbiana* Casual irruptive: recorded Great Plains, w. Great Lakes; accidental: LA, AL

Violet-green Swallow *Tachycineta thalassina* Casual: widespread records

Common House-Martin *Delichon urbicum* Accidental: recorded St. Pierre, SPM, 26-31 May 1989

Mountain Chickadee *Poecile gambeli* Casual irruptive: recorded Great Plains

Juniper Titmouse *Baeolophus ridgwayi* Casual: recorded w. Great Plains

Pygmy Nuthatch *Sitta pygmaea* Casual irruptive: recorded Great Plains

American Dipper *Cinclus mexicanus* Casual: recorded Great Plains; accidental: MN

Siberian Rubythroat *Luscinia calliope* Accidental: specimen Hornby, ON, 26 Dec. 1983

Stonechat *Saxicola torquatus* Accidental: recorded Grand Manan Is., NB, 1 Oct. 1983

Aztec Thrush *Ridgwayia pinicola* Accidental: recorded Port Aransas, TX, 30 Jan. 1979; Corpus Christi, TX, 16-20 May 1996

Phainopepla *Phainopepla nitens* Casual: recorded Great Plains; accidental: WI, ON, RI

Lucy's Warbler *Vermivora luciae* Casual: recorded s. and e. TX, LA, MA

Hermit Warbler *Dendroica occidentalis* Casual: widespread records

Grace's Warbler *Dendroica graciae* Casual: recorded c. TX; accidental: IL

Red-faced Warbler *Cardellina rubrifrons* Casual: recorded c. and s. TX; accidental: LA

Painted Redstart *Myioborus pictus* Casual: widespread records

Slate-throated Redstart *Myioborus miniatus* Accidental: recorded Corpus Christi, TX, 10 Apr. 2002 (two); Pharr, TX, 12-13 Mar. 2003

Hepatic Tanager *Piranga flava* Casual: recorded n., c., and s. TX, LA, IL

Flame-colored Tanager *Piranga bidentata* Accidental: recorded South Padre Is., TX, 11-14 Apr. 2002; Pharr, TX, 28 Feb. 2005

Sage Sparrow *Amphispiza belli* Casual: recorded w. Great Plains; accidental: NS

Golden-crowned Sparrow *Zonotrichia atricapilla* Casual: widespread records

Streak-backed Oriole *Icterus pustulatus* Accidental: recorded Iron Co., WI, early Jan. to 15 Jan. (when found dead) 1998; Brazos Bend State Park, TX, 12 Dec. 2004 to 8 Apr. 2005

Brambling *Fringilla montifringilla* Casual: widespread records

Acknowledgments

The editors and artists are indebted to the following individuals and institutions for their valuable assistance in the preparation of this book: Field Museum of Natural History (David Willard); Jon S. Greenlaw; Marshall J. Iliff; Liverpool Museum, UK (Clemency Thorne Fisher, Tony Parker); Los Angeles County Museum of Natural History (Kimball L. Garrett); Steve Mlodinow; National Museum of Natural History, Smithsonian Institution (James P. Dean); Natural History Museum, Tring, UK (Mark Adams); Bill Pranty; Royal Ontario Museum (Glen Murphy, Mark Peck); Slater Museum of Natural History (Dennis Paulson, Gary Shugart); John Sterling.

The editors and artists wish to thank the following individuals and institutions for their contributions to the *National Geographic Field Guide to the Birds of North America*, on which much of the current book is based: Mark Adams; Thomas A. Allen; David Agro; J. Phillip Angle; Jim Arterburn; Stephen Bailey; Lawrence G. Balch; Dr. Richard C. Banks; John Barber; Jon Barlow; Jen and Des Bartlett; Giff Beaton; Ken Behrens; Louis Bevier; Gavin Bieber; Eirik A.T. Blom; Daniel Boone; Jack Bowling; Edward S. Brinkley; Dawn Burke; Danny Bystrak; Richard Cannings; Steven W. Cardiff; Charles Carlson; John Carlson; Robin Carter; Allen Chartier; Graham Chisholm; Carla Cicero; Charles T. Clark; William S. Clark; Rene Corado; Marian Cressman; Ricky Davis; James P. Dean; Denver Museum of Natural History; Bruce Deuel; James Dinsmore; Donna L. Dittman; Robert Dixon; Peter J. Dunn; Peter Dunne; Cameron Eckert; Victor Emanuel; Richard Erickson; Doug Faulkner; Field Museum of Natural History; Dr. C. T. Fisher; Robert Fisher; John W. Fitzpatrick; David Fix; Rick Fridell; Kimball L. Garrett; Freida Gentry; Daniel D. Gibson; Peter Grant; John A. Gregoire; Jon S. Greenlaw; Britt Griswold; Dr. James L. Gulledge; Dr. George A. Hall; J.B. Hallett, Jr.; Robert Hamilton; Jo and Tom Heindel; Matt Heindel; Steve Heinl; Paul M. Hill; Chris Hobbs; Phill Holder; Steve N.G. Howell; Rich Hoyer; Rebecca Hyman; Frank Iwen; Greg Jackson; Alvaro Jaramillo; Joseph R. Jehl, Jr.; Ned K. Johnson; Colin Jones; Roy Jones; Lars Jonsson; Kenn Kaufman; Dan Kassebaum; Tom Kent; Wayne Klockner; Rudolf Koes; Lasse J. Laine; Daniel Lane; Dr. M. Largen; Greg Lasley; Paul E. Lehman; Nick Lethaby; Tony Leukering; Rich Levad; Mark Lockwood; Los Angeles County Museum of Natural History; Tim Loseby; Aileen Lotz; Louisiana State University Museum of Natural Science; Derek Lovitch; Rich MacIntosh; Bruce Mactavish; Laura Martin; Ron Martin; Guy McCaskie; Terry McEneaney; Mick McHugh; Ian McLaren; Doug McRae; Dominic Mitchell; Steve Mlodinow; Joseph Morlan; Killian Mullarney; Museum of Vertebrate Zoology, University of California, Berkeley; Glenn Murphy; National Museum of Natural History, Smithsonian Institution; Natural History Museum at Tring (UK); Harry Nehls; Kenny Nichols; Michael O'Brien; Jerry Oldenettel; Gerald Oreel; Mike Overton; A. Parker; Tony Parker; John Parmeter; Michael Patten; Brian Patteson; Patuxent Wildlife Research Center (USGS); Dennis Paulson; Mark Peck; Paul Prior; Peter Pyle; David Quady; Betsy Reeder; Dr. J.V. Remsen; Robert F. Ringler; Don Roberson; Mark Robins; Gary Rosenberg; Philip D. Round; Bill Rowe; John Rowlett; Rose Ann Rowlett; Royal Ontario Museum; Will Russell; San Diego Natural History Museum; Larry Sansone; Santa Barbara Museum of Natural History; Rick Saval; Robert T. Scholes; Brad Schram; Thomas Schulenberg; Scott Seltman; Larry Semo; David Sibley; Ross Silcock; Mark Stackhouse; James Stasz; Rick Steenberg; Andrew Stepniewski; John Sterling; Mark Stevenson; Doug Stotz; Sherman Suter; Peder Svingen; Thede Tobish; Dr. John Trochet; Charles Trost; Laurel Tucker; Nigel Tucker; Bill Tweit; Philip Unitt; University of Alaska Museum; Arnoud van den Berg; T. R. Wahl; George Wallace; Western Foundation of Vertebrate Zoology; Mel White; Tony White; Hal Wierenga; Claudia P. Wilds; David W. Willard; Jeff Wilson; Chris Wood; World Museum Liverpool (UK); Alan Wormington; Louise Zemaitis; Barry Zimmer; Kevin Zimmer.

Art Credits

Jonathan Alderfer: title page; 8-Short-billed Dowitcher; 10; 11-Lark Sparrow; 12-Goldeneye hybrid; 36; 41-Goldeneye hybrid; 57-displaying Sharptailed Grouse, displaying Greater Sage-Grouse; 65; 67-Clark's Grebe head, Western Grebe head; 69-Cory's Shearwater, Black-browed Albatross; 73-Cory's Shearwater, small flying figures of Cory's Shearwater, Black-capped Petrel, and Greater Shearwater; 75-Sooty Shearwater head, swimming Manx Shearwater, small flying Manx Shearwater; 81; 85; 99-flying Greater Flamingo; 137; 151; 161-standing Stilt Sandpiper, American Woodcock, Wilson's Snipe; 163; 207-swimming Thick-billed Murre; 209-Long-billed Murrelet, flying winter Dovekie, winter adult Black Guillemot *mandtii;* 213-Eurasian Collared-Dove, White-winged Dove, Mourning Dove (all with Schmitt); 267; 271-Rose-throated Becard; 281-flying Chihuahuan Raven, flying Common Raven; 301-Tail of female Blue-gray Gnatcatcher; 315-Common Myna; 398-except Garganey; 399-except Little Shearwater; 400-Gray Heron; 404-Jack Snipe; 405-Great Auk; 406-Zenaida Dove (with Schmitt), Passenger Pigeon, Carolina Parakeet; 408-Social Flycatcher; 409-Masked Tityra; 411-Mangrove Swallow; 412-Blue Mockingbird, White Wagtail; 413-Gray Silky-flycatcher. **David Beadle:** 8-Willow Flycatcher, Alder Flycatcher; 9-Acadian Flycatcher; 255; 257; 259; 261; 269-Gray Kingbird; 277-Philadelphia Vireo, Warbling Vireo; 285-Horned Lark; 289-flying adult Cave Swallow *pelodoma;* 333-fall male Bay-breasted Warbler; 361-Vesper Sparrow; 367-Dark-eyed Junco *montana* and *mearnsi;* 391-Gray-crowned Rosy-Finch; 402-Paint-billed Crake, Spotted Rail, Double-striped Thick-knee; 405-Scaly-naped Pigeon; 407-Antillean Palm-Swift; 408-Greenish Elaenia, Caribbean Elaenia, Cuban Pewee; 409-Loggerhead Kingbird, Thick-billed Vireo; 410-except Eurasian Jackdaw; 411-Orange-billed Nightingale-Thrush, Black-headed Nightingale-Thrush; 413-Tawny-shouldered Blackbird. **Peter Burke:** 9-Scarlet Tanager; 11-flycatcher tails; 13-Shiny Cowbird; 87-American Bittern, Least Bittern; 95; 97-Glossy Ibis (except flight figure), White-faced Ibis; 265-except Great Kiskadee; 275-Gray Vireo; 343-except Common Yellowthroat and Bananaquit; 345-except Western Spindalis; 347-except female White-collared Seedeater and first-winter male White-collared Seedeater; 349-Eastern Towhee, Spotted Towhee; 385-Shiny Cowbird; 387; 389; 409-Piratic Flycatcher, Variegated Flycatcher; 412-White-throated Robin; 413-Yellow-faced Grassquit, Crimson-collared Grosbeak; 414-Black-vented Oriole. **Marc R. Hanson:** 69-Northern

Fulmar, Band-rumped Storm-Petrel; 73-large Greater Shearwater figures; 75-flying Sooty Shearwater figures, large flying Manx Shearwater figures, Audubon's Shearwater; 77-except European Storm-Petrel; 129; 131; 133-except Purple Swamphen; 399-Little Shearwater; 401-Corn Crake; 402-Eurasian Coot. **Cynthia J. House:** 8-Lesser Scaup, Greater Scaup; 11-American Black Duck; 15; 17; 19-Brant, Canada Goose *canadensis;* 21; 23-except flying figures of Muscovy Duck; 25; 27-except American Black Duck head and Mottled Duck *fulvigula;* 29; 31; 33; 35; 37; 39; 41-except Goldeneye hybrid; 43; 45-except Egyptian Goose; 46-except Muscovy Duck; 47; 48; 49; 398-Garganey. **H. Jon Janosik:** 67-except Clark's Grebe head and Western Grebe head; 79; 83; 87-Anhinga; 143. **Donald L. Malick:** 7-except Cerulean Warbler; 13-except Shiny Cowbird; 101; 103; 107-except third-year Bald Eagle; 109-except flight figures; 111-perched juvenile Common Black-Hawk, Zone-tailed Hawk; 113-perched Short-tailed Hawk; 117-except flying figures of Red-tailed Hawk; 119-except dark-morph Ferruginous Hawk, flying adult White-tailed Hawk, and dark juvenile White-tailed Hawk; 121-Crested Caracara, perched figures of Aplomado Falcon, American Kestrel (except lower flying figure), Merlin (except flying figures); 123-except flying figures; 213-White-tipped Dove; 215-Common Ground-Dove, Inca Dove; 223-Barn Owl; 225; 227; 229-Eastern Screech-Owl, Elf Owl; 231; 243; 245; 247; 249; 251-except large figures of American Three-toed Woodpecker; 253; 406-Key West Quail-Dove, Ruddy Quail-Dove. **Killian Mullarney:** 139-standing Killdeer; 141-Northern Lapwing, Mountain Plover; 147-standing figures of Upland Sandpiper; 159-except flight figures; 165; 168-Phalaropes. **Michael O'Brien:** 69-Black-capped Petrel; 71; 73-Herald Petrel; 145-Willet; 291; 293-Tufted Titmouse, Black-crested Titmouse. **John P. O'Neill:** 293-Verdin, Bushtit. **Kent Pendleton:** 51-Wild Turkey; 53; 55; 57-except displaying Sharp-tailed Grouse and displaying Greater Sage-Grouse; 59-except Northern Bobwhite *floridanus;* 105-Snail Kite, Hook-billed Kite (except flying female); 123-all flight figures; 124-except Hook-billed Kite; 125; 126; 127. **Diane Pierce:** 89; 91-Snowy Egret, Cattle Egret; 93; 97-White Ibis and flying Glossy Ibis; 99-except flying Greater Flamingo; 135; 349-singing Rufous-crowned Sparrow; 353; 355; 357; 359-Seaside Sparrow; 361-Lark Bunting; 363; 365; 367-Snow Bunting, Dark-eyed Junco *aikeni, caniceps,* and *hyemalis;* 369; 371; 373; 375; 377; 391-except Gray-crowned Rosy-Finch; 393; 395; 397-American

Goldfinch, Lesser Goldfinch; 400-Jabiru. **John C. Pitcher:** 12-Greater Yellowlegs, Lesser Yellowlegs; 139-except Killdeer and flying figures; 141-Snowy Plover and Piping Plover (except flying figures); 145-Spotted Sandpiper and standing figures of Solitary Sandpiper; 147-standing Lesser Yellowlegs, Greater Yellowlegs; 153-Ruddy Turnstone; 155-except breeding female Semipalmated Sandpiper; 157-White-rumped Sandpiper and Baird's Sandpiper (except flying figures); 161-Purple Sandpiper (except flying figures); 404-Little Stint, Broad-billed Sandpiper. **H. Douglas Pratt:** 6-Worm-eating Warbler; 7-Cerulean Warbler; 211; 221; 223-Smooth-billed Ani, Groove-billed Ani; 237-Buff-bellied Hummingbird and adult Green Violet-ear; 239-except Ruby-throated Hummingbird wings and Black-chinned Hummingbird wings; 241; 263; 265-Great Kiskadee; 269-Eastern Kingbird, adult Fork-tailed Flycatcher, Scissor-tailed Flycatcher; 271-except Rose-throated Becard; 273; 275-except Gray Vireo; 277-except Philadelphia Vireo and Warbling Vireo; 279-except Western Scrub-Jay; 281-except flying ravens; 283; 285-Purple Martin; 287; 289-except flying adult Cave Swallow *pelodoma;* 295; 297; 299; 301-except tail of female Blue-gray Gnatcatcher; 303; 309-American Robin, Clay-colored Robin; 311; 313-Brown Thrasher, Long-billed Thrasher; 315-except Common Myna; 317-Cedar Waxwing, Bohemian Waxwing; 319; 321; 323-Nashville Warbler, Northern Parula, Tropical Parula; 325; 327; 329; 331; 333-except fall male Bay-breasted Warbler; 335-except Black-and-white Warbler; 337; 341-except Wilson's Warbler; 343-Common Yellowthroat, Bananaquit; 347-female White-collared Seedeater, first-winter male White-collared Seedeater; 381-except Bobolink; 383; 385-except Shiny Cowbird; 408-Bahama Woodstar; 410-Eurasian Jackdaw; 411-Bahama Swallow; 412-Rufous-backed Robin; 413-Black-faced Grassquit. **David Quinn:** 12-Redwing; 61; 63; 77-European Storm-Petrel; 91-Little Egret; 133-Purple Swamphen; 305-Northern Wheatear; 309-Redwing, Fieldfare; 317-American Pipit, Sprague's Pipit; 400-Western Reef-Heron; 402-Collared Plover; 403-except Eurasian Curlew; 404-Eurasian Woodcock, Gray-hooded Gull; 405-Whiskered Tern; 406-European Turtle-Dove; 411-Eurasian Blackbird, Song Thrush; 412-Citrine Wagtail; 414-Common Chaffinch, Eurasian Siskin. **Chuck Ripper:** 207-except swimming Thick-billed Murre; 209-Atlantic Puffin, Black Guillemot (except winter adult *mandtii*), Dovekie (except flying winter); 233; 235. **N. John Schmitt:** 9-House Sparrow; 19-Cackling Goose and Canada Goose

parvipes; 23-flying figures of Muscovy Duck; 27-American Black Duck head; 45-Egyptian Goose; 46-Muscovy Duck; 51-Plain Chachalaca; 59-Northern Bobwhite *floridanus;* 105-flying female Hook-billed Kite, Northern Harrier; 107-third-year Bald Eagle; 109-flight figures; 111-Common Black-Hawk (except perched juvenile), Harris's Hawk; 113-except perched Short-tailed Hawk; 115; 117-Red-tailed Hawk in flight; 119-dark-morph Ferruginous Hawk, flying adult White-tailed Hawk, dark juvenile White-tailed Hawk; 121-flying figures of Aplomado Falcon, lower flying American Kestrel, flying figures of Merlin; 124-Hook-billed Kite; 126; 127; 213-Eurasian Collared-Dove, White-winged Dove, Mourning Dove (all with Alderfer); 215-except Common Ground-Dove and Inca Dove; 216; 217; 219; 237-Chimney Swift and White-throated Swift; 269-immature Fork-tailed Flycatcher; 313-except Brown Thrasher and Long-billed Thrasher; 359-except Seaside Sparrow; 367-flying "Slate-colored" Dark-eyed Junco; 397-Eurasian Tree Sparrow, House Sparrow; 401-Eurasian Kestrel; 403-adult Eurasian Curlew; 406-Zenaida Dove (with Alderfer); 407-White-collared Swift, Common Swift. **Thomas R. Schultz:** 6-Yellow Warbler; 11-Common Tern; 12-Red-footed Falcon; 27-Mottled Duck *fulvigula;* 153-Red Knot and Sanderling (except flying figures); 155-breeding female Semipalmated Sandpiper; 157-Dunlin and Curlew Sandpiper (except flying); 171; 173; 175; 177; 179; 180; 181; 182; 183; 185; 187; 188; 189; 191; 193; 195; 197; 199; 201; 202; 203; 205; 229-Ferruginous Pygmy Owl; 251-large perched American Three-toed Woodpecker; 279-Western Scrub-Jay; 305-except Northern Wheatear; 307; 323-Virginia's Warbler and Yellow Warbler; 335-Black-and-white Warbler; 339; 341-Wilson's Warbler; 345-Western Spindalis; 349-juvenile Rufous-crowned Sparrow; 351; 361-Savannah Sparrow; 379; 381-Bobolink; 400-Great Frigatebird, Lesser Frigatebird; 401-Crane Hawk, Collared Forest-Falcon, Red-footed Falcon; 405-Belcher's Gull, Large-billed Tern; 407-Stygian Owl, Mottled Owl. **Daniel S. Smith:** 139-all flying figures; 141-flying figures of Snowy Plover and Piping Plover; 145-juvenile Sandpiper in flight; 147-flying figures; 149; 153-flying figures of Red Knot and Sanderling; 157-flying figures; 159-flying figures; 161-flying figures of Purple Sandpiper and Stilt Sandpiper; 166; 167; 168-except Phalaropes; 169; 403-juvenile Eurasian Curlew. **Sophie Webb:** 237-Green-breasted Mango, immature Green Violet-ear; 239-wings of Ruby-throated Hummingbird and Black-chinned Hummingbird.

Index

National Geographic Guide to the Birds of Eastern North America

Edited by Jon L. Dunn and Jonathan Alderfer

Published by the National Geographic Society

John M. Fahey, Jr., *President and Chief Executive Officer*

Gilbert M. Grosvenor, *Chairman of the Board*

Tim T. Kelly, *President, Global Media Group*

Nina D. Hoffman, *Executive Vice President; President, Book Publishing Group*

Prepared by the Book Division

Kevin Mulroy, *Senior Vice President and Publisher*

Leah Bendavid-Val, *Director of Photography Publishing and Illustrations*

Marianne R. Koszorus, *Director of Design*

Barbara Brownell Grogan, *Executive Editor*

Elizabeth Newhouse, *Director of Travel Publishing*

Carl Mehler, *Director of Maps*

Staff for This Book

Barbara Levitt, *Editor*

Jennifer Conrad Seidel, *Text Editor*

Jennifer Gibson Frink, *Art Director*

Paul E. Lehman, *Contributing Editor, Chief Map Researcher and Editor*

Sven Dolling, *Map Production*

Richard S. Wain, *Production Project Manager*

Marshall Kiker, *Illustrations Specialist*

Al Morrow, *Design Assistant*

Jennifer A. Thornton, *Managing Editor*

Gary Colbert, *Production Director*

Manufacturing and Quality Management

Christopher A. Liedel, *Chief Financial Officer*

Phillip L. Schlosser, *Vice President*

John T. Dunn, *Technical Director*

Chris Brown, *Director*

Maryclare Tracy, *Manager*

Nicole Elliott, *Manager*

Founded in 1888, the National Geographic Society is one of the largest nonprofit scientific and educational organizations in the world. It reaches more than 285 million people worldwide each month through its official journal, NATIONAL GEOGRAPHIC, and its four other magazines; the National Geographic Channel; television documentaries; radio programs; films; books; videos and DVDs; maps; and interactive media. National Geographic has funded more than 8,000 scientific research projects and supports an education program combating geographic illiteracy.

For more information, please call 1-800-NGS LINE (647-5463) or write to the following address:

National Geographic Society
1145 17th Street N.W.
Washington, D.C. 20036-4688 U.S.A.

Visit us online at
www.nationalgeographic.com/books

For information about special discounts for bulk purchases, please contact National Geographic Books Special Sales: ngsspecsales@ngs.org

For rights or permissions inquiries, please contact National Geographic Books Subsidiary Rights: ngbookrights@ngs.org

Library of Congress Cataloging-in-Publication Data
National Geographic field guide to the birds of eastern North America / edited by Jon L. Dunn and Jonathan Alderfer with Paul Lehman.
    p. cm.
    Includes index.
    ISBN 978-1-4262-0330-5
    1. Birds--East (U.S.)--Identification.
    2. Birds--Canada, Eastern--Identification.
    I. Dunn, Jon, 1954- II. Alderfer, Jonathan
    K. III. Lehman, Paul.
    QL683.E27.N38 2008
    598.0974--dc22

                                    2007050769

Printed in China

BIRDING WITH THE BEST

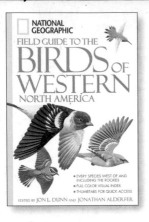

National Geographic's new **Field Guide to the Birds of Western North America** is the perfect companion for birding expeditions west of and including the Rocky Mountains. It provides in-depth coverage and full color illustrations of every bird recorded in western North America, including some 670 regular species, 100 casual and accidental birds, and 55 rarities. Packed with practical features—visual index on inside covers, extensively annotated art highlighting birds' key distinguishing characteristics, hundreds of new range maps, identification tip boxes, thumbtabs for speedy searches, and quick-reference flaps that double as placemarkers—the guide is a must-have resource for birders who want the most up-to-date information for their western birding adventures.

"Delightful...this is an essential book for all bird watchers."
—**Booklist**

Field ornithologists Jonathan Alderfer and Jon Dunn have crafted a masterful guide for the rapidly growing ranks of North American birders. This friendly, reliable guide teaches birders what to look and listen for, how to make sense of what they see and hear, and how to get the most from the experience. National Geographic's quality photography is a major highlight, supplemented by pencil drawings and full-color maps.

"...an awesome work...the most up-to-date field guide out there...birders can do no better than to tuck this book in their cars, backpacks, or bike sacks."
—**Bird Watcher's Digest**

This fully revised and updated edition of National Geographic's million-selling field guide has set the standard for nearly a quarter-century. Named by *Wild Bird* magazine one of the top 20 birding products of our time, it details more than 960 species depicted in 4,000 full-color illustrations by leading bird artists. New features are updated and enlarged range maps, extra-durable cover, thumbtabs, and a quick-find index.

Available wherever books are sold or call 1-888-647-6733
www.shopng.com/birdbooks